Women of Color and Hair Bias in the Work Environment

Kula A. Francis
University of the Virgin Islands, US Virgin Islands

Anna M. Clarke
University of the Virgin Islands, US Virgin Islands

A volume in the Advances in Human Resources Management and Organizational Development (AHRMOD) Book Series

IGI Global
PUBLISHER of TIMELY KNOWLEDGE

Published in the United States of America by
IGI Global
Business Science Reference (an imprint of IGI Global)
701 E. Chocolate Avenue
Hershey PA, USA 17033
Tel: 717-533-8845
Fax: 717-533-8661
E-mail: cust@igi-global.com
Web site: http://www.igi-global.com

Library of Congress Cataloging-in-Publication Data

Names: Francis, Kula A. - editor. | Clarke, Anna Maria - editor.
Title: Women of color and hair bias in the work environment / edited by Kula A. Francis, and Anna M. Clarke.
Description: Hershey, PA : Business Science Reference, [2024] | Includes bibliographical references and index. | Summary: "This book explores the experiences of professional women of color who have had experiences of uncertainty, self-consciousness, or differing treatment, and/or discrimination because of their natural hairstyle choices. The intent is to shine a light on the challenges professional women of color face, and how these experiences impact their hiring and/or work environment. This book will serve as an invaluable resource to organizations, practitioners, women, and students who are concerned about cultural competency, identity, equality, work biases, professionalism, and the position of women and the experiences they contended with. This book also allows women to be encouraged by stories of professional women who have overcome the societal burdens placed on natural hair"-- Provided by publisher.
Identifiers: LCCN 2023027792 (print) | LCCN 2023027793 (ebook) | ISBN 9781668487907 (hardcover) | ISBN 9781668487914 (paperback) | ISBN 9781668487921 (ebook)
Subjects: LCSH: Discrimination in employment. | African American women--Employment. | Women, Black--Employment. | Women professional employees. | Hairstyles--Social aspects. | Dress codes in the workplace--Social aspects.
Classification: LCC HD4903 .W66 2024 (print) | LCC HD4903 (ebook) | DDC 331.13/3--dc23/eng/20230615
LC record available at https://lccn.loc.gov/2023027792
LC ebook record available at https://lccn.loc.gov/2023027793

This book is published in the IGI Global book series Advances in Human Resources Management and Organizational Development (AHRMOD) (ISSN: 2327-3372; eISSN: 2327-3380)

British Cataloguing in Publication Data
A Cataloguing in Publication record for this book is available from the British Library.
All work contributed to this book is new, previously-unpublished material.
The views expressed in this book are those of the authors, but not necessarily of the publisher.
For electronic access to this publication, please contact: eresources@igi-global.com.

Advances in Human Resources Management and Organizational Development (AHRMOD) Book Series

ISSN:2327-3372
EISSN:2327-3380

Editor-in-Chief: Patricia Ordóñez de Pablos, Universidad de Oviedo, Spain

MISSION

A solid foundation is essential to the development and success of any organization and can be accomplished through the effective and careful management of an organization's human capital. Research in human resources management and organizational development is necessary in providing business leaders with the tools and methodologies which will assist in the development and maintenance of their organizational structure.

The **Advances in Human Resources Management and Organizational Development (AHRMOD) Book Series** aims to publish the latest research on all aspects of human resources as well as the latest methodologies, tools, and theories regarding organizational development and sustainability. The **AHRMOD Book Series** intends to provide business professionals, managers, researchers, and students with the necessary resources to effectively develop and implement organizational strategies.

COVERAGE

- Skills Management
- Change Management
- Corporate Governance
- Strategic HRM
- Process Improvement
- Upward Feedback
- Organizational Behavior
- Collaborative Method
- E-Human Resources Management
- Compliance

IGI Global is currently accepting manuscripts for publication within this series. To submit a proposal for a volume in this series, please contact our Acquisition Editors at Acquisitions@igi-global.com or visit: http://www.igi-global.com/publish/.

The Advances in Human Resources Management and Organizational Development (AHRMOD) Book Series (ISSN 2327-3372) is published by IGI Global, 701 E. Chocolate Avenue, Hershey, PA 17033-1240, USA, www.igi-global.com. This series is composed of titles available for purchase individually; each title is edited to be contextually exclusive from any other title within the series. For pricing and ordering information please visit http://www.igi-global.com/book-series/advances-human-resources-management-organizational/73670. Postmaster: Send all address changes to above address.

Titles in this Series

For a list of additional titles in this series, please visit:
http://www.igi-global.com/book-series/advances-human-resources-management-organizational/73670

Enhancing Employee Engagement and Productivity in the Post-Pandemic Multigenerational Workforce
Angela M. Even (Purdue University, USA) and Bryan Christiansen (Southern New Hampshire University, USA)
Business Science Reference • © 2023 • 464pp • H/C (ISBN: 9781668491720) • US $235.00

Utilizing Cloud Computing for SME Development
Jonathan G. Sinclair (HighRoads Ltd, UK)
Business Science Reference • © 2024 • 300pp • H/C (ISBN: 9781799896951) • US $250.00

Global Citizenship and Its Impact on Multiculturalism in the Workplace
Randa Diab-Bahman (Kuwait Technical College, Kuwait) and Abrar Al-Enzi (Gulf University for Science and Technology, Kuwait)
Business Science Reference • © 2023 • 351pp • H/C (ISBN: 9781668454367) • US $240.00

Managing Successful and Ethical Organizational Change
Dimitrios Belias (University of Thessaly, Greece) Ioannis Rossidis (Hellenic Open University, Greece) Christos Papademetriou (Neapolis University, Cyprus) Andreas Masouras (Neapolis University, Cyprus) and Sofia Anastasiadou (University of Western Macedonia, Greece)
Business Science Reference • © 2023 • 396pp • H/C (ISBN: 9798369302354) • US $250.00

Addressing Corporate Scandals and Transgressions Through Governance and Social Responsibility
Carlos Flórido Lopes (DEGEIT, University of Aveiro, Portugal & Research Centre on Accounting and Taxation (CICF-IPCA), Polytechnic Institute of Cávado and Ave, Portugal) Augusta Ferreira (ISCA-UA, University of Aveiro, Portugal & Research Centre on Accounting and Taxation (CICF-IPCA), Polytechnic Institute of Cávado and Ave, Portugal) Carlos Ferreira (DEGEIT and LASI/IEETA, University of Aveiro, Portugal) Helena Inácio (ISCA-UA and GOVCOPP, University of Aveiro, Portugal) and Carlos Santos (ISCA-UA, University of Aveiro, Portugal & Research Centre on Accounting and Taxation (CICF-IPCA), Polytechnic Institute of Cávado and Ave, Portugal)
Business Science Reference • © 2023 • 311pp • H/C (ISBN: 9781668478851) • US $250.00

For an entire list of titles in this series, please visit:
http://www.igi-global.com/book-series/advances-human-resources-management-organizational/73670

IGI Global
PUBLISHER of TIMELY KNOWLEDGE

701 East Chocolate Avenue, Hershey, PA 17033, USA
Tel: 717-533-8845 x100 • Fax: 717-533-8661
E-Mail: cust@igi-global.com • www.igi-global.com

To our mothers, Yvonne Maria Phillips Francis and Janet Joyce Amaro Clarke.

The first Queens of our Crowns.

Table of Contents

Detailed Table of Contents

Women of color have moved into professional roles to become engineers, lawyers, scientists, pilots, politicians, doctors, and professors. Despite the increase of women in professional settings, their proficiency has been put to the test. How Black women choose to wear their hair is a simple but significant phenomenon. Too often, women of color sacrifice their hairstyle to assimilate into their profession. Diversity among members in professional organizations might be advanced as the goal. With this socialized preference towards mainstream congruence, Black women have had to conform to the majority White society. This chapter looks at a professional woman of color, and her life-long journey to determine her hair as a significant part of her identity. Through a reflection on the author's hair life, this chapter discusses how imagery, mainstream culture, biases and expectations have played into her professional life. This chapter also discusses how future generations of professional women of color see contemporary accomplished women, and how they expect the world will see them.

This book chapter offers readers an opportunity to travel through time with the author on her personal hair journey. Readers will immerse themselves in the author's experiences from young adolescence through her adult professional life and have an opportunity to fully understand how those experiences impacted the author's feelings of self-confidence and self-esteem, which resulted in her going to great lengths to conform to what is considered acceptable and professional. The concept of hair bias will be examined and explored through the lens of the author's employment experience. Readers will discover how black hair has evolved from its natural existence to an altered state to conform to societal constructs, and how this has resulted in hair challenges for women of color.

What is it like to be a woman with wavy/curly hair in a country like India? Although hair stories are different for different women, one common hair story for all Indian women with wavy/curly hair is moments of insecurity regarding the normalcy and beauty appeal of their hair. Aside from the discrimination faced due to the texture of hair, Indian women also face restrictions and suffocations in terms of creative self-expression of hair. This chapter presents an overview of the hair culture in India from a historical perspective along with religious narratives. The nature of hair discrimination of women in India is discussed and the chapter also shed light on institutionalised illogical restrictions. The author's personal hair stories will serve as an example to underline the complexity of hair discrimination in India.

In this chapter, the author discusses a journey of natural hair acceptance. As a child, she struggled with not understanding how to care for her hair and the desire to have straight hair. She shares the challenges of conforming to Eurocentric beauty standards in institutions that require uniformity, such as cheerleading and military service in the United States Air Force. These experiences led her to focus on natural hair in her graduate studies. She discusses the challenges of wearing natural hair in graduate school and how discussions of professionalism and hair left her feeling isolated yet energized. Ultimately, she shares her recent experience with embracing her natural hair as a researcher and professional. As an assistant professor at a prestigious HBCU, she has increasingly fallen in love with her and other women's natural hair. She teaches students about the CROWN Act and has continued her research on natural hair experiences. Today, she credits her newfound confidence to spaces and people that accept and celebrate Black beauty and natural hair.

Rowe (2022) stated, "Perhaps a specific challenge for the advancement of Black women in higher education is correlated to how Black women are understood and assessed based on hair and hair texture" (p. 32). While higher education is often viewed as an institution to acquire new knowledge and understanding, cultivating a space of diversity and equality, the author's personal experience and the stories of other women in Rowe's article highlight the discrimination that exists while employed in higher education. In utilizing the conceptual framework of intersectionality, this chapter recounts the lived experience of a Black woman's struggle with unacceptance in higher education while pursuing her own self-acceptance. It tells the story of how her hair journey was one of the conflicting feelings of much pain, especially when the choice to go natural was not chosen by the one who had to represent it.

This chapter shares the personal experiences of the author as she worked her way up the corporate ladder while donning locs, aka dreadlocs. The goal of this chapter is to encourage Black women to embrace hairstyles that allow them to project confidence when being evaluated professionally instead of feeling pressured to conform to what the dominant culture narrowly defines as an acceptable professional appearance. The chapter discusses Black hair perceptions from pre-colonial Africa to the present, how these perceptions persist in corporate work settings in modern times, proposed legislation to police hair bias, and what leaders can do to influence their workplaces.

Hair is so culturally significant within the lives of Black women that the transition from high school to college forces Black female college students to make arduous decisions about how to care for and wear their hair in this untried and dislocated space. This chapter investigates the "turning point" or transition of Black female

Preface

As editors of this illuminating volume, *Women of Color and Hair Bias in the Work Environment*, we are delighted to present a comprehensive collection of personal accounts, research studies, and perspectives that delve deep into the complex relationship between professional women of color and their natural hairstyles. Our sincere hope is that this book will serve as a vital resource for all who are interested in the intricate dynamics of identity, equality, and cultural competency within the professional world.

This compilation has been painstakingly curated to address an issue of undeniable significance. It is a topic that has long been relegated to the shadows, where professional women of color have silently borne the weight of societal expectations and workplace biases concerning their hair choices. It is a topic that is both personal and political, as it touches upon issues of self-acceptance, authenticity, and the struggle to be recognized for one's professional competence, rather than outward appearance.

Professional women of color have, for too long, been thrust into the spotlight for their natural hairstyles, which often stand in stark contrast to mainstream Eurocentric norms. They have endured the weight of stereotypes, the pressure to conform, and the discomfort of having their identity scrutinized, all based on the way they choose to wear their hair. This book shines a light on their experiences, their resilience, and their ability to rise above the pervasive biases.

The viewpoints within this volume explore a wide array of themes, from personal hair journeys to the ethics of hair bias, from research studies of cultural acceptance to discussions on professional empowerment. They traverse the uncharted territory where self-identity and workplace expectations collide. The stories shared here are poignant, powerful, and, at times, painful. They highlight the challenges women of color face in a society that often equates professional appearance with adherence to certain beauty standards.

We firmly believe that understanding these experiences is crucial not only for the women who have lived through them but also for the organizations and individuals committed to fostering diverse, inclusive, and equitable workplaces. It is our hope that this book will provide insight and guidance for creating environments where every woman, regardless of her hairstyle, can thrive.

The intended audience for this book is as diverse as the women whose stories it encapsulates. It is for professionals in various fields, educators, business leaders, social scientists, and students. It is for anyone interested in the ethical, cultural, and diversity dimensions of the modern workforce.

The chapters contained within this volume offer a rich tapestry of narratives, insights, and recommendations. They explore the multifaceted issue of hair bias, and they challenge the status quo. They serve as a testament to the strength and resilience of professional women of color, who have navigated the turbulent waters of identity and acceptance in a world that sometimes fails to recognize their worth beyond their hairstyle.

In the pages that follow, you will find stories of triumph over adversity, reflections on the deeply personal nature of hair, and analyses of the societal constructs that have shaped our perceptions. We hope that readers will be inspired, enlightened, and empowered by the experiences shared within these pages.

Organization of Book

This work is divided into three sections.

Section One, (chapters one to six) focuses on personal hair accounts, including the struggles, heartaches, and realizations of women of color. This section uncovers delicate details of these women. Section Two (chapters seven to nine) covers research studies conducted on women of color from a variety of hair perspectives. The research from these chapters consider women of color from an assortment of backgrounds, including, college-level young women, to women employed in government agencies. Finally, Section Three (chapters ten to thirteen) draw attention to societal motivations, along with legal and governmental resolutions of natural hair.

Chapter 1

This chapter embarks on a journey of exploration into the life of a professional women of color. It examines the multifaceted roles women have taken on, breaking barriers and shattering stereotypes across various fields. However, it also delves into the less visible but equally significant challenge women face – the societal scrutiny of their hair choices. The author discusses how hair becomes a symbol of identity, addressing the pressures and biases that have forced many women of color to conform to mainstream standards. The chapter also looks at the impact on future generations, shedding light on how contemporary role models influence the expectations and perceptions of young professional women of color.

Chapter 2

This chapter offers readers a personal narrative of the author's lifelong hair journey, from her formative years into her professional life. Readers will gain insights into the author's struggles with self-confidence and self-esteem as she navigates societal standards of acceptability and professionalism. The concept of hair bias is examined through the lens of the author's employment experiences, shedding light on how black hair has transformed over time to conform to societal norms and how this evolution has presented challenges for women of color.

Chapter 3

This chapter explores the unique experiences of Indian women with wavy/curly hair, shedding light on the insecurities and discrimination they face regarding the normalcy and beauty of their hair. The authors provide a historical perspective on the hair culture in India, including its religious and societal narratives. The chapter delves into the complex issue of hair discrimination, highlighting institutionalized restrictions and sharing personal stories to illustrate the multifaceted nature of this challenge.

Chapter 4

In this chapter, the author takes readers on a personal journey of natural hair acceptance, starting from childhood struggles with hair care and a desire for straight hair. The narrative delves into the author's experiences in environments that emphasize Eurocentric beauty standards and the challenges faced in maintaining natural hair in such settings. The author's transformation, from isolation and insecurity to embracing natural hair as a researcher and professional, serves as an inspiring example of self-acceptance and empowerment.

Chapter 5

This chapter delves into the complex intersection of race, hair, and higher education. Using the lens of intersectionality, the chapter recounts the lived experience of a Black woman's struggle for acceptance in higher education, particularly regarding her natural hair. It highlights the conflicts and challenges faced by Black women who often find themselves representing a choice they didn't make, and how their journey is marked by pain, self-acceptance, and self-expression.

Chapter 6

This chapter explores the personal experiences of the author as she rises through the corporate ranks while proudly wearing locs. The central message of this chapter is to encourage Black women to embrace hairstyles that project confidence in professional evaluations, rather than succumbing to pressure to conform to narrow dominant cultural standards. The chapter delves into the historical perceptions of Black hair and their persistence in modern corporate settings, as well as legislative efforts to combat hair bias.

Chapter 7

This chapter explores the significant transition that Black female college students undergo when it comes to their hair choices as they enter a new professional setting. Through the narratives of 31 Black female participants, the chapter investigates the transformation from Eurocentric beauty standards to embracing their natural features. The study identifies connections between Black hair and identity through various themes, offering insights that can inform anti-bias training and policy changes on college campuses.

Chapter 8

This chapter delves into the impact of stereotypes, biases, and workplace policies on the self-expression and personal identities of Women of Color. Through a mixed methods approach, the chapter examines how textured hair is perceived as less professional, affecting self-expression and personal identities. The research offers valuable insights into how hair bias influences career choices and the experiences of women of color in the workforce.

Chapter 9

This chapter explores the role of hairstyle among African American/Black women working in government organizations. Drawing on qualitative data from focus group interviews, the chapter reveals the challenges and biases Black women face in the workplace. It also showcases how these women view themselves as leaders and advocates for change, even through their hairstyle choices.

Chapter 10

This chapter delves into the relationship between African aesthetics and natural Black hairstyles. It discusses how Black natural hairstyles, such as Afros, locs, twists, braids, and Bantu knots, align with African aesthetic principles. The chapter also addresses the discrimination and bias against natural Black hairstyles in the American workplace, offering an insightful perspective on the rejection of African aesthetics by European standards.

Chapter 11

This chapter deconstructs the assumptions and standards imposed on Black hairstyles in professional settings. Using an intersectional perspective, the authors examine the complex interplay of Black hair, culture, and identity. They explore the ways in which Black women experience external pressures to conform to whitewashed standards of professionalism and self-identity. The chapter also highlights hair discrimination lawsuits and concludes with equity-focused strategies.

Chapter 12

This chapter explores the complexities and simplicities of natural hair, focusing on the legislation designed to protect wearers from discrimination and bias. Through an examination of existing legislation and qualitative data, the chapter delves into the impact of discrimination and hair bias on individuals who choose to wear their natural hair.

Chapter 13

This chapter tackles the issue of hair discrimination and its implications for diversity, equity, and inclusion (DEI) initiatives in the workplace. The author explores the ways in which white supremacy culture shapes definitions of professionalism and the consequences of hair discrimination for Black women. Using an intersectional perspective, the chapter questions why banning afro-textured natural hair contradicts DEI initiatives and undermines Title VII of the Civil Rights Act of 1964.

Welcome to a journey that transcends hair and delves into the heart of identity, diversity, and professionalism.

Kula A. Francis
University of the Virgin Islands, US Virgin Islands

Anna M. Clarke
University of the Virgin Islands, US Virgin Islands

Acknowledgment

Thank you to the countless individuals who assisted in the formulation, preparation, and production of this book project. We are in deep gratitude to Dr. Kenny Hendrickson, Dr. Claudia Schrader, Dr. Latashia Edwards, Dr. Keisha Thompson, Dean Neijma Celestine-Donnor, Ms. Jocelynn Hessler, and finally, the CLASS Collaborative Initiative (CCI) of the College of Liberal Arts and Social Sciences at the University of the Virgin Islands.

Chapter 1
Mastering Matters of the Mane:
A Hair-Tale of a Professional Woman of Color

Kula A. Francis
https://orcid.org/0000-0002-7977-1769
University of the Virgin Islands, US Virgin Islands

ABSTRACT

Women of color have moved into professional roles to become engineers, lawyers, scientists, pilots, politicians, doctors, and professors. Despite the increase of women in professional settings, their proficiency has been put to the test. How Black women choose to wear their hair is a simple but significant phenomenon. Too often, women of color sacrifice their hairstyle to assimilate into their profession. Diversity among members in professional organizations might be advanced as the goal. With this socialized preference towards mainstream congruence, Black women have had to conform to the majority White society. This chapter looks at a professional woman of color, and her life-long journey to determine her hair as a significant part of her identity. Through a reflection on the author's hair life, this chapter discusses how imagery, mainstream culture, biases and expectations have played into her professional life. This chapter also discusses how future generations of professional women of color see contemporary accomplished women, and how they expect the world will see them.

DOI: 10.4018/978-1-6684-8790-7.ch001

INTRODUCTION

The experience of being a professional woman of color is significant. The struggles of how she adorns her hair bring a next level of consequences for women. Hair becomes a cruel hurdle for many women of color when considering that styling and caring for hair as it grows is not always accepted in many social and professional settings. The hairstyles of women of color serve as a direct form of communication as it quickly transmits messages of how they want to be seen (Powe, 2009). Drumond (2020) suggested that hair serves as a visual rhetoric that could positively describe a woman as having 'good hair' despite what society may not accept as such. In many instances, a woman's value is determined within moments of initial introduction, based on her appearance. A women's hair impacts their everyday outlook about themselves. Hair also affects how women are perceived. For a woman, how she wears her hair may affect her ability to land a job, the circle of friends she gains, her acceptance into social and professional groups, and even her spouse. In general, hair has the ability to determine so much about an individual in many black cultural settings. Understandably, the power of hair plays an important role in how women of color maintain and place emphasis on keeping hair groomed to their liking (Majali, 2017).

With hair holding so much influence, it is bound to become a major part of a woman's apprehensions. For many women of color, the inability to freely wear their hair in braids, cornrows, dreadlocks, or other natural styles is a challenge. Given that these natural styles are generally the most uncomplicated, healthiest, and less manipulative styles available for their hair (Henson, 2017). Unfortunately, these natural styles introduce many biases against women of color, and their capabilities. This chapter uncovers my personal hair story and offers perspective on hair as a professional woman. I also discuss conversations I have had with my daughter and nieces about how they view their mane, and what they expect the future of hair for women of color in the professional setting will be.

CHILDHOOD VIEW ON HAIR

The Banana Clip Fail

As a child, combing my hair was a task. I truly disliked every part of washing, clearing out, greasing, braiding, and even loosing out my hair. It was a process that early on felt like a punishment. At a young age, I had a thick full head of hair. The process of getting it combed felt like an eternity. As early as I can remember, my hair was washed and combed during the weekend for school during the week. This process was a weekly task that I believed was unfair. My brother didn't have this weekly routine, so why did I have to suffer through it while he could play outside, ride his bike, or enjoy any of his weekend time for himself? I remember complaining to my mother about how unfair it was. She would always respond with something reassuring, but I was always left with a sense of discontent. As I got older in elementary school, hair became more important to me. I wanted my hair to have styles and beads like other girls in my school. My mom would always fulfill my requests as best as she could. That is, until the third grade, when my request was to have it in a banana clip. Banana clips were the hottest look for girls during the end of the 1980's. Anyone who was anyone had one in their hair. My gracious mother happily purchased the clips in a variety of colors with all intentions of creating the style that I had wanted. I remember her brushing, and pulling, and giving it all she could, but the banana clip just could not clip. My significantly thick hair did not allow the clip to close. This was the first time I realized that hair did not come in one size fit all. My issue was not the length. By black girl standards, I had long hair; But even more important is that I also had very thick hair. Trying to keep up with the trends, my mother attempted another style with the banana clips, by parting my hair into what would most closely resemble the bunny ears style, with some of my hair out at the back. Still, the banana clips just would not hold. Unfortunately, the banana clip met the fate similar to many of the combs and brushes against my thick and wooly hair. The banana clip broke in two. As embarrassing as it sounds, breaking a comb, a brush, or a clip was somewhat of the norm for me.

Straighten me Yesterday!

Shortly after the banana clip hair fail, I became fixated on having my hair straightened. Based on my socialization in school, I had also seen many of my classmates have their hair relaxed. It was also common to see commercials on TV with beautiful little Black girls with "Just for Me" relaxer kits. I can still hear the jingle, as I sang along, "Just for Me"! I begged to get it, but my usually agreeable mom was not having it. As a matter of fact, both of my parents were very much against it. As they would say it, "You don't need to put chemicals in your hair". I remember being called Medusa because of the thickness of my hair when my mom neatly combed my hair in twists. My father was a proponent of natural hairstyles even when they had grown out of popularity from his generation. He grew up during the Civil Rights Movement, a time when the "Black is Beautiful" Movement helped to positively change the imagery people of African descent had of themselves (Roberson, 2022). For some, this period was a time of hair defiance. As a matter of fact, people with these hairstyles were thought of as defiant in general. Hairstyles included the afro, dreadlocks, cornrows, and puffs have been used to indicate rebelliousness in social and political spheres. This negative connotation has continued well into recent times.

In the highly publicized satirical cartoon drew by Barry Blitt, former First Lady Michelle Obama was portrayed as a militant, radical, gun carrying black woman by an illustration of her with an Afro as her hairstyle. (Johnson & Bankhead, 2014).

Despite my father's preferences for these styles, I simply wanted straight hair. I was attempting to conform to European standards of beauty, and intending to eliminate the beauty that was naturally my black hair (Carter, 2019). By the sixth grade, the social order of things at school started to become clear. Girls who had the straightened hair tended to be more popular. Historically, Black hair came with the connotation of 'bad' hair. Conversely, the kinkier the hair, the more negatively this hair became. This obsession meant that the closer to straight and white the hair, the more "good" the hair was considered (Majali, 2017). Bencosme (2017) posited that African American hair has a negative view because of its difference.

Another issue of hair became a competition of length. The longer their hair, the better. Growing up on the Caribbean island of St. Thomas, in the US Virgin Islands, the population was mainly African Americans. About 75-80% of my classmates were of African descent. There were at least 10-15% Hispanics (mainly Puerto Ricans and Dominicans), about 5-8% Indians (Mainly from Trinidad, are the descendants of Indentured Servants who moved to the Caribbean from India and South East Asia in the 1800's). Girls who were Hispanic, Indian, Native American and White generally had hair that was naturally straighter. If there were waves in their hair, it was not as tightly curled as the hair of Black girls. This meant they had "longer" hair. Longer hair meant better hair. Truthfully, longer hair meant overall, the girl was prettier. This was a problem among many within my elementary school. We were acculturated to believe there was a standard to how all hair should look.

Although there was beauty in all the varieties in my young world, our understanding was far from where we needed to be. Many of the Black girls, including myself, had parents who knew the importance of creating spaces to discuss self-love and individuality among mainstream acceptance. Even though my household was filled with positive assurances of the beauty of my brown skin, wide nose, thick lips, and bushy hair, I still felt a level of hair inadequacy among my peers. Still, like many of the Black girls in my school, I persisted. You would think being in a majority Black society would make it easier, but similar to the issues of colorism among the shades of blackness, it was just another area for Black girls to compare and reduce the spirit of other Black girls.

Hair Length Pissing Match

Hair became an extensive conversation during lunch and breaks. Girls would venture into, what I call "hair pissing matches", over whose hair was the longest. Generally, the length of straight hair was the only thing that would be considered. I truly believe we were too naïve to know that black hair had length, but it was curled into beautifully spiraled waves that hid its span.

My best friend in school was born in Dominica, and was mixed Black and Carib. Caribs are an aboriginal group, which is one of the few indigenous people found in the Caribbean today. She had thick and long flowing hair way beyond her back. She was the hair-envy of many of the other girls. Whenever the hair competitions began, all the other girls knew she had them beat. They would sometimes change the script, and exclude her from their pointless hair competitions. "Which Black girl in this class has the longest hair?" or "Jessica's hair is longer than Kenya's." were the types of conversations, drama, and initiations many young girls dealt with. Social pressures of believing Eurocentric features and hair begins at an early age through socialization (Bencosme, 2017). This again showed our immaturity and oblivious limited understanding of hair. The significance of hair length continued throughout the rest of my childhood, into junior and senior high school, college, and even early in my professional career.

Elementary school certainly played a big role in understanding how hair relates to societal ques, ignorance among others, gaining tolerance for bad behavior, and self-love. Hair is extremely important within the black community throughout the entire span of life. It is deeply rooted spiritually and culturally in how we view ourselves, how we communicate, and how we have perpetuated a well-established caste system that is determined largely by the texture of one's hair (Phillips, 2012).

Straight Hair Expectations

When I entered junior high school, the probability of straight hairstyle was eight straightened heads for every ten. Of course, my head was still natural. This was the age of exploration. These pre-teen girls wanted to try all the styles, and all the new fads. By this point, the blow dryer was the closest I got to straightening my hair. This came with some damage. Nonetheless, I enjoyed that my hair had a more desirable airy feel. The denseness of my natural hair was the enemy. I also was able to try using crimping hot curlers, a bang, which I held with a pink sponge roller at night, and the hot curler to curl the ends. This exploration was delightful for me. To some extent, it was an opportunity to discover how I wanted my hair to be styled. Although I was able to comb my hair, and complete quick braided styles, by junior high, even my best friend with the naturally gorgeous hair down her back had relaxed her hair. I continued to beg and plead with my parents to allow me to straighten my hair. They did not allow it. As the hair years went by, high school came with opportunities to participate in debutante balls, prom, senior picture day, and other events that required girls to always look their best.

My years of crying, begging, and giving all the reasons why I should be able to get a relaxer, was within hand's grip by my senior year. I had weighed down my mother. She understood! The struggle, my hair needs, my hair cries were generally directed to my mother. Still, my father was not in favor, and did not agree. In my eyes, he did not have an understanding of the difficulties women (and specifically me) went through to take care of hair. One Saturday morning during my senior year, without my father's complete consent, I secretly arrived to the hair salon. I arrived early - at least so I thought. Getting up on a Saturday earlier than I would during the weekday to get to school was absolutely abnormal. In general, Saturdays were my day to sleep in. I arrived at about 7:30 that morning. There was a sign-in sheet with eight names before mine. The entire waiting area was already filled. One by one, names were called. By the time I sat in the stylist's chair, it was already 10:00 am! The stylist hurriedly began to apply a base to my scalp. She parted my hair in four equal parts, and then proceeded to add a petroleum jelly-like substance to my head. She then asked me to return to the waiting area, where she did the exact same process with another lady who arrived behind of me. Once the stylist completed the latter lady's basing process, I switched seats with her. I was finally there!

The time I had been waiting for finally arrived. I was nervous and excited all at the same time. How will it look? Will I like it? How will my friends like it? What will my dad say? I remember the first dollop of the white cream being placed on my head. The stylist, a professional, effortlessly combed through my hair, from the root to the end of my hair, to get each strand of hair as straight as can be. As she worked her way through, she began to smooth the cream throughout my hair. She then placed me on the side, and told me, "You have thick hair, you are going to have to let this sit for a minute." She quickly called the lady whose hair had been based after mine. Again, she began the same process with the lady. I sat quietly and nervously, not knowing exactly what to expect. In the excitement of it all, I tried to ignore the tingling... No, I mean the burning that I was feeling in my head. I obliviously sat and wondered if I should say something. "Do I need to say something about the tingling?" "Should I speak up about the burn?" "Should I scratch my head?" "Should it hurt this much?" My mind was running a mile a minute. All the same time, the stylist would not even look my way. She was busy adding the relaxer to the lady's hair who came in after me. I started to become more and more antsy by the minute. The stylist finally looked over, and I instantly made eye contact. The stylist said, "Is it burning?" I quickly responded, "Yes!".

The stylist responded by saying that she will be with me in a minute. In that minute, I waited, expecting that she would wash out the relaxer that had now been in my head for at least 20 minutes. Within the minute, the stylist came over to where I was sitting, with a can of oil sheen hair spray. She asked me where was burning, and began to spray the oil sheen in that area. This was not at all what I expected.

Nevertheless, the sheen spray was not what I expected, but it did calm the burn; even if just a little. The lady who had come in after me was doing a process called a touch-up. Her requirements were not as overwhelming as mine. I looked away for a moment, and realized that she was now washing the relaxer out of her head. The stylist placed conditioner on her head, wrapped it with a shower cap, and placed her under a hair dryer.

Finally, I was called to get the relaxer out. The stylist washed it out, and conditioned it. As she applied the conditioner, I felt the glide of the comb go straight through my hair. I was screaming on the inside. The excitement! At that moment, I was so happy that my normally "break the comb" thick hair was no more. After sitting under the hot dryer for about 15 minutes for a full hair treatment and conditioner, I washed the conditioner out of my hair, and began adding plastic rollers to my hair. There is an obsession of straight hair plaguing many generations of women of color. They spend a great deal of money and hours in order to create the "good" hair distinction (Majali et al, 2017).

Once my hair was complete, about seven hours later, I felt like I had arrived. I had never in my entire life felt my confidence go so much through the roof. I felt beautiful, gorgeous, stylish, trendy, attractive, and on top of the world. I kept running my fingers through my hair. It was an amazing feeling! Again, the satisfaction of having long hair was of major importance of the process. I saw my hair become, what I thought was almost double in length.

The Reviews

Once I got home, I was met with my father's rejection to my new straight hairstyle. My father's disappointment played on his belief that people of African descent must love themselves as they are. He believed that my ability to love me should not require me to change who I was. He believed that my hair as it grew was a reflection of me – unprocessed and uncompromised. In reality, Black women and girls see their hair as "symbolic and an inseparable part of their identity" (Johnson & Bankhead, 2014, p. 89).

This was one time when his views did not matter. I mean, I couldn't stop looking in the mirror. I was happy, so I just wanted him to be happy too. At school, I received compliments everywhere I went. The girls, the boys, even the teachers approved of my new look. I could not be happier. Within a month, as the new growth came in, the luster and shine began to disappear. This was my first experience with why hair relaxers were called "creamy crack". Maintenance of the straightened hair required a touch-up or retouch. Once my hair was relaxed, I spent a lot of time and money in the hair salon.

Graduate School and Early Career

I attended an HBCU for my undergraduate degree. Although this choice made for a more conscious college experience, I was young in my understanding of how I wanted to be seen by others. Self-imagery paid a big part in this. I had grown accustomed to having Black professors with dreadlocks in their hair, and dashikis as their attire. I saw ample female professors, university employees and students wear braids and cornrows. It was a norm for me. It was not until I arrived at a Predominantly White Institution (PWI) for graduate school that I had full-on interaction with individuals who had no clue about black hair. It was my first need to describe black hair terminology to another person. It became a constant inquiry of my contemporaries.

In conversation with a small group of classmates, which included another Black graduate student, she discussed the process of greasing her hair. With all good intentions, our White colleague asked if it was done with the grease that she used to fry food. On another instance, I had traveled to New York City and gotten my hair braided. I mentioned something about burning the ends of the braids. The White colleague was completely shocked. She screamed out, "You burned your hair!" This really gave me a chuckle. There is no way that my White classmates would have had any idea of the process, products and time that Black women went through to get their hair done. After all, the customs, norms and activities of the Black minority had no bearing on the lives of the majority race in Ohio, or most of America for that matter.

Understanding that Whites were historically considered the dominant social group within my new environment, it became implicitly clear that the standards to determine what is professional, beautiful, and accepted was based on the physical characteristics of Whites (Koval & Rosette, 2020, p. 2). Moreover, conforming to what is accepted is an expectation of Blacks as a minority race. Blacks have had to obey, adapt, imitate and support white norms since their introduction to the Americas. Social control is embedded in a number of institutions that Blacks maneuver through on a daily basis (Joseph-Salisbury & Connelly, 2018; Oyedemi, 2016). Schools, clubs, and certainly workplaces preserve and perpetuate routines and requirements of Blacks as a normal part of the institution. Any deviation from the norm opens the possibility for missed opportunities for work advancements.

As I began my professional career, I became fixated with the frequency and type of styles I wore in my hair. I made it my business to schedule hair appointments to coincide with meetings, conferences, presentations, and other events related to my employment. McCluney et al. (2021) noted that it was common for African Americans to present themselves in such a way that they receive desirable outcomes. In the process of uncovering my appearance, I was compelled to alter my natural hairstyle as a method of conveying a positive impression. Aladesuru et al, 2020, posited that hair bias in professional settings does not only hold explicit bias, but also implicit predispositions. African Americans have been implicitly associated with intelligence aptitude below that of Whites. Afrocentric hairstyles bring additional focus to this categorization more than Eurocentric types of hairstyles (Aladesuru et al, 2020).

Although I enjoyed the convenience of wearing braids and cornrows, for any events outside of the classroom, I would remove the braids from my hair. Braids were taken out to ensure that I looked the part. The sentiments of looking the part is a common concern of Black women on many occasions. Michelle Obama realized that Americans 'weren't ready' for her natural hair (Oladipo, 2022). I did not want to encourage labels or become stigmatized as being the Black woman with the braids. Media already fed into the stigmas that change perceptions of many people who believe that Black women as ghetto if they braided their hair, young boys as hoodlums if they wore a hoodie, and Black men as marijuana smokers if they wore dreadlocks. It was important that others, whether Black or White, saw me as the professional that I had worked to become. In spite of everything, the perception of professionalism improves when the actions of the minority are similar to the majority in their organization (McCluney et al., 2021, p. 3).

Silky, Straight, and Limp

For almost two decades, I was a prisoner to relaxers. For the most part I enjoyed having straight hair. It allowed me to fit in – or at least feel like I was fitting in. I had somehow been brainwashed to believe the silky, straight hair was the only option. According to Carter (2019, p. 36), "Black hair in its natural form carry negative connotations of being unprofessional, unkempt, and messy." Eurocentric standards of beauty require people of color to take extreme actions to make and maintain unrealistic alterations to their natural self (Carter, 2019; Oyedemi, 2016). As the years went by, I realized that my hair was lacking the versatility that it was capable of having. My hair styles were limited to flat, limp styles, or a pony tail. My hair had no ability to defy gravity. The truth really was that I may have limited myself by having my hair relaxed.

Early in the 2010's, there became a number of research studies that discussed the harms that women who utilized relaxers were facing (Helm, 2019; McDonald et al, 2018; Zota & Shamasunder, 2017). There had been an increase number of women with fibroids, cancers, and other health complications. According to Helm et al (2018, p. 449), in the quest to conform to social beauty norms, Black women utilize hair products to straighten and moisturize their hair that is a potential source of exposure and health disparities. In 2023, the U.S. Food and Drug Administration reported that they intended to ban many of the products found in these hair products geared to Black women (Rabin & Jewett, 2023). Many of the chemicals found in the hair straighteners have been linked to possible developmental and reproductive disruptions, uterine cancers, and hormone altering effects (Chang et al, 2022; James-Todd et al, 2021; Helm, 2019).

I was quite concerned that the practice that I did every six-weeks could be harming me more than helping me. The chemicals found in these products often times are highly toxic, and contain formaldehyde (Aglan & Mansour, 2020). Knowing the academic findings on these hair straighteners was one thing. Being able to make a plan while maintaining a professional look was another issue. Once hair is relaxed, the only way out of the routine was to stop applying the relaxer, and letting hair grow from the root. In addition to physical damages, Donahoo and Smith (2019) suggested that Black women cause harm to themselves both physically and emotionally with hair straighteners, since the process reminds women of color that mainstream society does not accept or appreciate them as they naturally exist.

Although I knew I was on my way to ending my conceivably 'abusive' relationship with relaxers, I had not made the definitive assertion to stop. While getting my hair retouched with relaxer at a local Dominican salon, there was a major water line interruption. No water was coming through the pipes! Here I was sitting in the seat with the relaxer in my hair with no water to wash it out. Luckily there was a small convenience store next door, and the owner quickly purchased gallons of drinking water to wash the relaxer out of my hair. This served as my final relaxer. I did not feel that I needed to place possible injury on my body any longer in the name of having straight hair. I had finally made the decision to leave relaxers alone.

To accelerate the process of returning back to natural, some women do what is known as the big chop. In my eyes, only the brave could do this. Because of my insecurities, I transitioned my hair back to its natural state by the process of keeping my hair braided with extensions. As a matter of fact, extensions became my next security blanket. My hair eventually was completely liberated from any straight hair, but I realized that I had a new problem. I had not lived any of my adulthood with natural hair. How do I get my hair to the level of 'manageability' that I had grown accustomed to with relaxed hair?

Invasion of the Braids

As I transitioned out of the relaxer, I kept my hair braided. In addition to being a professional woman, I also became a mother. Any woman can attest to the time it takes to equally and effectively accomplish both. Nevertheless, it may require a great deal of effort, but being a professional working mother is certainly achievable. Braiding my hair became a security blanket and a quick solution to keeping my hair in order. My concerns with my new found style of convenience were threefold: First, I was concerned that braids may not come across as professional. As a Black female, it is quite easy to be perceived as unprofessional, not serious, or not prepared. I wanted to stay clear away from these types of biases. According to Koval and Rosette (2020), Black women face challenges in deciding how to present their hair more than most other races experience.

Although my role as an educator at an HBCU allows for some flexibility on hairstyles, there are times when interactions go beyond the acceptance of campus attire. In external meetings, national conferences, and presentations, I sometimes question if I will be taken seriously, or if assumptions are being made based on my hairstyle. The second concern that I had with braids is very similar to the research on hair relaxers. Academic resources have linked the plastics in the substances utilized in the synthetic hair extensions as toxic and harmful to the health of the wearers (Dike et al., 2022; Thomas, 2023). The man-made plastics and polymers create fibers that include a number of chemical components that may be doing more harm than women realize. In their 2022 study, Dike and collaborators found concentrations of heavy metals, including lead, cadmium, iron, zinc, vanadium, and high levels of nitrates in these popular synthetic hair packages (pp. 303-05).

Again, I find myself in a place where I attempt to ween myself off of the packaged, synthetic braid hair. I find myself returning back to them more than I sometimes intend. Additionally, as a mother of a daughter, I recognize that most of her peers wear hairstyles using this same packaged synthetic hair. It is a bit of a deja-vu because similar to how I begged for relaxers, as it was the "in thing", she is constantly requesting "braids". As a young girl, she asserts that she has grown out of barrettes, twists, cornrows and braids when done without hair extensions. As a parent, introducing anything that could cause harm is not practical. Although my daughter has worn synthetic braids on certain occasions, I hope she does not become attached to them as much as many women (including myself) in our communities are. The more versatile she becomes in her abilities to wear her natural hair in multiple styles, the less trapped into a specific hairstyle she will be. The third and final issue I have with braids with synthetic hair is that it encourages a perception that long hair is necessary or even better than natural hair. I have seen an increase in length of braids, and it again brings me back to my elementary school years of competitions of whose hair is longer than the other. Although with braids the extended lengths are an impossibility, culturally, it appears that there is something really important for braids to be long. I question if hair to a woman's knees could on any level be considered professional.

Conversation with the girls – Future Generation of Hair

During a recent family get together, I decided to ask a few questions to my nieces and daughter about their perception on Black hair. I also asked them about what a professional Black woman's hair looks like to them. Finally, I asked them in general, what they plan to do with their hair in the future during job interviews, weddings, and other important events. They all range in ages from 12 to 17. I also wanted to hear their views on what image professional women are passing on to young women. I was amazed by the commentaries they shared. One of my nieces, who is the most outspoken of the bunch, very talkative, and was a member of the championship debate team for her county, openly shared her experiences. She wears her hair in a natural afro. By most observers, her hair appears short in length and wooly. Of her sisters, she has the most tightly curled pattern of hair. The more tightly, generally spirally curled natural hair is, the more it is rejected by society, whereas, the more loosely curled natural hair falls, the more likely it is to be considered acceptable. According to Johnson and Bankhead (2014), "tightly coiled hair was considered deplorable when pitted against straight European hair that is considered beautiful and attractive" (p. 88).

Historically, African Americans have internalized the idea that natural hair was unacceptable (Byrd & Tharps, 2014). Despite her hair type having negative reference, my niece was overall optimistic about the future of her hair, but also admitted to sometimes having moments of strain because of her hair. In its natural state, it does not do the things most people around her have the ability to do with their hair. She mentioned that at her part time job, the requirement is that all women wear their hair pulled back off their shoulders, and into a neat bun. Based on her natural growth pattern, her hair would have to be relaxed, blow dried, or manipulated through an unwelcomed process, to get it pulled back into the appropriate requirements of her job. As the only Black employee in her store, she has never been reprimanded for failure to pull her hair back, but she realizes that it is probably because the policy was not written with people like her in mind, and her managers probably have little understanding of her hair. This brought on a lot of debate among the entire family, whom were all very engaged and appreciative of the discourse. Although it is not an issue for my niece, it has been for many women of color. "Policies and expectations that dictate styling guidelines for Black hair... outside of health and safety interfere with the rights of Black women" (Donahoo & Smith, 2019, p. 198).

The Crown Act (2022), Creating a Respectful and Open World for Natural Hair Act makes it illegal to discriminate based on a hair style or a person's hair texture. (H.R. 2116 – 117th Congress). I asked my niece if she could think of any person in the media that she would like to gain their level of success, that have hair that looks like hers. She was silent in her thoughts for some time on this question. She then intelligently said that there are few to no individuals who display their hair as she does that she could look up to. She also said that people who appear in the media are forced to change the way they look, just to be heard. She then mentioned that the only person who she could think of that has hair similar to hers was Kenyan actress,

Lupita Nyong'o. My niece quickly said that she has no interest in acting, but if she had to pick someone to look up to with hair like hers, that is the only person she could possibly think of. I felt really uneasy for that moment. It reminded me of my childhood, and not knowing many women who were considered someone to know that did not have long flowing hair.

My second niece, who is 15, has a different, more socially desired hair pattern to her older sister. She generally wears twist outs, wash and goes, and curly afros. Her comments were straight forward. She said, "Professional hair on Black women look just like my hair". She went on to say that, "Any hairstyle I choose to wear is professional." Finally, she said, "If I carry myself professionally, my hair automatically is professional." My thoughts took me back to her sister's position. It was easy for my second niece to form her opinion and give an answer because she did not have to deal with the issues or concerns her sister was facing. Had my second niece been in the job of her older sister, she could easily pull her hair into the required hairstyle. She could easily do many of the things with her natural hair that her sister could not do.

As I continued to lead the impromptu discussion, I asked the question, "What does a professional woman look like to you?" My daughter and my youngest niece, 12 and 14, respectfully, responded very similarly. When their opinions were combined, the image was a White woman with blonde flowing hair, a suit with a knee length pencil skirt, and two to three inch pumps on her feet. This made me realize that society still plays a major role in dictating what a professional woman should look like. As the conversation continued, with many tangential shifts in the direction, my youngest niece, the niece with the naturally loosest curls and longest observable hair said that she believed that she wore her hair in an afro. She then said that a White classmate had told her once that her hair isn't an afro because it does not stand up. Again, her hair was being defined by a White student, in a manner that she did not perceive for her own hair. For a moment, she felt like her identity as a Black girl was being questioned. I asked her then, if she ever felt that she needed to change her hair, or would be willing to change her hair to fit in, or in the future, to get a job. My 14-year-old niece's response was instant. "My hair is my identity. I am not willing to change my hair ever!" She snickered and said, "Anyone asking me to change my hair has committed a hate crime." The entire family burst out in laughter. In reality, although we found it amusing, a request to change our natural hair truly shows some level of hate against us. This is the level of bias that many women of color face on a daily basis in the workplace. In particular, Black women with natural hair struggle with issues of identity, based on their appearance. (Summers et al., 2022). These types of hair biases, according to Trusty, et al (2022) often occur both consciously and unconsciously among hiring managers, recruiters, leaders, and professionals.

I have seen the effects that social media has played on the development of these young girls in my family. I also see my hair-behaviors and habits become a piece of the puzzle that molds them. I know that hair is important to them. As for my daughter, I see how she uses her hair as a social device. How it is combed changes her level of confidence, changes how attractive she feels about herself, and she believes determines how the world will see her. As agonizing as her hair's power on her life has been at just 12 years, I understand; I have been there. I too have felt like I could command an audience during a presentation best with hair that flows. I too have felt a greater sense of being liked with straighter hair. I too have looked in the mirror at natural curls, and thought it not as attractive as I would like. What is important for me at this point in my life is to discontinue the power hair has had on generations of women of color. As I suppose that my daughter and my nieces will become professional women one day, I hope that they are able to enter the workforce as their natural and authentic selves. I hope that they focus on their career much more than on their hair. I hope that employers, coworkers, and the world, do not hold biases against them because of their hair.

CONCLUSION AND FUTURE

Although my personal hair journey is still complicated, emotional, difficult, and important to me in how I am perceived, I am hopeful that the future, and young girls of color will have more strength, confidence, and gumption not to be concerned about how others see them. My personal hair journey has repeatedly played over into my professional life. The fears, obstacles, preparation, and time spent focusing on hair has been significant. In as much as I am happy with my career advancements, had half of the 'hair-energy' been applied to research papers, presentations, grants, community service, and other professional requirements of my field, successes would have been over the moon. The transformations of contemporary professional women of color have not gone unseen. Black women are proudly adorning styles that they would have been fearful of wearing a generation ago. There is a small wave of African American women changing the appearance of professional black hair. Individuals such as Associate Justice of the Supreme Court, Judge Ketanji Brown Jackson, American politicians Ayanna Pressley and Stacey Abrams, have proven that hair should not be a variable of determining black competence. Certainly, my hope is that hair is not an indicator of a woman's intellectual abilities, job performance, or competencies. As far as I see it, the future will consist of women taking charge of defining our own beauty, for proving professionalism is not a cookie cutter formula, and demanding that what they present in any professional setting is what will be acceptable in hair. I enthusiastically anticipate that we can accept the magnitude of the hair that defies gravity.

REFERENCES

Aglan, M. A., & Mansour, G. N. (2020). Hair straightening products and the risk of occupational formaldehyde exposure in hairstylists. *Drug and Chemical Toxicology*, *43*(5), 488–495. doi:10.1080/01480545.2018.1508215 PMID:30208743

Aladesuru, B. H., Cheng, D., Harris, D., Mindel, A., & Vlasceanu, M. (2020). To Treat or Not to Treat: The Impact of Hairstyle on Implicit and Explicit Perceptions of African American Women's Competence. *Open Journal of Social Sciences*, *8*(10), 13–22. doi:10.4236/jss.2020.810002

Bencosme, Y. (2017). Beauty is pain: Black women's identity and their struggle with embracing their natural hair. *Perspectives*, *9*(1).

Byrd, A., & Tharps, L. L. (2014). When Black Hair is against the rules. *The New York Times*. https://www.nyti.ms/1hU86nF

Carter, K. (2019). Workplace Discrimination and Eurocentric Beauty Standards. *GPSolo*, *36*(5), 36–39.

Chang, C. J., O'Brien, K. M., Keil, A. P., Gaston, S. A., Jackson, C. L., Sandler, D. P., & White, A. J. (2022). Use of straighteners and other hair products and incident uterine cancer. *Journal of the National Cancer Institute*, *114*(12), 1636–1645. doi:10.1093/jnci/djac165 PMID:36245087

Dike Ijere, N., Okereke, J. N., & Ezeji, E. U. (2022). Potential Hazards Associated with Wearing of Synthetic Hairs (Wigs, Weavons, Hair Extensions/Attachements) in Nigeria. *Journal of Environmental Science and Public Health*, *6*, 299–313.

Donahoo, S., & Smith, A. D. (2022). Controlling the crown: Legal efforts to professionalize black hair. *Race and Justice*, *12*(1), 182–203. doi:10.1177/2153368719888264

Drumond, S. E. (2020). *Hair: How Naturals Are Using Social Media to Reshape the Narrative and Visual Rhetoric of Black Hair*.

Helm, J. S., Nishioka, M., Brody, J. G., Rudel, R. A., & Dodson, R. E. (2018). Measurement of endocrine disrupting and asthma-associated chemicals in hair products used by Black women. *Environmental Research*, *165*, 448–458. doi:10.1016/j.envres.2018.03.030 PMID:29705122

Henson, R. (2017). Are My Cornrows Unprofessional: Title VII's Narrow Application of Grooming Policies, and Its Effect on Black Women's Natural Hair in the Workplace. *Bus. Entrepreneurship & Tax L. Rev.*, *1*, 521.

H.R. 2116 – 117th Congress (2022). *Creating a Respectful and Open World for Natural Hair Act of 2022*. US Congress. https.www.congress.gov.bill/117th-congress/house-bill/2116/text

James-Todd, T., Connolly, L., Preston, E. V., Quinn, M. R., Plotan, M., Gandi, B., & Mahalingaiah, S. (2021). Hormonal activity in commonly used Black hair care products: Evaluating hormone disruption as a plausible contribution to health disparities. *Journal of Exposure Science & Environmental Epidemiology*, *31*(3), 476–486. doi:10.103841370-021-00335-3 PMID:33958708

Johnson, T. A., & Bankhead, T. (2014). *Hair it is: Examining the experiences of Black women with natural hair*.

Joseph-Salisbury, R., & Connelly, L. (2018). 'If your hair is relaxed, white people are relaxed. If your hair is nappy, they're not happy': Black hair as a site of 'post-racial' social control in English schools. *Social Sciences (Basel, Switzerland)*, *7*(11), 219. doi:10.3390ocsci7110219

Koval, C. Z., & Rosette, A. S. (2021). The natural hair bias in job recruitment. *Social Psychological & Personality Science*, *12*(5), 741–750. doi:10.1177/1948550620937937

Majali, Z., Coetzee, J. K., & Rau, A. (2017). Everyday hair discourses of African Black women. *Qualitative Sociology Review*, *13*(1), 158–172. doi:10.18778/1733-8077.13.1.09

McCluney, C. L., Durkee, M. I., Smith, R. E. II, Robotham, K. J., & Lee, S. S. L. (2021). To be, or not to be… Black: The effects of racial codeswitching on perceived professionalism in the workplace. *Journal of Experimental Social Psychology*, *97*, 104199. doi:10.1016/j.jesp.2021.104199

McDonald, J. A., Tehranifar, P., Flom, J. D., Terry, M. B., & James-Todd, T. (2018). Hair product use, age at menarche and mammographic breast density in multiethnic urban women. *Environmental Health*, *17*(1), 1. doi:10.118612940-017-0345-y PMID:29301538

Oladipo, G. (2022). Michelle Obama says Americans 'weren't ready' for her natural hair. *The Guardian*. https://www.theguardian.com/us-news/2022/nov/17/michelle-obama-natural-hair

Oyedemi, T. (2016). Beauty as violence: 'beautiful' hair and the cultural violence of identity erasure. *Social Identities*, *22*(5), 537–553. doi:10.1080/13504630.2016.1157465

Phillips, M. (2012). Black hair politics in White academia: With reference to Black studies. In M. Christian (Ed.), *Integrated but Unequal: Black Faculty in Predominantly White Space* (pp. 94–104). Africa World Press.

Powe, A. (2009). Beyond the pencil test. Transformations in hair and headstyles, or communicating social change. *Glocal Times*, (12).

Rabin, R. C., & Jeweth, C. (2022, October 16). F.D.A. plans to ban hair straighteners with Formaldehyde: The products, often marketed to Black women, have been linked to an increased risk of uterine cancer. *The New York Times*. https://www.nytimes.com/2023/10/16/health/hair-straighteners-black-women-fda.html

Roberson, A. (2021). White Hair Only: Why the Concept of Immutability Must Be Expanded to Address Hair Discrimination Against Black Women in the Workplace. *U. Det. Mercy L. Rev.*, *99*, 223.

Summers, L. M., Davis, T., & Kosovac, B. (2022). Hair we grow again: Upward mobility, career compromise, and natural hair bias in the workplace. *The Career Development Quarterly*, *70*(3), 202–214. doi:10.1002/cdq.12302

Thomas, C. G. (2023). Carcinogenic materials in synthetic braids: An unrecognized risk of hair products for Black women. *Lancet Regional Health. Americas*, *22*, 22. doi:10.1016/j.lana.2023.100517 PMID:37274553

Trusty, J., Ward, D. A., Good-Perry Ward, M., & He, M. (2023). Hair Bias in the Workplace: A Critical Human Resource Development Perspective. *Advances in Developing Human Resources*, *25*(1), 5–26. doi:10.1177/15234223221135557

Zota, A. R., & Shamasunder, B. (2017). The environmental injustice of beauty: Framing chemical exposures from beauty products as a health disparities concern. *American Journal of Obstetrics and Gynecology*, *217*(4), 418.e1–418.e6. doi:10.1016/j.ajog.2017.07.020 PMID:28822238

Chapter 2
Hair in My Feelings

Anna M. Clarke
University of the Virgin Islands, US Virgin Islands

ABSTRACT

This book chapter offers readers an opportunity to travel through time with the author on her personal hair journey. Readers will immerse themselves in the author's experiences from young adolescence through her adult professional life and have an opportunity to fully understand how those experiences impacted the author's feelings of self-confidence and self-esteem, which resulted in her going to great lengths to conform to what is considered acceptable and professional. The concept of hair bias will be examined and explored through the lens of the author's employment experience. Readers will discover how black hair has evolved from its natural existence to an altered state to conform to societal constructs, and how this has resulted in hair challenges for women of color.

THE NAPPY YEARS

Mbilishaka, et al. (2020), explain how African American women have had hair styling experiences with their mothers growing up that they internalize and can recount right through their adult years. My experiences confirmed what the authors informed as they are extensive, and I frequently recounted many to my own daughter as we shared hair experiences during her childhood. I recall one such experience that had such a profound impact on me and informed how different my hair texture was from that of which I loved.

My mother would frequently comment that my hair was thick and coarse as she would comb it for school or church. These two words were always used to describe my hair as a child. Of course, I did not know what those words meant,

DOI: 10.4018/978-1-6684-8790-7.ch002

and probably thought both were flattering until I realized what they meant later in life. Throughout my childhood, I hated my hair and wished I could change it, and I did, if only for a few minutes daily. Each day, I sat on the floor in front of our floor-model television, watching cartoons and living out fantasies in my head. Every day the colored television in our living room played the Johnson's Baby Shampoo commercial repeatedly, and I imagined myself as the girl in the commercial. Three words stuck in my head from that commercial - "soft, beautiful hair." The little white girl's hair in the commercial was long, silky, soft, and beautiful. Her hair draped over her shoulders. That is what I wanted, and that was what I imagined on myself as the commercial played, hence changing my hair for a few minutes daily. Each time the commercial came on, I sat glued to the television.

Do you know that Johnson's Baby Shampoo was the only shampoo my mother bought? The commercial said it was gentle enough to use daily, so I did. I washed my hair as often as possible since the commercial said it was gentle enough to use daily. In addition to what the commercial said, my mom told me that the shampoo would make my hair look like the girl's hair in the commercial if I washed my hair with it. Who would not believe their own mother? You know, if your mother said something, it was as good as gold; therefore, I believed her. So, I did; again, and again, and again. My hair never changed; rather, it remained the same each time I washed it…thick and coarse. I could not understand why. I was crushed. It was a severe blow to my ego. I did not like or want my own hair. In fact, I really hated it. What did I see reflected in the mirror? Black, coarse, short hair that would not move unless touched and, even then, would stand still. The worst part was going to the beach because it would look like a little black boy's hair when it was wet - short and nappy, with little peaks of hair sticking straight up, making me look like the heat miser from The Year without a Santa Claus. My hair made me feel ugly, and I was ashamed of it. I wanted her [girl in the commercial] hair because her hair made her look pretty, while that is not the feeling I got from my hair. Wong, Williams, Tolliver, & Potts (2023) tell us that a mark of identity for African American women is our hair and that it can seriously influence our self-perception. My perception of self was confirmed by the authors' point of view as I did not like my hair at all and felt badly about myself whenever my mother would comb and braid my hair. The combing process was a great challenge as it was physically painful. The physical pain was one challenge, but there was also an emotional component to it that was a completely different challenge and one that I believed would be my cross to carry for life.

THOUGHTS AND FEELINGS

Adolescence was a challenging time for me, as I was subject to bullying and teasing along with suffering with identity issues. Other girls my age would express their discontent with their hair as well, so I knew this challenge was not unique to me. There were other challenges that my friends experienced during that time that I did not understand at that age, but hair was one of those challenges that we would share about. My primary challenge was my hair that influenced how I felt about myself, which I later learned that I suffered with low self-esteem. The authors Phelps-Ward & Laura (2016) supports this notion as they suggest that black adolescent girls face many challenges that negatively impact their self-esteem daily, and some of these challenges hinder them from reaching their full potential. The way I felt about my hair was the last thing I expected to have to manage, and I did not realize home deeply it impacted my self-esteem.

Moreover, I did not realize that, as an adolescent, I would have to navigate the dominant societal narratives of what beautiful hair was, and I did not do it very well. I say this because comments about my coarse hair would hurt me deeply. My self-esteem plummeted, especially when my peers at school and within the island community would engage in hurtful, teasing comments about the texture, length, and hairstyles my mom would subject me to. Picky bo-bo! Nigga Naps! BB shots (the way the hair curls at the nape of the neck (your kitchen)!

Honeycutt & Wright (2017) discuss a concept referenced as positive teasing. This concept suggests teasing in the form of comments meant to influence bonding and relationships or express positive feelings of admiration. The teasing directed towards me seemed to be just the opposite of bonding, admiration, and building relationships. Rather, the teasing I endured hurt and humiliated me. This only added to my already low self-esteem. After much time and humiliation, my mother found a solution that eased my pain emotionally but added another layer of physical pain I could never imagine. Little did I know, help was on the horizon that would erase my emotional pain but give rise to a new kind of pain.

THE HEAVY METAL DAYS (HOT COMB)

Introducing…the hot comb! Yay! It was my mom's viable solution to all my hair problems, or so she thought. I am sure you can relate to the hot comb if you are a Silent Generation, Baby Boomer, or Generation X cohort member. I am also sure that most, if not all, of the girls my age at the time dreaded Saturday afternoons. Those afternoons were reserved for Sunday service preparation, which was mostly the "pressing your hair" routine.

The routine involved a kitchen chair, usually one from the dining room set you sat on, and a heavy metal hot comb. How it worked was that the hot comb was placed in the fire of the stove top burner to heat the metal comb part. The hair was twisted into about eight sections with Dax grease (Sulfur 8, Afro Sheen, Vaseline, or whatever grease your Mom thought was best) dabbed into the scalp and hair strands. Once the comb was heated in the stovetop fire, my mom glided it through a section of the hair at a time, leaving each section soft and straight to the ends. When the comb made contact with the grease, it created a sizzling sound, much like when the chicken was placed in hot vegetable oil to fry. This process was adequately described by Cox (2018) based on the Netflix movie 'Nappily Ever After' where the author references the smell of burning hair and keratin and the sound of the sizzle, snap, and crackle.

Moreover, If the hot comb was placed too close to my hair root or my ear, a new layer of pain ensued, causing me to pull away in a jerking movement that resulted in my mom apologizing and telling me to sit still. This would happen several times throughout the process, making it a dreaded routine, but one that I would like to think of as a necessary evil to get the end result of straight hair, which I absolutely loved. Cox (2018) confirms this feeling as she wrote about the character in the Nappily Ever After Netflix movie receiving compliments indicating her hair was long and pretty, after having to sit through an eight-hour hair straightening process. This was my reality as well.

Hot combing made my hair straight, gave it much more length, that a gentle breeze could blow through it, whereas it could not before. In those days, all black women and girls would use sponge rollers to curl our hair, which we called setting our hair. The next day, once the rollers were taken out, the result would be curls to style any way you'd like. I loved the sponge roller set as my hair would hang loosely, almost on my shoulders, much like the little girl in the Johnson's Baby Shampoo commercial. Most of all, hurtful teasing comments from my peers became a thing of the past, and my confidence level was through the roof with my newfound hair texture and various hairstyles. Increased self-confidence resulted in increased self-esteem which was a direct result of my hair/appearance.

Research confirms a relationship between hair and positive self-concept and self-esteem. A study was conducted with eleven female African American girls in foster care where hair and hair's association to the girls' sense of sense and self-esteem was examined. Several themes emerged, but the one theme that confirms a relationship between hair and self-esteem is the girls identifying their hair as important, and noted their appearance is connected to their appearance, it influenced who they are, and how they saw themselves as African American females (Mitchell Dove & Powers (2018).

CHEMICAL ADDICTION

The hot comb was a miracle worker for black women and girls like me, and I loved how my hair looked after the grueling process. It made me look good and feel better about myself and that was all that mattered to me. Little did I know then that I was conforming to society's standard of what beautiful hair was. At that time, I only knew I wanted my hair to feel soft, bounce, and blow in the wind like most girls my age.

While the hot comb was great, there was something that proved to be even better. I went from hot combing my hair to a chemical perm (short for permanent wave) or relaxer by the fifth grade because perming your hair became a "thing" at my school. I reference this period of time in my life as my chemical addiction because the more I had my hair permed, the more I loved and wanted perms, hence my reference to the perm as an addiction. My chemical addiction became my new reality as I remained on this destructive hair trajectory through my mid-thirties.

My chemical addiction remedied the love hate relationship I had with my hair over the years. I forced my hair to conform to the dominant societal narrative – straight hair. I had perms/relaxers, an S-Curl, Hawaiian Silky, finger waves, and anything else that achieved the accepted look of straight hair; that made it soft and beautiful; just as the Johnson Baby Shampoo commercial said. I loved the straight hair look and the compliments derived from it, so I continued my chemical addiction journey.

Perms were my new normal from school days throughout my mid-thirties. It was during that time, when I began experiencing severe headaches that forced me to seek medical assistance from a dermatologist. Per the dermatologist, the consistent years of perming resulted in a condition that made me experience migraine-like headaches and hair loss that she referenced as alopecia. The hair loss could be seen in different areas of my scalp, but especially in the crown or center of my scalp. She further explained that the damage resulted directly from the chemicals used in the relaxer.

The finding of my dermatologist is confirmed by authors Madu & Kundu (2014) who explain that various methods of hair grooming to include chemical relaxers, hot comb straightening, sew-in or glued weaves, tight braids, etc. result in damaged hair follicles and irritation to the scalp. Moreover, the authors Seité, Dantec, Demessant-Flavigny, & Kerob (2023) further explain that the chemicals used to treat hair cause harm to the hair shaft and scalp; that the possible consequences of this include irritation to the skin, allergic dermatitis, hair loss, and risk of cancer. Hindsight is twenty/twenty. Given this information, it appears that the risks of developing one of these conditions was not worth the beautiful straight-hair look.

I am certain that my mom did not know about these consequences associated with the prolonged use of chemical relaxers. The consequences were unknown to me before I began experiencing hair loss (alopecia) and severe pain (intense burning from the chemical perm during the perming process) in my scalp. I became increasingly concerned as my symptoms worsened, which prompted a visit to a different dermatologist for a second opinion. I flew to Puerto Rico for a second opinion due to lack of faith in the medical diagnosis of my local dermatologist. The decision to fly to Puerto Rico was the voice of our island mentality creeping into my head as we always believe medical care elsewhere is superior to our own. Once again, I was informed of the consequences of years of chemical relaxers and was encouraged to permanently refrain from relaxing my hair. Given the diagnosis and medical advice from both dermatologists, I thought it best to immediately cease perming my hair and return to a natural hairstyle, free of all hair chemicals that could result in further damage to my hair and scalp. Since I could no longer use hair chemicals, I had to find a natural hairstyle. After much thought, I settled for a braided hairstyle using hair extensions.

LADY OF EXTENSIONS

Isn't it funny how life repeats itself? Here it is I began my hair journey with my mom braiding my natural hair. I ran away from hair braiding to hot combing my hair, then using a chemical relaxer for a completely different look that I thought was best and most beautiful. Well, I was back to where I began with braiding, but this time, I had braids that were now a "thing," and hung loosely, giving me the long hair look, I wanted and deemed beautiful.

I wore braided hairstyles to avoid relaxing my hair, for obvious health reasons. Braids, better known as extensions, made my hair look as beautiful as a hot comb style and doubled the length, which I appreciated. The only downside was I had to sit in a chair for many hours while a stylist added store-bought, human hair to my own hair, forming singles or cornrows in a particular style of my choosing.

While my braided hairstyles were beautiful and a great alternative to having my hair permed, the first few days of pain after the initial braiding (especially around the edges) was a serious challenge I had to consistently navigate. The newly braided hairstyle would remain tight until the braided style loosened over several days with new growth. During that time, my scalp felt like someone took a razor and peeled off my skin. I do not know which was worse, the intense burning from the perm or the first few days after a braided hairstyle.

As my scalp improved, my edges began to disappear. This could have resulted from the tight braiding at my hairline each time I had a new style braided. Despite my disappearing edges, I continued wearing braided hairstyles until I was about forty years of age or in my mid-forties. I decided I could no longer tolerate the pain I've always had to endure during the braiding process and the loss of my edges.

Since I arrived at that conclusion, the next best decision to preserve the hair I had left was to grow my own hair in dreadlocs (locs for short).

What would be the benefits of growing locs? I would be growing my own hair. Also, there would be no stress to my hair follicles and scalp. Moreover, my hair and scalp would no longer be subjected to harmful chemicals. Lastly, the cost of perms and braided hairstyles and the many hours of sitting in a chair would be a thing of the past for me. These were all positive reasons to grow my own hair. With that said, I used my last braided hairstyle (single braids) as the foundation to begin my loc journey that I knew I could manage and maintain independently. When the single braids grew out from the root, I would twist the new growth at the root clockwise. The twisting of the hair root resulted in the hair strands being forced to fuse together and lock in place. Eventually, I had the beginning of locs with braids hanging loosely. This began my loc journey.

ROPING IT IN

Some people call them dreadlocs, dreads, or just plain locs. They are all the same hair strands that have a rope-like appearance once the hair is, fused, braided, or matted together (Glace & Waldstein, 2022). In fact, Wong, et al. (2023) further describe dreadlocs as a hairstyle that requires low maintenance, the hair "locks" into place, and it is a permanent hairstyle that requires individuals to cut their locs off.

How did this hairstyle come about? Marcus Garvey, a prophet and founding father of African nationalism, was a staunch advocate of Africans (those residing in America and the diaspora) wearing their hair in a kinky (natural) fashion. Just as the Afro did, dreads or locs became known as a way of disagreeing with or refusing white dominance and standard of beauty. Moreover, the prevalence of locs throughout the Caribbean and its diaspora is generally credited to the Rastafari movement, which made the hairstyle more popular through Reggae music (Glace & Waldstein, 2022). Locs have now evolved from solely attributed to the Rastafari religious movement to a popular hairstyle.

I loved the look of locs and watching others don the increasingly popular hairstyle. In fact, I believed the hairstyle would look great on me. Therefore, when my little locs grew to the point where they hung loosely but short (picky phase), I cut the braids off so they could grow naturally on their own from the loc'd roots. This phase of my loc journey was the most challenging and less fashionable as my loc'd strands could not be twisted in styles due to their limited length. I really disliked this phase of my journey and wished I did not have to go through it, but it was a necessary evil to reach the length I wanted; not unless I opted to wear scarves and/or hats, as most people did, until my locs grew longer, so I would not be so self-conscious about them.

Head scarves and hats did not seem a viable solution for my place of employment at the time, as I was employed at the Governor Juan F. Luis Hospital and Medical Center as a Medical Social Worker at the time of this momentous decision. Hats and head scarves did not conform to a professional appearance that aligned with the dress code, at least in my opinion. Therefore, I continued to don my short locs until I had enough length to twist them into different hairstyles.

BIASED BEYOND RECOGNITION

I was excited to work at the hospital and looked forward to becoming enmeshed in the hospital's culture. While I did not begin my tenure with my dreadlocs, I believed my self-expression would be embraced. Why? First, because of the total employee population - 95% were residents and as such, should be aware of and comfortable with the hairstyle. Second, there was such a large percentage of locals, they should be culturally sensitive and accepting of my self-expression. Lastly, I never heard of locs being an issue at any agency on the island before. Therefore, I did not believe I would encounter any issues with my new demonstration of identity and individuality.

However, I would soon realize that my belief was wrong. One day, I was walking in one of the hospital's halls in the administration section when a female administrator from the hospital's administration team saw me. She approached me with a look of disdain on her face as she inquired, why would you put those things in your hair? At first, I wondered if something was stuck in my hair that I was unaware of. After pausing to think about her question and patting my hair to see if something would fall out, I asked her what she meant by that. She responded by indicating that she was referencing my locs. Once again, she inquired as to why I would put those things in my hair, as she phrased it. She followed up her question by telling me that the look did not compliment me and that I would look much prettier with a perm. She went on to tell me how beautiful she thought I was and how she thought I dressed so stylishly; that she could not understand why I would want locs in my hair. She finished her rant by reminding me that I was in a professional environment, and that locs did not look good on me; that locs were unprofessional, and that I should take them out.

Her rant made me feel ashamed and embarrassed. Her judgment of my locs was harsh and unnecessary. This unpleasant encounter made the emotional pain I felt in the past resurface – the self-doubt and self-hatred were back, and this time, with momentum. Why was it so painful? It was painful because another black, local said it, but more importantly, another black female said it. I do not expect children to fully understand the impact of their words on others. However, adult professionals must be aware of their words' impact, especially if those words have a negative connotation.

Words can make us feel good or bad, happy or sad; therefore, women of color should be circumspect about the words that leave their lips. I firmly believe that you do not have to verbalize every thought that comes to mind, especially if those words could hurt the receiver. As a professional woman of color, I do not feel the need to speak on everything and keep some thoughts to myself in the interest of protecting the feelings of others.

As professional women of color, we should empower others, build each other up, and not tear each other down and make other women feel bad about themselves, much like what was done to me by the administrator. Her comments cut like a knife and made me feel so badly about the way I looked when I did not think it was a poor look on me. It was difficult working through the rest of the day. Whenever I entered a unit, I was worried that others would look at me and talk about how unprofessional my hair was and how terrible it looked. I wanted to go home but could not. It was the most uncomfortable feeling to remain at work when all I wanted to do was leave or have the earth open and swallow me whole. Moreover, as I walked the hospital's halls, each time I encountered someone, I became extremely self-conscious about how I looked. I was worried as I searched each person's face for some sign of disapproval. I felt paranoid all day until I left, worried that I looked like a mess in the eyes of others who may not be comfortable telling me how I really looked. I kept wondering why locs would not be seen as professional. After all, it is hair, black hair, at that, in a black community. It is loc'd black hair that can be pulled into a ponytail, braided, worn loosely, or twisted into many hairstyles. Is it, not the same as having permed hair that can be worn in a ponytail, loosely, braided, or in other styles but just a coarser texture? I would say yes, but the hospital and/or society may believe differently. Why would loc hairstyles be unacceptable and unprofessional to some?

What I experienced at the hospital affected my self-esteem and distorted my sense of professionalism. It is now considered an emerging barrier where women of color, who embrace their natural hairstyles, such as locs, are targeted at their places of employment; it is called natural hair bias. Natural hair bias is considered to be a form of social injustice where individuals who don natural, coarse, or Afro hair types are seen negatively and often perceived as looking unprofessional, unattractive, less beautiful or desirable, or even unclean (Summers, Davis, & Kosovac, 2022). Armed with the aforementioned information about hair bias, it is clear that this bias can affect the perception of beauty for women of color, their self-esteem, and their sense of professionalism.

HAIR HER-STORY (HISTORY)

As black women, we have historically been seen as not good enough, and everything about us, from our skin color to our features, has been criticized and judged. Remember what happened after emancipation? Dawson, Karl, & Peluchette (2019) inform us that there was a northern movement from the South, and having straight hair was associated with attaining a certain status in society. The authors further explain that those blacks with straight hair reaped socioeconomic benefits because of it. As blacks migrated from the rural South to more urban areas in the North, they fought hard to be accepted socially, which included exchanging their black Southern hairstyles (plaits, braids, and cornrows) for the northern straight hairstyles as they tried desperately not to look like an uneducated person from the South. Given this information, you can see that from slavery to today, we have been conditioned to believe our hair, the way we speak, our features, etc., do not meet certain social constructs. So, what have we done historically?

As blacks, we have consistently tried to conform to what society says is acceptable or meets its standard. It is sad but true that we have been conditioned to think that if it is white, it must be right. With this stated, historically, we have strived for soft, wavy hair that mirrors white women's hair. As black women wanting the look of white women, we would sear our ears weekly with hot combs to soften our coarse tresses and to have straight hair, like white women. When lye became a thing, we permed our hair burning our scalps raw, to have straight hair that would mirror white women's hair. It did not matter what we had to do; we did what was necessary, from perms to Jheri Curls and now weaves. By any means necessary, no matter the cost, to be accepted and achieve the "look." We have been conditioned for so long, jumping through hoops and torturing our beautiful black tresses to gain acceptance, that we reject our own natural black hair. Hence, the reason locs would be deemed unacceptable and/or unprofessional, that is, to some.

Black women have been subjected to and have had to manage negative stereotypes and biases aligned with their natural black hairstyles. Unfortunately, a great deal of these biases is still in existence in society today. As these biases increase and intensify, they have the potential to make black women feel more easily seen in their workplaces. What is considered to be the "norm" in workplaces usually supports a Caucasian culture (Karl, Peluchette, & Dawson, 2022).

PROFESSIONAL OR UNPROFESSIONAL?

Many agencies and organizations – public, private, and non-profit- have policies that speak to employees' expectations, which may include their hair (Onnie Rogers,

Versey, & Cielto, 2022). However, people should be free to express themselves however they want. Self-expression is important to me, and I felt ugly, ashamed, and embarrassed when my locs were judged and criticized. I can understand an agency policy that speaks to clothing. For example, a behavioral health agency may have a policy that prohibits short skirts/dresses and revealing clothing because clients receiving services there may present with sexual challenges. Therefore, it would be completely understandable if someone from HR approaches an employee with a concern about this type of clothing if worn to work. I can also accept a policy that dictates certain shoes be worn to work for safety reasons. Given the environment, a policy may address hair if it presents safety concerns, such as wearing a beard in areas in a refinery or at the Fire Department. However, as it relates to hairstyles, I have great difficulty trying to understand how a particular hairstyle could be considered unprofessional. I can understand how attire can be considered unprofessional as it is a social construct everyone aspires to and can attain, because it is all relative. In fact, all agencies have a dress code that employees must adhere to, but I am sure the dress code does not stipulate which hairstyles are acceptable and which are deemed unprofessional. Employees should feel empowered to express their personal style and individuality through their chosen hairstyle as long as the hairstyle is neat and clean.

My short locs hairstyle was neat and clean, so what made it look unprofessional? My position would be absolutely nothing, except for one female's irrelevant opinion based on her perspective of what she deems a "professional hairstyle" should look like. Unfortunately, I let that female's biased opinion influence my next decision. When I returned home from work that evening, I sat in my living room for hours, with a comb and brush, and combed each loc out. Her words weighed heavy on me. It felt like a sword cutting through my armor of confidence. As I brushed the last loc out, I went against medical advice and returned to a permed hairstyle to look professional, as the administrator suggested.

BURN, BABY BURN!

The following week, after having brushed out my locs and permed my hair, I returned to the hospital with a freshly permed hairstyle, and I was immediately complimented by the administrator. She complimented me on my hairstyle indicating that my hair looked much better than those picky locs I was sporting, as she so frankly put it. Although I was thinking she was a bit crass in her commentary, I politely thanked her as there was no need for further conversation with someone who makes me feel bad about myself one day and good the next.

Returning to a permed hairstyle was not the best decision, and I knew it, but I let this woman's crass comments force me back into pain and further hair loss (alopecia) to look a certain way and feel accepted. Each month, when I visited the hair salon to retouch my perm, it would consistently burn in the same area – the center (crown) of my scalp. This is where I experienced the most hair loss (alopecia), and it continued to worsen as time wore on. Why didn't I continue on the same natural hair journey? I would silently repeat this question to myself, often enough. I knew why but did not dare return to what I knew was best for my hair. I feared the backlash – negative remarks, criticisms, and judgments. Therefore, I suffered in silence for many months. It was not the easiest thing to do. However, my hairstyle received many compliments, so I thought the physical pain (severe burning from the perm) and continued hair loss (alopecia) were well worth it, as a permed hairstyle made me look good, receive many compliments, and conformed to the professional expectation at my place of employment. Obviously, the physical pain I was withstanding was sheer desperation for the emotional fuel necessary to boost my self-esteem. But at what cost? Research confirms the prolonged and permanent damage resulting from chemical relaxers. The damage is not only physical as women can also suffer emotional damage in the form of low self-esteem.

Yongyu He, Yu Cao, Binji Nie, & Junpu Wang (2023) discuss the effects of using chemical relaxers. Per the authors, while a perm produces the desired results of straight hair, there have been some associations with perms and hair and scalp issues for many years. The authors further explain that during the perming process, there may be some physical damage known as thermal damage to the hair and scalp; that this means if there is not an appropriate amount of the combined chemicals used during the process, the reaction when in contact with the scalp is that of a substantial amount of heat. The authors further indicate that the scalp is sensitive and fragile, and because of this, the heat generated feels like an intense burning to the woman undergoing the perming process, and that feeling may burn the scalp.

Per Yongyu He, et al. (2023), the scalp injuries resulting from the burning may look different. This may include redness of the scalp, blisters, and inflammation. If the damage is extensive enough, there may be damage to the skin; the hair follicles in the area where the damage occurred cannot be restored after being destroyed. This permanent hair loss is one of the most critical consequences of the burning and is referenced as alopecia, which occurs at the damaged site. This alopecia causes more than physical pain; it alters a woman's physical appearance, negatively influencing her emotions, such as low self-esteem.

Research supports the assertion that hair is critical to the development of identity and self-esteem. Negative hair experiences influence injuries to both as confirmed by the authors Mbilishaka & Apugo (2020). As I recall the many negative hair experiences from childhood and my emotional responses, such as embarrassment and shame to those experiences, it is obvious that those responses were carried over to adulthood when I encountered the negative loc experience.

Many women of color had the same and/or similar emotional responses as I did, when confronted with hair bias experiences. This issue is widespread for many women of color in the workplace as confirmed by research. For example, Dawson, et al. (2019) shared about a study that was conducted in the United States with 2,990 respondents who identified as either Black, Hispanic, Caucasian, or multiracial/multiethnic. Per the authors, the respondents were either engaged in part-time or full-time employment. The age range of the respondents, all of whom were from the United States, was indicated to be between 25-64 years of age, per Dawson et al., (2019). The results of the research study suggested that women of color shared the same position, which was that black hair is most likely to be judged as unprofessional and the respondents also felt that they had to wear their hair straight during job interviews to succeed, per the authors. This study confirms the feelings women of color express having to navigate to obtain and/or maintain employment. Per the authors, those feelings include fear of losing employment, being reprimanded, and/or denied employment. The feeling of being reprimanded fueled my decision to return to unhealthy hair practices, which in the long term proved to be the worst decision for me personally but seemed to be the best decision professionally. It was the consequences of that decision, that overshadowed what I was experiencing professionally, and resulted in my return to a natural hairstyle.

GROWTH

After receiving the dermatologist's second opinion, I decided to support my natural, healthy hair growth. After all, when you know better, you do better. It is a demonstration of personal growth. The only viable option at the time that would support a healthy scalp and thereby hair growth was a loc'd hairstyle, which worked well for me in the past. Therefore, I returned to growing locs once again.

In the past, there were many benefits derived from my loc'd hairstyle, but most important to me included avoiding all harmful chemicals and consequences associated with using chemical relaxers and saving money on hair appointments. Both were of paramount importance to me. Besides these reasons, given what I knew from research, both dermatologists, and my personal experiences with other hairstyles that warranted the use of chemicals and stressed the hair follicles, it would be hair suicide to continue the destructive hair trajectory I was on. Therefore, I returned to my loc'd hairstyle.

After a few years, I was able to attain the length I had the first time I had locs. In the absence of chemicals, my scalp improved. I enjoyed maintaining the hairstyle for over fifteen years with a length below my waist – healthy, natural hair growth.

I did so without ridicule or reprimand from anyone in any position of authority at the hospital. Surprisingly, the female administrator who was so moved to approach me in the past, criticizing my locs, complimented me many times on the styles I would twist my locs in and reminded me on a few occasions of her initial impressions. My self-esteem increased along with my confidence – personal growth.

When I returned to my locs hairstyle, I did so without ridicule or reprimand at the hospital. The administrator who felt so moved to judge my locs never had a disparaging word to say again. In fact, I was able to move beyond the negative comments and rebuild a positive, professional relationship with that administrator – professional growth.

I wore locs for over 15 years until alopecia surfaced and forced me to cut my locs due to losing so many as I experienced gross hair loss. The challenge of hair loss influenced efforts to seek alternative hairstyles to complement me personally and professionally. Weaves became my new normal for the past several years as I do not have the confidence necessary to shave my head. To date, I continue to suffer with excruciating scalp pain that sometimes lasts for two to three days. This is a direct result of the scalp burns from the years of chemical relaxers.

This chapter began with feelings that influenced low self-esteem to include hurt and humiliation. Both were quickly replaced with the word beautiful, as I tried different hair treatments and styles. Ultimately, it was my natural, black hair that I discovered was beautiful and made me feel good about myself. I sincerely hope other women of color may benefit from my story and would not allow hair bias experiences to negatively impact their self-esteem or alter their sense of what is beautiful and/or professional.

REFERENCES

Cox, E. (2018). Black Girl Magic sparkles again: Netflix's "Nappily Ever After" is the hair representation we've been looking for. *UWIRE Text*, 1.

Dawson, G. A., Karl, K. A., & Peluchette, J. V. (2019). Hair matters: Toward understanding natural Black hair bias in the workplace. *Journal of Leadership & Organizational Studies*, *26*(3), 389–401. doi:10.1177/1548051819848998

Glace, N., & Waldstein, A. (2022). Spiritual hair: Dreadlocks and the bodies multiple in Rastafari. *Journal of the Royal Anthropological Institute*, *28*(1), 279–296. doi:10.1111/1467-9655.13660

He, Y., Cao, Y., Nie, B., & Wang, J. (2023). Mechanisms of impairment in hair and scalp induced by hair dyeing and perming and potential interventions. *Frontiers in Medicine*, *10*, 1139607. doi:10.3389/fmed.2023.1139607 PMID:37275367

Honeycutt, J. M., & Wright, C. N. (2017). Predicting Affectionate and Aggressive Teasing Motivation on the Basis of Self-Esteem and Imagined Interactions With the Teasing Victim. *The Southern Communication Journal, 82*(1), 15–26. doi:10.1080/1041794X.2016.1265577

Karl, K., Peluchette, J. V., & Dawson, G. (2022). Why So Much Ado About a Hairdo? Examining How the Hair Choices of Black Women Vary by Occupation. *Journal of Business Diversity, 22*(1), 10–22. https://www.proquest.com/scholarly-journals/why-so-much-ado-about-hairdo-examining-how-hair/docview/2643280738/se-2

Madu, P., & Kundu, R. (2014). Follicular and Scarring Disorders in Skin of Color: Presentation and Management. *American Journal of Clinical Dermatology, 15*(4), 307–321. doi:10.100740257-014-0072-x PMID:24820821

Mbilishaka, A. M., & Apugo, D. (2020). Brushed aside: African American women's narratives of hair bias in school. *Race, Ethnicity and Education, 23*(5), 634–653. doi:10.1080/13613324.2020.1718075

Mbilishaka, A. M., Mitchell, D. S. B., & Conyers, C. (2020). Grandma's Hands: Memories of Hair Styling Interaction with African American Grandmothers: Research. *Journal of Intergenerational Relationships, 18*(2), 139–155. doi:10.1080/15350770.2019.1658008

Mitchell Dove, L., & Powers, L. E. (2018). Exploring the complexity of hair and identity among African American female adolescents in foster care. *Children and Youth Services Review, 95*, 368–376. doi:10.1016/j.childyouth.2018.10.043

Phelps-Ward, R. J., & Laura, C. T. (2016). Talking back in cyberspace: Self-love, hair care, and counter narratives in Black adolescent girls' YouTube vlogs. *Gender and Education, 28*(6), 807–820. doi:10.1080/09540253.2016.1221888

Seité, S., Dantec, G. L., Demessant-Flavigny, A., & Kerob, D. (2023). Survey of Hand Issues Encountered by Hairdressers and Hairdresser Related Professionals: From Epidemiological Data to Clinical Observational Survey Results. *Clinical, Cosmetic and Investigational Dermatology, 16*, 111–117. doi:10.2147/CCID.S385681 PMID:36698444

Summers, D., Davis, T., & Kosovac, B. (2022). Hair we grow again: Upward mobility, career compromise, and natural hair bias in the workplace. *The Career Development Quarterly, 70*(3), 202–214. doi:10.1002/cdq.12302

Wong, N., Williams, K., Tolliver, S., & Potts, G. A. (2023). Hair length in association with hair care regimen and healthy habits in Black women. *Journal of Cosmetic Dermatology, 22*(8), 2361–2363. doi:10.1111/jocd.15696 PMID:36994547

Chapter 3
Contemplating Hair:
Many Shades of Hair Oppression in India

Indumathi Somashekar
https://orcid.org/0000-0002-0340-1526
Christ University (Deemed), India

ABSTRACT

What is it like to be a woman with wavy/curly hair in a country like India? Although hair stories are different for different women, one common hair story for all Indian women with wavy/curly hair is moments of insecurity regarding the normalcy and beauty appeal of their hair. Aside from the discrimination faced due to the texture of hair, Indian women also face restrictions and suffocations in terms of creative self-expression of hair. This chapter presents an overview of the hair culture in India from a historical perspective along with religious narratives. The nature of hair discrimination of women in India is discussed and the chapter also shed light on institutionalised illogical restrictions. The author's personal hair stories will serve as an example to underline the complexity of hair discrimination in India.

INTRODUCTION

What is it like to be a woman with wavy/curly hair in a country like India? My hair stories are perhaps different from other Indian women with not-so-straight hair, but I am certain that it is replete with intense moments of disappointment and self-doubt. In India, hair is not just the crowning glory of a woman, but it also determines one's measurement of beauty, prospects of marriage, and even respect. In modern times, hair also determines a woman's measure of worth, and suitability in a workplace. It can also be used as an instrument of oppression.

DOI: 10.4018/978-1-6684-8790-7.ch003

My hair is complex and so is my relationship with it. It is not outright straight nor curly. Some parts of my hair are more straight than curly and vice-versa. Some people describe my hair as wavy. But I can never be sure. And there are days when it is frizzy, thanks to humidity. But my hair has a mind of its own and has never stayed the same way for as long as I can remember. My hair has always been a cause of worry for me right from childhood. To be more specific, it is not my hair, rather the people who make nasty comments about my hair. What puzzles me is that even in my 30s and in this 'neo-liberal' age, I find myself having to confront with hair bias and insults.

The most recent memory I have is of a confrontation I had in my workplace in February 2020. This was right before the pandemic raged and swept the world. It was a regular day at work except that I let my hair loose which is normally tied into a bun or half-tied, half-loose. As a college professor teaching journalism and communication, one would least expect to hear personal remarks especially about one's hair. I walked into my class brimming with confidence feeling extra special because of the open hair. The class went quite well. I walked out and took the elevator. My supervisor was there. She was a woman in her late 40s and for the three years, I worked with her, I thought of her as extremely conservative. She looked at me with disgust, and ordered, "Tie your hair. It does not look good." To which I retorted, "Do you tell other people to tie their hair?" Her immediate response was, "Don't argue with me. I just told you. It does not look good to go like that with your hair open when you go to class."

I was shocked at her condescending and derogatory remark. I was utterly speechless because, one does not hear such conversations, much less direct order to tie one's hair, in a civilised society. I was shocked at her crude behaviour. But I did not let it go. I was fuming and had to confront her. I waited till all my classes for the day got over. I told her clearly that I do not appreciate her personal remarks. But she got defensive and told me that that this was my problem and must have been so since childhood. Well, when things got ugly, she walked away without giving an explanation nor an apology. Later, I sent her a mail and called out her authoritarian and cultural bullying, only then could I breathe. There were two other female professors in the same department, and when I checked with them, they confided in me that they never received such directions from her. I was not surprised because both these professors had relatively straighter hair, and would often leave their hair loose.

The popular perception of an educational institution to dispel myths and create agents of change and transformation may not hold true to all the universities and colleges, especially in a country like India. Even a professor of journalism and communication who teaches the duties of press to lend voice for the voiceless, can get ridiculed in her workplace for her hair by another professor, and get away scot-free. For some people like me, it is relatively easy to fight the perpetrator head-on, and the self-doubts that arise as a result of such violation. But for others it can be scarring and debilitating.

In this chapter, I try to outline the hair culture in India by revisiting the history of hair along with religious narratives of hair. Hair has been an important cause for concern and discussion in both educational institutions and work places. The hair politics in these different institutions will be discussed. A discourse on issues is incomplete without personal stories that reflect the larger reality. My hair stories will keep us company as I delve into the complexities of hair style, texture, and colour for Indian women and the challenges that they face.

HAIR HISTORY

To begin with, a historical perspective of hair culture in India could serve as a background to understanding the hair politics in India. Hair is associated with beauty in India, and possessing thick and shiny hair is considered as a sign of beauty and vitality. According to history books, Indian women applied coconut oil to nourish their hair and for the glossy appearance (Nichols & Kenny, 2017). In fact, the ancient science of cosmetology is said to have originated in Egypt and India way back in circa 2500. Great importance was given to beautification and early records reveal the special herbal ingredients and remedies for hair growth, hair fall, premature grey and even hair dyes and perfumed hair wash (Patkar, 2008).

According to Patkar (2008), these herbal practices were associated with the daily activities of life in ancient India and was extended to not only hair but also the health of the skin. Herbal masks to improve the size of the breast, mouth freshners, and depilatory masks, were popular herbal treatments promoted to improve the beauty of women. These ayurvedic remedies were so popular that even the kings invested their time in testing their efficacy and documentation. For instance, the Raja Serfoji acquired the throne of erstwhile Thanjavur in the state of Tamil Nadu in India. The Raja spent time carrying out research and testing their potency on patients, and elaborate herbal remedies were recorded by him.

One of the herbal formulas recorded by the Raja for healthy hair is a combination of the juice of the popular Indian herbs *Bhringaraja, Triphala, Baheda, Lohakitta, Amla* to be cooked in oil. This concoction when applied to the scalp of head had the potential to treat itchy scalp, alopecia, cure dandruff and even darken premature grey hair. This is a typical example of importance attached to wellness and beauty in India.

The different Indian women hair types and styles were also prominently featured in the sculptures and artwork in the early Indian civilisations (2500–1700 BCE). Intricate hair styles were a dominant feature of women in the Indus Valley Civilisation as depicted in the bronze sculpture of the famous dancing girl from Mohenjodaro.

The bronze showcases a lady with a heavily coiled mane of hair emerging from the left ear that cascades over her right shoulder (Kalra, 2015).

The diverse nature of India is also depicted in hairstyles in different parts of the country at different time periods. During the Mauryan empire (322 BCE - 185 BCE), women either braided their hair or showcased shaved heads. Another popular hairstyle of women in ancient India was hair tightly coiled around head. Mauryan empire women were fond of head-dress and arranged the hair by pulling them on the top of their head in a knot. They also parted their hair in the middle which is common even today.

The Vijayanagara Period (1336 - 1646) in the Southern part of India was known for many things including its cultural extravaganza. One of the popular hairstyles during this period which is predominantly used at present is the long-braided hair look which is typical of a South Indian woman. The hair is adorned with sparkly ornaments. The Tamil Sangam literature describes women parting their hair into five sections, plaiting them separately, but tying them together at the back in a graceful manner (Patkar, 2008).

FAITH AND HAIR

Religion plays an important role in Indian culture, and religion also has control over hair practices in India especially on women. Since India is a multi-religious country, the different hair culture pertaining to specific religions could sometimes turn into a cause for controversy. In Hinduism, one of the dominant religions of the country, Hindu gods both male and female gods are depicted with long and loose hair, but strangely different interpretations are given to the state of hair in Hindu religious texts. For instance, loose hair that are untied is said to represent wild nature. That is why it was customary to oil hair, comb it thoroughly and keep it tied (Trüeb, 2017).

The Goddesses Lakshmi, the consort of Lord Vishnu, and popularly known as the goddesses of wealth and prosperity is often depicted in paintings with long curly hair which is let loose, but adorned with accessories. The Goddesses Saraswati, the consort of Lord Brahma is also portrayed having loose, long straight or curly hair, and her hair is adorned with a crown. Goddesses Kali, consort of Lord Shiva, is also shown having either long, curly, wavy or even straight hair that is let loose (Trüeb, 2017); (Choi & Choi, 2009).

In the early period, women sporting loose hair is considered as domestic nature connected with sexual intimacy. Sculptures portray erotic couples with loose hair. Men and mostly women are expected to not present themselves with loose hair in public. Rituals connected to hair and hair forming part of Hindu rituals is common in India. For instance, the Hindu babies undergo the first cut of their hair. The age of the babies differs among different families. It can range anywhere between a year old to even 3 years. The ceremony is grand, and food is offered to relatives and friends (Hiltebietel & Miller, 1998).

Such rituals are known as Samskaras which means the rites of purification. The head shaving ceremony is carried out to ensure that hair at birth is removed to enable the child to be free from the problems of the past life. Another reason for removing the hair is to promote good growth of hair. It is also common for men and women to shave their heads and offer hair to the Gods as a token. This custom is popular in temples such as Tirumala Venkateshwara Temple in Tirupati, Arulmigu Dhandayuthapaniswamy Temple in Palani, Tamil Nadu (Trüeb, 2017).

As a practicing Hindu, I have visited many temples in the southern part of the country. When I think of places of worship, what comes to my mind is of course the rituals, fragrance of incense, flowers, and most importantly peace in the presence of God. One would hardly imagine that a mere visit to a temple with your hair open can invoke the wrath of certain ladies at the temple. I can recall at least two such incidents in two different cities. One pleasant evening in the Summer of 2012, I visited a temple in Chennai along with my mother and aunt. I had left my hair loose, and I was just casually strolling through the temple, when a bunch of ladies gave me strange looks and after a point of time, it seemed as if there were writhing in suppressed anger. They almost screamed at me for letting my hair loose. They commanded me to tie my hair immediately. I felt humiliated and angered at complete strangers' yelling at me, and forcing me to tie my hair. But I had no choice, but to tie my hair, as I winked back my tears. I did not want to anger the mob further as there was no telling how extreme a situation could get.

I faced something similar the very next year, and this happened in my own city, Bangalore. My family visited a temple for performing certain rituals that helped with alleviating testing times. It was late in the evening, and a thick envelope of smoke from the yagna surrounded the temple. This was when a lady at the temple decided to tell me to tie my hair. It goes without saying that she was rude, and what was more puzzling was her reason for policing me. Apparently, it was unwise to leave one's hair open in the late evening, as it is a popular belief that ghosts often latch onto open hair. If you are wondering my reaction to it, I walked away from her, and did not force myself to listen to her command. I was done with people telling me how to style my hair. Of course, I considered it as a superstitious belief at that time. But I will not lie that there are times I am hesitant to leave my hair open in dark and isolated places in the night. That lady got to me on some level, much against my wish and expectation.

INSTITUTIONS AND INSTITUTIONALISED HAIR CONVENTIONS

Obedience is the norm for survival in this world, and to work in a company, one of the basic traits one must possess is of course compliance. 'Do not question nor answer back, you are only required to follow the rules' - this golden rule is taught at a very young age in schools and extends to colleges to get everyone work-ready. Almost every aspect of a child's life is controlled in terms of dress, hair, time, way of speaking, etc. In countries like India, the rules and regulations in educational institutions pertaining to hair among other things can be considered as a violation of personal freedom of choice and comfort. It is indeed unfortunate that such rules are normalised and even accepted by parents, and some parents even prefer such rules because they want their wards to grow into an 'obedient' person with no sense of personal choice.

SCHOOL IS WHERE IT BEGINS

The regressive practice of controlling hair in educational institutions in India is unfortunately normalised. For instance, it is a common rule in many of the schools in India to force school girls to part their hair and braid them into two plaits. In the recent past, this was contested by students who even filed complaints. Aside from prescribing uniform, many schools have been prescribing hair style for girls and when the rules are not followed, the students are reprimanded (Express News Service, 2016).

A twelfth standard school girl, Alsha in the state of Kerala in India filed a complaint against the school regarding the rule of compulsory plaiting of hair by female students. The complaint was filed with the Kerala State Commission for Protection of Child Rights (KSCPCR) in 2016. The KSCPCR came in support of the student and called the rule a violation of child's right. This further led to the Kerala Directorate of Higher Secondary Education and the Directorate of Vocational Higher Secondary Education passing an order that female students cannot be forced to plait their hair in higher secondary schools.

In her complaint with the KSCPCR, the student had raised some concerns with respect to the compulsory hairstyle which included the problem of foul odour that developed due to plaiting wet hair, lice infestation, and scalp issues. She also pointed out the practical difficulties involved in the plaiting the hair as that required her to seek help from her parents in the morning, and hair problems such as split ends. She also mentioned that the compulsory rule made the students to not wash their hair which further resulted in health problems. The student also called out the rule as gender discriminatory in nature ("Kerala school girl", 2016).

When I was a child, hairstyling was a never-ending nightmare. First, as a school going child, I had no freedom to wear the hair style of my choice, both at home and in school. I can think of numerous days when I went to school teary eyed because of the conflict between my choice, and my mother trying to groom my hair according to the school's regulations. There are many layers to the hair regulations of the schools back in the 90s. Girls must part their hair right in the centre and style it into two plaits. And for girl's whose hair was longer than shoulder length, it was necessary to plait them with a ribbon, and fold the plait secure it at the crown of the hair with the ribbon. In my opinion, this is a horrendous hairstyle which I loathed growing up. I hated everything about it, right from the way it looked to the way it felt. I could sense the tiny hair prick my scalp and the ribbon felt tight and tiresome. It was a humiliating experience that I had to endure every single day.

This was a strict rule and must be followed, and failure to do so would result in painful punishments such as kneeling in the assembly quadrangle. Teachers, especially the Physical education teachers were given the additional responsibility of enforcing these atrocious rules. Although I liked long hair, I would often pester my mother to cut it short to avoid wearing the folded plait hairstyle. When I completed my schooling, I was happy for more than one reason, including freedom of my hair choice, well, for the most part.

One would think that such hair regulations in schools are a thing of the past, but you would be surprised to note that even at present, some schools force girl children to wear a certain hairstyle, as evidenced in the news reports that I mentioned earlier. In fact, a few years ago, my niece came home crying because one of her teachers reprimanded her for parting her hair sideways rather than in the centre. However, one significant change is that some students and their parents instead of blindly succumbing to such illogical rules are revolting against dreadful practices of certain schools.

STRAIGHT HAIR MANIA IN COLLEGES

Growing up in the late 80s and early 90s, I always thought that curly hair was fashionable as every other model or celebrity on TV was sporting a spring curly hair look. But my opinion began to change in the late 90s and early 2000. Suddenly pin straight hair was considered not only stylish, but normal as well. This may not seem problematic, but when there is a general perception that anything other than straight hair is not normal or in other words pleasant-looking, this opens door for insecurity, bullying, among others.

As I entered college, I saw pretty girls with straight and shiny hair just like those perfect haired models in fancy shampoo advertisements. Little did I know that many of these girls had paid for their straight hair. Raised in a conservative family, my socialisation during school days was limited to school friends in schools and nothing beyond that. So, unlike other kids, I was ignorant of many of the modern fashion tips that many girls my age were privy to. It was only in college I realised that some girls ironed their hair to achieve straight hair look, and this is not the modern-age flat iron devices, but the iron machine used for ironing clothes. Although this came as a shock to me, I was desperate to straighten my hair because by then the mania for straight hair as a beauty and status symbol had struck me as well. I remember laying out my good and healthy hair on bed and ironing it with an iron box. At first, nothing seemed to change the texture of my hair. But then I could see some changes. I was happy with the result, and decided to leave the box on my hair for longer duration for faster results. The result was an almost burnt hair and smell. I soon developed dry hair with split ends, and never dared to straighten my hair with an iron box ever.

Since I hailed from a lower middle-class family, paying my college tuition fee was a challenge for my parents, and to expect them to pay for hair straightening never occurred to me. The best that people like me could manage was a quick visit to a nearest salon for a temporary straight hair during important college events such as ethnic day, graduation day or convocation. During my college days, I cannot remember a single soul complimenting my wavy hair. But I do remember people mocking my hair and resorting to name-calling. I can vividly remember a classmate, an immature boy calling my hair 'buddhi ke baal' in Hindi language. I did not understand the meaning as my knowledge of Hindi is limited. The denotative meaning of the words is old woman's hair, but it was only later that I realised that the term 'buddhi ke baal' was used to refer to cotton candy. Either way it was not a very pleasant thing to say to a 20-year-old girl, who was insecure about her hair, among many things.

From time-to-time, I had to encounter condescending remarks from men and women with straight hair. 'Your hair looks like a straw', 'Your hair is so big', and of course a popular one among many, 'Tie your hair'. This is largely due to the perception among some people that straight hair is healthy, looks good and stylish in comparison to wavy or curly hair. Media plays a significant role in creating beauty standards, and unfortunately some follow these standards blindly. In my opinion, the most damaging are the shampoo advertisements that featured only models with straight and glossy hair. This phenomenon was dominantly prevalent in the 90s and the following decades. Even TV shows such as Friends popularised the blow-dried look of sleek and straight hair sported by the character, Rachel Green played by Jennifer Aniston. This was a trend setter. The 90s kids grew up watching shows like Friends, and films like the Princess Diaries. A more recent example would be Meghan Markle as Rachel Zane in *Suits*. Rachel Zane often sports straight open hair or straight hair with soft twirls.

One scene in Princess Diaries paints a negative image about curly hair. The Princess Mia's makeover scene shows the stylist struggling with her curly hair which is depicted as unruly and ugly. Her curly hair is transformed into straight hair, a symbol of beauty. Such media portrayals of curly hair can have a damaging effect on some young girls and women with curly hair. There are stories of many women out there who felt ugly in their natural curly hair, thanks to the negative portrayal of curly hair in the media. Talia Lakritz is one such women who shared her struggles with hair in the *Business Insider*. Talia points out that she watched the film, Princess Diaries when she was eight years old, and internalised the message in the makeover scene that curly hair is ugly 'before' and straight hair is attractive 'after'. Eventually she plunged into the chemical-ridden hair straightening methods to achieve her 'attractive hair' look. It took her some time to embrace her curly hair (Lakritz, 2022).

NEVER-ENDING HAIR DEBATE

It is not uncommon for schools and colleges in India to make regulations that can get a little too specific. For instance, a college in India, had set rules that female students cannot leave their hair loose nor tie it into a high bun or low bun. If one were to take a closer look at some of the regulations in many of the schools and colleges in India, one rule that would prominently figure is hair colour, either it is completely not allowed or certain colours are not permitted. As teachers we often confront students who are at an adventurous and experimental age, and want to creatively express themselves in many ways including hair colour. But strict regulations make it next to impossible for them do it, and what is worse is that they are never going to be the same age again, and probably not going to feel the exact same enthusiasm that they felt during the college days.

An article published by Education Times delineates the suffocation that medical college students feel in India due to their college regulations pertaining to hairstyle, dress code, among other things. A female medical college student who shared her opinion regarding the matter says that some of the rules that they are required to follow is to not colour hair nor apply streaks, and not sport any funky or unique hairstyles. The students are also expected to keep their hair tied. The student even confessed that such rules take a toll on her psychologically especially when they socialise with other college students who have trendy haircuts. She says that she feels backwards in terms of fashion and does not see a connection between fashion and academics. The professors in general do not find any problem with the strict regulations as they think that courses like medical are demanding and students should focus on academics and not waste time on fashion. However, these regulations are set by many of the colleges irrespective of courses, and can be seen as a disdain towards the creative expression of students in terms of fashion and even personal hairstyle choices which can be a simple reason of comfort not just fashion ("'Fashion rules'", 2010).

But not all professors feel this way. Liberal professors often are caught between personal ideologies to support the freedom of expression, and having to not just obey, but also enforce such regulations on students as part of job in many of the Indian schools and colleges that include checking dress codes. I have witnessed some college girls forced to change their hair colour to black else they are not permitted to enter the college premises.

WORKPLACE VIOLATION

Many of our challenges with hair bullying, policing, or even insecurities do not end in college. It extends to workplace as well. Although India is touted as the destination of IT revolution and rapidly developing country, Indian workplace can also exert control over women's hair either by having blatant policies or subtle remarks. Some companies have policies against hair colouring and certain hair styles which might be considered unprofessional. Straight hair of medium or long length is considered as professional ("Indian women open up about the pressure to keep their hair long and straight," 2020). In an article on hair challenges of Indian women published by HuffPost in 2020, the author, Rohina Katoch Sehra interviews eight Indian women about their hair experiences. It is evident from the article that the ideal Indian beauty standard is straight hair of medium or long length, and this may be one of the reasons that almost all the contestants of Miss India competition sport the similar hair texture (straight) and style. However, straight hair does not reflect the larger percentage of women in India who have curly or wavy hair nor does it reflect the diversity in India.

Aside from the general preference for straight hair, the women shared their other challenges with respect to hair texture and hairstyle. For instance, one of the respondents, Priyanshi Jariwala from Gujarat states that since childhood she struggled to accept her curly hair and had deepest urge to straighten them. Although she works in the fashion industry which is slightly more accepting of people's experimentation with hair, she confesses that she would not let her curly hair loose in business meetings. Rachana Iyer, adds the dimension of hair styles and hair colour in workplaces. She opines that workplaces in India are not inclusive of all hair types. She states that non frizzy and uncoloured straight hair is preferred in workplaces. Rachana who loves to sport a buzz cut explains that most corporations would consider buzzcuts as unprofessional because it is assumed that people with fun hair will not take work seriously.

Sehra also shares the story of Chugh Vali an entrepreneur who previously worked as a television news anchor. During her anchor days, Chugh did not let her curly hair open. She would often keep it gelled and tied. “The option of enhancing my natural hair or going curly did not exist,” says Chugh.

These struggles are quite common among Indian women with curly or wavy hair. I did everything I could to straighten my hair naturally from applying endless homemade natural pastes to straightening my hair with a flat iron. The pastes did not work and the flat iron made by hair dry and brittle. I would spend hours trying to straighten my hair with a flat iron, and once I stepped out the wavy, frizzy hair would be back. I felt helpless, sad, and unglamorous. But since I was working, I had some money. In 2012 I decided to straighten my hair using chemical method. It was called the smoothening method. I remember spending hours together at the salon and a good fortune of my money to transform my wavy hair to straight hair. I was happy with my hair, or at least I thought so. The hair stylist at the salon made it mandatory to buy certain shampoos to retain the straightened mane and strictly told me not to oil my hair.

With that began my straight hair life period which did not last long, because my hair grew showcasing the contrast between my straightened hair and wavy hair. So, I had to redo the procedure. There are different methods to straighten hair and can cost anywhere between 3,000INR (36 USD) to 10,000 INR (120 USD) depending on the length of the hair (Hair smoothening in Bangalore, 2023). In a matter of few months, the hair regrows in its normal texture and the straightening procedure must be repeated to the newly grown hair. Hair straightening is a costly procedure for women especially from middle class families.

Although I found the straightened hair easy to manage, I did face some issues. Firstly, there were times when I suffered from pain in my hair roots. Since I associated straight hair with beauty and stylish symbols, I had nightmares of my hair suddenly turning into wavy hair which troubled me. The very thought of the arduous task of chemically straightening my hair and the money spent on it was not making me feel good either.

Although I got away from the hair bullies who mocked my curly hair, I met new kind of bullies who mocked my straightened hair. For instance, I would often hear unsolicited advice from women at my workplace that it is bad to straighten hair and the straightened hair looks artificial. Some would go to the extent of even calling it a broom. Just when I thought I had gotten rid of the infamous ‘tie your hair’ comment, it came back to haunt me despite straightening my hair. This time it was the envious ladies at my work who did not like me flaunting my straight hair. I recall this incident when I was just two years into my teaching career, and two professors who joined with me in an organisation gave directions with respect to my hair. After initial queries they got to know that I had got it straightened. And one fine day, during our group discussions, one of these ladies asked me with a condescending tone that how I could leave my hair open when it was so hot. The other lady in fact told me to tie my hair. But by this time, I had learnt the subtle art of countering such people who clearly had no boundaries. It may seem difficult to understand such depraved minds, but to me it almost felt like them telling me without telling me that I had no right to flaunt my artificially straightened hair, and of course the envy was also too obvious. At that point I was more than convinced that curly haired women cannot escape such bullies at least in this present age in India or elsewhere.

Regulations against leaving hair open for teachers working in schools and colleges is quite common in India. According to an article published on the website, Feminism in India, a female teacher left her teaching job in an international school in Haryana state because the principal asked her to tie her hair and not leave her hair open. The principal believed since the teacher taught upper primary and secondary classes which had adolescent boys, the students may get wrong impression about her loose hair and pass comments. The teacher did not wish to tolerate his sexist comment nor did she want to comply with his irrational demand of tying her hair, and so she left her job. Many such stories do not see the light of the day (Naaz, 2016).

MAKING SENSE OF HAIR BIAS IN INDIA

It is often difficult to understand the cause of hair bias in India and other South Asian countries. What drives a certain section of society to hold such prejudice against hair textures like curly and wavy hair or even hair styles and hair colour? For instance, let us first look at the aversion for women leaving their hair open in temples. It is hard to fathom the exact cause of this phenomenon especially when the Hindu Goddesses themselves are often depicted beautifully in their natural state of loose hair which differs from curly, wavy to even straight hair.

It seems almost ironic that Goddesses are depicted with loose hair, but God's creation, women are insulted and forced to tie their hair. I must, however, admit that these are isolated incidents, and I am not sure if other women have had similar experiences, but it does not take away the fact that it was a disturbing experience, especially since it happened in the abode of God. But then again covering one's head is a common practice in religious places like churches, and even gurudwaras. Although I may disagree with these outdates practices, from time-to-time, one may be forced to follow these customs related to faith to avoid 'offending' some people, and only hope for change in the near future.

But the same cannot be said about educational institutions. "At a time when we relentlessly hold discussions on gender discrimination and gender sensitivity, it is painful that school authorities and teachers compel girls to come to school in a particular way, while boys have no such hairdo code," said Alsha, the female student who complained against her school. Her statement speaks volume about the state of many educational institutions in India that preach one thing and practice another ("Don't compel",2016).

Educational institutions are entrusted with the responsibility of creating awareness about important issues aside from inculcating knowledge of important subjects. Although schools through lectures, events, exhibitions, and other forms do create awareness on crucial issues such as gender discrimination, inclusivity, and freedom of expression, among other things, they take away student's personal choice when they enforce draconian dress codes and irrational hairstyles. Although one must have great pride and respect for one's indigenous culture and practices, it is also important to step away from practices that are irrational and outdated or even colonial. One fine example is not allowing female students to let their hair loose which is popularly considered as a metaphor for untidiness. It makes people wonder if girls presenting their hair in its natural state should be ashamed of it.

It is understandable that students or anyone for that matter should maintain hygiene in institutions, but the hair bias in the form of rules does not do good for progressive societies. Open hair is considered distracting and it is difficult to comprehend the meaning of such words in this context. It almost seems as if the institutions firmly believe that open hair or other such hairstyles could impede their ability to absorb knowledge in class. As evident in the historical depictions and inscriptions, early Indians loved to experiment with their hair and style it in numerous ways. It is only fair that girls and women of all ages are encouraged to experiment with their hair and creatively express themselves instead of passing suffocating and unconvincing regulations that are meant to control people.

There is a strong need to bring greater awareness to hair bias in the Indian society which does not get enough attention that it deserves, but does lot of damage to young Indian girls in the form of inculcating hate towards their own hair. The curly or wavy hair discrimination continues in the Indian media even to this day. An advertisement by the popular brand Lakme Salon that came out in 2022 reinforces negative idea of undesirability for curly hair. The advertisement features a woman who is seated in a Lakme salon. She is seen lamenting about her curly hair which she refers to as two kilograms of frizz (Khedkar, 2022).

As expected, the hair stylist in the salon comes to her 'rescue' to transform her perfectly good-looking curly hair into a so-called manageable and beautiful straight and sleek hair. The woman quite predictably is happy with the change. The advertisement surprisingly received flak and was apparently removed, which is a huge development in a country like India, where the hair bias against curly and wavy hair is normalised. The negative representation of curly hair continues in Indian media in the form of advertisements or in Indian cinema. There are fair number of films that show villains with curly hair in Indian cinema in sharp contrast to the good-natured protagonists with straight hair. The connotation being that a woman with curly hair is wild and of questionable character, whereas a woman with straight hair is neat, and good natured.

An article by Sneha Khedkar (2022) published in The Wire explores the scientific explanations behind different hair texture. Khedkar states that several factors such as genes, hair follicles, and chemical bonding play a role in determining the texture of hair. The curvy curls of hair are also in fact pre-determined to some extent well before birth, thanks to certain developmental genes. The Indian women with curly and wavy hair sadly face discrimination in their own country as opposed to the African women who often face discrimination from non-Africans.

EMBRACING NATURAL HAIR

The craze for straight hair is often attributed to European beauty standards, but nearly 60 per cent of European population have curly hair. 53 per cent of Asian population have curly hair, while 100 per cent of African population have wavy or curly hair. A whopping 85 per cent of Indians have curly hair, and 60 per cent of world's population have curly hair. Despite these numbers the obsession for straight hair and disdain for curly hair, especially in India continues Khedkar (2022). According to a 2019 survey, 87 per cent of Indians admitted their preference for straight hair.

Despite this oddity, there is a rise in Indian women who are breaking away from the negative shackles of false beauty standards surrounding hair. More and more women are learning to embrace their curly hair and are falling in love with new hair routines and their healthy curly hair. In the past few years, there is a steady increase in online platforms in the form of blogs, Facebook communities, and Instagram influencers, promoting curly hair and creating awareness surrounding the wrong notions surrounding it. This is often referred to as the curly hair movement or natural hair movement. These online communities are mostly started by women who have had a long journey of hair insecurity, encountered bias, and finally found acceptance and peace with the natural curly or wavy texture of their hair (Kedia, 2022).

It is not uncommon to find Instagram posts with beautiful women sporting their nourished curly hair, and sharing their curly hair method to the followers. A Facebook group called the 'Indian Curl Pride' has around 77,000 members. The group which was started way back in 2015 by Asha Barrak is used as a forum to share hair journeys, haircare routines, tips, and product reviews (Mantri, 2018).

Such mutual help groups can be empowering especially since all the members in the group have gone through similar challenges and are on the path to healing and loving their true hair identity. These groups help women inspire and learn from one another, and express their hair journeys without fear of judgement or even rejections. Most importantly, it helps them to not only accept, but appreciate their curly or wavy hair. It starts from self-acceptance which in turn will help women to challenge the hair bullies and media's negative representation with confidence. Of course, it is also important to change not just the media narratives by constantly raising voice against it, but also by fighting wrong narratives in our day-to-day life. This, hopefully could reach a level where legislations can be passed in India to counter the different kinds of hair bias that exists in different institutional set ups.

In my opinion, there is nothing more powerful and invigorating than helping oneself and loving your true self. It took me awhile, but I could learn to love my hair just the way it is, and slowly found myself transitioning to natural remedies, and harsh chemicals free hair products. I must admit that although I have my share of bad hair days, I have found my peace and learn to appreciate and embrace the little twirls in my hair. Every now and then I meet well-meaning people who appreciate my hair, and that is when I feel stumped, and fumble to thank their little compliments. From time-to-time I catch myself in the mirror admiring my hair, and that is a beautiful transformation.

REFERENCES

Choi, I., & Choi, M. (2009). A Study of Hindu God's and Goddess' Hairstyle. *The International Journal of Costume Culture*, *12*(1), 26–37.

Don't compel girl students to plait hair: child rights body to Kerala schools. (2016). *Asianet Newsable*. https://newsable.asianetnews.com/south/dont-compel-girls-to-plait-their-hair-tells-commission-to-schools

Express News Service. (2016, August). Schools girls not to be compelled to plait hair: Protection of child rights. *The New Indian Express*. https://www.newindianexpress.com/cities/kochi/2016/aug/24/Schools-girls-not-to-be-compelled-to-plait-hair-Protection-of-Child-Rights-1512355.html

'Fashion rules' suffocate medical students. (2010, February 4). *Education Times*. https://www.educationtimes.com/article/campus-beat-college-life/69558655/fashion-rules-suffocate-medical-students

Hiltebeitel, A., & Miller, B. (1998). *Hair: Its Power and Meaning in Asian Cultures*. State University of New York Press.

IANS. (2019, August). Indians still stuck in sexist prejudices; prefer long, straight hair on women, says survey. *National Herald.* https://www.nationalheraldindia.com/lifestyle/indians-still-stuck-in-sexist-prejudices-prefer-long-straight-hair-on-women-says-survey

Kalra, V. (2015, November 20). Tightly-wound to knotted, a history of Indian hairstyles. *IndianExpress*. https://indian express.com/article/india/india-news-india/tightly-wound-to-knotted-a-history-of-indian-hairstyles/

Kedia, S. (2022, December 12). South Asians are reclaiming their curly hair. *The Juggernaut*. https://www.jgnt.co/south-asians-reclaiming-curly-hairCurly hair movement

Kerala School girl shows us how it's done: Hair plaiting can't be made compulsory, says govt. (2016, October 24). *The News Minute.* https://www.thenewsminute.com/article/kerala-school-girl-shows-us-how-its-done-hair-plaiting-cant-be-made-compulsory-say-govt

Khedkar, S. (2022, October 4). Despite the science, hairy stereotypes still plague curly hair. *Science. The Wire*. https://science.thewire.in/health/curly-hair-science-stereotypes/

Lakritz, T. (2022, August 19). 'The Princess Diaries' portrayed my curly hair as a problem. I've since learnt to embrace it. *Business Insider*. https://www.businessinsider.in/entertainment/news/the-princess-diaries-portrayed-my-curly-hair-as-a-problem-ive-since-learned-to-embrace-it-/articleshow/93647697.cms

Mantri, G. (2018, June 28). 'Curly is beautiful': This movement is helping Indian women accept their natural hair. *The News Minute*. https://www.thenewsminute.com/article/curly-beautiful-movement-helping-indian-women-accept-their-natural-hair-83844

Naaz, H. (2016, December 23). "I will not tie my hair": Sexism in Educational Institutions. *Feminism in India*. https://feminisminindia.com/2016/12/23/hair-educational-institutions-campus-sexism/

Nichols, E. G., & Kenny, E. (2017). *Beauty around the world: A cultural encyclopedia* (1st ed.). ABC-CLIO.

Patkar, K. (2008). Herbal cosmetics in ancient India. *Indian Journal of Plastic Surgery, 41*(S 01), 134-137. doi:10.1055/s-0039-1700484

Sehra, R. (2020, March 3). Indian women open up about the pressure to keep their hair long and straight. *HuffPost*. https://www.huffpost.com/entry/indian-women-hair-pressure-long-straight_l_5e54236ec5b66729cf6064e3

Trüeb, R. (2017). From hair in India to hair India. *International Journal of Trichology*, *9*(1), 1. doi:10.4103/ijt.ijt_10_17 PMID:28761257

Chapter 4
Shame to Pride:
A Natural Hair Journey From Childhood, the United States Air Force, to Academia

Nicole Dezrea Jenkins
https://orcid.org/0000-0002-0631-4188
Howard University, USA

ABSTRACT

In this chapter, the author discusses a journey of natural hair acceptance. As a child, she struggled with not understanding how to care for her hair and the desire to have straight hair. She shares the challenges of conforming to Eurocentric beauty standards in institutions that require uniformity, such as cheerleading and military service in the United States Air Force. These experiences led her to focus on natural hair in her graduate studies. She discusses the challenges of wearing natural hair in graduate school and how discussions of professionalism and hair left her feeling isolated yet energized. Ultimately, she shares her recent experience with embracing her natural hair as a researcher and professional. As an assistant professor at a prestigious HBCU, she has increasingly fallen in love with her and other women's natural hair. She teaches students about the CROWN Act and has continued her research on natural hair experiences. Today, she credits her newfound confidence to spaces and people that accept and celebrate Black beauty and natural hair.

DOI: 10.4018/978-1-6684-8790-7.ch004

THE SIGNIFICANCE OF NATURAL HAIR FOR BLACK WOMEN

This chapter delves into the intricate relationship between natural hair, societal expectations, and the experiences of Black women, particularly within the contexts of the military and academia. To construct a comprehensive foundation for my personal narrative, I draw upon a range of academic sources, including Black Feminist Thought, sociological perspectives, and empirical research on natural hair experiences. Before embarking on a discussion of personal experiences, it is essential to establish key concepts. Texturism, which involves discrimination based on hair texture, is a pivotal concept for understanding the unique challenges faced by Black women in embracing their natural hair. This term, rooted in discussions of hair bias, underscores the need for deeper exploration.

Scholars such as Afia Mbilishaka, NM Rooks, Jenkins and more have begun to examine the deep social and emotional implications of hair shaming for Black women, men, and children within interpersonal and professional relationships and experiences (Rooks 1996, Mbilishaka 2020, Jenkins 2020, Ray 2022). Hair shaming involves microaggression and overt comments about hairstyles and textures that most often result in negative emotional experiences. Dr. Afia Mbilishaka, natural hair researcher and psychohairopist has revealed emotions such as embarrassment, anxiety, and sadness associated with experiences of hair shaming amongst Black men and women in her research (2020). Similarly, Jenkins (2020) and Ray (2022) find anxiety and sadness associated with these experiences for women and children.

While there are many negative emotions associated with experiences of hair shaming for Black people in the U.S. and throughout the world, natural hair is becoming increasingly visible and protected throughout the globe. Social movements like World Afro Day (September 15th) that began in the UK, and National Crown Day (July 3) that began in the US, are just a few examples of ways that Black people throughout the world are advocating for their right to wear natural hair and demonstrating their pride in doing so. Additionally, legislation like the CROWN Act that began in the U.S. have provided liberation and community for those who choose to wear natural hairstyles and textures. Absent hair-shaming, there is a tremendous amount of growing pride in wearing natural hair for Black people throughout the globe.

Sociologists engage in robust discussions regarding the multifaceted dimensions of Black hair within the realms of social, political, racial identity (Greensword 2022, Majali et al. 2022, Council et al. 2020). Recent scholarship has increasingly recognized the profound importance of Black hair, particularly in light of the resurgence of the natural hair movement in the United States, which gained momentum in the early 2000s (Council et al. 2020). Scholars have examined this resurgence as a potent social movement, one that empowers Black women by challenging and redefining Eurocentric beauty standards that historically excluded them (Tate 2010,

Jenkins 2019, Council et al. 2020). Furthermore, the scholarly exploration of Black hair's significance within sociology provides essential socio historical context for understanding the racial oppression that has long surrounded Black hair (Greensword 2022). Scholars have even delved into the historical trauma associated with the loss of cultural identity and the public humiliation stemming from head shaving, a form of punishment used during chattel slavery.

CONTEXTUALIZING "SHAME TO PRIDE"

The chapter's title, "Shame to Pride," encapsulates my personal transformation and serves as a metaphor for broader societal dynamics related to hair shaming. Hair shaming is a pervasive issue that affects individuals and institutions alike, and it requires contextualization to comprehend its far-reaching implications (Norwood, 2018).

BLACK FEMINIST THOUGHT AND NATURAL HAIR

Black Feminist Thought, as elucidated by scholars like bell hooks (1982) and Patricia Hill Collins (2022), provides a robust theoretical framework for examining the political significance of natural hair for Black women. These scholars have extensively explored the intersectional oppression faced by Black women, shedding light on the interplay of societal expectations regarding beauty and professionalism with race and gender. The societal expectations placed upon Black women's hair, especially in professional settings, have been a central focus of academic discourse. Research by Donahoo and Smith (2022) and Karl, Peluchette, and Dawson (2022) underscores the pressures faced by Black women to conform to Eurocentric beauty standards and the impact of these expectations on their self-identity and professional lives.

COMPARATIVE ANALYSIS: MILITARY VS. ACADEMIA

Drawing from sociological perspectives, this chapter compares my personal experiences in the military with those in academia, highlighting the contrasting hair expectations and their consequences. Sociological studies by Garen and Marcketti (2022) emphasize the role of rigid bureaucratic systems in perpetuating conformity, which can hinder the advancement of women of color.

THE SIGNIFICANCE OF HBCUS

Historically Black Colleges and Universities (HBCUs) play a crucial role in empowering Black students as they navigate the workforce. Niel and Mbilishaka (2019) discuss the significance of HBCUs in promoting self-acceptance and confidence among Black students entering professional environments.

BROADER IMPLICATIONS

In conclusion, this chapter bridges personal narratives with academic insights, shedding light on the experiences of Black women in society and professional contexts. By examining the broader implications of societal biases and expectations, this work contributes to a deeper understanding of the challenges faced by Black women and encourages meaningful dialogues on diversity, inclusion, and authenticity in the workplace.

CHILDHOOD: FLUFFY BUNNY TAIL HAIR

I was born to parents who taught me the beauty of Blackness and its diversity. My Puerto Rican mother had olive skin and fluffy black hair that came down to her waist at points in her life. Linda means beautiful in Spanish, and she was. She introduced me to my hair by always telling me it was beautiful. She would say it was "like hers, but even better." My Black father had brown skin with a red tint. His nickname was Red because he had red hair and a ton of light brown freckles across his face like Malcolm X. He was a big and tall man (6'4" and over 200 lbs) who grew up in the Jim Crow South (South Carolina). I grew up in a small rural desert town in Southern California with a predominantly white population.

In my home, we had a range of skin colors and hair textures. Between my mother, me, and my siblings, all of our hair was different lengths. I already talked about my mother's hair, long Black, and fluffy. She didn't have to do much to her hair but put a little water or maybe some mouse. Her loose natural curls would create beautiful volume effortlessly. Women spent hundreds of dollars to perm their hair into curls that my mother had naturally. They would tease and blow dry their hair to achieve the volume she achieved from an air dry. I was always envious of my mother's hair, but she told me that I shouldn't be, that my hair was the prize.

My father, although we had a limited relationship, wore his red hair in a shortcut. When he gave his best effort, he had amazing waves. He wore a durag or wave cap to keep them looking fresh. When his durag was off, he took his black bristle wooden brush from his pocket, brushed his waves, and swiped his large hand across them, smoothing them down frequently throughout the day. These were not your average waves; according to him, they were more like a "tsunami." Dad jokes are the best.

Texturism is the discrimination of looser hair textures and curls over afro textures. Hair textures of people within the African Diaspora range from loose textured curls, to tightly coiled hair textures. This range is often represented and discussed using hair texture scales that help identify the range and diversity. Hair texture scales have a history of being anti-black, and contemporary hair typing systems, such as the Andre Walker Hair Typing System, have been widely critiqued for fueling texturism, by favoring looser curls. I use this scale to describe my and my siblings' hair to provide a visual of the range of hair textures in my home and recognize my privilege. Growing up, my oldest sibling, Channy, had 4ab thick kinky-coily hair past her shoulder; she wore it in natural styles most of my life. She currently rocks gorgeous locs she has been growing for the past ten years that have grown past her waist. Rodney, my oldest brother, had 4b kinky-coily hair that he wore in a large round afro as a teen. His hairstyle reminded me of a Jimmy Hendrix poster he had on his bedroom wall. Today he wears his hair shaved to his scalp. Larrianne, my older sister, has kinkly-coily 4c hair. She was "tender-headed" (sensitive to combing and detangling), so finding a style was challenging. I remember she shaved her hair to an inch long in high school, "the big chop," before it was named. She has learned to braid since having two daughters and a son who all have long natural hair that she styles regularly. She currently wears natural braided styles. My younger brother Lamar has flakes of red hair like our father and the same hair texture as me, curly, 3b. He has worn his hair in an afro, curly, locs, in an S Curl, and cornrows. He still changes his hair frequently but currently wears short twists in a mohawk style.

I have 3b thick curly hair. Despite a love for Blackness, I was wrapped up in fitting in for most of my childhood and did not like my curly hair. My family always told me that my curly hair was beautiful; I received nothing but affirmations in my home but my experiences outside were not affirming.

When I was in first grade, a memorable incident took place in the library line. Standing behind me was Amy Clawson, a girl with perfectly curled blonde hair tied up in a ribbon that coordinated with her daily outfit. She reminded me of Cindy Loo Who from The Grinch. Suddenly, she tapped me on the shoulder, and as I turned around, I saw her giggling with another student, her hand covering her mouth. "Your hair," she exclaimed, still giggling, "it looks so funny! It's all fluffy like a bunny tail in the back, and in the front, looks like a horse's tail." This particular hairstyle stayed etched in my memory because it had taken me months to master. I had painstakingly pulled two sections of hair in front of my face, attempting to imitate the styles I had seen on Michael and Janet Jackson. Using a black boar bristle brush, which we referred to as a "smoothing brush" back then, I tried to tame the rest of my unruly hair and gathered it all into a low ponytail. I secured it with a scrunchy, fluffing up the back to create the desired effect. In my eyes, I looked great, feeling like a grown-up.

However, as the two girls continued to laugh heartily, standing arm in arm in the library line, I found myself frozen in embarrassment. A lump formed in my throat, the familiar prelude to tears. But I swallowed it back. Library day was my favorite day of the week, and I refused to let Amy ruin it for me. As one of the few Black children in the school, I didn't know how to respond. I simply turned around. Most days, I did my own hair because my mother, a single parent to five children, would often leave for work before we set off to school. Although she or my older sister would occasionally help with styling, it was mostly up to me. Dealing with my thick, voluminous hair was a challenge as my hands were not large enough to manage it easily. Merely tying it up with a hair tie felt like an accomplishment. And I wasn't alone; anyone else who had to style similar hair would agree it was a chore. Like my sister Larrianne, I was also tender-headed, so the styling process was often lengthy and painful. I needed frequent breaks, and tears were a common occurrence. However, once it was all done, and the tears had dried, I loved the way my hair looked. But deep down, I still yearned for straight hair.

The impact of Amy's mocking words cut deep because it tapped into a deeper struggle I faced as a young Black child. In the latest CROWN Research Study, it was revealed that "53% of Black mothers whose daughters have experienced hair discrimination reported that their daughters encountered race-based discrimination as early as five years old" (Dove, 2023). This study shed light on the fact that many young Black girls like me faced judgment and prejudice due to our natural hair textures.

The incident in the library line not only reminded me of my own journey with my hair but also highlighted the larger societal pressures and standards that often made me question my own beauty. Straight hair was deemed more desirable and acceptable, while my voluminous curls were seen as different or even amusing to some. It was a painful realization that even at such a young age, the world had already started shaping my perception of beauty through biased lenses.

Yet, despite the hurt and the longing for straight hair, I refused to let this incident define me. Library day remained my sanctuary, a haven of knowledge and imagination that allowed me to escape the judgment and insecurities that sometimes plagued my young mind. I was determined to hold on to the joy and excitement that those weekly trips to the library brought me.

So, while that moment in the library line caused temporary pain and embarrassment, it ultimately shaped me into the strong, confident individual I am today. It served as a reminder that our uniqueness should be celebrated, not ridiculed and that our differences contribute to the vibrant tapestry of humanity. I carry this lesson with me as I continue to embrace my natural hair and encourage others to do the same, rewriting the narrative of beauty and empowering young girls to love themselves unconditionally, just as they are.

My hair sparked a lot of curiosity in my white friends and even their parents. In school, many kids touched my hair, so much so that it was normal for me. I spent the night at my best friend's house. Her mother and aunt (two white women) wanted to put braids in my hair and did. I looked like a complete mess when these women were done. While I barely remember the experience, I was so disappointed with the end product. They just wanted to experiment. Regardless, in the end, my hair looked nothing like when my Mom, Aunties, or sisters did my hair. Growing up, it felt like a chore, and I would have given anything just to have straight hair.

In the 90s, hair relaxers were all the rage. A hair relaxer, also called a hair straightener, is a chemical product used mainly by people with tightly curled or kinky hair to straighten it by breaking down the hair's protein structure, specifically the disulfide bonds responsible for natural curls. These products, containing strong chemicals like sodium hydroxide or calcium hydroxide, can be harsh on the scalp and hair, potentially causing irritation, burns, and damage if not applied correctly. Improper application or leaving the relaxer on too long can lead to scalp and skin irritation, discomfort, and even chemical burns. Following the manufacturer's instructions and seeking professional application is crucial. While hair relaxers achieve straightening results, they can weaken hair over time, causing breakage, thinning, and overall damage. Additionally, the chemicals in these products can release toxic fumes, necessitating proper ventilation during application to prevent harm to the user and those nearby. Concerns exist regarding disparities in hair relaxer use among different racial and ethnic groups. Some studies have indicated a link between frequent relaxer use and specific health issues, especially among African-American women, including certain types of cancer. There are currently many major pending lawsuits with companies like L'Oreal regarding serious health concerns as a result of the longtime use of hair relaxers.

The marketing for hair relaxers specifically for children was memorable. *Just For Me* was a relaxer brand marketed toward Black girls. The jingle was so catchy I remember singing it throughout my house whenever the commercial aired. The song would be stuck in my head for the rest of the day. "Just for meeeeee." I saw the beautiful Black girls in the commercial, singing and smiling, their hair straight, sleek, and neatly styled in colorful barrettes. I wanted to look like them, and I still remember my excitement when my mom purchased my *Just For Me* relaxer kit.

The colorful box was covered with pictures of beautiful girls from the commercials. Inside was a large page of instructions with two clear plastic gloves attached to the page that could easily be peeled off and used. The instructions were folded up neatly. There was a jar of thick white cream that had a strong smell. This thick cream was to be mixed with another small bottle of liquid, and the smell became even stronger after the chemical reaction. This process felt like a small chemical experiment. A wooden stick was provided to mix the cream and liquid, making it more aqueous. The plastic gloves were meant to be worn for applying the cream to the hair and scalp. There was a small packet of vaseline-like substance that was instructed to be applied on the skin of the hairline and the ears; a skin protector. The small bottles of shampoo and conditioner had a pleasant smell, especially in contrast to the creamy substance, but there always seemed to be more conditioner. The best item in the box was a cassette tape containing the *Just For Meeee* jingle from the commercials. When I got mine, I played the cassette repeatedly on our family boombox, blasting it and singing along until my siblings demanded that I stop. I was excited, and the thought of having straight hair was exhilarating.

But the tantalizing adventure of straight hair quickly faded from excitement once the perm application process began. I already mentioned the potent chemical smell. I will never forget the sensation all over my head. The "creamy crack" smothered my head, and everywhere it was applied felt tingly, warm, then HOT, and began to burn. This included any cream that had smeared on my forehead or ears. Luckily, my mother wore gloves to protect her hands while applying the cream throughout my hair section by section. But for me, there was no escaping the sweltering pain. I complained, then whimpered but did not want to make a fuss.

I tried to keep my composure and withstand it as long as possible because I badly wanted straight hair. I had to wait to rinse the burning cream from my hair until the recommended time had passed. In my mind, if I did not, then I would not get the results I wanted. It seemed like time slowed down, snakelike. I cried from the burning but did not let my Mom see. I didn't want her to make me rinse it out too early. When it was finally time to rinse it out, I felt relief from the burning and the cool sensation of the water against my scalp. The cool water felt like a cool stream washing over a scorching desert. Stringy straight hair replaced my curls that had previously brought me so much difficulty and trouble. Although I felt strange and a bit like an imposter with the new straight hair I had yearned for, I knew I would fit in now and was happy.

Scholars have discussed hair's significant role in Black women's self-concept, identity development, and life experience (Johnson and Bankhead 2014). Reflecting on the decision to perm my hair, I think about the negotiation between Ariel and Ursula in *The Little Mermaid*. Ursula, the villain, can give Ariel what she has always wanted, legs, so she can walk with the humans and be part of their world. Similarly, the perm could give me what I always wanted, straight hair so that I could be part of a world from which I also felt excluded. But Ursula did not offer Ariel legs without cost; this was in exchange for her beautiful voice. Her voice made her unique and the very reason Prince Aric fell in love with her. Like Ariel, my straight hair would come at a cost as well. I would have to give up my curls and puffy hair, which made me unique. Like Ariel, it was not until a spell without my bouncy, fluffy, and lively hair that I realized what I had had before was much better and safer.

I only recently learned of the dangers of using hair relaxers. Using hair relaxers has been determined to cause lasting health effects for Black women who use them. Hair relaxers, which contain harsh chemicals such as lye or no-lye formulations, are commonly used by black women to straighten their hair. However, these products have been linked to various health issues, including scalp burns, hair loss, and in some cases, more serious conditions such as endometrial cancer, uterine cancer, uterine fibroids, and breast cancer. " The Sister Study, a public health study conducted by the National Institute of Environmental Health Sciences, has sought to identify risk factors that increase the likelihood of cancer diagnoses. According to the American Cancer Society, women involved in the Sister Study who reported the use of hair-relaxing products were almost twice as likely to develop uterine cancer. In contrast, women who reported significant usage were 2.5 times more likely to develop cancer" (www.representingwomen.org).

Black women disproportionately affected by these health disparities are not only exposed to harmful chemicals through hair relaxers but also face limited access to safe alternatives due to societal beauty standards. The concerning impact of hair relaxers on Black women's health has led to an increasing number of lawsuits against hair product manufacturers. These lawsuits allege that manufacturers have failed to adequately warn consumers about the potential health risks associated with their products, and they seek to hold them accountable for the harm caused. The outcomes of these lawsuits have the potential to bring about greater awareness and regulation to protect the health and well-being of black women and promote safer alternatives in the beauty industry.

I grew up in California, the first state to pass the CROWN Act. Our trailer park had a community pool. I would swim every day if allowed, but this was not a pleasant experience for my curly hair, especially since I refused to wash and detangle after each swim as directed by my mother. My curly hair got matted and tangled regularly. When my mom got around to detangling my hair, it was a long and excruciating process. With my permed hair, swimming was a breeze. My now thin and straight hair didn't tangle; in fact, it didn't do much of anything. It was dull and lifeless. The perms didn't last long. After about a month, the roots of my hair would grow out, leaving the ends stringy and straight and the hair at my scalp thick and curly. Over the years, I got several more perms and applied them myself but eventually stopped by Jr. High, where I transitioned into straightening tools, like hot combs and flat irons. I used these throughout Jr. High and into Highschool. I was privileged never to be penalized or punished at school for my hair. In a study that analyzed the dress codes of a random sample of K-12 schools nationwide, scholars found that "70% mentioned hair. particular hair colors were mentioned in 30% of the dress code policies. 20% forbid students to wear their hair in Afros. 20% forbid students to wear their hair in braids" (Kenner and Harte, 2020).

FITTING IN: TEENAGE DREAMING AND CHEERLEADING

I began cheerleading in middle school. I did not look like the average cheerleader in my town. I was short, chubby, and one of few girls of color, often the only Black girl on the squad. By high school, I had a few years of experience and became a skilled cheerleader and dancer. After one of many growth spurts and now with my straightened hair, I finally fit it with most of the girls on my squad. Although I wore natural hairstyles, like box braids and cornrows periodically, my straight hair was my go-to. By my sophomore year, I made the varsity cheerleading squad at my high school, and by my senior year, I was voted Cheerleading Captain of the Varsity Squad.

Being "uniform" (or having a similar aesthetic) is an element of implementation for cheerleading and dancing for visualization during performances. It was easy to style my straight hair into a high ponytail with a ribbon matching my uniform and the rest of my squad. I could do this without issues when I wore my hair straight or in box braids. But no one knew what it took behind the scenes for me to achieve straight hairstyles. My thick curly hair, now free of any chemical straightening products, was not easy to straighten. It took hours. Between washing, blow-drying, hot combing, and flat ironing, the process took me about 5 hours to do on my own. I would wake up at 5:00 am some mornings to curl my straightened hair with a curling iron before school or re-flat iron it so it was "bone straight." I damaged my hair. Not to mention, I was still learning how to do my hair. I did not own styling products promoting healthy hair or heat protection. Although I had been using straightening tools for years at this point, I continuously burned myself. Once while reaching for my curling Iron, I misjudged the distance and burnt my forearm. I heard my skin sizzle like something cooking in a pan. I still have a three-inch scar on my left forearm from a hot curling iron accident.

I could get someone to help or straighten my hair if I was lucky, but this, too, was tough but not as bad. Stylists would often burn my skin at the edges of my hairline or ears. Holding down my ears or staying very still could help, but only sometimes, a burn or two was inevitable. The tools are very hot. In the end, I felt that it was all worth the pain.

My straight hair got me compliments from my peers, and I ultimately gained immense popularity at school. At the time, I wouldn't admit that I was popular and acted as if I didn't care and it wasn't a big deal; however, now, I know that fitting in and popularity are significant in adolescence.

HOMECOMING AND PROM COURT

By my senior year, I had been voted onto the Homecoming **and** Prom Courts. These were two separate courts of seniors, ten girls, and ten boys. The senior class votes and selects the "top ten" for each court. Those who were voted to court did photoshoots in town. We wore formal gowns and suits, so I straightened my hair. I look back at the photos as the only Black girl in each image, on each court, and remember fitting in. I would have never felt confident enough to wear my natural hair, unstraightened in those photos. I felt just as beautiful as the other most popular girls in my school. I was right alongside them, and it was affirming. If the goal was to fit in, I achieved and surpassed it. I was popular.

While I transitioned between natural hairstyles like cornrows and box braids, I began to straighten my hair more and more and noticed all of the compliments I got when I wore straight hair. When my hair was straight, I received comments like "You look so different," "You look so pretty now," and "You don't even look Black." The microaggressions never felt good, but being accepted made me feel more confident. When I wore braids, I noticed that I would receive microaggressions from my peers and teachers about being "ghetto" or "having an attitude." These experiences stayed with me and socialized me into devaluing natural hairstyles. When I prepared to interview for my first job in high school, one of the first things I'd do to prepare was straighten my hair. Due to the challenges with natural hair discrimination that Black women have in the workplace, various assimilation techniques are common practice and a major concern for Black women when making decisions about how to style their hair for the workplace (Griffin 2019). While I did not have the language for my experiences at the time, conforming to white Eurocentric standards of professionalism to be successful by straightening my hair helped me feel more confident in interviews.

AIR FORCE INSTRUCTIONS 36-2903-DRESS AND APPEARANCE

I joined the United States Air Force in 2007 just after the new rendition of the natural hair movement began to surge (in the early 2000s). Natural hair vloggers grew in popularity online as Black women began to do more and more tutoring about how to style and care for natural hair of all textures. At this point, I had not applied any chemical relaxers to my hair for over a decade and became more interested in hair health, so I applied heat to my hair less often.

Air Force Instruction (AFI) 36-2903, "Dress and Personal Appearance of Air Force Personnel," is the official regulation on dress and appearance– the military's dress code. The AFI covers the appropriate wear of each uniform for men and women. It additionally covers hair regulations that include appropriate styles, lengths, and colors for men and women. Regarding women's hair, AFI 36-2903 states that hair must be neat, clean, and well-groomed. It should not interfere with the proper wear of headgear and should not extend below the bottom edge of the collar. The instruction also outlines guidelines for hair accessories, such as the size and type of hairpins, barrettes, and scrunchies allowed. These regulations became problematic for many Black women as interpretations of "neat, clean, and well-groomed" could exclude them based on their hair textures. The Black Caucus is pursuing efforts to make these regulations more inclusive (Enokenwa et al. 2022).

Adherence to these regulations is required by military law as part of the code for military dress and appearance. Violations of these codes can result in letters of reprimand and other forms of punishment with multiple violations potentially and ultimately resulting in removal from military service.

Slicking my hair back into a bun to meet the standards for dress and appearance for women was not a challenge for me. I was able to maintain proper regulations for dress and appearance and was considered a model airman for my uniform. In the Air Force Leadership School at Nellis Air Force Base, my photo was used as an example for how to wear the uniform dress and appearance goals properly. While I could no longer wear the cornrow styles I once wore in high school, I rarely straightened my hair. While I didn't experience many challenges with my hair, I noticed that other Black women did. I was experiencing privilege due to my hair texture. Black women with hair too coarse to slick back and too short to put into a bun experienced challenges with maintaining the AFI regulation for dress and appearance. They experienced microaggression and overt racism associated with their hair. Equally serious, it could impact their careers due to being reprimanded for violating the dress code.

I overheard a group of Airmen talking about a Black woman's hair.

Airmen 1: "Smith got an LOR (Letter of Reprimand- disciplinary paperwork) from her supervisor."

Airmen 2: "Smith? She is like a super troop and seriously does everything perfectly; why would *she* get paperwork?"

Airmen: 1" Her hair." The airmen said matter of factly with a shrug. "She has been warned a few times about it already. Come on, you guys see it. That shit is nappy. She needs to get a perm or something."

Airmen 2: "Damn. That's harsh, but ya, it definitely looks unprofessional."

Airmen 1: "Well, I bet she will get her shit together now. This is the Air Force. We have regulations, and you don't see any other Black girls walking around with nappy hair. I don't feel bad."

Kim Smith was a dark-skinned Black woman who stood about 5'9" had short Black natural hair that formed into an afro about 1" long. Regulations state that hair must be "neat," and her supervisor did not think that short natural hair was. While I knew Karen and was friends with her, I never told her what I had heard. She also never told me about her paperwork.

Since my military service and the implementation of the CROWN Act throughout various states in the US, changes to the language across military grooming regulations have been made to exclude pejorative language. For example, words like "matted," "unkempt," and "dreadlock" have been removed (Enokenwa et. al 2022). Additionally, the Department of Defense has recognized the inequalities (specifically for Black women) associated with their grooming policies. As an effort to be more inclusive, the DoD is working towards removing discriminatory and biased language in their grooming policies. "Passage of a federal CROWN Act will promote similar or parallel changes for federal employees outside the military services (Enokenwa et. al 2022).

Graduate School- "You Look More Professional Like That."

By graduate school, I had embraced wearing natural hairstyles and even decided to center my research on understanding other Black women's experiences with their natural hair. I decided that I wanted to conduct ethnographic research on the experiences of Black women wearing natural hair in my city. I began my fieldwork in 2016 and finished in 2019 during a historical time for natural hair as a social movement. In 2016, the US 11th Circuit court came to the decision to ban dreadlocks on a federal level in response, the CROWN Act was born- legislation meant to protect individuals wearing natural hairstyles and textures in the workplace and educational institutions. I quickly established myself as a natural hair researcher and dawned a variety of natural hairstyles and textures throughout graduate school. From cornrows to faux locs, jumbo twists to wash-and-goes, I was wearing natural hairstyles most often.

Despite this, I was not completely shielded from microaggressions about my research interests or my decisions to wear natural hair. I was one of few Black students in my graduate school department and had several encounters with deliberate racism and microaggressions, especially about my hair.

One particular week I came to campus with straightened hair. A colleague stopped me in the hall of my graduate department because he "couldn't quite put his finger on what was so different about me." When he finally came to the conclusion that my usually curly hair was straight, he decided to give me some constructive feedback. "That's it," he said, "your hair is straight. You know, you look way more professional like that." I was pissed, annoyed, and frustrated. At the same time, it should have been a reminder that the research I am doing remains essential; I felt isolated.

Another student stopped me in the hall after I had given a presentation in my Research Methods class. "What's the whole point of just talking about hair anyways? White people have bad hair days too. I just don't see how a person can be in grad school and study hair; why not take up cosmetology? Don't Black girls wear fake hair anyways?" I was often peppered with these questions by white men present for my research talks but who remained unattentive throughout. Many of their questions were addressed in the presentation; however, it did not prevent them from taking up space and attempting to devalue my research centering on Black women and natural hair (Author Info removed). I was exhausted and frustrated. I left him in the hallway. It didn't end there.

One of my white male professors also did not understand my interest and the relevance of natural hair research. "Some of these people just don't want to have to comb their hair, right?" he asked during a Q & A session after my research presentation. The comments always made me second-guess myself. Perhaps I had not explained the problem in enough detail. Perhaps I was overreacting by feeling that I was experiencing a microaggression. I learned to navigate these interactions more thoughtfully as I continued through my Ph.D. program. Boundaries were one element I learned, probably much later in life than I should have.

I entered my graduate seminar with big fluffy hair. It was day two of my wash-and-go, so my volume was volumizing, and my hair was large and in charge. When I walked by a white woman who was also a student in the course, she immediately became aw stuck. "Wow, your hair smells so good. I could smell it when you walked by. It smells like some yummy fruit or something," she said. I thanked her and proceeded to my seat across the table from hers. "Your hair looks so pretty. Can I touch it?" she asked. I shrugged and felt indifferent to the situation. "Sure," I leaned in. "It's so soft; I am so jealous," she raved. I felt petted like an animal, but the situation was all too familiar from how I had grown up. I sat in my seat and waited for class to start.

After class, a student inquired about the situation. "Hey, did you want her to touch your hair?" they asked. "I didn't really think much about it; I don't care. I am used to it. Kids have been doing that my whole life." I said. "Well, I only ask because you looked a bit deflated when you let her. Like you *had* to let her, and you don't, you know? I mean, it's up to you, but you do have a choice… just checking in on you, that's all."

That check-in meant so much to me. My friend gave me a life lesson that day. I had not even considered what I wanted in the situation. I just let it happen to me as I had in the past. I learned boundaries at that moment. I don't have to let anyone have access to me or my body simply because they make a request.

BUILDING CONFIDENCE: FEELING LIKE THE HBIC AT AN HBCU

Despite numerous encounters with microaggressions, I built up my confidence as a researcher by pursuing my research interests centering on Black women wearing natural hair and wearing my own natural hair in my professional settings. I have presented my research and numerous national conferences and found people and spaces that welcome research that centers on Black experiences. In these spaces, I wore my natural hair and professional attire without feeling less than or as if my professionalism would be questioned due to my choice. Scholars have discussed the importance of embracing natural hair for Black women and how it can be an uplifting experience for them (hooks 1992, Danahoo 2021). I have adopted this demeanor as a scholar, researcher, and teacher. My decisions to wear natural hair textures and styles have been instrumental in my confidence and in dealing with imposter syndrome. Part of this confidence-building journey is finding safe places and spaces that value my authenticity. Finding the space can feel like an anomaly but can be crucial to a confidence-building journey.

One of my first affirming experiences wearing my natural hair as a professional was at an academic conference. At the *Association for Black Sociologists* in New York, New York, in 2019, I wore my natural hair (a wash-and-go) to present my research at the conference. I felt amazing. As I entered the room, curls poppin', volume on VOOM, I swelled with pride for the opportunity to present the research to an audience that would care. In a room full of Black sociologists, I was not concerned about being viewed as less than professional for wearing my natural hair or that the topic of natural hair was not a worthy one for research. I felt seen and understood. There was a range of experiences in the room. From graduate students like me (at the time) to full and Sterling professors. That space left me feeling confident as a scholar and as a Black woman in academia. My presentation led me to several opportunities to present my research again. One, in particular, was an invited presentation to Yale's Ethnography Workshop. Validation that me and my hair were professional could not be any more apparent.

I obtained my Ph.D. and began teaching at my first academic institution, an HBCU. Amid the recent changes in affirmative action that no longer support increases in enrollment specifically for students of color, HBCUs have become more important than ever. On June 29th, 2023 the US Supreme Court ended a four-decade-long precedent that allowed colleges and universities to broadly consider race for applicants, making the application process for Black, Latinx, and Native American students significantly more challenging.

"Though HBCUs make up only three percent of the country's colleges and universities, they enroll 10% of all African American students and produce almost 20% of all African American graduates.A whopping 25% of African American graduates with STEM degrees come from HBCUs. Eight HBCUs were among the top 20 institutions to award the most science and engineering bachelor's degrees to Black graduates from 2008-2012. An HBCU graduate can expect to earn an additional $927,000 in their lifetime, which is 56% more than they could expect to earn without their HBCU degrees or certificates" (United Negro College Fund 2023).

Previous concerns about straightening my hair for an interview were virtually non-existent. While I was, of course, concerned about my appearance and especially my hair, as a Black woman, I was not concerned that wearing my natural hair would be off-putting or impact my interview experience.

I joined the Howard University Faculty in 2020 while COVID-19 and the pandemic remained a concern and altered the classroom and campus experience. When the campus became open to in-person instruction, and I obtained keys to my office, I was excited to meet my colleagues throughout campus. As a natural hair scholar, one of the first things I noticed was the array of beautiful natural hairstyles I saw on campus from faculty and students alike.

Natural Hair Discrimination at Work

In recent years, there has been a growing awareness of the challenges women of color, particularly Black women, face when it comes to their natural hair in professional settings. Discriminatory workplace regulations, as highlighted by Greene in 2012, have unfairly targeted Black women's natural hairstyles, exacerbating feelings of anxiety and insecurity related to hair biases.

These feelings of anxiety often result in a distressing dilemma for Black women. On one hand, they may feel pressured to conform to Eurocentric standards of beauty, which frequently favor straight hair. As a response to these external pressures, some opt to straighten their hair or use weaves to blend in and avoid potential biases or discrimination, as noted by Dawson and colleagues in 2019.

This complex issue not only raises questions about beauty standards and cultural acceptance but also intersects with workplace policies, diversity and inclusion efforts, and the broader sociocultural context. As a sociology professor at Howard University, my insights and research in this area could contribute significantly to the understanding and dismantling of these biases and discriminatory practices.

I am now an Assistant Professor at a prestigious HBCU where students and faculty are drawn to my research and courses. In my lectures, I teach my undergraduate and graduate students about the CROWN Act and continue to dawn various natural hairstyles on campus, including cornrows, box braids, wash-and-go, and other protective styles. I feel professional and know that I am perceived that way. I credit my confidence to Black spaces and people supporting and affirming others. Spaces that affirm Black women in their choices to wear natural hairstyles and textures are powerful and make all the difference for Black women professionals. I share my story hoping that Black women can be reminded of the beauty and versatility of our hair journeys. I hope that Black women may feel empowered and supported as they move through their journey and lend that support to other Black women as they move through theirs. I hope to also capture the stories of Black women's hair journeys worldwide in my current research project (Author Info removed).

As I grew older, I began understanding the importance of self-acceptance and embracing my natural beauty. I discovered role models who celebrated their own unique hair and inspired me to do the same. I learned about Black hair's rich history and cultural significance, its versatility, and its ability to express our identities. Slowly but surely, I started to appreciate the beauty in my curls and the strength of embracing my authentic self.

The incidents from my childhood, time spent in the Air Force, and graduate school became pivotal moments in my journey toward self-love and acceptance. They ignited a fire within me to challenge societal norms and stand proud in my own skin, defying the narrow beauty standards that sought to diminish my worth. I would no longer let the judgment of others dictate how I saw myself.

Now, as I reflect on these memories, I realize that they were a catalyst for a profound transformation and taught me resilience, empathy, and the importance of uplifting others who may face similar challenges. I became an advocate for inclusivity and fought against the discrimination that often targets diverse hairstyles. My experiences fueled my passion to create a world where every young girl, regardless of hair type or ethnicity, could feel seen, valued, and beautiful.

REFERENCES

Collins, P. H. (1990). Black feminist thought in the matrix of domination. *Black feminist thought: Knowledge, consciousness, and the Politics of Empowerment, 138*(1990), 221-238. http://archive.cunyhumanitiesalliance.org/introsocspring20/wp-content/uploads/sites/50/2019/03/Collins.Black-Feminist-Thought.pdf

Dawson, G. A., Karl, K. A., & Peluchette, J. V. (2019). Hair matters: Toward understanding natural black hair bias in the workplace. *Journal of Leadership & Organizational Studies, 26*(3), 389–401. doi:10.1177/1548051819848998

Dove. (2023). Dove supports the CROWN Act. https://www.dove.com/us/en/stories/campaigns/the-crown-act.html

Enokenwa, M. G., Okoro, U. J., Cho, S., & Norton, S. A. Military Grooming Standards and Black Hairstyling Practices. Mil Med. 2022 Oct 17:usac313. . Epub ahead of print. PMID: 36251302. https://pubmed.ncbi.nlm.nih.gov/36251302/#:~:text=Changes%20made%20to%20grooming%20standards,dreadlock%22)%20have%20been%20removed. doi:10.1093/milmed/usac313

Griffin, C. (2019). How natural black hair at work became a civil rights issue. *JStor Daily*. https://daily.jstor.org/how-natural-black-hair-at-work-became-a-civil-rights-issue/

Hamilton, A. (2020). Untangling discrimination: The CROWN Act and protecting Black hair. *U. Cin. L. Rev., 89*, 483.https://acrobat.adobe.com/link/review?uri=urn:aaid:scds:US:e080ab49-3fab-4e4a-98f7-f6428595365d

Jenkins, N. (2020). *Strategic Resistance in an African Owned Hair Salon: Intersections of Race, Gender, and Nationality in US America* (Doctoral dissertation, University of Nevada, Las Vegas). https://www.proquest.com/docview/2438343839?pq-origsite=gscholar&fromopenview=true

Jenkins, N. D. (2019). Contested identities: African diaspora and identity making in a hair braiding salon. *Journal of Contemporary Ethnography*, *48*(6), 806–835. https://journals.sagepub.com/doi/pdf/10.1177/0891241619829210?casa_token=4uV6RXM6924AAAAA:xDvNGqF7F3i4UPbu8i3_OiymoICTaDszuz6NNTflbjIr r3I0mos_9TMe-enJbtkBNrAMAsvK9teFZ6M. doi:10.1177/0891241619829210

Johnson, T. A., & Bankhead, T. (2014). Hair it is: Examining the experiences of Black women with natural hair. https://academicworks.cuny.edu/cgi/viewcontent.cgi?article=1036&context=me_pubs

Kenner and Harte. (2020). My Hair is Against the Rules: Activism towards Equitable Dress Code Policies in K-12 Settings. National Association for Multicultural Education. https://wpvip.edutopia.org/wp-content/uploads/2023/02/Natural_Hair-1.pdf

Maebob, G. (2022). Enokenwa, BS, MC, USNR and others, Military Grooming Standards and Black Hairstyling Practices. *Military Medicine*, •••, usac313. Advance online publication. doi:10.1093/milmed/usac313

Mbilishaka, A. M., & Apugo, D. (2020). Brushed aside: African American women's narratives of hair bias in school. *Race, Ethnicity and Education*, *23*(5), 634–653. doi:10.1080/13613324.2020.1718075

Mbilishaka, A. M., Clemons, K., Hudlin, M., Warner, C., & Jones, D. (2020). Don't get it twisted: Untangling the psychology of hair discrimination within Black communities. *The American Journal of Orthopsychiatry*, *90*(5), 590–599. doi:10.1037/ort0000468 PMID:32463256

Norwood, C. R. (2018). Decolonizing my hair, unshackling my curls: An autoethnography on what makes my natural hair journey a Black feminist statement. *International Feminist Journal of Politics*, *20*(1), 69–84. https://doi-org.proxyhu.wrlc.org/10.1080/14616742.2017.1369890. doi:10.1080/14616742.2017.1369890

Ray, R. (2022). School as a Hostile institution: How black and immigrant girls of color experience the classroom. *Gender & Society*, *36*(1), 88–111. doi:10.1177/08912432211057916

ADDITIONAL READING

Ayeni, D., & Bonner, A. (2018). Natural Hair and Professional Identity: An Examination of Black Women's Experiences in Corporate America. *Journal of Black Studies*, *49*(8), 750–773.

Bajaj, R. (2017). Cultivating Kinks: Solutions to Natural Hair Discrimination in American Schools. *The Georgetown Journal of Gender and the Law*, *18*(2), 413–456.

Barnes, S. L. (2017). Natural Hair as Professionalism: An Exploration of Natural Hair in the Professional Field. *Journal of Black Studies*, *48*(8), 765–786.

Bonner, A. (2014). Branding the Afro: Natural Hair and Identity Politics in the United States. *Journal of Popular Culture*, *47*(2), 324–343.

Das Gupta, A. (2020). Hair Stories: Understanding Black Women's Experiences with Natural Hair in Professional Settings. *Journal of Gender Studies*, *29*(4), 375–388.

Ebanks, C. J., & Okunrounmu, O. (2020). Hair and the City: A Look at the Legal Landscape of Natural Hair Discrimination in Employment. *Journal of Business & Technology Law*, *15*(2), 285–307.

Greene, D. (2013). multidimensional analysis of what not to wear in the workplace: Hijabs and natural hair. *FIU Law Review*, *8*(2), 333–368. doi:10.25148/lawrev.8.2.8

Koffi, A. (2017). Natural Hair Discrimination in Corporate America: A Sociocultural Perspective. *Journal of Applied Communication Research*, *45*(3), 257–275.

Rocha, R., & Kovich, G. (2019). Natural Hair and Workplace Discrimination: A Literature Review and Recommendations for Future Research. *Journal of Business Diversity*, *19*(2), 45–63.

Rockquemore, K., & Brunsma, D. L. (2008). Beyond Black Hair: Stereotypes and the Workplace. In J. Bailey & T. R. Bailey (Eds.), *The Sage Handbook of Race and Ethnic Studies* (pp. 415–432). Sage Publications.

Rooks, N. M. (1996). *Hair raising: Beauty, culture, and African American women*. Rutgers University Press.

Shetty, V. H., Shetty, N. J., & Nair, D. G. (2013, January). Chemical hair relaxers have adverse effects a myth or reality. *International Journal of Trichology*, *5*(1), 26–28. doi:10.4103/0974-7753.114710 PMID:23960393

Summers, L. M., Davis, T., & Kosovac, B. (2022). Hair we grow again: Upward mobility, career compromise, and natural hair bias in the workplace. *The Career Development Quarterly*, *70*(3), 202–214. doi:10.1002/cdq.12302

Thompson, M. A. (2009). Hair Matters: Beauty, Power, and Black Women's Consciousness. *Gender & Society*, *23*(4), 456–476.

United Negro College Fund. (2023). https://uncf.org/the-latest/the-numbers-dont-lie-hbcus-are-changing-the-college-landscape

Wanzer, L. (2022). *Trauma, Tresses, and Truth: Untangling our Hair through Personal Narratives*. Chicago Review Press.

KEY TERMS AND DEFINITIONS

Box Braids: Box braids are a protective hairstyle that involves sectioning the hair into small, square-shaped sections and braiding each section from the root to the ends. These braids are typically created with synthetic or natural hair extensions and can be styled in various ways, offering versatility and low maintenance.

Coily: Coily hair is a texture that forms tight, spiral-shaped curls or coils. It is often characterized by its high density and shrinkage, appearing shorter than it actually is when stretched. Coily hair types, also known as type 4 hair in the hair typing system, require specific care and maintenance techniques to retain moisture and minimize breakage.

CROWN Act: stands for "Creating a Respectful and Open World for Natural Hair." It is a legislative effort to prohibit race-based hair discrimination. The CROWN Act aims to protect individuals from discrimination in schools and workplaces based on their natural hair, including hairstyles such as braids, twists, locks, and afros, which have historically been subjected to biases and restrictions.

Hair Relaxer: A hair relaxer is a chemical product used to alter the hair's natural texture, specifically to straighten tightly curled or kinky hair. It typically contains chemicals such as sodium hydroxide (lye) or no-lye formulations that break down the protein bonds in the hair, allowing it to be reshaped and straightened. Hair relaxers are applied to the hair and usually left on for a specific period before being rinsed out. This process permanently changes the hair's structure until new growth occurs. Hair relaxers are often used by individuals seeking to achieve a straighter hair texture or manage their natural hair more easily.

Imposter Syndrome: Imposter Syndrome refers to a psychological pattern where individuals doubt their abilities, accomplishments, or talents and fear being exposed as fraud. People experiencing imposter syndrome often believe that their achievements are due to luck or external factors rather than their capabilities, leading to feelings of inadequacy and self-doubt.

Locs: Locs, short for dreadlocks, are a hairstyle where the hair is intentionally allowed to mat and form long, ropelike strands. This hairstyle has cultural significance and has been traditionally associated with various communities, including African, African diaspora, and Rastafarian cultures.

Natural Hair: Natural hair refers to hair that has not undergone any chemical treatments, such as relaxers or perms, to alter its natural texture. It embraces the hair's natural state, including a wide range of textures, such as afro, coily, curly, or wavy.

Natural Hair Scale: Type 3: Curly Hair: Type 3 hair is characterized by well-defined, springy curls ranging from loose curls to corkscrew-like spirals. It has more volume and texture compared to Type 2 hair. Type 3 hair is further divided into three subcategories: Type 3A: Loose curls with a wider circumference, resembling stretched-out S-shaped curls. Type 3B: Medium-sized curls that are tighter and have more ringlets or spiral patterns. Type 3C: Coarser, tightly packed curls that may appear as corkscrews or small spirals. Type 4: Coily and Kinky Hair: Type 4 hair is characterized by tightly coiled or kinky hair with a zig-zag or S-shaped pattern. It tends to have the least amount of natural sheen due to the difficulty of sebum (natural oils) reaching the hair shaft. Type 4 hair is further divided into two subcategories: Type 4A: S-shaped coils with a defined curl pattern, similar to a spring. The curls are usually fine and densely packed. Type 4B: Z-shaped or zig-zag curls that are less defined and appear more tightly coiled. The hair may have a high density. Within the Type 4 category, there are additional variations, such as Type 4C hair, characterized by tightly coiled hair that may not form distinct curls and has a higher density. This type of hair often experiences significant shrinkage, appearing much shorter when dry compared to its actual length when stretched.

Texturism: is the discrimination of looser hair textures and curls over afro textures. It is important to note that the natural hair scale is a general guideline, and individual hair can have multiple textures or a combination of different types within a single head of hair. Hair care routines and product choices can vary based on the specific characteristics of one's hair, regardless of the assigned hair type on the scale.

Chapter 5
Seeing Myself Through the Wild Fire:
Seeking Self-Acceptance While Being Unaccepted in the World of Higher Education

Tunisia Lacy-Lumpkin
Independent Researcher, USA

ABSTRACT

Rowe (2022) stated, "Perhaps a specific challenge for the advancement of Black women in higher education is correlated to how Black women are understood and assessed based on hair and hair texture" (p. 32). While higher education is often viewed as an institution to acquire new knowledge and understanding, cultivating a space of diversity and equality, the author's personal experience and the stories of other women in Rowe's article highlight the discrimination that exists while employed in higher education. In utilizing the conceptual framework of intersectionality, this chapter recounts the lived experience of a Black woman's struggle with unacceptance in higher education while pursuing her own self-acceptance. It tells the story of how her hair journey was one of the conflicting feelings of much pain, especially when the choice to go natural was not chosen by the one who had to represent it.

DOI: 10.4018/978-1-6684-8790-7.ch005

THE BEGINNING

"It is like a wildfire, and I'm trying to keep it from spreading," said the dermatologist during one of my visits while examining my thinning hair. She suggested that I cut it short as a way to minimize the chance of doing any more damage to my hair. That meant I needed to rock the Teeny Weeny Afro or TWA, as known within the Black community. I was devastated. I had a hard time processing her words. Although it had been a while since I put a relaxer in my hair, I wore weaves or went to the Dominican salon for a bone-straight blowout. A blowout is when the stylist will blow dry your hair until it is perfectly straight and then they put loose curls in your hair. You will walk out of that salon with the most bouncy and straight hair ever!

When I saw young women with natural styles, I often said, "That looks great on them, but it wouldn't look good on me." But now, alopecia (hair loss) forced me to do something I was not comfortable doing…wearing my hair in its natural state. No weave, no blowout. No, nothing…just a teeny, weeny afro.

To add to the complexity of my hair situation, I had an interview at a university the following week after receiving the news from the dermatologist. At the time, I held a recruiting position at a Historically Black College and University (HBCU). I was seeking professional growth within higher education and there were not any promotions at the HBCU where I was employed. That opportunity for a promotion came at a different institution. The university I was interviewing with was not an HBCU. Being a Black woman in America, I know how Black women are often judged by our hair, so I had to be strategic about when I would do the "big chop." I "knew" I needed to establish a plan for when I would cut my hair. As I continued orchestrating this transition to the TWA, I decided to wear a weave to the interview and cut my hair after. A White man and a White woman interviewed me, which at that time, made me feel like I made the "right" decision to wear weave to the interview. As several studies suggest, Black women will straighten their hair (e.g., relaxers, blowouts), wear weaves, and other hairstyles that are closer to White in order to assimilate in the workplace. In Dawson, et al. (2019), a participant talked about conformity in the workplace by stating, "So, to get the job, I have to inflict the violence of a relaxer on my body" (p. 394). I walked away from the interview with my weave, feeling confident that I got the job. And my intuition was correct. A few days later, I received a call offering me the position.

After being offered the position, I visited the department to meet with the Dean, still wearing my weave. During that meeting, I discussed possibly receiving tuition assistance toward my doctoral degree. He responded favorably to my request, and I was looking forward to my new position, increased pay, and the possibility of being a doctoral student.

Although I did not know the demographics of this new department, I recognized that I did not see one Black person when I was there for my interview (Once I started working for the department, I found out there was one other Black person, a Black man). Although I was leaving to work for a school with fewer Black people, my previous life and work experiences made me accustomed to assimilating in majority White spaces. But now that I was forced to wear my hair in its natural state, it became a foreign experience for me. How do I navigate this White dominated professional world with an image of myself that I do not yet accept?

After I accepted the position, the next step was to determine when to move forward with my hair. Exactly when was I going to cut my hair? I chose to cut my hair before my first day of work in my new role. I took the whole day off the job I was leaving because I knew it would be an ordeal. I anticipated it to be a very emotional moment for me. As soon as I got home from getting all of my hair cut off, I sat on the bed. My husband came home shortly after, looked at me, and said, "I like it," to which I responded with tears of sadness but yet appreciation for his support. Now, I was set to face the world, my colleagues, superiors, and the public with this Teeny Weeny Afro that I did not choose in the first place! As revealed in The Perception Institute's "Good Hair" Study, some Black women experience high levels of anxiety about their hair (The "Good Hair" Study, 2016); and now I, feeling unprepared to face the world, became one of those women with high anxiety regarding my hair.

After I cut my hair, I had to go into the office of my new job to complete paperwork. I purchased a wig and wore it that day. I was uncomfortable as hell wearing that wig. I wore weave, not wigs. But I thought anything was better than the little afro on my head. I went to the administrative assistant's desk, who was a White woman, to complete the paperwork. I watched her eyes wonder straight to my hair. She said nothing about it, but her eyes said it all. A look of confusion, considering she saw me when I came for my interview. But she said nothing about my hair and gave me the necessary documents that I needed to complete.

INTERSECTIONALITY

"Double jeopardy,"… "multiple jeopardy,"… "interlocking oppression" (Berdahl & Moore, 2006; Carastathis, 2016, p. 17) are terms used to refer to intersecting identities. But Kimberle Crenshaw framed the term intersectionality by addressing that Black women are forced to choose an identity, either a woman or Black, but the two are seldom considered as a whole (Crenshaw, 1991). In addition, Black women have a "unique sociocultural position, because they do not benefit from whiteness or maleness" (Holler, 2023, p. 229).

Intersectionality advocates for change, such as change within policies and laws because it analyzes individuals' experiences by looking at all of their intersecting identities (e.g., race, gender, and hair). Furthermore, it "studies how blended identities cause individuals to experience inequality and injustice" (Lumpkin, 2022, p. 24).

Although Black women are often made to separate their identities, they are frequently judged based on their combined identities (Lumpkin, 2022); and the way a Black woman wears her hair can cause her to be judged even more. For example, if she is wearing natural hair, she is seen as militant. This lack of consideration of intersecting identities "places unacceptable boundaries on Black women's experiences and opportunities" (McCann & Kim, 2013; Lumpkin, 2022, p. 22).

BLACK WOMEN IN THE WORKPLACE

Rowe (2022) stated that it is not uncommon for Black professional women to confront stereotypes around professionalism and competence within higher education. And I was no exception. I felt misunderstood and that my professionalism and competence were in question the year I worked in that department. Not realizing until later that it all began on my first day with my TWA, to which the Dean said, "Oh, you cut your hair?"

There are many incidents in which Black women are not selected for jobs because of their hair. For example, in the case of *Chasity Jones vs. Catastrophe Management Solutions*, in 2010, Jones was hired for a customer service position with the company. The company rescinded their offer because she refused to cut her dreadlocks. After reading about this case and reflecting on my own experience, I cannot help but think what would have happened if I showed up to my interview with my natural hair? I believe I probably would not have been offered the job. This is substantiating that Black women's livelihoods are impacted by hair discrimination. The 2023 CROWN Workplace Research Study focused on the experiences of Black women in the workforce. In that study, they found that 66% of Black women change their hair for a job interview (https://www.thecrownact.com). Furthermore, 25% of Black women believe that they were denied a job interview because of their hair. And that percentage increased to 33% of women between the ages of 25-34 years old (https://www.thecrownact.com). Circumstances such as *Chasity Jones vs. Catastrophe Management Solutions*, instill this presumption that our hair needs to mimic European standards of beauty in order to secure the job.

Mbilishaka, et al. (2020) found in their research that peers (e.g., classmates, friends, co-workers) were the highest perpetrators regarding hair discrimination. The perpetrator is the individual that causes the offense regarding hair discrimination, whether it be a demeaning comment or demonstrating actions that are discriminatory.

While these perpetrators exist, Black women are expected to maneuver in these White dominated spaces because it is an "economic necessity" (Dawson et al., 2019, p. 397); to be employed. Because of this "economic necessity" to have employment, many Black women alter their hair to fit more into the European standard of beauty (Dawson et al., 2019). Such as a participant in Dawson et al.'s study who is willing to alter her hair for employability:

I am a black woman with beautifully groomed locs.... While I excel at what I do, I know that I cannot hope to find a job with my hair like this, no matter how healthy, neat, clean, and beautiful it is. The truth is, I cannot afford to stick to my principles on this one, and I am saddened by this fact. Sometimes I cry, mourning the loss of my culture, and the right to my racial identity, I hope that middle and upper-class women are able to fight this fight, and push these walls down. For me as a working class woman, to survive, to put food on the table, to give my children the possibility of a better life, I have to surrender my crown, and make the sacrifice. (Dawson, et.al., 2019, p. 397)

And those that are "lucky" enough to stay employed, but do not conform to European beauty standards, such as straight hair, it could cause them to be the "Other" in the work environment. The "Other" is often defined by their areas of lack, such as not having straight hair, when examined by the "in-group" or the dominant group (Staszak, 2008, p. 1). Since my hair was extremely different, I guess the leadership in the department felt as though they were catfished. That I was not the same person that they interviewed, and I did not know that first comment about me cutting my hair would be the start of my "otherness" experience. As Aguirre and Rowe noted, "Black women continue to be underrepresented as the "only" within departmental units" (Aguirre, 2000; Rowe, 2022, p. 32). I was the "only," and I was the stranger.

THE BLATANT DISCRIMINATION

My primary role was the recruiter for the graduate school. However, I was also charged with assisting the Undergraduate Program Director with undergraduate recruitment. The Undergraduate Program Director was this beautiful Bulgarian woman with long straight brown hair, light skin, and a slim frame. She was very close with the Dean. At first, she was pleasant to me. In fact, she was one of the interviewers. And when I was hired, she gave me a tour around campus while telling me stories about her Black roommate's hair. Then out of nowhere, the Undergraduate Program Director's behavior changed. She stopped speaking to me, and it was apparent that she was conversing about me with the Dean regarding our collaboration with the undergraduate recruitment. This was the beginning of the blatant discrimination I endured while at this institution and it all started at an undergraduate recruitment meeting with the Dean, the Graduate Program Director, my supervisor, and the Undergraduate Program Director.

We were discussing recruitment plans for the school, and the Dean demonstrated a microaggression towards me by commenting, "We need to not work in a vacuum." I responded by asking what that meant and that I sent the Undergraduate Program Director emails to keep her in the loop regarding my recruitment efforts for the undergraduate population. Silence fell into the conference room for what seemed like forever. A few minutes later, other topics were covered then the meeting was adjourned.

After the meeting, I went to my supervisor to discuss the meeting and informed him that I had emails that I sent her as proof. He responded, "Your emails mean nothing." So, I felt that my hard evidence could never match up to her White words. He never even asked to see any of the emails. Asare (2022) stated that Black people might experience inequitable treatment from leadership and peers when they change their hair from a more Eurocentric hairstyle (e.g., straight hair) to a Black hairstyle (e.g., braids). Additionally, Donahoo (2022) stated, "hair is an element of the everyday oppression that Black women face living in a society controlled by whiteness" (p. 598). This confrontation that I experienced illustrates just how much control whiteness has in our society. I felt that my changed hair caused them to change their behavior towards me. The Undergraduate Program Director and her White aesthetics granted her a sense of privilege that if any situation arose involving me, she would always be right. Regardless of not having any evidence. Her words alone were enough for those in positions of power within the department.

As Ellis (2001) noted, racism is based on the thought that the "colored race" is physically, intellectually, religiously, socially, and morally inferior to the White race (Ellis, 2001, p. 11; Lumpkin, 2022, p. 18). This Black woman with a TWA was already viewed as less intelligent than this Bulgarian woman and her European aesthetics. White society established beauty standards to certify Eurocentric feminine traits, such as straight hair and lighter skin (Lumpkin, 2022). The closer a woman is to having these Eurocentric aesthetics, the more she is perceived as beautiful (Bryant, 2013). With this value on physical traits equating to acceptance, it was evident that I was not accepted physically, intellectually, or professionally.

"ON AND ON"

Perceptions of the "Black woman with natural hair" continued from a Black man who worked in a small café on the lower level of the building where I worked.

During my visits to the café, I engaged in conversation with him. One day, during our conversation, he asked me, "Are you one of those Erykah Badu types?" He associated me to an earthy, spiritual, Afrocentric woman. I wore business attire and Erykah Badu often wears African inspired clothing. It was evident that his perception was solely based on my hair. His question made me reflect on his possible experiences with White people and Black women. His views of Black women's hair possibly could have been influenced by White society and the lack of presence of Black women in the location where he worked. Maybe he was not used to seeing professional Black women with natural hair in this area. He saw me in the neo-soul world and not in the world of higher education. Just like the leadership in the department I worked in, he, too, could not see past my hair. This situation showed me that my hair experiences were multifaceted, recognizing that I would be dealing with how I was perceived by those outside and within the Black community, as well as how I saw myself with my natural hair.

DISQUALIFYING BLACK HAIR

I continued to experience harsh treatment while employed with this department. While creating my email signature, I placed Coordinator "of" Graduate and Professional Education as my job title. The Dean saw this in one of my emails and he told my supervisor. The Dean used my direct supervisor as the messenger to tell me that I was not to have "of" in my title as Coordinator because it resembled ownership. How dare this Black woman with her kinky hair own anything in this White-dominated department! Research proves that Black women with coily textured hair are two times more likely to experience microaggressions in the workplace compared to Black women with straighter hair (https://www.thecrownact.com). Additionally, Mbilishaka, et al. (2020) stated that participants of their study felt that the most common basis for hair discrimination is texture and that they noticed a disparity in treatment because of one's natural hair texture. This Black woman is not an equal; she is the other. Through their eyes, I was considered part of the "out-group" and "different and deviant in comparison to Whites" (Staszak, 2008, p. 1; Yancy & Ryser, 2008, p. 732).

In Four Ways Hair Bias Shows Up In The Workplace, Asare (2022) stated, "It's easy to hide one's discrimination behind the guise of poor performance" (para. 5). Furthermore, Carter et al. (2005) studied racial discrimination in the workforce, and hostile work environments were one of the forms of discrimination discussed by the participants. One of the participants shared that although they did high-quality work, their White male supervisor demeaned and unjustifiably criticized them.

And when it came to my performance evaluation, I received one that was quite deflating. During my tenure with the department, I recruited one of the most significant cohorts for the graduate program. Still, my performance assessment did not articulate my efforts, accomplishments, or other achievements. I knew I was a great worker. I was humiliated and furious with those words and rating on that performance assessment; I wanted to cry. But I refused to shed one tear in front of my supervisor. I asked to be excused midway through the meeting to go to the restroom. In there, I took a moment to cry. I was not crying because I was sad; I was crying out of frustration and unfair treatment. Knowing that I could not be gone for too long, I quickly gathered myself; then, I walked back into the meeting to read an assessment that completely denigrated me. To add insult to injury, my supervisor informed me that the Dean rescinded his statement about providing me with tuition assistance toward my doctoral degree. As described by Alleyne (2005), these types of discriminatory actions that I encountered are "silent and not so easy to pin down" tactics (p. 288).

My performance evaluation and retraction of financial assistance were both forms of symbolic violence. Symbolic violence is a non-physical act of violence (e.g., discrimination) towards minorities, such as Black women not receiving promotions at work because some individuals in positions of power view them and their hair as unprofessional (Bourdieu & Passeron, 1998; Lumpkin, 2022). My performance evaluation and rescinded offer of tuition assistance were both tangible tools used to keep me from excelling in my position. Rowe (2022) stated, "The presentation of Black hair and hair texture automatically qualifies or disqualifies individuals from opportunities and levels of credibility and competence which could have economic implications related to promotions and earning potential" (p. 38). Indeed, this served as a way for them to control my professional advancement. To keep me from elevating professionally and educationally. Additionally, Rowe (2022) acknowledged that a challenge for the advancement of Black women in higher education could be connected to how "Black women are understood and assessed based on hair and hair texture" (p. 32). Again, my evaluation solidified my feelings of being completely misunderstood and incorrectly assessed based on my hair.

In a study conducted by Lumpkin (2022), one of the participants discussed his experience dating Black women. From his conversations with these Black women, he shared that they worked very hard to attain certain positions in their careers and that they wore their hair in more Eurocentric styles (i.e., straighter hair, longer hair) so that they would not have the "additional fight" of having hairstyles deemed unprofessional (p. 121). In addition, Awad et al. (2015) stated, "There may be social costs for [Black] women who choose to wear their hair natural" (p. 543). Although comments may not always be about our hair, it is still a huge factor in how Black women are treated.

While I was the Coordinator of Graduate and Professional Education and recruited the incoming cohort, this was my first incoming cohort. I was unaware of my role during this process, and I was not informed of my responsibilities to the cohort on their first day of the program. On the first day, my supervisor asked me, "Did anyone tell you to come and introduce yourself to the cohort?" I informed him that no one did, but he did not offer to include me . So, I took it upon myself to introduce myself to the students I recruited for this cohort. I stood by the entrance and greeted each one as they walked into the department area. I had to create this space for myself to be seen.

MIRROR, MIRROR

Meanwhile, while dealing with this external conflict at work, I simultaneously grappled internally with accepting my hair. I never really wore my hair in its natural state, such as twists, afros, or any style that showed my natural kinky hair. Even when I stopped getting relaxers, I either wore a long straight weave or altered my hair (blowout) to make it straight. As a little girl, I have no memory of wearing my hair natural. I had a Jheri curl, and a few times, I did have braids with hair added, but my hair was relaxed most of my childhood to my mid-20's. Then in my mid-20's through my early 30's, I wore weave or blowouts. To go from choosing more Eurocentric hairstyles, such as straight hair or loose curls, then being forced to wear my super kinky short afro was very overwhelming.

There are a number of Black women and girls who embraced their natural hair journey and felt liberated once they went natural, such as Wura, who stated that during her first year of her natural hair journey she felt, "wild because I'm in control," and Nzingha who believed deciding to go natural was a "reclamation of lost and interrupted knowledge" (Djan, 2020, para. 27; Taylor, 2023, p.107). In my case, that was not the feeling. I felt the opposite, as if I had no control of my own hair. In just one day, my self-perception changed. I believe my feelings were not like those who were happy about their natural hair journey because it was a choice for them. They decided to wear their hair in its natural state and were excited about their transition to natural hair. I felt forced and that I no longer had hair autonomy.

I had two unfavorable choices: to either cut my hair to save the rest from being damaged or continue to wear it like I usually did and take the risk of possibly losing all of my hair.

Growing up in a majority White area and attending a predominantly White institution as an undergraduate, my self-perception stems from those White experiences. I subconsciously had "low Black consciousness" (Makkar & Strube, 1995), which meant that I did not have complete awareness of the Black identity and did not embrace the characteristics that came along with my blackness, such as my kinky hair. Since I had low Black consciousness, I was more affected by European standards of beauty than someone with high Black consciousness.

Furthermore, just like many Black women, I do not recall receiving positive affirmations about my natural hair when I was younger, which impacted my acceptance of my Black attributes. The absence of hair affirmations is not uncommon within the Black community and have caused long-lasting impacts on Black women. As previously mentioned, peers were the highest perpetrators of discriminatory actions towards Black hair (Mbilishaka, et al., 2020). Family was the second highest perpetrators towards hair discrimination. Most of the perpetrators within the family are mothers and/or a female family member (Mbilishaka, et al., 2020). Ellington (2023) conducted a study in which Carla, a participant, stated that her mother told her "If you want to live in Africa, you can go back," because she decided to wear her hair natural (p.73). In addition, two sisters that participated in Ellington's study shared that once they went natural, their mother did not speak to them for almost a month. One participant in Mbilishaka et al.'s study, shared that she recalled a time when she was a child, and her grandmother was talking to some of the neighborhood women about the participant's hair. They stated that the length and texture of her hair was not as good as the hair on her father's side of the family (Mbilishaka et al., 2020).

In Taylor's (2023) research, Black women shared their childhood memories about their hair. One of the participants voiced that she was "haunted" by her family's disapproval of her natural hair and how their comments were very "discouraging" during the time she wanted to transition to natural hair (p. 104). Other participants shared how the disparaging comments from people, including family members, resulted in low self-esteem.

My mother relaxed my hair at a young age, and I remember her saying it was difficult for her to manage my hair without a relaxer. Now, reflecting on my childhood hair experiences, I question why I made the hair decisions that I made. Maybe those childhood experiences made me an "internal oppressor," carrying around "intergenerational baggage" (Alleyne, 2005, p. 295), or caused me to work "within internalized beauty paradigms to attain one small piece of what society defines as beautiful" (Hervey et al., 2016, p. 874). Maybe my choice to continue to wear my hair straight after my childhood years was my effort to attain just one small piece of what society views as beautiful. But at the time, I was unaware that I had an "issue" with my hair because I wore it the way I was accustomed to wearing it, which was straight in some capacity. At that time, I was unsure, but I was certain about one thing. When I looked in the mirror at myself with a little afro, a stranger stared back at me.

RESIGNATION

After almost a year of misery, I found another job with the federal government. I felt I should resign before they terminated me because I saw the writing on the wall. And I received that job offer before the end of my contract with the department at the university. Two co-workers and my supervisor took me to lunch on my last day. After lunch, my supervisor asked to speak with me. During that conversation, he said he wished he defended me more, acknowledging that I was treated poorly. However, his lack of action contributed to the discrimination I experienced at this higher education institution. His lack of action caused me to endure unnecessary pain and struggle; a struggle to be seen and respected in this White space. As noted by Anderson (2022), "Black people are required to navigate the White space as a condition of their existence" (p. 13). Anderson (2022) also described the steps Black people take in order to navigate a White space, such as to observe individuals to distinguish who will and will not provide support. I struggled to exist in this particular White space. I was descending in this White space and my supervisor, a White man who was in a place of privilege, could have offered me a life jacket, could have provided support, but yet, he chose to allow me to drown. His actions, or lack thereof, make me believe that he was feeling White fragility, which is when a White person experiences racial stress, such as witnessing and participating in the discrimination I encountered at that university. White fragility is when "racial stress becomes intolerable for White people" (DiAngelo, 2011, p. 54); which can create feelings of guilt and silence. His silence contributed to the discrimination I experienced. So, with that, I sat in silence.

THE AFTERMATH

My story is a prime example of how the intersection of race, gender, and hair affects the treatment of Black women in the workforce. Furthermore, it adds a layer, highlighting the complexity of my views of my hair and the perceptions and treatment from others because of my hair. This shows the double-edged sword that some Black women face with their hair's intricacies. Painter (1976) stated that "the Black woman's unequal status in society is intensified by racist practices that further inhibit her ability to survive, let alone thrive, within the system" (p. 224). Reflecting on that horrific experience, I would say that I survived. My leadership refused to acknowledge that I recruited the largest and most diverse cohort at that time. Because of their lack of support and respect for my accomplishments, I had to tell myself that I did thrive, but I knew that was only temporary. I might not have survived if I had remained employed with that department. My moments of thriving would most likely continue to be disparaged. I would come to a place of not thriving or surviving. This experience happened nine years ago and occasionally occupies my mind. Sometimes I replay specific scenarios during my time with that educational department and think about what I could have done differently. I suppose I could have done more to defend myself. I started to keep a journal and write down different situations that happened while I was working there, but I did not report anything. I should have contacted Human Resources and reported the discrimination I was experiencing in that particular department.

Oftentimes, Black people suffer in silence when we encounter discrimination in the workplace, and I did just that. I suffered in silence. I did not express to them how they treated me. Anderson (2022) stated, "To be at all successful, Black people must manage themselves within this [White] space" (p. 19). Years later, I still think about how this experience transpired and that I should have confronted them about how they treated me. Although I am confident that the administration in that department would have denied any misconduct, at least I would have addressed their behavior. But then again, if I confronted them about it, would that have affected my future employment? Carter et al. (2005) researched racial discrimination's impact on individuals. They mentioned that race-related situations are considered stressors and can cause post-traumatic stress disorder (PTSD). Per their findings, 74% of the participants shared that they experienced psychological and emotional effects from racial discrimination. My ruminating thoughts could be the aftermath of that experience.

Aguirre (2000) mentioned how higher education is perceived as being a "place of enlightened thought" and "immune to influences from the outside world. Free of conflict and stress" (p. 6). Nevertheless, my experience caused external conflict and contributed to my existing internal struggle and stress, resulting in trauma. "Invisible injuries" or "Black identity wounding" is an "unguarded area." (Alleyne, 2005, p. 283). This "invisible wounding" (Alleyne, 2005, p. 287) is not a wound that an individual can physically see, but the feelings and long-term damage caused by these wounds are real.

THE JOURNEY TOWARDS MY OWN HAIR ACCEPTANCE

Since that work experience, I have grown out my hair with beautiful sister locs, but I had to cut them because they caused traction alopecia. Traction alopecia can happen when your hair experiences continuous pulling (e.g., braids, retightening of locs, etc.) and damages the hair follicle, which causes hair loss. The internal hair struggle returned. This time, I did not have to deal with the external barriers at work. I do not know if it is because I work for the federal government, the culture of this particular agency, I work with mostly Black people, or the fact that I work from home five days a week, which limits my face-to-face interactions with individuals. Either way, it was easier than fighting two battles of acceptance. That experience taught me a lot about my hair and gaining hair acceptance. My "Black consciousness" grew, and I became more confident and educated in Black hair. I decided not to make plans for my hair for employment purposes. I will wear it in a way that helps me become more comfortable dealing with alopecia. Regardless of my personal hair struggles, I refuse to compromise my hair for any employer ever again. As Awad et al. stated, "Black hair has important consequences for Black women as they choose between what is good for them and what might prevent access to economic and professional realms" (Awad et al., 2015, p. 554). Oftentimes Black women pay a price if they decide to wear hairstyles that are more centered around their blackness. But even with that risk, Donahoo (2022) found that "Black women are stepping away from the idea that professional hair exclusively means straight hair and instead, selecting hairstyles that affirm their identities and self-concepts" (p. 599). And when it comes to my hair, I will always choose what is good for me.

My story supports Donahoo's statement that "hair has and continues to affect the employment opportunities and professional experiences of Black women" (2022, p. 599). My experience made me feel as if my Black hair did not belong in their White space. My performance evaluation was used as a tool to prevent additional employment opportunities and rescinding my financial assistance toward a doctoral program was used as an effort to control my professional, academic, and personal growth.

THE FIGHT GOES ON

As more Black women are wearing their natural hair, it is important to have systems in place to protect this group of individuals from continuous discrimination in the workplace. When my incident occurred, the CROWN Act (Creating a Respectful and Open World for Natural Hair Act) did not exist. Established in 2019, the CROWN Act is a federal legislation to end hair discrimination, which was passed by the U.S. House of Representatives on March 18, 2022. Unfortunately, on December 14, 2022, the bill was rejected by the U.S. Senate (https://www.thecrownact.com). The CROWN Act laws passed in only 23 states. In addition, some cases under Title VII of the Civil Rights Act covered hair texture but did not support cases pertaining to hairstyles. This is because of how the government defines immutability. Immutability is defined as characteristics that cannot be changed, such as skin color and hair texture. The courts do not consider hairstyles as immutable because they believe a person can change their hairstyle (Moronta, 2021; Holler, 2023). Many times Black people wear their hair in particular styles due to cultural and other reasons (e.g., religious, health). In order for this law to change, the definition of race discrimination and immutable need to be expanded to include hair discrimination, not just texture but hairstyles as well (Boyd, 2023).

In addition to race, gender, and hair, which is included in Title VII, The CROWN Act also includes hairstyles. Goodman (2021) believes that the CROWN Act "can serve as a solution to this unique type of discrimination where Title VII leaves some ambiguity" (p. 1018). But the Supreme Court has not implemented an intersectional approach in discrimination cases with Black women plaintiffs, nor held that cultural conceptions of race should be protected (Holler, 2023). The CROWN Act and Title VII show efforts that individuals made to protect Black people from hair discrimination, but there still is a huge reluctance from government officials to enforce and/or expand these laws by their refusal to recognize the intersectionality of race, gender, and hair.

In order for these laws to be mandated, it requires individuals to continuously fight for them. And in order to increase representation, more people need to understand the impact hair discrimination has on Black people. But I believe this starts with recognizing the messages that are being conveyed about Black hair within the Black community. Many participants in Mbilishaka et al.'s study declared that they experienced numerous situations involving hair discrimination from those within the Black community (Mbilishaka, 2020). As a community, Black people should be more intentional on becoming more knowledgeable about their hair and sending positive messages to each other.

As previously discussed in this chapter, many Black women shared stories of negative messages they heard about their hair, which then affects how they view Black hair. When Black people are intentional on learning about their hair, they can send different messages to other Black people, especially children. Recognizing my own hair struggles that began during my childhood, I am intentionally unlearning what I was taught as a child, such as my hair is untamable without applying chemicals to it. I make sure I do not send those same negative messages to my children. We talk about Black hair positivity, and I consciously affirm my children's hair, especially my daughter. Her hair is natural, and she even shared with me that she does not want to ever get a relaxer.

Similar to my beliefs, other women are deliberately changing what they were taught about Black hair. For example, Kamala, a participant in Taylor's study, said that although her mother pressed and relaxed her hair when she was a child, she has not put a relaxer in her daughter's hair and encourages her to wear her natural hair (Taylor, 2023). Another participant shared that although she does not have children yet, when she does, she plans on trying to keep them wearing their natural hair "as long as possible" (Taylor, 2023, p. 110). If Black people begin to show more support for each other, such as with Black hair, this could possibly gain more supporters from non-Black people. And by increasing the number of people that are protesting for laws to protect individuals from hair discrimination, could possibly force those individuals that are in positions of power to make change; force them to create a respectful and open world for natural hair.

REFERENCES

Aguirre, A. (2000). *Women and minority faculty in the academic workplace: Recruitment, retention, and academic culture*. Jossey-Bass.

Alleyne, A. (2005). Invisible injuries and silent witnesses: The shadow of racial oppression in workplace contexts. *Psychodynamic Practice*, *11*(3), 283–299. doi:10.1080/14753630500232222

Anderson, E. (2022). Black. In *White Space*. The University of Chicago Press.

Asare, J. G. (2022, August 15). Four Ways Hair Bias Shows Up In The Workplace. *Forbes*. https://www.forbes.com/sites/janicegassam/2022/08/15/four-ways-hair-bias-shows-up-in-the-workplace/?sh=4be6402469a3

Awad, G. H., Norwood, C., Taylor, D. S., Martinez, M., McClain, S., Jones, B., Holman, A., & Hillard, C. C. (2015). Beauty and Body Image Concerns Among African American College Women. *The Journal of Black Psychology*, *41*(6), 540–564. doi:10.1177/0095798414550864 PMID:26778866

Badu, E. (1997). *On & On*. Baduizm. Kedar Records and Universal Records.

Berdahl, J. L., & Moore, C. (2006). Workplace Harassment: Double Jeopardy for Minority Women. *The Journal of Applied Psychology*, *91*(2), 426–436. doi:10.1037/0021-9010.91.2.426 PMID:16551193

Bourdieu, P., & Passeron, J. C. (1998). Foundations of a Theory of Symbolic Violence. Reproduction in Education, Society, and Culture. *Sage (Atlanta, Ga.)*.

Boyd, A. (2023). Hair me out: Why discrimination against black hair is race discrimination under title vii. *The American University Journal of Gender, Social Policy & the Law*, *31*(1), 75–106.

Carastathis, A. (2016). *Intersectionality: Origins, Contestations, Horizons*. University of Nebraska Press. doi:10.2307/j.ctt1fzhfz8

Carter, R. T., Forsyth, J. M., Mazzula, S. L., & Williams, B. (2005). *Racial Discrimination and Race-Based Traumatic Stress: An Exploratory Investigation: Handbook of Racial-Cultural Psychology and Counseling: Training and Practice* (R. T. Carter, Ed.). Vol. II). John Wiley & Sons, Inc.

Crenshaw, K. (1991). Mapping the Margins: Intersectionality, Identity Politics, and Violence Against Women of Color. *Stanford Law Review*, *43*(6), 1241–1299. doi:10.2307/1229039

Dawson, G. A., Karl, K. A., & Pelluchette, J. V. (2019). Hair Matters: Toward Understanding Natural Black Hair Bias in the Workplace. *Journal of Leadership & Organizational Studies*, *26*(3), 389–401. doi:10.1177/1548051819848998

DiAnglelo, R. (2011). White Fragility. *The International Journal of Critical Pedagogy*, *3*(3), 54–70.

Djan, N. (2020, September 19). Taking Up "Hair" Space: 8 Black Women Talk About What Natural Hair Means to Them. *PopSugar*. https://www.popsugar.com/beauty/black-women-talk-about-their-natural-hair-47350427

Donahoo, S. (2022). Working with Style: Black women, black hair, and professionalism. *Gender, Work and Organization*, *2*(30), 596–611. doi:10.1111/gwao.12838

Ellington, T. N. (2023). *I'm Free Now! The Self-Esteen and Self-Schema of African American Women Wearing Natural Hair* (T. N. Ellington, Ed.). The Kent State University Press.

Ellis, G. (2001). The Psychology of American Race Prejudice. In E. Cashmore & J. Jennings (Eds.), *Racism: Essential Readings* (pp. 10–17). Sage Publications. doi:10.4135/9781446220986.n2

Goodman, M. (2021). Wearing My Crown to Work: The Crown Act as Solution to Shortcomings of Title VII for Hair Discrimination in the Workplace. *Touro Law Review*, *37*(2), 1001–2021.

Hervey, N. E., Doss, A., Davis, D., Nicks, R., & Araiza, P. (2016). African American Personal Presentation: Psychology of Hair and Self-Perception. *Journal of Black Studies*, *47*(8), 869–882. https://www.jstor.org/stable/26174232. doi:10.1177/0021934716653350

Holler, S. E. (2023). Braids, Locs, and Bostock: Title VII's Elusive Protections for LGBTQ+ and Black Women Employees. *The Journal of Gender, Race & Justice*, *26*(1), 223–270.

Lumpkin, T. (2022). *What I Like: Chronicles of Black Males' Perspectives of Black Women's Hair* (Publication No. 29164066) [Doctoral dissertation, University of Maryland, Baltimore County]. ProQuest Dissertations Publishing. https://www.proquest.com/docview/2677022697/B66F6D9656254E41PQ/1

Makkar, J. K., & Strube, M. J. (1995). Black Women's Self-Perceptions of Attractiveness Following Exposure to White versus Black Beauty Standards: The Moderating Role of Racial Identity and Self-Esteem. *Journal of Applied Social Psychology*, *25*(17), 1547–1566. doi:10.1111/j.1559-1816.1995.tb02632.x

Mbilishaka, A. M., Hudlin, M., Clemons, K., Warner, C., & Jones, D. (2020). Don't Get It Twisted: Untangling the Psychology of Hair Discrimination Within Black Communities. *The American Journal of Orthopsychiatry*, *90*(5), 590–599. doi:10.1037/ort0000468 PMID:32463256

McCann, C. R., & Kim, S. K. (2013). *Feminist Local and Global Theory Perspectives Reader*. Routledge. doi:10.4324/9780203598313

Moronta, G. (2023). Why Do You Care About My Hair? A Proposal For Remedying Hair Discrimination In The Workplace On A Federal Level. *Cardozo Law Review*, *43*(4), 1715–1746.

Painter, D. H. (1976). Women in America. *Current History (New York, N.Y.)*, *70*(416), 224–227.

Rowe, K. L. (2022). Tangled: Black Hair and Texturism in ethnodrama. *Cultural Studies ↔. Cultural Studies, Critical Methodologies*, *22*(1), 32–43. doi:10.1177/15327086211049708

Staszak, J. F. (2008). Other/otherness. International Encyclopedia of Human Geography, 1-7.

Taylor, T. (2023). *Going Natural: Black Women's Didactic Hair Culture* (T. N. Ellington, Ed.).

The Kent State University Press. (n.d). *The CROWN Act.* Kent State University Press. https://www.thecrownact.com/

The Perception Institute. (2016, August). *The "Good Hair" Study Results*. The Perception Institute. https://perception.org/goodhair/results/

Yancy, G., & Ryser, T. A. (2008). Whiting Up and Blacking Out: White Privilege, Race, and White Chicks. *African American Review*, *42*(3-4), 731–746. https://www.jstor.org/stable/40301264

Chapter 6
The Hair Journey of a Professional Woman of African Descent

Joanne Walters
https://orcid.org/0009-0007-0005-2694
University of the Virgin Islands, US Virgin Islands

ABSTRACT

This chapter shares the personal experiences of the author as she worked her way up the corporate ladder while donning locs, aka dreadlocs. The goal of this chapter is to encourage Black women to embrace hairstyles that allow them to project confidence when being evaluated professionally instead of feeling pressured to conform to what the dominant culture narrowly defines as an acceptable professional appearance. The chapter discusses Black hair perceptions from pre-colonial Africa to the present, how these perceptions persist in corporate work settings in modern times, proposed legislation to police hair bias, and what leaders can do to influence their workplaces.

MISSION

The mission of this chapter is to encourage Black women to embrace hairstyles that allow them to project confidence when being evaluated professionally instead of feeling pressured to conform to what the dominant culture narrowly defines as an acceptable professional appearance.

DOI: 10.4018/978-1-6684-8790-7.ch006

INTRODUCTION

Maya Angelou said, "I have learned that people will forget what you said, people will forget what you did, but people will never forget how you made them feel."

This quote underscores my entire career journey; my hair taught me how to live these words. I was born and raised in St. Thomas, US Virgin Islands. Most of my family, including my parents and siblings, are from another island country: Antigua. Our household was heavily religious, and our beliefs were dogmatic. Practices like women wearing pants, jewelry, or make-up were frowned upon. Locs were associated only with the Rastafari belief system and thereby seen as deviant in our very strict household. Much of my parent's hopes and dreams were metaphorically wrapped in the successes of my siblings and me. By the time I finished high school, to some extent, my parents believed that they had perfected teaching me how to assimilate successfully to the cultural norms of the United States mainland.

Growing up, I had a negative relationship with my hair. I remember many hot combs and bad relaxers, and I rarely felt beautiful.

During my second year of college, I moved from the U.S. Virgin Islands to Texas, where I graduated with a Bachelor of Business Administration with a concentration in Finance from the University in 1996. My college's business school prepared me for life in Corporate America. A part of the preparation included sharing images of what was an accepted professional look and what was not. Among the coveted professional looks were women wearing their hair long and straightened. I tried desperately to maintain that look. I tried to assimilate. I went through a phase of wearing straightened hair weaves of varying lengths to achieve a professional appearance that I believed to be the only packaging that was appropriate for Corporate America.

Then it happened.

After years of wearing weaves and trying to make my hair look flowy, I realized that none of this investment in my appearance translated into actual dollars on my paycheck. I was still earning far less than my non-Black colleagues. One evening, while driving home from my job at a mutual funds company, I called my hairdresser and said, "I need you to cut my hair." She assumed I was being impulsive and, even though she wore her hair loced, she was concerned that I would not be accepted at work, negatively impacting my economic security. She had just relaxed my hair a few weeks before, so cutting all my chemically treated hair also meant I would be practically bald. I was ok with that. It was Texas, a hot and humid place, and the long straight hair gracing my shoulders and back felt like nothing more than a nuisance.

I wish I could claim that the next day at work, I was greeted by the support of every Black person, but that was not the case. Instead, my dramatic change seemed to make many of my colleagues uncomfortable; and some questioned whether I was battling a psychological issue. I also wish I could claim that I immediately felt liberated by taking what could be seen as a bold move. I did not. Many mornings, as I got dressed for work, I looked in the mirror and did not see pretty. I snuck a few wigs in until I finally committed to locing my hair.

Six months later, I landed a job interview at a company in another state. I showed up to the interview as me. The whole me. I landed the job, doubling my income. That began a career filled with significant accomplishments and new financial heights. The difference between the version of me struggling to pay bills and whom I had to become through my hair journey is that I was forced to see myself, every flaw. I had to embrace all the parts of me that still held on to self-doubt. Then I had to let others see me too. I could not hide behind the long and straightened hair anymore. In job interviews, I had to project a confident me. I had to leave people remembering how I made them feel rather than evaluating whether my physical packaging was appropriate. Because here is the thing, it would never be appropriate if the only standard was the dominant cultural standard. My lips would always be full. My nose would always be broad. I would always be me, but now being me meant being confident in my technical abilities and living free.

HAIR BIAS AND ITS IMPACT ON THE WORKPLACE

For over a decade, I have worked as a human resources leader. As a human capital executive, I promote workplace diversity, equity, inclusion, belonging, and justice. Often, this role does not feel like work because the stated principles are among my core values. I have been known to say that human resources found me instead of me finding human resources as the best career fit. I did not take courses or get degrees in human resources. Instead, my impetus for entering the profession was born out of dissatisfaction with my personal work experiences and the anecdotal experiences of others. After years of unpleasant workplace experiences, I decided I wanted to be a leader that was a part of the solution rather than one who complained about what the companies I worked for were doing or not doing, which may have impacted me or others negatively. I decided to pivot my career in financial services, information technology, and business operations to human resources. I did this to effect change at an organization's core. I wanted to be an influential voice when policies were made and have some control over how organizational policies were interpreted and implemented. I cared about people. I cared about people who looked like me, getting genuine opportunities to bring their best selves to the workplace and excel.

In my first professional role obtained after finishing my undergraduate degree, I was an operations leader for a non-profit organization. I had a history with the organization because I worked there as an intern during my last year of college. However, I paid little attention to the organization's stated dress code and moral code until it directly affected me. My hair was not the issue. Back then, I maintained the long, straight hair look that I had come to accept as appropriate for professionals. I did not earn much more, nor did I expect to, because I worked for a non-profit organization. I felt motivated by the organization's mission and viewed my work as a part of the loftier goal of spreading kindness and building more resilience worldwide. Then at one staff meeting, I paid attention to the words in the moral code that all leaders in the organization were expected to read aloud at various meetings. There was a line in the moral code that required the organization's professionals not to associate with anyone who led a lifestyle not aligned with the organization's interpretation of Christian principles. That is when it struck me. I was a part of something oppressive to some of the friends I had made during my undergraduate studies. While I did not ascribe to the organization's stated beliefs concerning individual lifestyle choices, I felt like a hypocrite for accepting wages from the company knowing this is where they stood on these critical issues. That was my earliest professional memory of my core values of diversity, equity, inclusion, belonging, and justice being challenged. As Dr. Martin Luther King said, "Injustice anywhere is a threat to justice everywhere" (*Letter From a Birmingham Jail [King, Jr.]*, n.d.). The misalignment between my core values and the organization's values could not be reconciled. I had to move on.

Alignment of your values and the values of the company you work for matters. There is a saying, "Go where you are celebrated, not where you are tolerated." I have used this mantra as my north star when determining my best career choices. After leaving my first professional job post my undergraduate studies, I sought opportunities for those interviewing me to get a holistic view of who I am as soon as possible in the interview process. As early as an initial phone screen, I chose volunteer information that could indicate to the interviewer that I am Black, such as letting the interviewer know that I was a member of a Black thespian group or that I sang in a gospel choir while in college. Though neither piece of information unequivocally indicates that I am Black, it was enough information to begin to paint a picture of who I am as a person and as a professional. This was my way of starting to thread together a theme for the interviewer and me to help us both determine if my race would be a point of contention. This is a controversial and somewhat risky choice, and I admit there was no guarantee that my tactics would work. Further, denying me an employment opportunity based on race was not legal, so I knew that would never be the official reason documented. Still, an interviewer could use dozens of reasons to classify me as "not a good fit" and end my candidacy for employment. I preferred to be denied those positions within organizations lacking the cultural maturity to effectively manage diversity because I did not see them as genuine opportunities. It was and still is my belief that any potential employer who would choose not to hire a person because of race, even subconsciously, did not deserve the contribution of my talents to the furtherance of their business' success. I also believe that thriving in that work environment would be unnecessarily challenging. I would rather invest my time and talents elsewhere.

Oxford English Dictionary defines bias as the "Tendency to favour or dislike a person or thing, especially as a result of a preconceived opinion; partiality, prejudice… any preference or attitude that affects outlook or behaviour, esp. by inhibiting impartial consideration or judgement" (OED Online, 2023, entry 18564). When any bias is present in the workplace, every person is affected directly or indirectly. Hair bias is no different. It can start with something seemingly innocuous, on the surface, such as a company dress code. Dress code policies are inherently designed to police personal grooming and hygiene. Many dress code policies require employees of an organization to maintain a clean and neat appearance. It is up to leaders in an organization to interpret what is deemed an acceptable appearance for employees and take action on those physical appearance choices that appear misaligned with an organization's dress code policy. This dynamic leaves room for bias that may be intentional or unintentional.

Disparate or adverse impact is an unintentional bias that is present when a protected class of people is disproportionally affected by an employment policy or practice (*Section VII- Proving Discrimination- Disparate Impact*, 2021). The Equal Employment Opportunity Commission (EEOC) clarifies that "…employment discrimination based on race, color, religion, sex (including pregnancy, sexual orientation, or gender identity), national origin, age (40 or older), disability and genetic information (including family medical history)" is prohibited under U.S. federal law (*Who Is Protected From Employment Discrimination?*, n.d.). A dress code policy that requires employees' hair to be neat can potentially result in a leader of the organization defining locs or other natural hairstyles as unkempt. Therefore, given that Black people are most likely to have hair textures that can form the loced look, this dress code will have a disparate impact on Black people. I have spent a significant part of my human resources career helping other leaders interpret the word "neat" when referring to employees' hair. Using "neat" or "well-groomed" in dress code policies to define acceptable workplace attire must be balanced with clear examples of what those words mean, or companies will consistently risk engaging in disparate impact.

Historical Context of Black Hair

Hair is an integral part of human identity. For the worldwide Black community, hair carries cultural significance that should be respected in the workplace. Dating back to thousands of years B.C., how we wore our hair identified our social standing, which society we were members of, defined our self-image, and served as a means for us to communicate (Tchenga, 2021). Additionally, our hair signified our spiritual connection to higher powers. Children born with knotted hair or locs were considered incredibly blessed. They were revered and believed to symbolize wealth to their family. The child's hair was not washed or combed, preserving its original loced state, thereby retaining the blessings (Tchenga, 2021). However, colonialism negatively impacted the perception of Black hair.

The slave trade was particularly traumatic for Africans psychologically. One of the first actions by European captors was to shave the heads of kidnapped Africans. Given that so much of an African person's identity was encapsulated in how we wore our hair, the ritual of shaving our heads resulted in the intended impact of breaking our spirit (Johnson & Bankhead, 2014). Then in the late 1800s and 1900s, words such as wooly and matted emerged from comparing Black hair to European hair, and the very existence of our hair, the way it naturally grows out of our heads, was racialized (Johnson & Bankhead, 2014). This aversion to the appearance of our hair continued through to life after slavery.

During the Civil Rights era, there was a shift towards people of African descent finding pride and honor in wearing their hair in its natural state. There was a surge of afros, non-chemically straightened hair and a re-emergence of the African long-toothed combs of our ancestors in the form of afro-picks. The concept of good hair was redefined from straight, soft, and wavy to tight coils that were not chemically processed or manipulated by heat. During this era, the Civil Rights Act was passed with Title VII of the Act identifying classes of people protected from employment discrimination based on specific characteristics such as race and gender. However, Title VII did not include characteristics specific to a race of people, such as hair texture, leaving open the possibility that acceptable hair texture may be interpreted as hair close to the Eurocentric beauty standard that persisted in American society throughout U.S. history.

In my own life, I recall numerous occasions where I was celebrated by others when I wore my hair, most similar to a European beauty standard. Growing up on a Caribbean island, where the majority population was people of African descent, did not insulate me from the effect colonialism had on the perception of Black hair. On every special occasion at church, my hair was pressed with a hot comb to make it straight, then curled with foam rollers to give me a full loose curl style. It was a painful process that I willingly endured just to be pretty. Many Black girls share similar experiences. The church elders and other kids would compliment me on how beautiful I was when my hair was straightened. Straight hair became synonymous with good hair in my subconscious.

Shortly after graduating from my undergraduate program in Houston, TX, I visited my childhood home in St. Thomas, USVI. My hair was chemically relaxed. I received many affirmations that I had grown up so beautifully. It was clear that my church family, my biological family, and my friends were proud of the young woman I had become. In later years, after I loced my hair, the reception I received starkly contrasted my prior visit. Someone expressed their deep concern for my soul to one of my family members because it appeared as if I had abandoned my Christian faith and was "a Rasta now." Straight hair was equated to good, pure, and Christian, while loced hair was suspicious, unclean, and deviant. This leads one to conclude that a disconnect exists between the wealth and good fortune locs represented in pre-colonial Africa and how locs are perceived in modern times.

Impact of Implicit Bias on Professional Black Women

Oxford English Dictionary defines implicit bias as "Any unconscious or unacknowledged preference that affects a person's outlook or behaviour; an unconscious favouritism towards or prejudice against people of a particular race, gender, or group that influences one's actions or perceptions" (OED Online, 2023, entry 88686775). Implicit bias influences hiring practices, promotional decisions, and how employees are evaluated, and can profoundly affect daily interactions. Further, Black women are constantly combating the complexities of the intersectionality of race, gender, and class and experience stereotype threat which is to be "…at risk of confirming, as self-characteristic, a negative stereotype about one's group" (Steele & Aronson, 1995, p. 797).

Implicit bias can prevent Black women from launching their careers. In one of my early career positions, I was in a client-facing financial services sales role and was the only Black woman on the team. I asked a co-worker for advice on how to increase my sales, and among many great suggestions was a recommendation that I settle on a more "polished" style. I feared being rejected so much that I did not want to ask what she meant by polished, yet I knew it was essential to know if my goal was to give myself the best chance at reaching my sales targets. When I asked for clarification, she encouraged me to let my hair grow longer and style it differently. I promptly went to the local flea market and purchased hair extensions and glue. The following Monday, my hair was long and flowy. I made my sales targets that quarter and quit the job right after. I did not quite have the words to express what did not feel right about the work environment. I did not associate the hair conversation with her as having anything to do with my dissatisfaction with the job until years later.

I only knew that selling financial services was challenging. The only type of sale that I thought would be more difficult was selling used cars. For my well-being, I knew I had to leave that job.

At another point, early in my career, I secured a job as an auditor for a furniture and appliance rental company. I was genuinely excited about where the role could take me professionally, as there appeared to be significant growth potential for a person with my training and ambition. I was the person who uncovered bookkeeping errors and potential misuse of company money, which, of course, meant that store managers did not appreciate my presence in the stores they managed. I was not discouraged by this because I viewed the auditor position as a chance to launch my career. Surprisingly, at the end of my three-month probationary period, my manager told me she had concerns about my progress and acclimation to the company. She noted that despite satisfactory work quality, I did not seem enthusiastic. I was confused by the characterization and inquired further to no avail. I was left to speculate about what I needed to do differently to be a cultural "fit" for the organization. I eventually lost motivation and transitioned to a new role. This was another position where I did not have enough time to establish myself because of implicit bias.

Eventually, I stopped using hair weaves, chemical relaxers, and heat manipulation to achieve a "polished" look. I was in my mid-20s when I made the shift, and I struggled to feel beautiful and confident wearing my natural hair consistently. I felt powerful the first day I wore a very short afro to work, but I began second-guessing my decision by day two. After some time, I realized I did not know my hair. It seemed strange to be alive for a quarter of a century and not know what my hair looked like in its natural state or how to groom it. My natural hair was foreign to me, and it could be argued that I felt like my hair was not an actual part of me. As many Black women do, I had spent a lifetime covering up my hair or changing its texture. I had to choose to embark on a journey of understanding my hair and falling in love with its uniqueness. This began my path of professional self-discovery. Embedded in the tight curls of my 4c hair, I found my professional strength. I found freedom.

With a new perspective on my hair, I searched for a new position in a city where many Black people were already in visible public leadership roles. This city also marketed itself as one with a remarkably educated, Black, and upper-middle-class population. On the day of my job interview, I took many deep breaths and interviewed with short locs. I was offered the position at an annual salary that was twice what I was currently making. This was my first time interviewing for a role with my hair loced. Without relaxed hair and weaves to hide behind, I had to project courage, competence, and likeability in my interview. It was a new space for me, and I felt powerful. The success I experienced in that interview helped me gain the confidence I needed to continue to wear my hair in its natural state in professional settings. Due to the work, I was exposed to in that job, I decided to pursue my next degree, an MBA with a concentration in technology management, further solidifying my position as a professional to be respected for my competence.

Then a strange phenomenon happened as my locs grew, causing me to find myself at a crossroads once again. The longer my locs grew, the more visible they were, and the more self-conscious I became about how I would be perceived at work. I started wearing my locs pulled back into a ponytail and away from my face so they would be somewhat hidden. Even after years of wearing my locs in professional settings, the length unearthed emotions and my unconscious bias about what long, free-form locs represented in society. The internal conflict between the often-unsolicited authenticity message I willingly espoused to colleagues and the woman now fearful of losing a well-paying position if she did not find a way to conform was overwhelming. After a while, I became convinced that it was time to distance myself from my locs, and I cut them. A few weeks later, I started to regrow my locs.

No one is immune to feeling insecure about their professional appearance. When I was in lower-paying positions, the risk of reinventing myself or starting over in a new role did not outweigh my drive to be authentic. Once I began to fill more competitive roles, the belief that I needed to assimilate to maintain my standard of living returned. Cutting my locs forced me to reflect on my values and place those in their rightful place in my decision-making process. In other words, I had to be honest with myself and accept that my locs had become a principal part of my identity.

HAIR BIAS FROM A LEGAL PERSPECTIVE

In many U.S. states, denying employment and educational opportunities to Black women who wear their hair in natural hairstyles is legal. In a 2023 research study conducted by the personal hygiene company Dove, and professional social networking giant, LinkedIn, it was reported that Black women's hair was more likely to be identified as unprofessional in the workplace (Dove LinkedIn 2023 Workplace Research Study, 2023). The same study further extrapolated that two-thirds of Black women change their hair for job interviews, moving from curly to straight and Black women with natural hairstyles were more prone to workplace microaggressions. Black women who are more junior in their careers feel the most pressure of conformity. Almost half the women interviewed for this study who were also under age 34 believed that they needed a professional headshot with hair that was more Eurocentric. A third of the women in this age group also thought they were passed over for job opportunities because of their natural hair (*CROWN Act Resources — the Official CROWN Act*, n.d.). I identify with this sentiment completely, as I had that exact feeling at the start of my career. It can feel like there is an all-out assault on our hair.

For Black women, workplace hair discrimination not only impacts how we choose to present ourselves but can also lead to practices that are detrimental to our health. There are class action lawsuits against the cause of ovarian, uterine, and endometrial cancer. The Sister Study, conducted by the National Institutes of Environmental Health Sciences (NIEHS), confirmed that frequent use of chemical hair straighteners doubled the risk of developing uterine cancer (*Hair Straightening Chemicals Associated With Higher Uterine Cancer*, 2022). Combined with the fact that Black women use hair straighteners more frequently than other racial groups in the study and started using straighteners at a much earlier age, Black women's exposure was higher than other racial groups. Further, the results of the Sister Study enabled researchers to draw a causal link between the regular use of chemical relaxers and uterine cancer, ovarian cancer, and any other hormone-driven health conditions. The chemicals contained in many hair relaxers have also been linked to infertility, immune disorders, cognitive issues, endometriosis, and metabolic syndrome in the person exposed and their future children (*The Sister Study: Home*, n.d.). The results of this study have since led to a class action lawsuit, and there is an expectation that in 2023, hair relaxer lawsuits will continue to increase exponentially.

Advances are being made concerning ending discrimination based on hair texture, though more is needed. The Create a Respect and Open World for Natural Hair or the CROWN Act is the most notable of those movements. The CROWN Act is a legislative intervention that would protect Black people from hair discrimination at work and school. As late into the 20th century as 2019, it was still legal to discriminate against employees based on hair. Then on July 3, 2019, Governor Gavin Newsome signed the CROWN Act into law (California, 2019). Since then, 19 other states and the U.S. Virgin Islands have followed suit, and over 40 local governments have enacted laws prohibiting hair discrimination. However, Federal level hair discrimination protections continue to fail to pass the U.S. legislative branch.

Additionally, the Equal Employment Opportunity Commission (EEOC) has begun exploring claims alleging race discrimination based on hair bias under the existing provisions of Title VII of the Civil Rights Act. In 2016, the EEOC sued Catastrophe Management Solutions for rescinding the job offer of a woman who refused to cut her locs as a condition of employment. The EEOC's position was that the CMS's actions were tantamount to race discrimination because locs are physiologically and culturally unique to people of African descent. The 11th Circuit Court of Appeals in the Southern District of Alabama upheld the decision of the lower courts, ruling that CMS was not in violation of Title VII of the Civil Rights Act (*Equal Employment Opportunity Commission V. Catastrophe Management Solutions, No. 14-13482 (11th Cir. 2017)*, 2017). Though the plaintiff did not prevail in this case, the willingness of the EEOC to commit to pursuing available legal avenues to find just resolutions to these incidences of racial discrimination is promising.

Black professional women are uniquely positioned to use our lived experiences to give voice to the need to normalize our presence as respected professionals while showcasing our naturally textured hair. I did not set out on a political journey when I loced my hair. In contrast, I sought a lower maintenance way of getting ready for work daily and wanted to be myself. However, like colonial times, the very presence of my hair seemed offensive to company decision-makers and, at times, used as a measure of my competence despite multiple academic degrees and experience. However, I persisted, and I encourage all Black women to do the same.

HAIR BIAS FROM A LEADERSHIP PERSPECTIVE

I am a business leader and have been for close to two decades. I know that little changes in a work environment without the organization's leadership modeling the behaviors we want to see and holding those not demonstrating the organization's values accountable for their choices. I have chosen to leverage the discomfort and fear I have felt in interviews to coach other Black women on professional authenticity. However, leaders have a more significant responsibility. Leaders should utilize their positions of influence to impact change on the broadest scale possible. Specifically, human resources leaders can spearhead changes to company policy to ensure the language is inclusive and lead training for teams to help them gain a more holistic understanding of workplace inclusivity. Most importantly, leaders should model the behaviors they expect from their teams.

Companies also have a responsibility to demonstrate good corporate citizenship. Good corporate citizenship is a business imperative. Social media allows consumers to know what companies are doing in real-time, and socio-political matters such as equality and justice have redefined what society sees as acceptable. The Millennials and Generation Z combined represent the most influential consumer groups and comprise most of the workforce. Multiple studies have been conducted on their buyer and worker behaviors. The results are consistent; alignment of personal and company values matters. The Deloitte Global 2023 Gen Z and Millennial Survey (2023) reported that these generations would not support organizations whose values do not align with their own. Approximately 40% of Gen Zs and Millennials left jobs because of a misalignment of values (*The Deloitte Global 2023 Gen Z and Millennial Survey*, 2023). In the 2022 Millenial and Gen Z Survey, 46% of Gen Zs and Millennials in senior leadership roles refused job offers or other assignments for the same reason. Further, these generations believe that business leaders must be pivotal in addressing society's most pressing problems, such as inequality (*The Deloitte Global 2022 Gen Z and Millennial Survey*, 2022). Therefore, organizations that take a public stand against hair bias and advocate for the passing of the CROWN

Act at the federal level are demonstrating their commitment to evolving inclusive practices within their communities. These are attractive values to the Millennial and Gen Z consumer base.

Black women leaders are in an opportune position to influence how junior Black professionals interpret the meaning of professionalism, starting with hair choices. I had witnessed Black people visibly exhale multiple times in my career when I was introduced as their new leader. I recall one team member, who has since become a friend, sharing with me that the way she experienced my leadership helped her gain the courage to stop wearing hair weaves and try natural hair. She was also educated to believe that she had to conform but rarely felt comfortable. This was her first time having such close interactions with a Black professional, with locs, that other leaders appeared to respect. This is how we change the narrative about accepting locs and other natural hairstyles in professional settings by choosing excellence, authenticity, and confidence instead of blind obedience to dominant culture standards.

STANDING IN YOUR POWER

In my professional career of over 20 years, I have learned that the interview process is partly what you know and partly who you project yourself to be. As a Black woman, the goal should be to acquire the technical skills needed to be ready for a role and master the art of exuding confidence when competing for a new position or promotion. Marcus Garvey, Jamaican founder of the Universal Negro Improvement Association (UNIA), once said, "If you have no confidence in self, you are twice defeated in the race of life. With confidence, you have won even before you started." This was the fundamental missing ingredient for me as I navigated the employment landscape in America. The wigs, the weaves, and the chemical relaxers helped me achieve a look similar to the Eurocentric beauty standards I was taught to embrace but did not consistently support the level of confidence I needed to fuel my career.

Throughout the years, I have had other Black women whom I admired and sought to emulate. Multiple Black women who were more senior to me in the organizations I worked for chose to serve as mentors for me. Once I ascended to middle management, I could turn to them for regular coaching on how to have effective performance conversations and attain the training and on-the-job experiences critical to position me for future senior management roles. Establishing executive presence was central to many of those conversations and was peppered with respect for my perspective on authenticity. These women guided me toward becoming a better version of myself, bridging the gap between authenticity and corporate assimilation. In a series of those career conversations about how I presented myself as a leader, including what my hair signified for me and others, it became apparent that if I was going to continue to grow in both influence and money, I needed to stay open to alternative career paths and diversify my income mix. This was the beginning of my entertaining opportunities to contribute to educational manuals and explore online training as another avenue for income generation. That decision has allowed me to establish myself as an indisputable expert in my field.

Employment experiences affect all areas of our lives. It is impossible to compartmentalize emotions felt because of work friction and how we show up in our personal lives. My decision to loc my hair exposed my character to myself by compelling me to confront dogmatic beliefs that were not grounded in facts. To be a woman of African descent and to equate innate characteristics of African people with abhorrent words like ugly or filthy is outrageous. Nevertheless, those connections were an integral part of my thought pattern that even after experiencing some career success with my hair loced, I still convinced myself that the length of my locs would pose a new threat to my advancement to the C-Suite. Being courageous and confronting my internal hypocrisy facilitated the mindset shift I needed to transform personally and professionally.

CONCLUSION

Promoting diversity, equity, inclusion, belonging, and justice in the workplace is onerous, yet satisfying as a woman who has had to navigate the unconscious bias that permeates American business. As a teenager, I dreamed of becoming an international human rights attorney and potentially working for the United Nations, improving global human outcomes. As I began to grow a career in human resources, it made sense that my penchant for ensuring people were treated fairly and equitably would be central to my practice. Change and compromise are constant in life, and that includes the workplace. I choose authenticity. As I evolved, my interpretation of authenticity shifted. That is growth; growth is what you want because you are metaphorically dying if you are not growing. As a Black woman, you will encounter obstacles because of race, gender, and perceived class. None of those obstacles are insurmountable. You navigate those obstacles by being clear about personal values. Know what is important to you and project confidence. Then you can also be a beacon to other Black women who may question their worth in the workplace.

References

California S. O. (2019, July 3). *Governor Newsom Signs Legislation to Protect Employees from Racial Discrimination Based on Hairstyle*. California Governor. https://www.gov.ca.gov/2019/07/03/governor-newsom-signs-legislation-to-protect-employees-from-racial-discrimination-based-on-hairstyle/

CROWN Act Resources — The Official CROWN Act. (n.d.). The Official CROWN Act. https://www.thecrownact.com/research-studies

Dove LinkedIn 2023 Workplace Research Study. (2023, January). The Crown Act. https://www.thecrownact.com/research-studies

Equal Employment Opportunity Commission v. Catastrophe Management Solutions, No. 14-13482 (11th Cir. 2017). (2017, December 5). Justia Law. https://law.justia.com/cases/federal/appellate-courts/ca11/14-13482/14-13482-2017-12-05.html

Hair straightening chemicals associated with higher uterine cancer. (2022, October 17). National Institutes of Health (NIH). https://www.nih.gov/news-events/news-releases/hair-straightening-chemicals-associated-higher-uterine-cancer-risk

Johnson, T., & Bankhead, T. (2014). Hair It Is: Examining the Experiences of Black Women with Natural Hair. *Open Journal of Social Sciences*, *02*(01), 86–100. doi:10.4236/jss.2014.21010

Letter from a Birmingham Jail [King, Jr.]. (n.d.). UPenn. https://www.africa.upenn.edu/Articles_Gen/Letter_Birmingham.html

Oxford University Press. (2023, March). *Bias*. OED Online. www.oed.com/view/Entry/18564

Oxford University Press. (2023, March). *Implicit Bias*. OED Online. https://www-oed-com.fgul.idm.oclc.org/view/Entry/88686775

Section VII- Proving Discrimination- Disparate Impact. (2021, February 3). CRT Department of Justice. https://www.justice.gov/crt/fcs/T6Manual7#D

Steele, C. M., & Aronson, J. (1995). Stereotype Threat and the Intellectual Test Performance of African Americans. *Journal of Personality and Social Psychology*, *69*(5), 797–811. doi:10.1037/0022-3514.69.5.797 PMID:7473032

Tchenga, D. S. N. (2021). Black women's hair and natural hairstyles in the workplace: Expanding the definition of race under title vii. *Virginia Law Review*, *107*, 272–299.

The Deloitte Global 2022 Gen Z and Millennial Survey. (2023, May 17). Deloitte. https://www.deloitte.com/global/en/issues/work/genzmillennialsurvey-2022.html

The Sister Study: Home. (n.d.). Sister Study. https://sisterstudy.niehs.nih.gov/English/index1.htm

Who is protected from employment discrimination? (n.d.). US EEOC. https://www.eeoc.gov/employers/small-business/3-who-protected-employment-discrimination

Chapter 7
Transitioning:
Examining Black Women's Hair Stories in Entering Higher Education

Kernysha L. Rowe
American University, USA

Afiya Mbilishaka
PsychoHairapy, USA

Destiny Bell
Georgia State University, USA

Whitney Harris
University of the District of Columbia, USA

Camaron Loritts
University North Carolina at Greensboro, USA

ABSTRACT

Hair is so culturally significant within the lives of Black women that the transition from high school to college forces Black female college students to make arduous decisions about how to care for and wear their hair in this untried and dislocated space. This chapter investigates the "turning point" or transition of Black female college students as it relates to their choices to wear their hair in this new professional setting. Through a phenomenological approach, the hair narratives of 31 Black female participants were collected through an online survey entitled the Hair, Health, and Heritage Study. Researchers engaged in a thematic content analysis in which Black women voiced their experiences of shifting from a Eurocentric beauty standard to embracing their natural features. This study asserts a connection between Black hair and identity through five themes. These insights direct anti-bias trainings on college campuses and student engagement through policy.

DOI: 10.4018/978-1-6684-8790-7.ch007

INTRODUCTION

Hair is so culturally significant within the lives of Black women, that the transition from high school to college forces Black female college students to make arduous decisions about how to care for, and wear their hair, in this untried and dislocated space (Ellis-Hervey et al., 2016; Mbilishaka & Apugo, 2020; Murrey & Taylor, 2020). Described by Greene (2011, p. 406), Black women must actively make decisions about their hair through their lifetime to relax or press it; to wear it straightened or natural; to cut it or grow it long; to braid or wear it out; to wrap it, roll it, or plait it; to put a weave in it or put a wig over it; to twist, braid, or lock it; to color, highlight, or not color at all.

Unfortunately, Black women are faced with making these decisions in the face of anti-Blackness and the potential consequence of being seen as unprofessional (Ellis-Hervey et al., 2016; Mbilishaka et al., 2020). Repeated studies suggest that Black women spend more time, money, and emotion on manipulating the texture, length, and style of their hair within a context of Eurocentric biased beauty ideals than any other group of women (Johnson & Bankhead, 2014; Lewis, 1999; Mbilishaka, 2018a; Neil & Mbilishaka, 2019). Still, little is known about Black women's thought processes concerning grooming practices related to their hair during the college years.

Not only does Black hair and hair texture visibly communicate race, ethnicity, and beauty (DeLongoria, 2018), it impacts personal and professional development opportunities. In predominantly white institutions, Black women are at risk for shifting (Shorter-Gooden, 2003), a process in which Black women navigating racial and gender expectations alter their true selves through excessive compromising—or because of fighting against these expectations which can be a draining process. Black women's stories about their hair experiences in higher education are often excluded from research on increasing institutional engagement among students, faculty, and university administrators. An emerging literature has begun to centralize the role of Black hair in navigating K-12 educational spaces (Essien & Wood, 2021; Rogers, Versey & Cielto, 2021; O'Brien-Richardson, 2019; Davis Tribble et al., 2019; Muhammed & McArthur, 2015; Mbilishaka & Apugo, 2020; Apugo, Mawhinney & Mbilishaka, 2020), but to date there is no published psychological study on Black female students' hair stories and higher education. Unpacking the meaning and impact of Black hair is critical for Black women in higher education because it may be the seed for establishing a professional and career identity.

Acknowledgement of the varied experiences of Black women and their hair can guide institutions of higher education to be more inclusive, by highlighting the complexity of college experiences of people from underrepresented communities. Black women face a spectrum of concerns related to hair that include but are not limited to: impacts on personal relationships (Garrod & Gomez, 2013; Mbilishaka,

2018b), self-inflicted hair abuse (Brice et al., 2007), anxiety (Garrod & Gomez, 2013), and hair stress (Winfield-Thomas & Whaley, 2019). Furthermore, career development, racial identity, and hairstyles of Black women are intertwined (Farley, 2016). Hair presentation is explicitly connected to identity and self-esteem for Black women (Ellis-Hervey et al., 2016; Johnson & Bankhead, 2014), and so it stands to reason that the combined psychological stressors may pose a threat to the success of Black collegiate women.

While the aforementioned consequences and implications have significant influences on the racial-gender identity development of Black college women, hair also offers space for empowerment.

Research has yet to pinpoint and unpack moments within the collegiate years which lead Black women to make the choice to wear natural and Afrocultural hairstyles. In a significant action of aesthetic resistance (Sekayi, 2003), Black women making the decision to embrace natural[1] Black hair is a result of a positive sense of self and connection to the larger African Diaspora (Maynard & Jules, 2020; Young, 2015). This qualitative study on this "turning point" related to hair aims to: (1) expand the literature about Black women's identity development in the context of hair politics, (2) document the narratives of Black college women navigating higher education while taking a conscious stance to resist European beauty standards, and (3) inform institutional policies by reducing racial barriers and consequences for Black women who are navigating hair decisions in higher education. To grasp a deeper understanding of the origins of hair stress for Black women in transitioning to college, historical context related to hair praise and bias must be provided.

THE ROOTS OF HAIR BIAS

In traditional African societies, the hairstyles of Black women and girls were often used as a language system to communicate dimensions of identity and initiation (Byrd & Tharps, 2014). In addition to the visual and oral documentation of hair rituals in Africa by African people, many European male emissaries documented what they considered ostentatious hairstyles of Black women, despite their illiteracies around African culture (Dabiri, 2020). For example, amongst the Yoruba of Nigeria and Benin, all female children were taught how to braid hair. Girls who demonstrated early mastery of the art become the caretakers of all the physical and spiritual heads of the community (Dabiri, 2020). For the Mende of Sierra Leone, female adolescents were separated from their birth families to engage in an initiation into womanhood, with the final demarcation of adulthood being the wearing of ornate hairstyles (Dabiri, 2020). When a Maasai adolescent girl matured enough to participate in marriage, she had her hair ceremonially shaved to mark a turning point in her relationship readiness

(Beckwith & Fisher, 1999). Due to hundreds of years of colonization in Africa and the enslavement of African people in the Americas, most of these rituals were lost in translation (Byrd & Tharps, 2014). Even still, enslaved African women who were transported in the belly of slave ships still engaged in hair grooming to communicate messages about identity after arriving to the unknown world (Oyedemi, 2016). Upon their arrival to the New World, Black women's heads were shaved to depersonalize and dehumanize them (Byrd & Tharps, 2014). Elements of dehumanization persisted on most plantations where enslaved African women were not permitted to wash and style their hair (Byrd & Tharps, 2014). Black women faced oppression in openly expressing their self-concept and culture through their hair.

Black hair is, and always has been, political in America (Morrow, 1990), specifically as it relates to texture. Oriowo (2016) defines 'texturism' as a hierarchal system that values straight hair over coiled hair, while Leath (2021) adds that texturism is the social phenomenon in which specific types of natural hair patterns are preferred or considered more beautiful.

Enslaved Africans were placed in a caste system of hair texture based upon the textural approximation to Whiteness (Morrow, 1990). Enslaved Africans with long, straighter hair were often responsible for household duties, while enslaved Africans with short, tightly-coiled hair were typically forced into manual labor in the field (Byrd & Tharps, 2014). This texture-based social system translated into the post-enslavement period, in which Black people with looser curls had more access to educational opportunities and employment. This is still occurring today (Mbilishaka et al., 2020; Opie & Phillips, 2015).

Wilson and colleagues (2018) argue that the environment impacts whether or not Black hair texture is embraced or celebrated, such as a cultural collegiate environment which encourage cultural pride, hair self-esteem can work against the grain of the historical pattern of texturism and pro-white bias. For example, Orey and Zhang (2019) found that dark-skinned individuals with less European characteristics sporting straight hair, a twist-out, or locs were considered more attractive, compared to their lighter-skinned counterparts with the same hairstyles. Lighter-skinned women, regardless of hairstyle, were perceived as less supportive of Black Nationalist views, while Afrocentric aesthetics (dark skin or highly textured hair) were perceived as harder working and more progressive (Orney & Zhang, 2019). The authors also attribute the Black Lives Matter Movement, and the popularization of natural hairstyles to Black college women embracing Black aesthetics.

Snider and Rosenberg (2006) examined the relationship between skin color and hair texture. They found that in racially diverse groups, lighter skin shades are considered more beautiful, and that "good" hair, defined as hair that is closer to straight, was considered an indication of good genes fit for marriage and procreation. Correspondingly, Luney (2021) identified how challenging university environments are for Black women with dark-skin and coiled hair. Darker-skinned Black women with locked hair received differential treatment, were ignored by university administration, and encountered stricter requirements to conform while on campus to avoid mistreatment (Luney, 2021). Simultaneously, all Black women received a type of support through the presentation of natural hair by university administrators (Luney, 2021). These studies highlight the hair bias in educational institutions and the prognosis for Black female students as they enter the workforce.

BLACK HAIR AND 'PROFESSIONALISM'

When it comes to equitable employment, hair has been, and continues to be, a barrier for Black women (Dove, 2019; Opie & Phillips, 2015;). Over 80% of Black women have had to alter the natural appearance of their hair for a job (Dove, 2019). Black women are often held to a Eurocentric standard of beauty when it comes to their hair, meaning that straight hair is seen as ideal and professional, while natural Black hair is seen as unkempt and unprofessional (Byrd and Tharps; 2014). This can have devastating effects when it comes to chances of employment after college for Black women, especially those who wear their hair natural. Black women with natural textures may be seen as less professional than their counterparts with straight hair (Swangan, 2013).

Although images of natural Black hair are gaining visibility in media and popular culture, Black hair and hair texure is often still stigmatized in the workplace, even by institutions that purport to promote diversity and inclusion (Gray, 2017). Biases and stereotypes play a role in creating norms of what is accepted as professionalism, a descriptive category which rarely includes natural Black hair characteristics. Again, the "hair hierarchy" suggests that there is a higher social value placed on hair that more closely resembles Eurocentric standards (Farley, 2016). As a result, many Black female college students may feel the need to straighten their hair in order to be competitive in the post-college job market. Despite a preference for wearing their hair naturally, Black women still believe that wearing it straight for job interviews will give them a competitive edge (Dove, 2019; McGill et al., 2017).

Black female adolescents have been included in research studies about thoughts of attractiveness and professionalism of Black hair. In the article "Developing a critical consciousness: Black women and the intersection of hair and power", Swangan (2013) argues that hair bias is fueled by fear and this fear impacts believed access to upward mobility. Other studies support this claim as well. Bellinger (2007) interviewed fifteen African American teens, ages 16 to 18 and reported that many of them were hesitant to wear their natural hair for fear of the negative reactions of employers. Bellinger reported that the teens were willing to spend more money on styles that were seen as more acceptable in the workplace. One participant explained "I think it has to do with the fact that the people in America who do the hiring aren't always racially sensitive." To be promoted in the workplace, African American women feel that they have to adopt a certain look. Looking "neat" equates to a very short afro, or expensive, permed hair (Bellinger, 2007). Bellinger (2007) further argues that the top earning women more often wear their hair straight, while working class women are more likely to wear their hair in natural styles, like braids. Indeed, even if they went natural in college, some students may revert back by temporarily or permanently straightening their hair, wearing a wig, or wearing a weave.

NAVIGATING BLACK HAIR IN HIGHER EDUCATION

The educational system, inclusive the elective branch of higher education, is an extension of the existing racist, sexist, and elitist structures that are interwoven into the fabric of America. Thus, the experiences for Black students are reflective of the experiences of Black Americans in the United States. Black students may have a hard time feeling like they belong in higher education spaces, which can lead to imposter syndrome (Lowe & Bernard, 2019), where belonging is questioned due to comparison to Eurocentric idealized standards of professionalism. Additionally, there is copious research which illustrates that Black student experiences are radically different from their counterparts in all facets, including social, financial, academic, professional, mental, and psychological.

Moreover, young Black adults are constantly exposed to sociocultural stressors such as racism, discrimination, and oppression. These barriers place them in a marginalized position that increases the likelihood of them experiencing stress (Stokes et al., 2020). The lack of positive gendered and racial socialization for Black women translates directly into the practice of toxic, chemical processing of their hair through products and techniques formulated to damage the overall health of textured hair and scalp (Mbilishaka & Apugo, 2020) to achieve straightness/whiteness. The ideology of texturism is present in the classroom and in the psyches of some teaching faculty and their pupils. Black women with natural hair are often targets for hair shaming from educators and peers, while also withstanding the consequences of hair damage. These negative hair experiences in schools, which are critical sites of socialization, magnify the implicit injuries of racial and gender marginalization (Mbilishaka & Apugo, 2020). Still, anti-bullying school policies often fail to include hair shaming (Mbilishaka and Apugo, 2020).

Hair bias experienced by Black girls at school remains a source of trauma and identity negotiation, causing disharmony within their microsystem of relationships and limiting healthy social-emotional development (Hilliard, 1979; Mbilishaka &

Apugo, 2020). Self-conscious emotions, such as embarrassment and anxiety emerge, causes discomfort in school and interpersonal relationships. This, in turn, may lead Black girls to have feelings of inadequacy and breed mental health conditions such as depression and dissociation, as they attempt to repress the aesthetic traumas they experience (Mbilishaka & Apugo, 2020). Hair, gender, and race are critical points of intersection for Black girls and women; therefore, it is urgent that Black girls and women be given space in which to voice their experiences of intersectionality (Crenshaw, 1991), both internally and within the academic environment.

RESEARCH DESIGN

The purpose of this study is to apply phenomenology to the examination of Black women who experienced a psychological turning point in the transition of hair during college. Hence, the "meaning, structure, and essence" (Patton, 2002, p. 104) of the hair stories of Black college women will be presented. The *Hair, Health, and Heritage Study* is a qualitative study which elicits memories and stories related to hair. This study was approved by the institutional review board and data was collected between February 2017 and February 2018. A research team from a psychology research lab recruited participants through social media (i.e., Twitter, Facebook, and Instagram) and through Black hair salons and barbershops in the Washington, D.C. metropolitan area. All surveys were administered digitally through *SurveyMonkey*. The average participant took 40 minutes to complete the full survey.

DATA COLLECTION

Criteria was established by the principal investigator in the original research study for the recruitment of participants, through the identification of 92 different Black-owned hair care settings in Washington, D.C. Before entering the hair care setting, all research assistants engaged in training on how to standardize the data collection. The team engaged in role play sessions about how to speak to potential participants and addressed frequently asked questions, authentically and ethically engaging with community members. Research assistants were required to: (1) request permission from the owner to recruit participants in their place of business, (2) place fliers in the hair care space, and (3) directly ask patrons to complete the survey with a digital link. Recruitment was most effective on Friday evenings and holiday weekends. In addition, convenience sampling occurred through posting the link on the personal social media accounts of the research team. Participants were virtually directed to complete the survey link at one location and in one sitting.

PARTICIPANTS

With a total of 233 participants who completed the study out of the 527 participants who started the survey (a 44% completion rate), this study included a sampling of the larger study. The inclusion criteria for this study included participants who: (a) identified as African American or Black, (b) identified as female, (c) were at least 18 years old, and (d) stated "college" or "university" in their "turning point" narrative (noting that the college and university can be interchanged). Thirty-one Black women fit the criteria and were moved forward for data analysis and satisfied sampling saturation (Morse, 1991). These participants ranged in age from 18 to 47 years old, with a mean age of 26. All participants completed high school, while some had gone on to earn professional degrees. All self-identified as heterosexual, and the majority resided in the mid-Atlantic region of the United States at the time of completion (58%). All participants were eligible to be entered into a raffle for ten $20 Amazon.com gift cards.

MEASURE

All participants completed the *Guided Hair Autobiography,* or GHA, (Mbilishaka, 2014) and a demographic questionnaire. The GHA is a modified adaptation from McAdams' (1997) *Guided Autobiography* (GA). The GA elicits stories through a life-story-telling model of the most salient episodes of the life story. The turning point prompt encourages participants to reflect on a time when they experienced a major shift in how they process the world and themselves. For the GHA, this measure elicits stories about hair. Participants completed the prompts, telling stories about their earliest memory of hair, a low point or "nadir" related to hair, and a turning point in how they thought about their hair. All narratives included in this study were in response to the following prompt:

In looking back on one's life, there is often a key turning point or episodes through which a person undergoes substantial changes with their hair. Please identify a particular episode in your life story when you underwent an important transition with respect to your understanding of yourself and your hair. It is not necessary that you consciously saw the event as a turning point when it actually happened. What is important is that you now see this particular event as a turning point in your hair story. If you feel that you have experienced no dramatic turning points in your hair story, then describe a particular episode in your life that comes closest to qualifying as a turning point. Please describe: what happened, when it happened, who was involved, what you were thinking and feeling, why this experience is significant, and how it shaped you as an individual.

Participants in the present study are those who mentioned college or university in their response to this prompt. Although this prompt does not directly ask the participant to write about educational environments, participants described those moments that pinpointed higher education and the developmental period of college in their lives.

RESEARCHERS' POSITIONALITY

The data analytic team for this study included four members, all women of African descent. The team consisted of two doctoral students studying higher education, one faculty member in journalism, and one undergraduate psychology student. Researcher A is of Caribbean heritage, was born in the UK, has worn her hair in locs for the past 16 years, is employed at a northeastern university, and is enrolled in a doctoral program. Researcher B is an African American undergraduate student at a southern university and wears her hair in afros or braids while on campus. Researcher C is an African American college professor at a northeastern university, is a broadcast journalist, and has worn her hair in locs for the past four years. Researcher D is an African American university staff member and doctoral student at a southeastern university and has been wearing her hair in locs for one year.

DATA ANALYSIS

Qualitative methods offer a scholarly approach to investigating research questions in a way which honors the nuanced perspectives of participants often neglected in quantitative research. Phenomenology specifically examines the essence of a lived experience or identified phenomenon (Jones et al., 2014). Phenomenology is influenced by constructivist epistemology, situated by the socially constructed realities of participants (Glense, 2011). Phenomenology is both a school of philosophy and methodology. Schools of phenomenological thought are splintered along the lines of the interests of Hans-Georg Gadamer's work concentrating on philosophy and history, Edmund Husserl's work centered on transcendental psychology, and Maurice Merleau-Ponty's work focusing on existential phenomenology (Jones et al., 2014). Educational research, in particular, is situated within Martin Heidegger's work on hermeneutic phenomenology, "the interpretation of an object for the purpose of understanding" (Jones et al., 2014, p. 88). Additionally, Heidegger's (1962) analysis of "being," inspired Schwandt (2001) to encourage phenomenologists to capture "careful description of ordinary conscious experience of everyday life (the life-world), a description of things (the essential structures of consciousness) as one experiences them" (p. 191). Therefore, phenomenological research focuses on the essence within the lifeworld of people who have experienced the same phenomenon (Creswell, 2013), thus making meaning of being within the world.

Phenomenology requires the researcher to unpack the lived experience of a phenomenon, often suggesting meaning beyond what is told by the participants. To this end, a great deal of reflexivity is needed on behalf of the researcher during data analysis (Jones et al., 2014). In phenomenology, this process is described as epoché and bracketing; distinct but inter-related research steps (Jones et al., 2014). Epoché, introduced by Moustakas (1994), involves internal reflection and conscious placement of personal assumptions, as well as preunderstandings, resulting in a "phenomenological attitude shift" (Jones et al., 2014; Patton, 20020, p. 485). Following epoché is the process of bracketing, or a phenomenological reduction (Jones et al., 2014). Derived from Husserl's work it allows for diligent inquiry of the phenomenon (Patton, 2002).

All narratives from the turning point episode that used the word "college" or "university" from the targeted sample were saved in a blinded Excel file. Using the phenomenological approach described above, a multi-rater system of four researchers gathered to familiarize themselves with each story, compose a list of meaningful terms, establish code definitions, distinguish themes (i.e., new environment versus new experience), and then to produce a report.

RESULTS

Based on the 31 responses from Black women, five themes emerged from the data: navigating shifts in resources, adjusting to new environments, emancipation from conformity, refocus on positive imagery, and openness to new experiences. The themes presented are interrelated, in that a college woman may have experienced more than one of the five themes in her recollection of a personal turning point in her hair story. To illustrate each theme, selected significant statements are presented.

Navigating Shifts in Resources

Navigating shifts in resources describes access to or restriction from resources, which may have triggered a turning point for college women. College women are at a unique junction in their lives because the transition to college and matriculation through college can determine one's level of access to resources (i.e., beauty salons, products for specific hair types, or stylists with specific expertise)—or that person's struggle to gain access to them. A consistent thread for all the college women is that access to or restriction from resources was critical for a healthy transition, or turning point, in the hair story.

The women listed 'resources' as a critical factor in their decision to transition from chemically straightened hair to unprocessed hair. For example, one woman refers to the process of getting a relaxer as a negative, painful experience that also became time-consuming and expensive. The process of perming her hair caused hair breakage, which resulted in her cutting off all her hair, starting over, and wearing it in its natural state for almost a decade after that. Another woman stated "when I went to college in NC there was a significant gap in salons skill set compared to DC stylist. At that moment I went natural began making my own wigs and doing my own hair." This woman took control of her own haircare practices by independently maintaining and styling her hair with wigs as an accessory during the transition to college. This woman required an interim hairstyle that would physically cover the turning point, the process of 'going natural' from processed hair.

One of the experiences resulting from the interim styling of wigs is that comments from peers about the realness of the wig hair were a source of personal embarrassment for the participant, which led to her future choice of short haircuts or braids to avoid these interactions and insecurities. Another woman confirmed similar sentiments when transitioning from permed hair to natural hair. This person was surrounded by natural-haired peers and family members before entering college, thus she desired to also wear her natural hair. This woman stated

I told her [her best friend] I was ready to be natural but not ready to wear it out yet. She finally said let me big chop your hair, cut off the permed ends. I was hesitant but agreed. She cut it, I unexpectedly cried and hugged her for helping me make that decision.

Although this woman admits to not wearing natural hair out for public view until a year later, this emotional experience with a best friend paved the way to her complete acceptance of self and the rejection of others' future influence on her physical appearance. Similarly, another student confirmed the value of a best friend during her hair transition to natural hair from relaxed hair. This friend provided hair strategies which facilitated her safe experimentation with hair care practices.

Adjusting to New Environments

Environment is critical to centering hair and identity for Black college women. In other words, the representation of images and characteristics which are reflective of individual students creates positive affirmation and self-worth among those students. A student who previously wore weaves (synthetic or human hair sewed into the scalp) stated that while attending a Historically Black College and University (HBCU), the HBCU environment was the first setting she had been in, in which others celebrated her hair texture and recognized her as attractive. “It was in college where I finally put the flat iron down and embraced my natural texture.” Another woman shared that it was not until a peer commented on how envious she was of this woman’s natural curls, that she began to embrace her hair. Other women stated that being socialized in an environment—in a community and/or family—in which the majority of people shared their same hair textures, prevented self-destructive thoughts about hair and allowed them to be less self-conscious. “I felt extremely comfortable with myself [and] how I looked with my hair.”

Furthermore, the existence of a sub-group of Black women sharing similar hair stories in the environment affirmed and supported the development of positive emotions of the participants towards their own natural hair. “When I went to college, I was around a lot more black people and they wore their natural hair more often than not. I got more used to seeing natural hair and then I started seeing my own hair as ok or at least not the tragedy that I viewed it as before.”

Emancipation From Conformity

Several women described a ‘freeing’ emotional response that pointed to the theme of emancipation, freedom or relief from how they previously conceptualized their hair. The first overlap of theme emerges between *emancipation* and *resources,* as a student transitioned to natural hair from chemically treated hair. This student had experienced a significant scalp issue, pain during the perm process, and poor customer service during hair treatments. “I do remember asking myself why I was putting myself through this type of torture.” Another woman also remembered disliking the salon experience while wearing straightened hair, therefore she transitioned to natural hair. “I became natural because my friend was, and she was telling me how much better it was… I also thought it’d be easier to handle. This helped me to understand what my hair needs, and I started watching YouTube for hair help.” Another student also bore a generally negative disposition toward blow-drying her hair straight every day, and opted to wear her natural hair as curls. “I switch it up a lot and enjoyed the flexibility… definitely a positive experience.” Another student felt liberated when creating hair care products. She devised a hair ritual made her feel empowered and “free to love [her] natural hair.”

Some of the women who experienced feelings related to ‘emancipation’ also mentioned liberation from parental expectations about hairstyles. A student stated, “I feel that starting my locs was such a significant portion of my life because I’d always wanted locs and was never allowed to get them - and this served as the first adult decision I'd made on my own and against the wishes of my parents." The process of taking a hair journey of discovery allowed this student to gain a love of self and hair in ways that were previously blocked by parental rule. Confronting parental figures allowed personal identification of self-determination. Another woman also confirmed that being in college allowed her to make independent decisions regarding her hair, "I had more freedom to cut, color, and style my hair the way I wanted to without my parents monitoring it as closely or judging it." These moments of experimentation laid the foundation of a healthy adult relationship with hair; one which involved confidence, haircare knowledge, and pride.

In college, I did lots of research on natural hair care and decided to chop all of my heat-damaged hair off despite pushback from my family because they were used to me with really long hair. After the chop, I loved my hair more than I did before it and decided to never straighten it again. I feel more like I'm being myself with my hair this way. I also feel that my natural hair is an expression of my cultural identity and that the pride that I have in it translates to improved overall confidence.

Refocus on Positive Imagery

Women also experienced *positive imagery*, a theme which refers to a process in which women undergo self-actualization and acceptance of the beauty of their hair. During this process, women embraced their natural hair color and length, they did the 'big chop' (cutting off chemically straightened hair to a short style) as an initiatory moment in embracing their natural hair, they shed insecure, younger versions of self, they achieved complete acceptance of their hair—including its texture, they recognized and broke through unknown barriers impacting self before transitioning.

I learned to appreciate my thick wavy hair entering college. I just realized it was beautiful and it was who I was. It was me and there's nothing wrong with me. When I was in graduate school, I had a boyfriend who was really into all things natural. He convinced me that I would be beautiful without my relaxed hair...The boyfriend and I broke up not too long afterward, but it was liberating to get to know my natural hair and free myself from the need to look and be a particular way...My graduate school natural experience opened me to the possibilities that my hair was both an important reflection of myself [and] just hair.

I wanted to free myself from the way I felt at my last school as an outcast and be a confident me regardless of my hair and if my clothes were in style... I wanted to allow myself more freedom to be confident in who I was without feeling pressure to still look a certain/acceptable way.

I love my hair. My junior year of college my hair was flourishing in its natural state. I rarely straightened my hair but when I did, it was beautiful.

I had just developed a beautiful relationship with one of [my] close friends at school who had been natural since she was 12. After exchanging stories and voicing our insecurities we realized how tired we were of limiting ourselves....I feel free. I feel beautiful. But most importantly, I feel like me.

I respect and protect [my hair] and they adorn me. I feel like I'm wearing a billion small roses around my face. Very beautiful, my hair is one of the most beautiful things on my body.

I finally realized that my natural hair was beautiful, and I like my hair natural way more now than when it is straight.

Openness to New Experiences

For other women, a range of new experiences inspired a turning point in their personal preferences of how their hair should be styled or worn. One student acknowledged that length was important to her. After cutting her hair short, she recognized the importance of hair length and regretted the cut. "A few months in adapting to my new hair cut was no fun, there was constant styling, and I was not planning on adding heat to my new hair cut so I kept my hair up in a bun." Another woman stated that despite her ability to grow natural, long, thick curly hair, envied by others, the feminine characteristics which were commonly ascribed to her hair were not in alignment with her self-view. This woman opted for a short, pixie style, stating that "masculine hair makes me feel tougher and like I'm not hiding.... I think people assume I'm more interesting and tougher because of it." An added benefit in shedding the socially determined 'feminine' characteristics of long, curly hair is the appreciation of the ways in which the new hairstyle deterred attention from specific kinds of men.

Other women had mixed experiences as a result of shaving their heads. One woman discovered that hair had little meaning when it needed to be shaved to compete in a swim meet. Another woman stated that a significant moment for her was shaving her head after severe hair breakage from coloring. This student stated, "I loved my shaved head. It went so well with my 'cool' aesthetic. I thought it automatically made me stand out, and it made me feel awesome." Later when her shaved head was introduced to familial figures, it was met with disapproval, and the regrowth of hair was strongly encouraged as a way of being accepted in professional settings. "I felt so... ordinary with a normal hairstyle." This student was harshly critiqued in personal environment which supports the previous claims that negative experiences in certain environments can hinder healthy hair transitions for college women. Additionally, the process to regrow hair became a hidden process for her, intersecting with her need for access to resources during a transition for a healthy transition. This student refused to straighten her hair and opted to wear wigs until she determined that the regrown hair was appropriate for public view. Because this student accepted her parent's wishes, she suppressed the expression of her authentic hair presentation and conformed to what her parents believed should be acceptable for hair presentation.

Women move through numerous points of hair transition either before entering college or during college. The environment(s) in which hair transitions occur is critical to how one will perceive one's own hair and can have an immediately impact on self-esteem. Emotions about hair are heavily influenced by peers, who do and do not affirm that college women should embrace their natural hair, whether that is hair texture, hair color, or a particular hairstyle. In contradistinction to this, college women also confront and negotiate parental expectations of hair, which may be tied to a generational adherence to respectability politics. When college women can break through fear, doubt, or anxiety about transitioning from one hair choice to another, however, they experience an overwhelming feeling of liberation and certainty. This is the point at which women reject any and all attempts at policing their hair choices. They refuse to live by other people's standards.

DISCUSSION

The findings of this research study support the argument that college represents an environmental shift, which in turn, can cause a shift in the way Black women think about and care for their hair. The turning point or transition in hair choice, as detailed in the Black women's narrative data, reveals the ways Black women navigate shifts in resources, adjust to new environments, emancipate themselves from conformity, refocus on positive imagery, and identify a personal openness to new experiences.

Upon entry to college, there is a sense of freedom that is often felt once a student arrives. Students feel free to create or recreate who they want to be (Winston et al, 2004). When newfound freedom is met with a sense of Black pride or pathways to the actualization of Black beauty, a student's new identity welcomed due to this new association. In other words, this freedom, coupled with the appreciation for Blackness, facilitates a positive self-actualization that translates into a new appearance in a Black woman college student. The student not only feels comfortable and new within herself, but she also feels comfortable and proud as a Black woman. The hair choices shift due to this new appreciation for Black hair and aesthetics, generally.

People in one's circle and environment can have a significant impact on one's self-perception and self-esteem (Ellis-Hervey et al. 2016). The people in your circle can impact the way you view yourself and the way that others view you. Thus, there is a connection to how the people around them also appreciate and celebrate blackness and black hair. If people in a person's environment are celebrating Blackness and Black hair, it can unconsciously encourage a person to do the same. External encouragement and positive imagery of Black hair can influence a person towards going natural or appreciating their Blackness. Through the encouragement and positive self-imagery, it enhances and motivates the student to think positively about themselves as well. Thus, the person makes the shift and reaches the turning point in their own journey.

UNIVERSITY IMPLICATIONS AND RECOMMENDATIONS

University staff plays the most integral role in shaping the experiences of Black students. Staff contribute to every facet of the college experience, from admissions to graduation, as they play a different but equally important role to faculty. University staff are the complementary other half to faculty, as they often facilitate the true college experience that happens outside of the classroom. They make policies, rules, and decisions that directly impact Black students.

Thus, to analyze the of university staff in identity development and hair requires a critical, intersectional lens to look at their part in the experiences a black student. Their role cannot be taken lightly or overlooked when analyzing the direct and indirect impact they have on black college students' experiences.

A lack of Black staff and mentors can have a damaging impact on Black students. The university and staff's commitment to and stance on issues can make students feel invisible, undervalued, and isolated, or it can make them feel valued and included. Experiencing unique situations and circumstances without adequate support and understanding can be detrimental to the psychological and mental state of Black students. Lack of support can severely impact how Black students show up in spaces because it reinforces the racist institution. Outside of faculty experiences, university staff can play a role in discrimination against Black students by management, housing, job, and other ways.

University staff have a responsibility to engage with Black students in an appropriate, productive manner University staff must be attentive to Black students' experiences because their experiences offer a unique, intersectional perspective that can inform decision making. As universities reckon with their whitewashed structure and identity, more student programming in offices have been created to combat the disproportionate circumstances that black students face.

To strengthen engagement with/among Black women students, university staff should:

(1) Invite hair care professionals to campus to style students hair or offer free transportation to local hair salons/barbershops.
(2) Invite hair care professionals and hair scholars to campus to discuss the complexity of hair within Black lives.
(3) Fund clubs on campus for Black women, in order to provide encouragement and support to peers around the transitioning-to-college process and the hair issues therein.
(4) Include orientation information related to Black hair and hair care.
(5) Offer hair product giveaways on campus.
(6) Display images in offices and university materials of Black women with a variety of hair textures and lengths.

LIMITATIONS

While this research study offers innovative approaches to reaching Black women in higher education, there are certain limitations to the methodology. The research study did not directly aim to engage Black college students, but rather it encourages Black women to narrate past experiences about their college years. By including individual interviews and focus groups with Black women, a richer data set could address these concerns. Additionally, the hair salon and barbershop sites of recruitment were community samples off campus. Intentional recruitment on college campuses may have elicited data which was more directly related to university life.

FUTURE DIRECTIONS

Areas for future research include exploring turning points in how Black men wear their hair, as well as turning points experienced by Black women at other pivotal moments in their lives, such as during pre-college programs, directly after completing college, and upon entering the workforce.

There is a growing body of research that evaluates hair-related experiences of Black women, but research on this topic for Black *men* is extremely limited. Dating back to slavery, however, hair has played a pivotal role for Black men, who were degraded for their "wool-like" hair, many of whom learned to specialize in hair grooming. Some even used profits from barbering to buy their own freedom and the freedom of their families (Byrd & Tharps, 2014; Mbilishaka, 2018). In modern times, Black men still experience bias, discrimination, and self-esteem related issues related to their hair. It is a safe presumption then, that Black men may also have a turning point at which they learned to reject Eurocentric norms and embrace their natural hair, with styles such as locs, afros, and braids. In fact, researchers argue that both barbershops, and beauty salons are powerful resources; indeed they are entry points into mental health dialogue for Black men and women alike (Mbilishaka; 2018). Future research could explore turning points for Black collegiate men and any similarities and differences between their experiences and that of their Black women counterparts.

CONCLUSION

In conclusion, many Black women expressed experiencing turning points in college. College is where they decided to reject Eurocentric standards of beauty with regards to their hair, and instead wear it in its natural state. Through this study, several themes emerged, including: resources, environments, emancipation, positive imagery, and new experiences. These themes illustrate that several aspects of the college experience can lead to higher self-esteem and positive identity. More specifically, these experiences at college can lead Black women to embrace their unique natural beauty and hair.

REFERENCES

Banks, B. M., & Landau, S. E. (2021). Cognitive effects of racial microaggressions directed at Black college women. *The Journal of Negro Education*, *90*(1), 84–95.

Bellinger, W. (2007). Why African American Women try to Obtain "Good Hair.". *Sociological Viewpoints*, 63.

Brice, A. L., Mansueto, C. S., & McCombs Thomas, A. (2007). *Hair pulling and its affective correlates in an African-American university sample*. Science Direct. https://www.sciencedirect.com/science/article/pii/S0887618506001204. doi:10.1016/j.janxdis.2006.08.004

Byrd, A., & Tharps, L. (2014). *Hair story: Untangling the Roots of Black Hair in America* (Second Edition, Revised). St. Martin's Griffin.

Crenshaw, K. (1991). Mapping the Margins: Intersectionality, Identity Politics, and Violence against Women of Color. *Stanford Law Review*, *43*(6), 1241–1299. doi:10.2307/1229039

Creswell, J. W. (2003). *Research design qualitative, quantitative, and mixed method approaches* (2nd ed.). Sage.

Davis Tribble, B. L., Allen, S. H., Hart, J. R., Francois, T. S., & Smith-Bynum, M. A. (2019). "No [right] way to be a Black woman": Exploring gendered racial socialization among Black women. *Psychology of Women Quarterly*, *43*(3), 381–397. doi:10.1177/0361684318825439 PMID:35237026

DeLongoria, M. (2018). Misogynoir: Black Hair, Identity Politics, and Multiple Black Realities. *Africology*, *12*(8), 39–49.

Everett, J. E., Camille Hall, J., & Hamilton-Mason, J. (2010). Everyday conflict and daily stressors: Coping responses of Black women. *Affilia*, *25*(1), 30–42. doi:10.1177/0886109909354983

Farley, Y. O. (2016). *An exploration of the identity and career development of African American women in higher education leadership: Does hair style make a difference?* (Publication No. 10248737). [Doctoral dissertation, Old Dominion University.] ProQuest Dissertation Publishing.

Garrod, A., Kilkenny, R., & Gomez, C. (2013). *Mixed: Multiracial college students tell their life stories* (1st ed.). Cornell University Press. doi:10.7591/9780801469169

Gillespie, C. H. (2013). *Down to the roots: A qualitative analysis of the psychological impacts of messages black women receive regarding their hair.* (Publication No. 3587989). [Doctoral Dissertation.] ProQuest Dissertations Publishing.

Glesne, C. (2011). *Becoming qualitative researchers: An introduction* (4th ed.). Pearson.

Gray, S. (2017). *"To curl up or relax? That is the question: Tenured Black female faculty navigation of black hair expression in academia.* (Publication No. 10266906). [Doctoral dissertation, Southern Illinois University Carbondale]. ProQuest Dissertation Publishing.

Heidegger, M. (1962). *Being and time*. Harper & Row.

Hilliard, A. G. (1979). Respect the Child's Culture. *Young Children*, *34*(5), 2–3. https://www.jstor.org/stable/42642722

Johnson, C. M. E. (2019). *"Each New Curl Howling a War Cry": Black Women, Embodiment, and Gendered Racial Formation*. (Publication No. 27802372, [Doctoral dissertation, University of Southern California].ProQuest Dissertations Publishing.

Johnson, T. A., & Bankhead, T. (2014). Hair It Is: Examining the Experiences of Black Women with Natural Hair. *Open Journal of Social Sciences*, *2*(1), 86–100. doi:10.4236/jss.2014.21010

Jones, C., & Shorter-Gooden, K. (2003). *Shifting: The double lives of Black women in America*. HarperCollins.

Jones, S. R., Arminio, J. L., & Torres, V. (2014). *Negotiating the complexities of qualitative research in higher education: fundamental elements and issues* (2nd ed.). Routledge. doi:10.4324/9780203123836

King, V., & Niabaly, D. (2013). The politics of Black womens' hair. *Journal of Undergraduate Research at Minnesota State University, Mankato*, *13*(4), 1–19.

Leath, S., Jerald, M. C., Perkins, T., & Jones, M. K. (2021). A qualitative exploration of jezebel stereotype endorsement and sexual behaviors among Black college women. *The Journal of Black Psychology*, *47*(4-5), 244–283. doi:10.1177/0095798421997215

Luney, L. T. (2021). *Coping to survive in the "wild west": Black college womxn and femmes enduring anti-black gendered racism in a university of the American West*. (Publication No. 28549089). [Doctoral dissertation, University of Colorado]. ProQuest Dissertations Publishing.

Mbilishaka, A. (2018). Black Lives (and Stories) Matter: Race Narrative Therapy in Black Hair Care Spaces. *Community Psychology in Global Perspective*, *4*(2), 22–33.

Mbilishaka, A., & Apugo, D. (2020). Brushed aside: African American women's narratives of hair bias in school. *Race, Ethnicity and Education*, *23*(5), 634–653. doi:10.1080/13613324.2020.1718075

Merriam, S. B. (2009). *Qualitative research: A guide to design and implementation*. Jossey-Bass.

Moustakas, C. (1994). *Phenomenological research methods*. Sage. doi:10.4135/9781412995658

Norwood, C. R. (2018). Decolonizing my hair, unshackling my curls: An autoethnography on what makes my natural hair journey a Black feminist statement. *International Feminist Journal of Politics*, *20*(1), 69–84. doi:10.1080/14616742.2017.1369890

Oathes, D., & Ray, W. (2008). Dissociative Tendencies and Facilitated Emotional Processing. *Emotion (Washington, D.C.), 8*(5), 653–661. doi:10.1037/a0013442 PMID:18837615

Okazawa-Rey, M., Robinson, T., & Ward, J. V. (1986). Black women and the politics of skin color and hair. *Women's Studies Quarterly, 14*(1/2), 13–14.

Orey, B. D., & Zhang, Y. (2019). Melanated millennials and the politics of Black hair. *Social Science Quarterly, 100*(6), 2458–2476. doi:10.1111squ.12694

Oriowo, D. O. (2016). *Is it easier for her? Afro-textured hair and its effects on Black female sexuality: A mixed methods approach.* (Publication No. 10120152). [Doctoral dissertation, Widener University]. ProQuest Dissertations Publishing.

Patton, M. Q. (2002). *Qualitative research and evaluation methods* (3rd ed.). Sage.

Randle, B. (2015). I am not my hair: African American women and their struggles with embracing natural hair. *Race, Gender & Class (Towson, Md.), 22*(1-2), 114–121.

Rowe, K. L. (2021). Tangled: Black Hair and Texturism in Ethnodrama. *Cultural Studies ↔ Critical Methodologies.* . doi:10.1177/15327086211049708

Schwandt, T. A. (2001). *Dictionary of qualitative inquiry* (2nd ed.). Sage.

Sekayi, D. (2003). Aesthetic resistance to commercial influences: The impact of the eurocentric beauty standard on Black college women. *The Journal of Negro Education, 72*(4), 467–477. doi:10.2307/3211197

Snider, S. R., & Rosenberg, J. (2006). The relationships of skin tone and hair to perceived beauty among African American students. *The University of Alabama McNair Journal,* 201-211.

Stemberger, R. M. T., Thomas, A. M., Mansueto, C. S., & Carter, J. G. (2000). Personal toll of trichotillomania: Behavioral and interpersonal sequelae. *Journal of Anxiety Disorders, 14*(1), 97–104. doi:10.1016/S0887-6185(99)00028-6 PMID:10770238

Stokes, M. N., Hope, E. C., Cryer-Coupet, Q. R., & Elliot, E. (2020). Black Girl Blues: The Roles of Racial Socialization, Gendered Racial Socialization, and Racial Identity on Depressive Symptoms among Black Girls. *Journal of Youth and Adolescence, 49*(11), 2175–2189. doi:10.100710964-020-01317-8 PMID:32955702

Swanagan, M. (2014). *Developing a critical consciousness: Black women and the intersection of hair and power* (Publication No. 1571649). [Master's thesis, Southern Illinois University at Edwardsville.] ProQuest.

van Manen, M. (1990). *Researching lived experience: Human science for an action sensitive pedagogy*. SUNY Press.

Wilkins, A. C. (2012). Becoming Black women: Intimate stories and intersectional identities. *Social Psychology Quarterly*, *75*(2), 173–196. doi:10.1177/0190272512440106

Wilson, I.-P., & Mbilishaka, A. M., & Lewis, M. L. (2018). "White folks ain't got hair like us": African American mother–daughter hair stories and racial socialization. *Women, Gender, and Families of Color, 6*(2), 226–248.

ENDNOTE

1 Natural hair is hair that has not been chemically altered

Chapter 8
Hair and Career:
The Impact of Hair Bias on Women of Color

Cryshanna A. Jackson Leftwich
https://orcid.org/0000-0001-5527-7152
Youngstown State University, USA

Nicolette Powe
Youngstown State University, USA

Amanda E. Fehlbaum
https://orcid.org/0000-0003-1247-031X
Youngstown State University, USA

ABSTRACT

The purpose of this chapter is to examine the impact of stereotypes, biases, and workplace policies on the perceptions of Women of Color in regards to self-expression and personal identities. This research aims to address the question: How does the implicit bias of hair impact the decision making of Women of Color as they currently navigate the workplace and/or prepare to enter the workforce? What experiences have these women faced in previous employment situations that may influence their career choices? This chapter is a case study analysis that consists of a mixed methods approach. Qualitative data was collected using focus group interviews with women of color who are entering or have already entered the workforce and quantitative data was collected using an occupational prestige survey. The research found that textured hair was perceived as less professional having a negative impact on the respondents' self-expression and personal identities.

DOI: 10.4018/978-1-6684-8790-7.ch008

INTRODUCTION

According to Jones (2020), employment discrimination based on hairstyles disproportionately impacts People of Color. Racial discrimination may be unlawful, but hair discrimination still exists. This type of bias forces People of Color to either compromise cultural expression or choose to be seen as employable to the masses. Microaggressions, racial stereotypes, and discrimination in American society are part of everyday life for African Americans living in the United States. The history of America is unfortunately rooted in white supremacy and white culture. As a society that aims to promote life, liberty, and freedom for all, the ability for one to be able to wear their hair how it grows out of their scalp goes against this very notion. Cultural expression is a form of empowerment that allows individuals to be their true authentic selves and add diversity to a mainstream culture. Hair discrimination, especially in the workplace is problematic because such discrimination works against providing safe spaces and equity in the workplace. In public and private workplaces, the goal of employers should to be ensure social equity. Social equity is defined as the fair, just, and equitable management of institutions that serve the public with the commitment to promote fairness, justice, and equity through public policies (Rice, 2004). Workplace policies that ban hairstyles, especially hairstyles that disproportionately impact people of color is unethical and can have a negative impact on places of employment.

Furthermore self-expression and personal identities are critical to college students who often spend time figuring out who they are and how to express themselves, all while figuring out what types of career paths they want to explore upon graduation. Experiences gained by these students will impact them for years to come. If a college student's cultural identity is defined by a hairstyle that is seen as "unprofessional" in the workplace that may impact the career choices that student makes. This may result in individuals avoiding majors and or careers where they cannot be their true authentic selves. In a world that has become increasingly diverse and where representation matters this unintended consequence may steer African American Students to fields where they are overrepresented and away from careers where they are underrepresented. This study examines to what extent hair bias and discrimination impact self-expression and personal identity.

BACKGROUND

There are many studies (Goodman, 2021; Berkemeyer, 2020; Moronto, 2022; Summers et al, 2022) that have examined the prevalence of hair bias and discrimination in the workplace. The hair bias caused by these policies in America has been intentionally and deliberately put in place by systems that impact Women of Color in terms of self-expression and personal identity. Self-expression is a large part of how individuals identify in different settings and European standards of beauty often influence mainstream society's perspective (Moronta, 2022). These standards have put self-expressions for women wearing their natural hair in the forefront by categorizing hair as being "good" or "bad" based on texture, and these definitions have influenced the way African Americans view hair and express themselves (Moronta, 2022). The research on the impact of hair also must factor in the importance of hair on personal identities and the long history of grooming policies, racism, and microaggressions we currently see today. According to Berkemeyer (2020), African civilizations used hairstyles for social status, including to honor traditions and identify tribes. Along with the historic importance of hair in African societies, hair can have a profound impact on the personal identities of African American women who develop self-perceptions and wear their hair in society to define their identity in relationship to gender and class, making the hair dilemma an even greater hurdle to overcome to gain social acceptance and conform to societal norms (Jeffries & Jeffries, 2014). Patton (2006) argues that the creation of unique hairstyles by Women of Color such as curls, dreadlocks, plaits, weaves, etc. is a form of resistance to the status quo and a way of expression that other cultures are unable to obtain. Furthermore, these Afrocentric hairstyles may be associated with stereotypes and biases setting up a catch-22 of sorts where African American women can either wear their natural hair as a form of self-expression or be seen as acceptable to the masses (Dawson, 2019).

The origination of the natural hair movement can be traced back to the 1960's as a part of the Black Power movement for Civil Rights (Jones, 2020). This is when women of color embraced their natural hair and went away from chemical straighteners. The hair bias and discrimination of People of Color eventually led to backlash and pushback. Jones (2020) defined natural hair as hair that has not been altered by chemicals, such as relaxers and texturizers. Goodman (2021) discussed the importance of the 1960s and 1970s when the "Black is Beautiful" movement began. This first wave of the natural hair movement popularized natural hairstyles like the Afro, rooted in Black Power as a call to embrace self-love and not self-hate. This evolved to the 1970s when the natural hair movement now included popular braided hairstyles, and in the 1990s, many African American women reverted to processed hairstyles and weaves; however, the natural hair movement regained steam in 2010, in an attempt to redefine beauty standards and promote healthy hair that for years had been damaged by heat and chemicals (Jones, 2020).

The African American community relies on their hair as a form of self-expression and an artform (Mornota, 2022). Historically, hairstyles have been important in defining characteristics of African culture, using hair as a type of self-expression and expression of personal identity. For example, Jefferies & Jefferies (2014) found that identity formation is intrinsically connected to hair and cultural beauty standards, and for women whose hair does not fit the culturally created beauty standards, the effect can be oppressive, resulting in lower acceptance of oneself.

Women of Color in America are faced with a standard of beauty that does not represent or fit the images of themselves; the standards of beauty set in the United States require Women of Color, especially Black women, to conform to European standards when trying to manage their images, especially in the workplace. This requires Women of Color to straighten or chemically alter their hair (Dawson et al, 2019). The reality is that beauty is subjective and determined by the class that is in power, thus failure to meet the enforced code of beauty can result in societal consequences such as loss of job, societal unacceptance, and decreased self-expression (Patton, 2006). Implicit bias is the brain's automatic association of stereotypes or group identity on a subconscious level (Johnson et al, 2021). To improve policies and continue dialogue to ensure everyone is being treated in an equitable manner, it is crucial to understand how implicit bias impacts individuals on a daily basis.

Self-expression is used by individuals to find acceptance and fit into society. In previous research, there are several historical examples of using hair for self-expression. For example, some African tribes had shaved heads until marrying age and other tribes braided their hair to prepare for war, while in other cultures hairdressing was done daily involving braids, twists, wraps and curls because unkempt hair was a sign of illness or mourning (Moronta, 2022). During the natural hair movement even though an increased number of African Americans were embracing their natural hair, those individuals had to face the backlash because of what was considered acceptable (Jeffries & Jeffries, 2014). While some People of Color joined the natural hair movement as a sign of resistance, one study reported that the journey for some African Americans, especially women was a lengthy process that required support, self-exploration, and courage (Summers & Kosovac, 2022).

Many Women of Color also used self-expression to conform or assimilate into mainstream values. African American women began to chemically straighten and press their hair; some even chose to wear weaves or wigs to replicate the status quo to fit into what society deemed acceptable (Patton, 2006). Goodman (2021) found that African American women are thirty percent more likely to receive direct information in relation to their employer's appearance or grooming policies and they are one-and-a-half times more likely to be sent home from work due to hairstyle infractions. This has resulted in African American women choosing to conform to European standards of beauty not because they want to but because they find it a necessary evil for economic mobility and the need to stay employed (Dawson et al, 2019). This choice to conform to certain acceptable standards has been exacerbated by company policies that target natural and textured hairstyles.

To add further context to the pressure felt by African American women, there is no federal remedy that is available to anyone who faces work discrimination based on their natural hairstyle. According to Berkemeyer (2020), companies have adopted "grooming" policies in the workplace that aim to undermine natural and textured hair. The beauty product company Dove conducted a study in 2019 that found that African American women's hair is policed more often than their white counterparts, reiterating the impact of workplace bias and corporate policies aimed at Black women (Moranta, 2022). Grooming policies are systematically put in place to perpetuate the stereotypes that kinky, curly, natural textured hair, predominantly found on People of Color, is not suitable for the workplace environment. These policies have been found to disproportionately discriminate against People of Color (Goodman, 2021). This is problematic for those individuals who use their hair as a form of expression and as a type of identity. Policies that disproportionately impact one group over another is a violation of social equity and fairness in the United States.

The previous studies mentioned above provide several examples that hair types typically associated with African Americans historically are not seen as acceptable in the United States. There is also the issue of white lawmakers who believe that African Americans are socially, economically, and politically inferior, and so is their appearance. For example, Mornota (2022) notes that New Orleans passed a law requiring that Black Creole women with natural hairstyles to wear a scarf over their heads. These laws have now taken the form of grooming policies put in place in several companies across the United States threatening self-expression and personal identity.

Grooming policies come in the form of formalized guidelines or informal dress codes designed to address the ways in which employers expect employees to physically present themselves at work. Employers are not allowed to legally discriminate based on race, but if an employee fails to meet the standards of the grooming policy, that gives the employer a basis to reprimand, suspend or even terminate the employee. Berkemeyer (2020) found that while grooming policies do not specifically target African American employees, terms such as "neat" and "professional" hairstyles can be construed as applying to straight hair and allowing hairstyles such as braids, locs, and Afros to be seen as "messy" and therefore unprofessional. Over the years, African Americans have tried to assimilate into a culture that consistently attacks and belittles them. Hair discrimination is another way to imply inferiority among a group in society, when hair is such a powerful tool for self-expression and personal identity.

While Women of Color may have numerous options of ways in which to style their hair, they may face punitive measures by employers if they do not pick a style deemed acceptable. While it has been argued that hair should not carry the same cultural significance it once did years ago, the "natural" or textured hairstyles remain a large political debate (Randle, 2015). According to Summers et al. (2022), there are more African American women in the workforce than other women, yet even with the highest numbers in the workforce, African American women are underrepresented at the higher levels, overlooked at greater rates for promotion, and receive little to no support from their bosses. The CROWN Act, legislation at the federal level passed to combat this discrimination, has only been adopted by a few states (Goodman, 2021). This leads to an interesting discussion of how Women of Color and especially African American women will fit into the workforce and if college students preparing to go into the workforce will alter their appearance to meet the status quo.

RESEARCH QUESTIONS AND HYPOTHESES

The purpose of this study is to address the questions: How does the implicit bias of hair impact the self-expression and personal identity of Women of Color as they currently navigate the workplace and/or prepare to enter the workforce? What experiences have these women faced in previous employment situations that may influence their career choices? To answer the questions, data was collected using a mixed methods approach of qualitative and quantitative data. Qualitative data was collected from a focus group and quantitative data was collected from a survey that measured professionalism and occupational prestige.

METHODOLOGY

Procedure and Participants

The study contained two components: a survey and a focus group. These are discussed in more detail below.

Survey

For the survey, the following hypotheses were tested:

Hypothesis One: Ratings of each hairstyle's professionalism will be positively correlated with levels of that hairstyle's occupational prestige.

Hypothesis Two: Hairstyles with more texture will be associated with lower levels of professionalism.

Hypothesis Three: Hairstyles with more texture will be associated with occupations with lower prestige scores.

Hairstyles with more texture were defined as Afros, locs, twist outs, and braids. Hairstyles with less texture were defined as straight hair, long curls, short curls, and pixie (Johnson et al., 2020).

Respondents were presented with stock photo images of Black women with various hairstyles (see Fig 1-9). For each of the nine photos, the respondents were asked to describe the perceived professionalism of the individual's hair, then select which career they thought the individual held based on their hairstyle.

Figure 1. Twist hairstyle
Source: Shutterstock (2023)

Figure 2. Afro-out hairstyle
Source: Shutterstock (2023)

Figure 3. Afro-tight hairstyle
Source: Shutterstock (2023)

Figure 4. Locked hairstyle
Source: Shutterstock (2023)

Figure 5. Braid piled hairstyle
Source: Shutterstock (2023)

Figure 6. Braid down hairstyle
Source: Shutterstock (2023)

Figure 7. Loose curls hairstyle
Source: Shutterstock (2023)

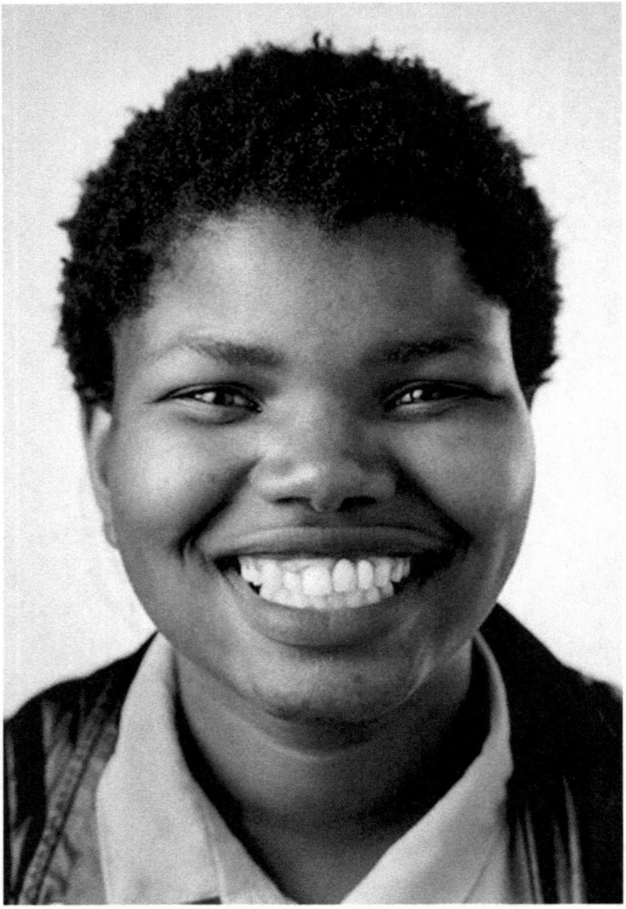

Figure 9. Straight pulled back hairstyle
Source: Shutterstock (2023)

Figure 8. Straight hairstyle
Source: Shutterstock (2023)

The stock photo images show each woman from the shoulders up against a gray background, similar to that of a driver's license. The purpose of using stock photos was to minimize the chance participants would try to use other contexts or cues (clothing, posture, setting, etc.) to determine the person's occupation.

Assessing the level of professionalism associated with a hairstyle builds off the findings of Johnson et al (2017). Black women in their study showed a preference for smooth hairstyles over textured hairstyles in professional settings. Furthermore, they reported that Afro hairstyles were considered significantly less professional compared to long curls. As jobs can vary in their level of professionalism, styles of hair can also vary in how professional they are perceived to be. Survey respondents were asked, "How would you describe this person's hair?" and given the options of professional, semi-professional, and not professional.

The careers were selected based on their Occupational Prestige Rating score (Hughes, et al 2022). Occupational Prestige Rating scores are a way of assessing the amount of status a person holds based on their occupational role, with higher numbers indicating more prestige than lower numbers. Scores are attained by surveying a sample of a population and asking them to rank or rate a set of occupations or jobs with the amount of respect, social standing, or prestige each has (Treiman 1976). Occupations with higher levels of prestige tend to be associated with power and privilege as they "require a high degree of skill or which entail authority over other individuals or control over capital" (p. 288).

The Occupational Prestige Rating scores used here are based on a 2022 index of 1029 specific occupations (Hughes, et al 2022). Occupations for the survey were chosen at the high (80.46-88.15), middle (51.4-56.07), and low (14.5-27.35) ends of the index (see Table 1 for the choices). They were assigned – one high, one middle, one low – at random to the options for the second question: "Based on this person's hairstyle, I think they are a(n) _________."

Table 1. Occupation options for each hairstyle and the corresponding prestige score

	Low Prestige Option	**Medium Prestige Option**	**High Prestige Option**
Twist	Barista (27.35)	Dental Hygienist (54.74)	Judge (80.86)
Afro – Out	Waitress (26.99)	Emergency Response Dispatcher (51.4)	Physicist (82.66)
Afro – Tight	Janitor (23.62)	Pharmacy Technician (56.07)	Nuclear Engineer (81.45)
Locked	Cashier (25.77)	Real Estate Broker (52.57)	Surgeon (88.15)
Braid – Piled	Parking Lot Attendant (19.46)	Social Worker (51.34)	Neurologist (87.94)
Braid – Down	Telemarketer (15)	Photographer (54.56)	Pediatrician (81.82)
Loose Curls	Housekeeper (22.66)	Legal Secretary (51.43)	Biochemist (83.93)
Straight	Fast Food Cook (20.51)	Medical Assistant (55.25)	Aerospace Engineer (83.83)
Straight Pulled Back	Dishwasher (14.5)	Veterinary Assistant (52.09)	Obstetrician (81.4)

Focus Group

The focus group part of the study was conducted in May 2023. Black women participants were recruited through snowball sampling; there were 21 participants in the focus group.

For the focus group participants were asked to expand upon the following five questions:

1. Where do you think the word "normal" or "professional" hair came from, and why?
2. Do you feel as though you've adjusted the way you've styled your hair when you appear at certain places such as school, work, or social events? Why?
3. How often do you see Women (and Men) of Color wearing their natural hair in the workplace?
4. Do you feel empowered seeing Women (and Men) of Color wearing their natural hair in the workplace?
5. What do you consider "appropriate" in regard to the way that a Person of Color chooses to wear their hair? Is there such a thing as "too much"?

Focus group participants were recruited via social media and text messaging using a convenience sampling approach based on their availability to participate in the focus group at the designated time using the Internet. The focus group was conducted via WebEx and the respondents participated in an hour-long session in which the above questions were asked, and the participants were able to verbally respond or respond in the chat. The transcript was created from the recording and used to identify common themes line by line and moved into categories referred to as the grounded theory approach.

RESULTS

The researchers launched the survey part of the study in March 2023 and collected responses through the end of April. Respondents were recruited through outreach on a university app as well as through the researchers' social networks. Of the 189 survey responses, 119 were from those who indicated they consider themselves to be Black or African American women. After cleaning the data, 110 valid responses remained (see Table 2 for detailed demographic information).

Table 2. Demographic information

	n	%
Age		
18-24 years old	22	20
25-34 years old	12	10.9
35-44 years old	16	14.5
45-54 years old	34	30.9
55-64 years old	12	10.9
65+ years old	14	12.7
Highest educational level		
High school diploma or GED	6	5.5
Some college, but no degree	16	14.5
Associates or technical degree	8	7.3
Bachelor's degree	28	25.5
Graduate or professional degree	52	47.3
Race		
Black or African American	95	86.4
Black or African American + White or Caucasian	6	5.5
Black or African American + Other	4	3.6
Black or African American + American Indian/Native American	2	1.8
Black or African American + Native Hawaiian or Other Pacific Islander	1	0.9
Black or African American + White or Caucasian + American Indian/Native American	1	0.9
Black or African American + American Indian/Native American + Other	1	0.9

$N = 110$

In the survey, participants were asked to describe the level of professionalism of a pictured hairstyle and asked which career they thought the person had based on that hairstyle. For the analysis of the data, each answer choice was assigned a number (3 = professional, 2 = semi-professional, 1 = not professional) and the occupation was assigned a number based on the level of prestige (3 = high prestige, 2 = medium prestige, 1 = low prestige).

Hypothesis 1: Ratings of each hairstyle's professionalism will be positively correlated with levels of that hairstyle's occupational prestige.

To test hypothesis one, researchers conducted a bivariate correlation analysis. The resulting Pearson Correlations are in Table 3.

Table 3. Correlation of a hairstyle's professionalism with the occupational prestige of the career associated with the hairstyle

	Professionalism									
		Twist	Afro – Out	Afro – Tight	Locked	Braid Piled	Braid Down	Loose Curls	Straight	Straight Pulled Back
	Twist	.542**	.398**	.316**	.269**	.311**	.152	.078	.143	.024
	Afro – Out	.317**	.440**	.219*	.181	.082	.029	.014	.187	.084
	Afro – Tight	.348**	.324**	.326**	.292**	.23*	.312**	.142	.193*	.237*
Occupational Prestige	**Locked**	.059	.297**	.172	.324**	.005	-.017	.072	-.053	.133
	Braid-Piled	.187	.182	.184	.063	.268**	.201*	-.112	-.061	.06
	Braid-Down	.187	.074	.108	.097	.182	.286**	-.019	.102	.067
	Loose Curls	.116	.195*	.092	.218*	-.069	.024	.168	.135	-.028
	Straight	.243*	.218*	.187	.179	-.053	.12	.126	.29**	.09
	Straight Pulled Back	-.164	.083	.129	.165	-.057	.007	.031	-.124	.347**

* = $p < .05$
** = $p < .01$

These results show that, except for loose curls, the perceived professionalism of the hairstyle is positively correlated with the occupational prestige of the career respondents associated with the hairstyle.

The strength of the association between hairstyle professionalism and occupational prestige is strong for twist ($r = .542, p < .01$), Afro – out ($r = .44, p < .01$), Afro-tight ($r = .326, p < .01$), locked ($r = .324, p < .01$), and straight pulled back ($r = .347, p < .01$). The strength of the association is moderate for braid piled ($r = .268, p < .01$), braid down ($r = .286, p < .01$), and straight ($r = .29, p < .01$).

The results also demonstrate that the level of a hairstyle's professionalism has positive, statistically significant correlations with the occupational prestige of careers associated with other hairstyles. For example, the braid down hairstyle's professionalism shows a strong association with the occupational prestige of the Afro – tight hairstyle. In other words, respondents were likely to give the professionalism of the braid down hairstyle the same answer, and they were likely to give the Afro – tight hairstyle the same occupation, though this does not mean they highly rated both hairstyles.

Hypothesis Two: Hairstyles with more texture would be associated with lower levels of professionalism.

Hypothesis Three: Hairstyles with more texture would be associated with occupations with lower prestige scores.

To test hypotheses two and three, researchers compared the means. Higher means indicate higher levels of professionalism or association with an occupation with a higher level of prestige.

Table 4. Comparison of means for professionalism of hairstyles and occupational prestige of career associated with hairstyles

	Professionalism		Occupational Prestige	
	M	*SD*	*M*	*SD*
Twist	2.42	.424	1.89	.696
Afro – Out	2.23	.820	2.35	.736
Afro – Tight	2.58	.709	2.32	.565
Locked	2.74	.482	2.38	.699
Braid-Piled	2.9	.330	2.43	.498
Braid-Down	2.94	.280	2.59	.732
Loose Curls	2.96	.228	2.33	.511
Straight	2.8	.424	2.26	.526
Straight Pulled Back	2.83	.567	2.72	.492

N = 110

Overall, the results support hypotheses 2. Hairstyles with more texture – twist, Afros, and locked – have lower means and are thus associated with lower levels of professionalism. However, braids are also considered to have more texture and they are rated above the lower texture, straight hair styles. Loose curls, a low texture style, is rated as having the highest level of professionalism.

Hypothesis three is not supported, as there is no consistency in the occupational prestige of the careers associated with the hairstyles. Some of the hairstyles with more texture are associated with careers with lower occupational prestige, and the straight hairstyle is also rated low. Straight pulled back, a low texture style, is rated highest.

In sum, hypothesis 1 was strongly supported, hypothesis 2 was supported and hypothesis three was not supported. Except for loose curls, hairstyle professionalism showed statistically significant correlations with occupational prestige. Hairstyles with more texture were associated with lower levels of professionalism, though braids were had higher means than straight hair styles. Occupational prestige of careers associated with hairstyles was not consistent.

These findings show not only that the perceived professionalism of a hairstyle has a relationship to a hairstyle's occupational prestige, but that hairstyles with more texture like Afros and locs are associated with lower levels of professionalism. This may have consequences for the way that Black women style their hair in certain occupations. That is, Black women may feel more pressure to wear their hair straighter or in braids so that they are seen as more professional.

The findings from the survey are supported by those of the focus group. Example quotes for common themes from the focus groups are displayed in Table 5. These common themes were identified as: normal or professional hairstyles, preconceived judgement, hairstyles dictating work ability, and natural hairstyle acceptance.

Table 5. Sample quotes from focus group

Common Themes	Example quote
Personal Identity: Normal or professional hairstyles	"But I always think too, how was my hair stopping me from being a hard worker? It's not distracting me from doing my job so it shouldn't bother anyone else, especially if I'm behind the desk." (Tykieena) "Straight hair loose hair is what is considered normal because they are considered, I guess, the standard of [normal hair]." (Gloria)
Self-Expression: Preconceived judgement	"We were talking about the interview for a job for a company that would be considered Fortune 500. I knew that if I walked in there. They would have preconceived judgment about me. Regardless of what my experience is, regardless of my education. They probably wouldn't have seen past my 'unprofessional' hair. So, I did change my hair that day." (Tiara)
Grooming Policies: Hairstyle dictates professionalism	"Your hairstyle does not reflect your intellect. I think that the new Supreme Court Justice [Ketanji] Brown Jackson [that] brought to life. She is such an intelligent woman, and she came with her natural hair. That just spoke volumes to me. I hope that it's sent to message to others that you can wear your hair any style that you like and that should not be compared." (Ruthie)
Grooming Policies: Natural hairstyle acceptance	"It is important as we start to rise into more executive level, leadership level roles that we become more courageous in wearing our hair and natural because we're blazing a trail for our young people to wear their hair in ways that can help them express themselves in, in ways that, help them feel more comfortable as African American young ladies." (Beatrice)

Common themes were also drawn from each question posed to the focus group, as seen in Table 6.

The focus groups asked the question, "Where do you think the word 'normal' or 'professional' hair came from, and why?" The respondents discussed determinant factors such as the European white beauty standard of straight hair, having hair that would lay smooth, and that hairstyle dictates work or ability. These responses imply a need to have discussions about rebranding what is considered "good" hair in society and being more inclusive. This includes how the hair is styled by brushing the hair down to meet the European white beauty standard of straight and loose hair. This could be an indication that some Women of Color struggle to with personal identify and self-expression.

When asked, "Do you feel empowered seeing Women (and Men) of Color wearing their natural hair in the workplace?" The respondents expressed support for natural hair from others and a promotion of natural hairstyles for acceptance. This indicates that representation matters and a sense of empowerment for Women (and Men) of Color when they see similar hair textures to their own. This reinforces the idea that natural hairstyle is more common, accepted and celebrated in minority communities.

Everyone should be free to have a certain level of self-expression. Focus group participants were asked, "Do you feel as though you've adjusted the way you've styled your hair when you appear at certain places such as school, work, or social events? Why?" Responses varied, but the participants expressed looking for low maintenance hairstyles and changing from their natural texture to avoid preconceived judgements. Respondents did admit that hairstyles can be used as a form of self-expression. Self-expression could be highlighted through the hairstyles and color selection among Women (and Men) of Color. The utilization of hairstyles and color selection as a form of self-expression could be viewed as another form of personal identity supporting cultural social equity beauty standards.

When discussion grooming policies focus group participants were asked "How often do you see Women (and Men) of Color wearing their natural hair in the workplace?" The responses said that natural hairstyles are more common and acceptable in the workplace. The focus group respondents also felt that in future careers natural hair would be accepted. This suggests that grooming policies/ grooming standards that stipulate in one way or another how an employer would like its employees to present themselves physically at work (Berkemeyer, 2020) should not include standards for hair. This supports the need for enactment of state legislation to accept diverse cultural hairstyles through company policies.

Table 6. Common themes from focus group findings

Questions	Summary Theme
Normal or Professional Hair	
1. Where do you think the word "normal" or "professional" hair came from, and why?	· European white beauty standard of straight and loose hair · Brush hair down · Shades of color hair · Hairstyle dictates work ability
2. Do you feel as though you've adjusted the way you've styled your hair when you appear at certain places such as school, work, or social events? Why?	· Minimal maintenance · Certain styles and color · Preconceived judgement · Work settings expect certain hairstyles · Express yourself using hairstyles
Wearing Their Natural Hair in the Workplace	
3. How often do you see Women (and Men) of Color wearing their natural hair in the workplace?	· Natural hairstyle more common · Hairstyle dictates workability · Natural hairstyle acceptance
4. Do you feel empowered seeing Women (and Men) of Color wearing their natural hair in the workplace?	· Support for natural hair from others · Natural hairstyle acceptance · Natural hair celebration
5. Think about the future career you want to have. What kind of hairstyle do you think is expected in that career?	· Natural hairstyle acceptance · Natural hair celebration

SOLUTIONS AND RECOMMENDATIONS

This study aimed to address how the implicit bias of hair impacted the self-expression and personal identity of Women of Color as they currently navigate the workplace and/or prepare to enter the workforce. The solutions and the recommendations are derived from the data collected from this study. Looking at personal identities, self-expression, and grooming policies, it is important to maintain a dialogue about the impact of hair bias on Women of Color.

Personal identities are considered unique to an individual and distinguish one individual from another. These identities are also socially constructed; however, the research has shown that an African American woman's identity is linked to her hair (Dawson et al, 2019). This shows the importance of examining the impact of hair bias on society. For example, Ciarah explained:

I'm a second year now in college, but I go to like the STEM (Science, Technology, Engineering, & Math) Expo and every time I go, I definitely get worried about what hairstyles I should do. I often just resort to the low slick back. I feel like that's as low as possible. The last time I finally put my hair up in, a half-part down. Which is kind like a step closer to wearing my natural hair, but I think about that every time I go to interview or something, I think about what they're going to think when they see my hair.

This and other examples show the difficulty Women of Color have when determining how to style their hair in the workplace. The results imply that women of color must change the way the identify to fit what is acceptable to the status quo, taking away their personal identities and self expression.

Respondents also noted that their ability to experiment with their hair was limited. One of the participants expressed how they felt that white women are allowed to play with color such as purple or pink hair but for African American women the idea of platinum blonde hair is deemed highly unacceptable in the workplace (Focus Group, Tiarra). These types of stereotypes should be addressed in any written grooming policy that a company may have. If there are hair colors along with hairstyles that are not seen as "professional," then policies must be consistent across the board and not subjective or left up to interpretation. This would be an area for future research because this study focused mainly on the textures of the hair.

There are, however, possibilities for change. The focus group respondents provided insight into potential solutions and recommendations in their answers about their future career and hairstyle expectations. For example, Tykieena said:

So, my dream is to be an attorney. That is already rare because we don't see many Black [or] African American women as attorneys. It's mostly a white, male-dominant area. But when I do see [Black women], it is mostly straight, pressed hair. And I don't think I can do that, because I get bored with straight hair - quick. So, I think I'm going to keep my hair however way. Currently, I need to slip up, down, whatever I need to do. Because the thing about Black woman here that we forget: We defy gravity. We can versatile and we can have and embrace straight, curls, ponytail, puffball. We can wear it any way and that's what I want to do. So, if I do see a girl with a little bit like me, they can know they can really have any career. No matter what kind of hair they have.

In other words, some African American women who enter high prestige occupations are adamantly against having a certain type of hair. Many voiced the importance of representation and the power of seeing someone with natural hair who is in a role or occupation where you want to be. This is especially important, they noted, in occupations where Black women are underrepresented, such as registered dieticians and licensed opticians.

FUTURE RESEARCH DIRECTIONS

This study, which utilized snowball sampling and focus groups, specifically focused on Black women. The majority of this study's sample was highly educated and aged 45 or older. Future research could replicate the study with individuals from other racial and ethnic groups, genders, educational attainment, and ages to determine if the findings are significantly different. A study could also be directed towards current traditionally aged college student preparing for careers after graduation and hair color could also be examined.

The extent to which respondents may have been influenced by factors in the photos other than hairstyle (age, skin tone, size, etc.) is unclear. Future research could utilize the same model in each photo and have their hairstyle be the only difference, as Johnson et al (2020) did. This would take away a certain amount of bias.

Future research could also be conducted with the employers of high-prestige, medium-prestige, and low-prestige occupations to ascertain whether their sense of a hairstyle's professionalism differs from what this study found. Such research could help make clear how high or low the barrier to entry is for African American women who want to wear their hair in more natural styles. That is, if employers' attitudes have not changed, this may indicate cultural lag and an obstacle for African American women to overcome in the workplace. Data could also be collected from these employers to see if they have workplace/grooming policies in place and if there is any mention of hair in these policies.

Last, future research could examine the meaning of "health" when it comes to Black hair. Some of the participants mentioned that if hair is worn naturally, it needs to be healthy – but it is unclear what healthy hair means and what role that plays in being considered professional.

CONCLUSION

Hair bias against natural or textured hair has a distinct impact on Black women for whom textured hair is their "normal." (Johnson et al, 2021). Self-expression and personal identity significantly affect how Women of Color see themselves and express personal identities through hair. Workplace grooming policies exacerbate these views because they are overwhelming biased against women of color. Exploring the role that implicit bias against certain hairstyles worn by Women of Color is a crucial step in addressing prejudice and discrimination in the workplace. Grooming policies in the workplace can be examined and those policies policing hair should be removed.

Due to continued bias against more textured hairstyles, Women of Color must make certain compromises with their hair, limiting their self-expression and personal identity in the workplace. This research examined how the stereotypes, biases, and workplace discrimination that Women of Color experience have impacted the way they style their hair. The study was composed of two parts: quantitative and qualitative both methods reinforced the notion of hair bias restricting self-expression and personal identity.

The quantitative survey data showed that the perceived professionalism of a hairstyle was highly correlated with a hairstyle's occupational prestige. Furthermore, it showed that most hairstyles that have more texture – Afros and locs – were associated with lower levels of professionalism. This implies that there is still not the level of acceptance with textured hair even with the current natural hair movement. These responses support the previous literature that has said textured hair is not as acceptable as smooth styles and Women of Color, African American women especially fill pressure to choose hairstyles that are seen as more professional as opposed to self-expression.

The quantitative focus groups revealed several themes throughout, these common themes were identified as: normal or professional hairstyles, preconceived judgement, hairstyles dictating work ability, and natural hairstyle acceptance. The participants in the focus group gave several examples of how they have had to alter their hair for interviews or chose to alter their natural hair to fit into situation to find acceptance. The respondents also expressed satisfaction in seeing natural and textured hairstyle represented in the workplace and seeing them more often. This is a positive result and shows that there is still much more to do to see natural hair as the norm and not the exception to the rule.

Federal legislation such as the CROWN Act not adopted in all 50 states may be the best chance to bring about policy changes on the state and local level to start to facilitate social change throughout society. However, if the women in this study's focus group are representative of more Women of Color, they are not going to wait for legislation to facilitate social change. They embrace the ethos of being the change they want to see in the world. They will wear their hair as they want, without an apology, so that they can be role models to others.

Michelle sums it up best when asked if she feels empowered seeing Women of Color wear their natural hair in the workplace:

So, for me, I absolutely love it. Okay. I'm the one now. I will be like, "Hey, Sis!" "Hey, Queen!" I say you like, that's me, because I just feel. We just need to hear it from each other because the number one thing with women -- they sometimes women hate on each other. Right? That's what. The talk is all the time, so I just love encouraging other women. Like, I see you. I absolutely love that. You are embracing you unapologetically whether you have locs or you [are] rocking your curls, whatever it is (Michelle, Focus Group)."

As argued by Summer et al (2022) there are social challenges in embracing natural hair that African American women are not taught to do at an early age. The very notion of offering encouragement and words of affirmation can work wonders in affirming cultural expression and personal identities. The findings from this study demonstrated that women are supporting women and empowering each other to be their authentic selves, using self-expression and personal identity are the first steps in overcoming implicit biases and having candid conversations about hair. Women supporting and empowering each other encourages the opportunity for creativity through self-expression and a display of unique personal identity that is supported by company policies that foster culturally accepted beauty standards for all Women (and Men) of Color.

REFERENCES

Berkemeyer, C. (2020). New Growth: Afro-Textured Hair, Mental Health, and the Professional Workplace. *The Journal of the Legal Profession*, *44*(2), 279–292.

Dawson, G. A., Karl, K. A., & Peluchette, J. V. (2019). Hair matters: Toward understanding natural black hair bias in the workplace. *Journal of Leadership & Organizational Studies*, *26*(3), 389–401. doi:10.1177/1548051819848998

Goodman, M. (2021). Wearing my Crown to Work: The Crown Act as a Solution to the Shortcomings to the Title VII for Hair Discrimination in the Workplace. *Touro Law Review*, *37*(2), 1001–1025.

HughesB. T.SrivastavaS.LeszkoM.CondonD. M. (2022, September 28). Occupational Prestige: The Status Component of Socioeconomic Status. doi:10.31234/osf.io/6qgxv

Jeffries, R. B., & Jeffries, D. (2014). Reclaiming our roots: The influences of media curriculum on the Natural Hair Movement. *Multicultural Perspectives*, *16*(3), 160–165. doi:10.1080/15210960.2014.926747

Johnson, A. M., Goff, P., Tropp, L., MacFarlane, J., & Godsil, R. (2020, June 17). *The "good hair" study*. Perception Institute. http://www.goodhairstudy.com/

Jones, R. (2020). What the Hair: Employment discrimination against black people based on hairstyles. *Harvard Blackletter Law Journal*, *36*(12).

Lee, J. (2017). Self-esteem and reflected appraisals of Women's Hair in College Women. *Journal of Interdisciplinary Undergraduate Research, 9*. https://doi.org/https://knowledge.e.southern.edu/jiur/vol9/iss1/2

Moronta, G. (2022). Why do you care about my hair? A Proposal for remedying Hair Discrimination in the Workplace on a Federal Level. *Cardozo Law Review*, *43*(4).

Patton, T. O. (2006). Hey girl, am I more than my hair? African American women and their struggles with beauty, body image, and hair. *NWSA Journal*, *18*(2), 24–51. doi:10.2979/NWS.2006.18.2.24

Randle, B. A. (2015). I am not my hair; African American Women and their Struggles with Embracing Natural Hair! *Race, Gender & Class (Towson, Md.)*, *22*(1), 114–121.

Rice, M. (2004). Organizational culture, social equity, and diversity: Teaching public administration education. *Journal of Public Affairs Education*, *2*(2), 143–154. doi :10.1080/15236803.2004.12001354

Scott-Ward, G., Gupta, N., & Greene, E. (2021). *back to natural* and the intergenerational healing of the natural black hair movement. *Journal of Humanistic Psychology*, *62*(6), 925–941. doi:10.1177/00221678211009078

Summers, L. M., Davis, T., & Kosovac, B. (2022). Hair we grow again: Upward Mobility, career compromise, and natural hair bias in the workplace. *The Career Development Quarterly*, *70*(3), 202–214. doi:10.1002/cdq.12302

Treiman, D. J. (1976). A Standard Occupational Prestige Scale for Use with Historical Data. *The Journal of Interdisciplinary History*, *7*(2), 283–304. doi:10.2307/202737

Chapter 9
"People Are Watching": Hairstyle and Black Women's Experiences Working in Local and State Government

Kimalee C. Dickerson
University of North Carolina at Chapel Hill, USA

ABSTRACT

As more organizations encourage their employees to bring their authentic selves to work, this chapter explores the role of hairstyle among African American/Black women working in government organizations. This qualitative study draws from seven focus group interviews conducted in 2022 with 38 Black women employed by local or state governments in a southeastern state. Results indicate that like other industries, Black women working in government experience bias against natural hair and respond in various ways. Although hairstyle at work continues to be a "dilemma" for many Black women, they also view themselves as leaders and recognize the opportunity to influence the culture in their workplaces and communities through their hairstyle choices.

Coming just as we are when we're the first, the only, the different, or one of the few can prove too risky, so we wear the costume. We keep the truer parts of ourselves hidden. We straighten our curly hair for interviews. We pick up hobbies we do not enjoy. We restate our directives as optional suggestions. . . . We omit parts of our stories, we erase parts of ourselves. Our histories and present realities show this to be the best path for success.

DOI: 10.4018/978-1-6684-8790-7.ch009

–Jodi-Ann Burey, Why You Should Not Bring Your Authentic Self to Work, TEDxSeattle

INTRODUCTION

In recent years, organizations have increasingly encouraged employees to bring their full selves to work and to be authentic in the workplace. Authenticity refers to the degree to which a person acts in agreement with their true self (Harter, 2002), and research links authenticity at work with positive outcomes including wellbeing, self-esteem, increased engagement and job satisfaction, perceptions of belongingness, and intentions to stay with an employer (Bettencourt & Sheldon, 2001; Cha et al., 2019). However, Burley's quote highlights the realities of what many Black women experience at work and why they continue to "wear the costume".

This chapter explores hairstyle as a specific aspect of the costume that Black women wear to work. While there is some existing research on Black women's hair in different industries such as law, advertising and academia (Karl et al., 2022; Koval & Rosette, 2021; Lewis, et al., 2016), the author has found no research on Black women's hairstyles in government organizations. Responding to recent calls to apply an intersectional lens to better understand Black women's experiences in the field of public administration (Bearfield, 2009; Blessett et al., 2019; Breslin et al., 2017), this qualitative study examines Black women's experiences with hairstyles and hair bias in state and local government workplaces.

NORMS OF PROFESSIONALISM AND CODE SWITCHING

Authenticity is a state that varies based on work culture, environment, and role. Therefore, an employee's workplace context and culture impact their willingness to be authentic at work (Fleeson & Wilt, 2010; Santiago et al., 2021). Relatedly, beliefs about what it means to be "professional" in the workplace create biases that can influence authentic expression. Being perceived as a professional, meaning possessing specialized knowledge, character and capacity, is beneficial because it generates respect in one's field, status, power, and access to networks and resources (McCluney et al., 2021; Roberts, 2005). However, White men in Western countries have historically held the power and authority to shape the norms of professionalism (Carton & Rosette, 2011; McCluney et al., 2021). Because most professional work environments are predominantly White and are characterized by White professional appearance standards that value lighter skin, straighter hair texture, smaller facial features, and thinner body frames, it is difficult for visibly Black women to meet these standards (Karl et al., 2022) Thus, individuals from underrepresented and historically marginalized groups, especially Black women, may feel pressure to adjust their self-presentation and hide their more authentic selves to adhere to these norms so they can be perceived as professional (McCluney et al., 2021).

There are many terms to describe the practice of adjusting one's self-presentation to align with norms of professionalism. In the 1960s, Erving Goffman introduced the term "covering" to describe an individual's choice to render their stigmatized characteristics less salient to preserve their status in a social order (Yoshino, 2001). Other scholars have referred to downplaying or concealing marginal identity traits so others only see their chosen professional identity as wearing the "mask of the professional" (Roberts, 2005; McBroom, 1986). Hewlin (2009) refers to "facades of conformity" as suppressing one's personal values and pretending to embrace organizational values when there is a discrepancy between personal and organizational values. According to Hewlin (2009), facades of conformity are more likely to occur in situations where employees perceive that there is greater subjectivity in how decisions are made about rewards, including monetary awards, promotions, social acceptance, and recognition.

The term "code switching" has also been used to describe this behavior. The concept of code switching originated in linguistic studies to describe language fluency or selecting/altering linguistic elements based on social context (Nilep, 2006). However, usage of the term has grown to include the "the temporary 'switching on' or adjustment of behaviors to optimize the comfort of others in exchange for a desired outcome" (McCluney et al., 2021). Code switching can be viewed as a survival technique for Black people in the workplace (Santiago et al., 2021). To advance in professional roles, Black people might temporarily adjust how they dress, think, act, and express themselves in exchange for fair treatment, employment opportunities, and quality service (McCluney et al., 2021). Examples of code switching among Black employees include adjusting one's preferred hairstyle, name choice, dress, or style of speech. For example, a Black woman may choose to wear a straight hairstyle to work rather than wearing braids or a short afro style.

BLACK WOMEN'S EXPERIENCES AT WORK

Black women often face disparate treatment in the workplace and, relatedly, tend to perceive their work environments more negatively than other demographic groups. This phenomenon is well established in the private sector (Elliott & Smith, 2004; Reynolds-Dobbs et al., 2008). A recent survey showed that in comparison with men and women from other racial/ethnic groups, Black women are the least likely to feel valued and treated with respect at work and to feel that there's a climate of fair treatment among coworkers (Lloyd, 2021). Moreover, Black women are the least likely to be classified as "thriving" in terms of wellbeing, compared with all other racial/ethnic groups (Lloyd, 2021).

Given these experiences, code-switching represents Black women's agentic response to workplace norms that do not value their social identities (McCluney et al., 2021). In other words, Black women choose to adjust their appearance or behavior to "look the part" to prove that they deserve to be in the workplace (Rosette & Dumas, 2007). For Black women, detracting attention from their race and gender may dispel negative stereotypes of incompetence and help their coworkers to see them as a potential leader (McCluney et al., 2021). Karl and colleagues (2022) argue that the likelihood of identity shifting for Black women depends on various factors including one's visibility, the number of Black women in the work environment, and the strength and formality of one's profession and/or organizational appearance norms. When Black women are extremely visible due to underrepresentation (hypervisibility) and face strong appearance norms, they are more likely to engage in code switching.

While covering or suppressing one's social identity or personal values may provide certain professional benefits or successes, it may have other negative psychological, relational, and organizational impacts. For Black women, code switching requires suppressing their cultural identity, which is emotionally, psychologically, and physically exhausting (Hewlin, 2009; McCluney et al., 2021; Wingfield, 2015). Deception or inauthenticity can also increase one's cognitive load or the amount of mental energy associated with impression management. Using additional mental energy for impression management is related to decreased task engagement (Roberts, 2005). Additionally, inauthenticity may impact the ability to develop trusting and high-quality relationships with colleagues (Roberts, 2005). Moreover, Black employees may also unwittingly reinforce White norms and culture as professional so that code switching becomes an expected pathway to advancement and success (McCluney et al., 2021). On the other hand, authentic expression of one's distinct gender and racial identities may promote personal well-being (McCluney & Rabelo, 2019).

BLACK WOMEN'S HAIR IN THE WORKPLACE

One area that many Black women choose to adjust in the workplace is their hairstyles. Hair is both a powerful signifier of ethnic or racial group and a means of identity and self-expression (Ellington, 2015). For many Black women, "hair is deeply symbolic, and its meaning extends into multiple dimensions of Black culture and life." (Johnson & Bankhead, 2014, p. 86; Rosette & Dumas, 2007). Additionally, unlike relatively immutable phenotypic traits such as skin color, eye color, nose width and lip size, hair texture is mutable allowing Black women to choose more easily to adjust it (Opie & Phillips, 2015).

The natural hair texture of most Black women is kinky, wooly, or tightly curled (Rosette & Dumas, 2007). Accordingly, a great deal of time and expense is required to transform Black hair so that it aligns with White workplace appearance standards and looks more like the hair of White counterparts. Black women can achieve straight-looking hair by using chemicals or thermal tools, or by using hair extensions and weaves. However, these style options are not without their costs (Rosette & Dumas, 2007). In addition to the financial costs, straightening their hair can result in hair breakage or skin diseases.

Like other forms of codeswitching or covering at work, research suggests that Black women experience dissonance and even "a dilemma" regarding their hair and how to manage their professional identity (Dawson et al., 2019; Rosette & Dumas, 2007). By conforming to White standards of appearance by altering or straightening one's hair, Black women gain the benefit of fitting in and ensuring employability. On the other hand, they may struggle with inauthenticity and the cost and physical challenges associated with maintaining the look (Dawson et al., 2019).

Historically, Black women's hair choices have been largely influenced by societal pressures to adopt White standards of beauty which idealize long, straight hair and light skin (Byrd & Tharps, 2014; Dawson & Karl, 2018). In the United States, during slavery, long and straight hair was associated with enslaved people with mixed heritage who often worked inside, instead of outside in the fields (Dawson et al., 2019; Koval & Rosette, 2021). After slavery, straight hair continued to be associated with status and was often a means to socioeconomic benefits (Dawson et al., 2019). During the 1960s, afros, braids, and other styles that allowed Black women to display the natural texture of their hair became popular and positively associated with the Civil Rights and Black Power movements (Opie & Phillips, 2015). The idea that Black was beautiful and that Black people no longer had to conform to White beauty standards gained popularity. At the time, these hairstyles were considered a bold political stance and a rejection of the status quo (Dawson & Karl, 2018). As the momentum behind the Black Panther Movement faded, straight hairstyles gained popularity once again during the 1980s and into the new millennium. The contemporary movement around natural hair started in the late 2000's and has largely grown through Black women communicating and posting information about caring for natural hair on the internet (Byrd & Tharps, 2014; Ellington, 2015).

Research shows that Black women's hairstyles impact various aspects of their work experiences. Overall, the research suggests that race-based hair discrimination - from hiring practices to daily workplace interactions - remains a systemic problem in the workplace that disproportionately impacts Black women's employment opportunities and experiences (Byrd & Tharps, 2014; Donahoo & Smith, 2022; Opie & Phillips, 2015).

Hair and Hiring

Opie and Phillips (2015) conducted a series of experimental studies to examine the influence of hairstyle and participant race on ratings of an employment candidate's professionalism and dominance. Across three studies, they found that employment candidates with Afrocentric or natural hairstyles were rated as less professional and less likely to succeed than employment candidates with Eurocentric hairstyles by both White and Black evaluators. Moreover, Black women evaluators were even more critical of Afrocentric/natural hair than White women evaluators (Opie & Phillips, 2015).

Perhaps it is not surprising then that a study by Dove (2023) found that of the approximately two-thirds (66%) of Black women who reported changing their hair for a job interview, 41% changed their hair from curly to straight (Dove, 2023). Similarly, Jones and Shorter-Gooden (2003) found that Black women expressed a sense of obligation to straighten their hair before job interviews to avoid backlash.

Hair and Workplace Interactions

There is evidence that bias against Black women wearing natural hairstyles to work also continues after employment begins. A recent study found that Black women with coily or textured hair are two times more likely to experience microaggressions in the workplace than Black women with straighter hair (Dove, 2023). Even Google's algorithm has been found to be biased against natural Black hairstyles, with a search for "unprofessional styles for work" resulting in many images of Black women with natural hairstyles and a search of "professional hairstyles for work" resulting in images of mostly White women (Sini, 2016). Historically, discrimination due to Black women wearing natural hair styles has even led to loss of employment (Byrd & Tharps, 2014). Over the last several decades, many Black women have gone to court seeking legal remedies for employment and racial discrimination issues related to their hair (Donahoo & Smith, 2022).

Some research indicates that Black women experience hair bias from White colleagues and other Black colleagues, while other research suggests that Black women are less biased against natural hairstyles compared to other groups. In one study, Dawson and colleagues (2019), analyzed comments posted to online discussion boards about Black hair at work. Although the researchers found that some Black women are embracing natural hairstyles, many felt pressured to conform to Eurocentric hairstyles and some had experienced negative consequences stemming from their natural hairstyle choices. The researchers found that the posted comments reflected hair bias or the notion that natural Black hairstyles were viewed as deviant, different, or unacceptable from the majority. Some commenters indicated that Black women with natural hair received more negative reactions and comments from other Black people as opposed to White people. In comparison, McCluney and colleagues (2021), found when asked to imagine a hypothetical coworker, Black women reacted more positively to a fictitious Black woman coworker that chose to wear her natural hair compared to White women participants, and Black women agreed more strongly with the natural hair choice compared to the straightened style.

Hair Across Different Industries and Occupations

Research suggests that while bias against natural hair occurs across different occupations and industries, the level of bias in a particular field or workplace depends in part on the formality of the profession and organizational appearance norms (Koval & Rosette, 2021). In a study of Black women employed in four occupations (finance, medicine, law, and technology), Karl and colleagues (2022) analyzed photos of Black women posted on professional lists on the internet. They found that Black women were more likely to adjust their hairstyle to mirror White standards of professionalism in more conservative and formal work environments. Specifically, technology professionals were significantly more likely to wear natural hairstyles than any of the other three occupations, and Black women lawyers were significantly less likely than either physicians or women in technology to wear natural hairstyles.

Koval and Rosette (2021) similarly conducted a series of four studies on natural hair bias in job recruitment. The researchers found that in comparison to Black women with straightened hairstyles, those with natural hairstyles were perceived as less professional and less likely to be interviewed for a job, and this bias was particularly salient in industries with strong dress norms. In comparison to the advertising industry which has more relaxed dress code norms, Black women with natural hair in the consulting industry, which is known for strong norms of wearing conservative business attire, received more negative evaluations when they applied for a job (Koval & Rosette, 2021).

Black women's hair in the workplace has also been studied in the public sector, particularly among Black women in academia. Several studies have found that Black women experience microaggressions (i.e., subtle and everyday verbal, behavioral, and environmental expressions of oppression based on one's social identities) (Sue & Spanierman, 2020) and assumptions about professionalism related to their hair. In a study exploring the ways in which faculty members' social identities impact their experience in the university, Ford (2011) found that Black women faculty overwhelmingly discuss hair and attire as potential impediments to being respected as qualified professionals. Similarly, a study of gendered racial microaggressions among Black women at a predominantly White university found that Black women experienced microaggressions that involve assumptions about their physical appearance, including hairstyle, body size, and facial features (Lewis et al., 2016). While there is some existing research on Black women's hair in different industries, there are many fields that have yet to be studied, including Black women working in government organizations.

BLACK WOMEN IN WORKING IN GOVERNMENT

Much like law and consulting (Karl et al., 2022; Koval & Rosette, 2021), government remains a more conservative industry with more formal appearance standards. The public sector has been called an "equalizing institution" because it has historically offered more career opportunities for people of color and women than the private sector (Cooper & Wolfe, 2020; Laird, 2017). As a result, Black people and women constitute a disproportionately large share of the state and local public-sector workforce (Cooper & Wolfe, 2020; Llorens et al., 2008). However, Black people remain underrepresented in certain sections of the public sector while they are concentrated in others, including the shrinking sectors of the economy (Blessett et al., 2019; Laird, 2017; Riccucci, 2009).

Moreover, Black workers are often at risk of being the "last hired, first fired" (Couch & Fairlie, 2010), particularly during challenging economic times. A study of 16 million applicants for state and local government jobs in 2018 and 2019 found that among candidates deemed qualified, Black women were 58 percent less likely to be hired than White men (Cohen, 2021). A study of public sector employment after the Great Recession of 2007-2009 found that Black public sector workers were more likely than White and Hispanic workers to experience job loss (Laird, 2017). Additionally, among unemployed workers who most recently worked for the public sector, Black women were the least likely to transition into private sector employment (Laird, 2017). Scholars have warned that Black workers and women may again be disproportionately harmed by state and local public sector budget cuts following the Covid-19 pandemic (Cooper & Wolfe, 2020).

Although Black women have historically comprised a disproportionate share of public sector employees, they remain underrepresented in management and leadership positions. Riccucci (2009) found that women of color are underrepresented in leadership positions across federal agencies and concentrated in certain agencies and in lower-paying and less prestigious jobs. Similarly, a study of cities and municipalities in the United States found that while all women are underrepresented at the administrator level, Latinas and Black women show the lowest levels of representation (Miller et al., 2010). While there are many potential reasons for the underrepresentation of Black women in leadership positions, Rosette et al. (2016) argue that stereotypes of Black women as less intellectually or technically competent and aggressive and vocal may serve as barriers to leadership opportunities. These stereotypes are closely related to perceptions of professionalism.

Additionally, a study of federal employees found that women of color have less access to networking and mentoring opportunities with decision makers (Daley, 1996). Like the private sector, the extant research on women of color working in government shows they often face disparate treatment in the workplace and, relatedly, tend to perceive their work environments more negatively than other demographic groups. A study of employees at a federal agency found that people of color and women report higher levels of discrimination and perceive organizational climate as less inclusive, supportive, or encouraging compared to White males (Soni, 2000). Similarly, Oberfield (2016) concluded that across federal agencies, people with different social identities viewed diversity climate differently, and women of color were least likely to perceive their organizations as being committed to diversity.

Among the few studies which consider the intersection of race and gender in experiences of workplace incivility, a subtle form of discrimination that can selectively target historically marginalized groups, findings are more mixed (Smith et al., 2021; Welbourne et al., 2014). However, several studies show that women of color in public organizations report higher levels of workplace incivility than White employees (Cortina et al., 2001, 2013) and men of color (Cortina et al., 2013; Smith et al., 2021). In a review of the literature about Black women working in government, the author did not find any literature focused on Black women's hairstyles.

Recognizing the need for additional research about Black women's experiences working in government organizations, several scholars have called for the application of intersectionality in public administration (Bearfield, 2009; Blessett et al., 2019; Breslin et al., 2017). A review of 25 years of public leadership literature found a limited application of intersectionality and a lack of attention to power relations and the processes that produce and maintain inequities (Breslin et al., 2017). Although some studies considered how gender interacts with public leadership, scholars have found the literature poorly accounted for the representation of women of color within public administration or the biases and barriers that shape their unique experiences (Breslin et al., 2017). While the study of race and gender is not new to public administration, Bearfield argues that the "future of social equity research lies in questions that address the intersection of race and gender as opposed to approaches that deal with them as separate categories" (Bearfield, 2009, p. 383-84).

This chapter seeks to respond to that call. This chapter is part of a larger study that broadly explores the experiences of Black women working in local and state government. Building on existing research about Black women's experiences with hair and hair bias in the workplace, this chapter focuses specifically on Black women working in state and local government organizations.

THEORETICAL FRAMEWORK

Intersectionality, a term coined by legal scholar Kimberlé Crenshaw (1991), refers to the ways in which social identity categories such as gender, race, class, sexuality, and ability, interact to shape one's experiences and outcomes. By emphasizing multiple and simultaneous dimensions of inequity, intersectionality highlights the unique experiences of individuals who occupy multiple marginalized social categories (Breslin et al., 2017). Intersectionality can be used to explore and provide solutions to range of pressing public administration issues including how institutions perpetuate inequities, why communities of color experience disparities on a range of quality-of-life indicators, and how different women lead (Blessett et al., 2016; Breslin et al., 2017).

While intersectionality can be applied to a range of identities, much of the extant intersectionality literature focuses on the intersections of race and gender, particularly among Black women (Breslin et al., 2017). Black women often face a "triple jeopardy" of race, class, and gender, which can subject them to multiple, simultaneous forms of oppression (King, 1988). Indeed, intersectionality developed from Black feminism and was first introduced as a theory to better understand the unique experiences of Black women in the United States (Hill Collins, 2000).

METHODS

Data Collection

This qualitative study draws from seven semi-structured focus group interviews conducted with 38 African American/Black women employed by local or state governments located in one southeastern state in the United States. The purpose of the study was to explore the experiences of Black women working in government generally, and this chapter focuses specifically on their experiences with hair and hair bias. Focus groups were conducted virtually via Zoom in 2022. The size of the focus groups ranged from three to eight participants. Each focus group was recorded, transcribed in its entirety, and reviewed to ensure accuracy. The interview protocol explored topics including career path and advancement, motivations for public service, what it means to be a Black woman working in government, authenticity at work, and challenges and empowering experiences working in government organizations.

Participants discussed hair and hair bias in relation to several questions about their experiences at work.

The 38 participants in this study ranged from early career government workers to recently retired from government service within the last two years. During the focus group interviews, the participants wore a range of hairstyles from shoulder length or longer straightened hair to braids and short natural curls. While the author observed a range of hairstyles during the interviews, data were not recorded about each participants hairstyle, and a few interviewees noted that they wore different hairstyles to work than they wore to the focus group interview. The participants worked in a variety of positions, and most worked in supervisory and leadership roles within local government organizations in the southeastern state. The size of the local government organizations ranged from small jurisdictions that serve populations less than 10,000 people to much larger jurisdictions serving over 500,000 people. All participants were given pseudonyms for reporting purposes. See Table 1 for characteristics of study participants and their employers.

Participants were recruited primarily through snowball sampling. After obtaining approval to conduct human subject research, the author sent an email invitation to an email list of Black women working in state and local government who had been meeting regularly as a group for the last several years. Group members were encouraged to share the opportunity to participate in the study with their networks. All participants received a $25 Visa gift card for participating in the study.

Table 1. Characteristics of study participants and their employers

Participant Pseudonym	Participant's Career Stage	Size of Jurisdiction
Renee	Early	Midsize
Marcella	Mid	Midsize
Keisha	Mid	Midsize
Loretta	Late	Large
Charlene	Late	Midsize
Betina	Mid	Midsize
Naomi	Early	Midsize
Vanessa	Mid	Large
Tina	Late	Small
Laura	Mid	Large
Roberta	Late	Small
Imani	Early	Small
Destiny	Mid	Midsize
Bridget	Mid	Small
Grace	Mid	Large
Luna	Mid	Large
Kayla	Early	Small
Serena	Late	Midsize
Claudette	Mid	Large
Nadine	Retired	Large
Leah	Late	Large
Pilar	Late	Large
Chantel	Mid	Midsize
Shante	Mid	Large
Raquel	Early	Large
Ebony	Mid	Large
Aliyah	Mid	Midsize
Angel	Mid	Small
Alex	Mid	Small
Nia	Mid	Midsize
Deja	Mid	Small
Jada	Mid	Midsize
Asia	Mid	Large
Patricia	Mid	Midsize
Jasmine	Late	Large

Continued on following page

Table 1. Continued

Participant Pseudonym	Participant's Career Stage	Size of Jurisdiction
Gabrielle	Late	Midsize
Tiana	Early	Large
Layla	Mid	Small

Note: Early career stage is defined as 10 years or less of employment experience in government or other sectors, mid-career is defined as between 11 and 30 years, and late career is over 30 years. For jurisdiction size, small refers to governments that serve a population of less than 50,000 people, midsize refers to populations between 50,000 and 200,000 people, and large refers to population over 200,000.

Data Analysis

Analyses were conducted using a grounded theory approach, which requires researchers to suspend any preexisting theoretical expectations and let the data dictate the formulation of the theory (Corbin & Strauss, 2008). The author began with open coding to identify initial concepts and group them into categories (Corbin & Strauss, 2008). Whenever possible, in vivo codes (i.e., actual language used by the participants) were used (Corbin & Strauss, 2008; Saldaña, 2013). Next, the author conducted axial coding, which involved searching for relationships among the categories and identifying higher order themes (Corbin & Strauss, 2008). Specifically, the author searched for themes that centered on Black women's hair in the workplace.

RESULTS

The findings demonstrate that hair is a significant consideration for Black women working in state and local governments. Hairstyle was primarily discussed in relation to what it means to be a Black woman working in government and being authentic at work. Many of the participants reported personally experiencing and/or observing differential treatment or negative workplace interactions due to wearing natural hairstyles. These interactions occurred with White colleagues and other Black colleagues. The continual interest and scrutiny that Black women experienced about their hair led to a heightened awareness of their hair, which several participants described as "exhausting" to have to think about. Interviewees responded to this scrutiny in various ways, from expressing resignation about straightening their hair to resisting White appearance norms by wearing natural hairstyles. Moreover, many

Black women viewed their hair style choice as an opportunity to encourage other people to be more authentic in government workplaces.

Hairstyle and Authenticity

Across the seven focus groups, participants associated their choice of hairstyle with the ability to be authentic as a Black woman in the workplace. In almost every focus group, the topic of hairstyle and wearing a natural versus straightened hairstyle emerged in connection with either a discussion about what it means to be a Black woman working in government or a discussion about bringing their authentic selves to work without the facilitator specifically asking about hair. For example, when asked what it means to be a Black woman working in government, Angel responded,

So, being a Black woman in local government, I feel like I'm a leader, I feel like people are watching what I say and what I do. And I'm very intentional about things. This is going to seem off, but I think I would like to share it, when I first started with the [local government], I had relaxed hair and I never thought I would have any other type of hair. During the pandemic, I went natural.

For some women, experiencing differential treatment based on hairstyle was a key factor in feeling like they could not bring their full authentic self to work. Alexis explained,

I absolutely notice that people treat me differently based on if my hair's long or short, or things of that nature. I'm always going to dress professional. I'm always going to have the same knowledge in my head. I'm always going to present professionally. So, the only thing that could be different is that you're seeing something visually and making assumptions based on that. So, I'll never bring 100% of myself. I hope that one day... we have a granddaughter who's a few months old, I hope that she can, as a Black woman, do that. But I just don't think it's in the cards for me for the rest of my career. And that's just being 100.

The connection participants made between the topics of hairstyle, what it means to be a Black woman in government, and authenticity at work highlights how central and important hairstyle was for their work experiences.

Experiences and Impacts of Hair Bias

Like Alexis, some of the study participants reported personally experiencing differential or discriminatory treatment based on their hairstyle. Specifically, several women described microaggressions and negative interactions and assumptions related to their hair. These women often expressed strong emotions related to their experiences, including frustration and sadness. Patricia explained,

Depending on how I have my hair, et cetera, a lot of the other people [at work] think that I'm this young girl, I don't know anything. And so, I just sit there and listen and observe. And then once I give my input, it's like, oh well whoa, wait a minute. And it's like, why does it have to be that way?

In addition to describing her interactions with coworkers, Patricia questions why she has to endure such experiences. Similarly, Roberta shared,

To me, that's sad that we'll receive one way or another based on your hair. When I wear the long straight hair, I'm one of the girls so to speak, and you get so many compliments when your hair is like the non-Blacks. But when you wear the braids, and you get stares, and you get stares, and you get questions, "How is that up there? How is that done?" But it's sad that that happens.

None of the participants reported personally not being hired or promoted or being fired due to their hairstyle. However, a few observed how hairstyle impacted other Black women's career opportunities. Claudette revealed,

I think Black people can maybe be the hardest on us about what we look like. I remember once I had a boss that was Black. I actually loved him. He was phenomenal, but he wanted to refer this woman for a job and she had braids in her hair because she had just come from vacation. He said, "She wasn't ready."

Like Claudette, a few other interviewees noted that the hair bias they experienced or witnessed came from other Black people. Alexis also described an instance of intra-racial hair bias. She stated,

the pitting of Black woman to Black woman, that is so real. My old director left, who happened to be a Black female. The person that we ended up hiring, also a Black woman and she has straight hair, has said to me, "I've seen pictures when you had your hair different. You should do this, you should do that." I'm like, "Really, sis?" "Really?"

Given the number of participants who experienced hair bias at work, it is not surprising that Black women were aware of the interest and scrutiny related to their hair and often gave significant thought to their hairstyles. Some found it exhausting to have to think so much about their hair and potential consequences of different styles. One shared,

So, the natural thing was a huge step for me because I am just getting comfortable bringing some of myself into the work environment. Not all, I don't think I ever bring all, part of that is because I'm in human resources, but part of it is being a Black woman. I literally think about if I'm going to get braids for vacation, do I want to wear those into the office? Because I don't want to hear those questions, I don't want to hear that being a conversation. And I'm very aware that it is going to be that. So, it's exhausting that you have to think about it. Whereas my colleagues that are White, don't have to think about any of that.

Although Pilar reported wearing a short and curly natural hairstyle for several years, she similarly acknowledged, "I'm very mindful of how I change up my appearance, and it can be very exhausting." Pilar's quote demonstrates that even among some of the Black women who regularly wore natural hairstyles, hairstyle choice and the impact of that choice remain a source of cognitive effort and exhaustion.

Responding to Hair Bias: Resignation and Resistance

The Black women who reported experiencing or witnessing hair bias responded in various ways. A few responded to biases against natural hair with code switching by straightening their hair in certain situations in an attempt to avoid discrimination. For example, Alicia explained,

My hair's natural, I will straighten my hair because I am more well received that way than if I have the puff. There are certain jobs that I don't feel like I would've gotten had I walked in natural. So, this is the life I'm living right now. I'm hoping that I can change that and be a light to somebody else. But in this stage of my career, it's just not looking positive in that area.

Alicia's explanation of why she sometimes straightened her natural hair demonstrates a level of resignation to the existence of bias against natural hair.

Other women, particularly those who had been natural for a long time, resisted professional norms around straightened hair and wearing natural hairstyles regardless of potential hair bias. These women shared various reasons for not adjusting their hairstyles. Keisha explained, "I've always felt comfortable in that way. I've been natural since 2000, so it's like take it or leave it for me. I feel like people should be accepted of what grows out of your head." Keisha directly challenges the idea that Black women should change their hair to conform to certain work environments.

In comparison, some Black women chose to wear a natural hairstyle for convenience or to fit their lifestyle. For example, Pilar reported,

I went natural years and years ago more so because relaxers were getting to be too expensive, and plus, with my active lifestyle, working out and everything, I just couldn't hold the perm anymore. And so, I just got rid of it and just went short and curly. I don't necessarily think local government is ready for Black women to bring their authentic selves because that means something totally different. They could say all they want to 'bring your authentic self.' No, no. Black people have been having to put on different hats for years when it comes to being the workplace person versus being the at-home person. Whereas our White counterparts can go fluidly between without problem.

Pilar's quote highlights that while she viewed hairstyle as related to authenticity, choosing to wear a natural hairstyle to work did not necessarily equate to feeling comfortable or welcome to bring her full authentic self to work.

Role Models in the Natural Hair Movement

Despite the challenges and emotional energy associated with hair, some of the Black women who embraced wearing their natural hair viewed themselves as role models for colleagues and their community. Almost all the study participants felt that their colleagues and the community they served were constantly watching and scrutinizing them. Several of the women were also the first Black woman to occupy their position within their government organization. While this hypervisibility caused additional feelings of pressure and stress for some, many women also viewed it as creating an opportunity and responsibility to be a role model and to open doors for others, especially younger Black women.

This perspective also extended to being a role model for natural hairstyles. For example, Bridget described her experience starting a new government position:

When I came in, I was like, "Okay, I need to change my hair." I know you're looking at the [Zoom] picture like my hair is straight. My hair is really not straight. So, when I came in and I had my natural hair, that was a concern for me. What I noticed was other people who were actually natural began to come out with their hair. They stopped doing their hair weaves. That's what happened with me.

Angel shared a similar experience of recognizing her visibility as a Black woman in local government and wanting to serve as a role model to others. She explained,

When I first started with the [local government], I had relaxed hair and I never thought I would have any other type of hair. During the pandemic, I went natural. And I'm not going to lie, I was a little bit fearful as to how some people would treat me. But the strength of my mom and other people reminded me, if not me, who? And so, I think about the young Black girls who come into the building, and they're with their mom or dad paying their electric bill, and I want them to see that I work here and I'm proud of who I am. And no shade, I may get a relaxer next year, I don't know, but it was really important to me to recognize people are watching and what do I want to portray? So, for me, being a Black woman in local government means people are watching, I stand on the shoulders of other people, and I want to be representative of all things good, but all things true as well.

In addition to being an inspiration to others, several women were inspired to bring more of their authentic selves to work by other Black women wearing natural hair and White colleagues who embraced non-traditional hairstyles. Shante reported,

I feel like when I came here, I'd heard some stories about women with natural hair and the impact of what that was for them. I don't have natural hair, I still perm it. I know. Creamy crack. I get it. But their experience of coming into this space with their natural hair and then witnessing a White woman here in the [local government] with vibrant pink hair and vibrant purple hair and her ability to be able to do that then encourage them, and their stories then encourage me to be more of my authentic self.

Similarly, Claudette recalled,

I worked for a Jewish man who would let people come with blue green hair, any color. He just really cared about your ability. So, that taught me very early that I was going to show up as my whole self. If they didn't like it, it just wasn't the match for me. I just didn't like having to shrink or be different as a Black person and that not be something that others have to do.

DISCUSSION AND CONCLUSION

This study extends the existing research about Black women hair in the workplace. Much like the private sector and academia, Black women working in state and local government organizations experienced differential treatment – from being asked inappropriate questions about their hair to assumptions of incompetence and employment discrimination – depending on their hairstyle (Dawson & Karl, 2018; Ford, 2011; Jones & Shorter-Gooden, 2003; Opie & Phillips, 2015; Rosette et al.,

2016; Sue & Spanierman, 2020). Specifically, Black women working in government reported more negative interpersonal interactions and treatment when wearing their hair in natural and braided hairstyles. Thus, Black hair remains an ongoing "dilemma" (Rosette & Dumas, 2007) for many Black women in government workplaces.

While many of the study participants wore their hair in natural styles to work and expressed support for other Black women wearing natural hairstyles, several had experienced or witnessed bias against natural hair from other Black people. This dichotomy reflects the apparent inconsistency in prior studies with some research finding that Black people reacted more negatively to natural hair in the workplace than White people (Dawson et al., 2019), while other research showed Black women reacted more positively to a Black women wearing a natural hairstyle compared to straight hair than White women (McCluney et al., 2021). As natural hairstyles continue to gain popularity and become more accepted at work, more Black people may also become more accepting of such styles.

This study also sheds light on the different ways that Black women are impacted by and respond to hair bias in local and state government workplaces. Consistent with prior research, the interviewees associated hairstyle choice with the concept of authentically expressing themselves at work. Moreover, much like the literature finding impression management at work to be exhausting and associated with increases in cognitive load for marginalized people (Hewlin, 2009; Roberts, 2005; Santiago et al., 2021), Black women reported feeling exhausted about having to think about their hairstyle and how it may impact their experiences and opportunities at work. Even some of the women who regularly wore a natural hairstyle to work reported spending mental time and energy thinking about their hairstyle. When faced the actual or potential bias against natural hairstyles, Black women responded in various ways. Like Black women in other industries (Dove, 2023; Jones & Shorter-Gooden, 2003), some women decided to code switch by straightening their hair, while others resisted the pressure to conform to White professionalism standards of straight hair.

Lastly, this study contributes to the existing research by highlighting the importance of work culture and environment in Black women's decision of how to style their hair for work. (Fleeson & Wilt, 2010; Santiago et al., 2021). As primarily local government employees, with several of them serving as the first Black woman in their role, the women in this study described themselves as leaders and recognized the opportunity to influence the culture in their workplaces and communities. Accordingly, several of them viewed their hairstyles choice as not just a personal decision, but an opportunity to encourage others to be proud of their natural hair and bring more of their authentic selves to work. Similarly, a few of the women felt more comfortable with wearing their natural hair after their White colleagues and/or supervisors donned unique hair colors and styles at work.

While this study helps to expand our understanding of Black women's experience around hair, code switching, and authenticity in the workplace, there are several limitations. First, all the study participants worked for state and local governments located within one state in the southeast. It is possible that their experiences with hair at work are not representative of Black women working in government in other geographical areas. Second, while hair was a frequent topic among the participants, this study did not focus exclusively on hair but rather Black women's experiences working in state and local government. Future research should investigate the experience of Black women related to hair at work in a range of geographic areas and in other public sector fields and occupations. Additionally, future research studies should focus exclusively Black women's hair at work to gain an even deeper understanding of on the role of hair in Black women's work experiences.

As one participant noted, being a Black woman in government means that "people are watching", including how they wear their hair. As more organizations strive to create inclusive and healthy work environments for all employees, this study suggests the benefits of using an intersectional lens to understand the unique experience of Black women working in government and the important role hair plays in their work experiences.

REFERENCES

Bearfield, D. A. (2009). Equity at the intersection: Public administration and the study of gender. *Public Administration Review*, *69*(3), 383–386. doi:10.1111/j.1540-6210.2009.01985.x

Bettencourt, B. A., & Sheldon, K. (2001). Social roles as mechanism for psychological need satisfaction within social groups. *Journal of Personality and Social Psychology*, *81*(6), 1131–1143. doi:10.1037/0022-3514.81.6.1131 PMID:11761313

Blessett, B., Dodge, J., Edmond, B., Goerdel, H. T., Gooden, S. T., Headley, A. M., Riccucci, N. M., & Williams, B. N. (2019). Social equity in public administration: A call to action. *Perspectives on Public Management and Governance*, *2*(4), 283–299. doi:10.1093/ppmgov/gvz016

Breslin, R. A., Pandey, S., & Riccucci, N. M. (2017). Intersectionality in public leadership research: A review and future research agenda. *Review of Public Personnel Administration*, *37*(2), 160–182. doi:10.1177/0734371X17697118

Byrd, A., & Tharps, L. (2014). *Hair story: Untangling the roots of Black hair in america* (Second Edition, Revised). St. Martin's Griffin.

Carton, A. M., & Rosette, A. S. (2011). Explaining bias against Black leaders: Integrating theory on information processing and goal-based stereotyping. *Academy of Management Journal, 54*(6), 1141–1158. doi:10.5465/amj.2009.0745

Cha, S. E., Hewlin, P. F., Roberts, L. M., Buckman, B. R., Leroy, H., Steckler, E. L., Ostermeier, K., & Cooper, D. (2019). Being your true self at work: Integrating the fragmented research on authenticity in organizations. *The Academy of Management Annals, 13*(2), 633–671. doi:10.5465/annals.2016.0108

Cohen, P. (2021, March 18). Black women were half as likely to be hired for state or local jobs than White men, a report says. *The New York Times*. https://www.nytimes.com/2021/03/18/business/black-women-hiring-discrimination.html

Cooper, D., & Wolfe, J. (2020, July 9). Cuts to the state and local public sector will disproportionately harm women and Black workers. *Economic Policy Institute*. https://www.epi.org/blog/cuts-to-the-state-and-local-public-sector-will-disproportionately-harm-women-and-black-workers/

Corbin, J., & Strauss, A. (2008). Basics of qualitative research: Techniques and procedures for developing grounded theory, 3rd ed (pp. xv, 379). Sage Publications, Inc. doi:10.4135/9781452230153

Cortina, L. M., Kabat-Farr, D., Leskinen, E. A., Huerta, M., & Magley, V. J. (2013). Selective incivility as modern discrimination in organizations: Evidence and impact. *Journal of Management, 39*(6), 1579–1605. doi:10.1177/0149206311418835

Cortina, L. M., Magley, V. J., Williams, J. H., & Langhout, R. D. (2001). Incivility in the workplace: Incidence and impact. *Journal of Occupational Health Psychology, 6*(1), 64–80. doi:10.1037/1076-8998.6.1.64 PMID:11199258

Couch, K. A., & Fairlie, R. (2010). Last hired, first fired? Black-White unemployment and the business cycle. *Springer, 47*(1), 21.

Crenshaw, K. (1991). Mapping the margins: Intersectionality, identity politics, and violence against women of color. *Stanford Law Review, 43*(6), 1241–1299. doi:10.2307/1229039

Daley, D. M. (1996). Paths of glory and the glass ceiling: Differing patterns of career advancement among women and minority federal employees. *Public Administration Quarterly*, 143–162.

Dawson, G., & Karl, K. (2018). I am not my hair, or am I? Examining hair choices of Black female executives. *Journal of Business Diversity, 18*(2), 46–56.

Dawson, G. A., Karl, K. A., & Peluchette, J. V. (2019). Hair matters: Toward understanding natural Black hair bias in the workplace. *Journal of Leadership & Organizational Studies*, *26*(3), 389–401. doi:10.1177/1548051819848998

Donahoo, S., & Smith, A. D. (2022). Controlling the crown: Legal efforts to professionalize Black hair. *Race and Justice*, *12*(1), 182–203. doi:10.1177/2153368719888264

Dove. (2023). *2023 CROWN Workplace Research Study*. The official CROWN Act. https://www.thecrownact.com/research-studies

Ellington, T. N. (2015). Social networking sites: A support system for African-American women wearing natural hair. *International Journal of Fashion Design. Technology and Education*, *8*(1), 21–29. doi:10.1080/17543266.2014.974689

Elliott, J. R., & Smith, R. A. (2004). Race, gender, and workplace power. *American Sociological Review*, *69*(3), 365–386. doi:10.1177/000312240406900303

Fleeson, W., & Wilt, J. (2010). The Relevance of Big five trait content in behavior to subjective authenticity: Do high levels of within-person behavioral variability undermine or enable authenticity achievement? *Journal of Personality*, *78*(4), 1353–1382. doi:10.1111/j.1467-6494.2010.00653.x PMID:20545814

Ford, K. A. (2011). Race, gender, and bodily (mis)recognitions: Women of color faculty experiences with White students in the college classroom. *Journal of Higher Education (Columbus, Ohio)*, *82*(4), 444–478. doi:10.1353/jhe.2011.0026

Harter, S. (2002). Authenticity. In *Handbook of positive psychology* (pp. 382–394). Oxford University Press.

Hewlin, P. F. (2009). Wearing the cloak: Antecedents and consequences of creating facades of conformity. *The Journal of Applied Psychology*, *94*(3), 727–741. doi:10.1037/a0015228 PMID:19450009

Hill Collins, P. (2000). *Black Feminist Thought | Knowledge, Consciousness, and the Politics of*. Routledge. https://www-taylorfrancis-com.libproxy.lib.unc.edu/books/mono/10.4324/9780203900055/black-feminist-thought-patricia-hill-collins

Johnson, T. A., & Bankhead, T. (2014). Hair it is: Examining the experiences of Black women with natural hair. *Open Journal of Social Sciences*, *02*(01), 86–100. doi:10.4236/jss.2014.21010

Jones, M. C., & Shorter-Gooden, K. (2003). *Shifting: The double lives of Black women in America*. HarperCollins.

Karl, K., Peluchette, J. V., & Dawson, G. (2022). Why so much ado about a hairdo? Examining how the hair choices of Black women vary by occupation. *Journal of Business Diversity*, *22*(1), 10–22.

King, D. K. (1988). Multiple jeopardy, multiple consciousness: The context of a Black feminist ideology. *Signs (Chicago, Ill.)*, *14*(1), 42–72. doi:10.1086/494491

Koval, C. Z., & Rosette, A. S. (2021). The natural hair bias in job recruitment. *Social Psychological & Personality Science*, *12*(5), 741–750. doi:10.1177/1948550620937937

Laird, J. (2017). Public sector employment inequality in the United States and the Great Recession. *Demography*, *54*(1), 391–411. doi:10.100713524-016-0532-4 PMID:28092072

Lewis, J. A., Mendenhall, R., Harwood, S. A., & Browne Huntt, M. (2016). "Ain't I a woman?": Perceived Gendered racial microaggressions experienced by Black women. *The Counseling Psychologist*, *44*(5), 758–780. doi:10.1177/0011000016641193

Llorens, J. J., Wenger, J. B., & Kellough, J. E. (2008). Choosing public sector employment: The impact of wages on the representation of women and minorities in state bureaucracies. *Journal of Public Administration: Research and Theory*, *18*(3), 397–413. doi:10.1093/jopart/mum020

Lloyd, C. (2021, March 5). *Black Women in the Workplace*. Gallup.Com. https://www.gallup.com/workplace/333194/black-women-workplace.aspx

McCluney, C. L., Durkee, M. I., Smith, R. E. II, Robotham, K. J., & Lee, S. S.-L. (2021). To be, or not to be…Black: The effects of racial codeswitching on perceived professionalism in the workplace. *Journal of Experimental Social Psychology*, *97*, 104199. doi:10.1016/j.jesp.2021.104199

McCluney, C. L., & Rabelo, V. C. (2019). Conditions of visibility: An intersectional examination of Black women's belongingness and distinctiveness at work. *Journal of Vocational Behavior*, *113*, 143–152. doi:10.1016/j.jvb.2018.09.008

Miller, W., Kerr, B., & Reid, M. (2010). Descriptive representation by gender and race/ethnicity in municipal bureaucracies: Change in US multiethnic cities, 1987–2001. *Journal of Women, Politics & Policy*, *31*(3), 217–242. doi:10.1080/1554477X.2010.496641

NilepC. (2006). "Code Switching" in sociocultural linguistics. *Colorado Research in Linguistics*. doi:10.25810/hnq4-jv62

Oberfield, Z. W. (2016). Why are some agencies perceived as more committed to diversity than others? An analysis of public-sector diversity climates. *Public Management Review*, *18*(5), 763–790. doi:10.1080/14719037.2015.1045017

Opie, T. R., & Phillips, K. W. (2015). Hair penalties: The negative influence of Afrocentric hair on ratings of Black women's dominance and professionalism. *Frontiers in Psychology*, *6*, 1311. doi:10.3389/fpsyg.2015.01311 PMID:26379612

Reynolds-Dobbs, W., Thomas, K. M., & Harrison, M. S. (2008). From mammy to superwoman: Images that hinder Black women's career development. *Journal of Career Development*, *35*(2), 129–150. doi:10.1177/0894845308325645

Riccucci, N. M. (2009). The pursuit of social equity in the federal government: A road less traveled? *Public Administration Review*, *69*(3), 373–382. doi:10.1111/j.1540-6210.2009.01984.x

Roberts, L. M. (2005). Changing faces: Professional image construction in diverse organizational settings. *Academy of Management Review*, *30*(4), 685–711. doi:10.5465/amr.2005.18378873

Rosette, A. S., & Dumas, T. L. (2007). The hair dilemma: Conform to mainstream expectations or emphasize racial identity makeup, identity performance & discrimination. *Duke Journal of Gender Law & Policy*, *14*(1), 407–422.

Rosette, A. S., Koval, C. Z., Ma, A., & Livingston, R. (2016). Race matters for women leaders: Intersectional effects on agentic deficiencies and penalties. *The Leadership Quarterly*, *27*(3), 429–445. doi:10.1016/j.leaqua.2016.01.008

Saldaña, J. (2013). *The coding manual for qualitative researchers* (2nd ed.). SAGE.

Santiago, R., Nwokoma, N., & Crentsil, J. (2021). Investigating the implications of code-switching and assimilating at work for African American professionals. *Journal of Business Diversity*, *21*(4), 72–81.

Sini, R. (2016, May 15). Wear a weave at work—Your afro hair is unprofessional. *BBC News*. https://www.bbc.com/news/uk-36279845

Smith, A. E., Hassan, S., Hatmaker, D. M., DeHart-Davis, L., & Humphrey, N. (2021). Gender, race, and experiences of workplace incivility in public organizations. *Review of Public Personnel Administration*, *41*(4), 674–699. doi:10.1177/0734371X20927760

Soni, V. (2000). A Twenty-first-century reception for diversity in the public sector: A case study. *Public Administration Review*, *60*(5), 395–408. doi:10.1111/0033-3352.00103

Sue, D. W., & Spanierman, L. (2020). *Microaggressions in everyday life*. John Wiley & Sons.

van den Bosch, R., & Taris, T. W. (2014). Authenticity at work: Development and validation of an individual authenticity measure at work. *Journal of Happiness Studies*, *15*(1), 1–18. doi:10.100710902-013-9413-3

Welbourne, J., Gangadharan, A., & Sariol, A. (2014). Ethnicity and cultural values as predictors of the occurrence and impact of experienced workplace incivility. *Journal of Occupational Health Psychology*, *20*(2), 205–217. Advance online publication. doi:10.1037/a0038277 PMID:25365631

Wingfield, A. H. (2015, October 14). Being Black—but not too Black—in the workplace. *The Atlantic*. https://www.theatlantic.com/business/archive/2015/10/being-black-work/409990/

Yoshino, K. (2001). Covering. *The Yale Law Journal*, *111*(4), 769–940. doi:10.2307/797566

Chapter 10
The Aesthetics of Natural Black Hairstyles

Carolyn Allen
University of the Virgin Islands, US Virgin Islands

ABSTRACT

The chapter considers the three African aesthetic principles of polyrhythm, curvilinearity, and repetition and applies the aesthetic principles to natural Black hairstyles. Aesthetics are associated with the conception of beauty or what is considered beautiful. Afros, locs, twists, braids, and Bantu knots are natural hairstyles considered beautiful in the African aesthetic. However, natural Black hairstyle have been disparaged in the American workplace. Discrimination and bias against natural Black hairstyles will be reviewed. The purpose of the chapter is to discuss the links between African aesthetics and natural Black hairstyles. Further, the chapter explores bias against natural Black hairstyles and the rejection of African aesthetics by European standards.

INTRODUCTION TO BLACK WOMEN'S NATURAL HAIRSTYLES AND AESTHETICS

In a 2014 study of 200 African American women living in a metropolitan midwestern city in the United States, 40% of the research respondents report having natural hairstyles (Gathers & Mahan, 2014). Afros, locs, twists, braids, and Bantu knots are natural hairstyles traditionally dawned by Black women. Previously, it has been asserted that less than 30% of African American women choose natural hairstyles (Callender, McMichael & Cohen, 2004). Natural hairstyles seem to be growing in popularity in the 2000's and the hairstyles are part of an African aesthetic.

DOI: 10.4018/978-1-6684-8790-7.ch010

Aesthetics are associated with the conception of beauty or what is considered beautiful. Furniss (2015) argues that what is considered beautiful is culturally defined. Importantly, notions of beauty are more a representation of learned cultural values rather than a matter of personal taste. The European aesthetic of beauty has been linked to qualities such as linearity, precision, balance, and lifelessness (Sibley, 2007). Conversely, the African aesthetic of beauty is different and has been associated with qualities such as polyrhythm, curvilinearity, repetition, and polycentrism (Thompson, 1984). While both the European and African aesthetic principles are legitimate and internally consistent, they produce different expressions for beauty.

Art, music, dance, and literature can all express a cultural aesthetic. Leonardo da Vinci's painting *Mona Lisa*, Ludwig van Beethoven's orchestral work *the Fifth Symphony*, Mikhail Baryshnikov's performance in the *Nutcracker* ballet and Ernest Hemingway's novel *The Sun Also Rises* can be analyzed for their linearity, precision, and balance. These famous works are judged to be beautiful based on the European aesthetic and deservingly so. In contrast, Aaron Douglas' painting *Into Bondage*, Miles Davis's musical arrangement *So What*, Judith Jamison's dance performance in Alvin Ailey's *Revelations* and Toni Morrison's novel *Beloved* can be analyzed for their polyrhythm, curvilinearity, repetition, and polycentrism. These eminent works are judged to be the superlative examples of the African aesthetic of beauty and rightly so. The judgement of aesthetic value is best accomplished by using the history and culture of the people studied (Garber, 1995). Failing to use cultural orientation in the analysis of aesthetics can lead to misunderstanding and stigmatization of the group studied (Dawson, Karl, Peluchette, 2019).

Just as art, music, dance, and literature can express a cultural aesthetic, hairstyles also can express a cultural aesthetic. Afros, locs, twists, braids, Bantu knots, short naturals and other styles are not only a part of a historical cultural tradition for Black people, but the hairstyles also express African aesthetic principles. The chapter defines the African aesthetic principles of polyrhythm, curvilinearity and repetition. The African aesthetic principles are extended to an understanding of the beauty in Black natural hairstyles. Further, discrimination and bias against Black natural hairstyles will be considered. Discussion is offered which links the bias against Black natural hairstyles to the rejection of African aesthetics by European standards. Concepts from the disciplines of linguistics, Afrocentricity and the Arts are included in the discussion to evoke images for the reader.

DEEP STRUCTURE AND SURFACE STRUCTURE

Noam Chomsky (2009) forwarded the development of transformational generative grammar theory which incorporates notions of deep structure and surface structure.

Deep structure refers to concepts, thoughts, and ideas. Surface structure is represented by words and language. Deep structure exists in the long consciousness of humans while surface structure is expressed by the contemporary words and the language of a people. Concepts, thoughts, and ideas are abstract whereas words and language provide concrete representations of the abstract. In other words, deep structure concepts, thoughts and ideas are translated to surface structure words and language. Deep structure concepts, thoughts and ideas can exist across long time spans. Surface structure words and language are more ephemeral.

The concepts of deep structure and surface structure amply apply to the beauty found in Black natural hairstyles. Polyrhythm, curvilinearity and repetition are deep structure while the actual hairstyles, (e.g., locs, twists, braids, and Bantu knots) are surface structure. Locs, twists, braids, and Bantu knots visually evoke polyrhythms. The hairstyles counter a straight-line progression that represents beauty and instead, bring to mind curves, bends and arcs found in nature's bounty. Patterns are repeated in the hair curls and twists and the repetition adds intensity.

The notion of deep structure and surface structure have been applied in several disciplines such as linguistics, psycholinguistics, and Afrocentrism. An understanding of how deep structure and surface structure are used in other disciplines is worthwhile to review so the reader may further conceive of how the concepts can be applied to Black natural hairstyles.

Afrocentric theorist Melefe K. Asante (2006) applies deep structure and surface structure to an understanding of Ebonics. Previously, Ebonics was understood to be the nonstandard English spoken by African Americans (Kaplan,1969). Use of nonstandard English was thought to be a product of low economic status and was seen in groups who do not have societal power such as African Americans and Mexican Americans. Asante applied surface structure and deep structure to the analysis of Ebonics and reached a different conclusion. Ebonics uses the surface structure of English words and language laid upon the deep structure of African languages grammatical rules (Asante, 2006).

Asante asserts that during the African enslavement period, multiple African ethnic groups needed to communicate, however, they did not share a common language. Yoruba, Asante, Ibo, and Hausa learned to use English words while retaining the syntax and grammar of African languages. For example, many African languages are tonal, whereby, the meaning of the word can be changed based on the tone spoken. Asante contends the deep structure tonal quality of language is present in Ebonics. If an Ebonics speaker wanted to communicate the sentence, "I saw a very long train.", the speaker might say, "I saw a loong train". The emphasis on the long vowel sound changes the meaning of the word "long" to connote "very long". In this way, English words are transcribed onto African grammar. Asante argues this is deep structure African language rules on surface structure English words.

Blackshire-Belay (1996) joins Asante's argument and extends the discussion of deep structure features of language to an understanding of Creole and Pidgin languages in the Caribbean and African diaspora. Blackshire-Belay proposes there is a family tree of Ebonics languages.

Deep structure and surface structure are relevant to the disciplines of linguistics and psycholinguists because they connect languages across time and regions. Similarly, deep structure and surface structure can assist in an understanding of Black natural hairstyles connection to African aesthetic principles. People across the African diaspora who reside in Africa, Eurasia, the Americas, or the Caribbean islands appreciate the beauty of natural Black hairstyles. Natural Black hairstyles have endured in past centuries and in the new millennium.

Akin to Asante's discussion African grammatical rules expressed as the deep structure grammar of Ebonics, Thompson (1984) describes how continental African art aesthetics is expressed in the artistic creations of contemporary Black people in the United States and the Caribbean. For example, the Mande people of western African traditionally made rhythmized textiles whose patterns have been reproduced by Black Caribbean and Black American communities. Barbadian aprons and African American bed quilts display the same rhythmized patterns as Mande textiles. The Mande textiles are narrow strips of cloth sewn together so the accent of one strip of cloth does not exactly repeat in the adjacent strip of cloth. Instead, the accent skips one strip and is referred to in other strips. The accents, colors and patterns are visually vibrant and often intentionally clash according to Thompson. The juxtaposition of accents, colors and patterns adds visual interest. The suspended, off-beat pattern produced is highly regarded in the African aesthetic.

Suspended patterning also is found in Barbadian articles of clothing and African American bed quilts. In both Barbadian aprons and African American bed quilts, strips of cloth are sewn together to create a polyrhythmic textile that has the suspended patterning feature. The stitching of pieces of cloth to create a textile could be viewed as a matter of necessity for economically oppressed communities. However, such an interpretation would fail to recognize that the suspended patterning feature represents the deep structure African polyrhythm aesthetic. Mande textiles, Barbadian aprons and African American bed quilts are the surface structure expressions of a deep structure African aesthetic that crossed generations and regions. Just as deep structure and surface structure can be used to analyze language and the arts, deep structure and surface structure can be used to understand the aesthetics of Black women's hairstyles in terms of polyrhythm, curvilinearity and repetition.

POLYRHYTHM IN THE AFRICAN AESTHETIC

As the term implies, polyrhythm is the simultaneous presence of multiple rhythms (Møller, Stupacher, Celma-Miralles, & Vuust, 2021). Polyrhythms have two or more isochronous beats. Polyrhythms are present in African visual arts such as paintings, performing arts such as dance, African diaspora music such as jazz, blues, reggae, juju, and highlife, and in architecture (Thompson, 1984).

In polyrhythm, the absence of accent or beat is as important as the beat or accent. The absence, disruption or suspension of a pattern brings excitement and expectation. In contemporary Hip Hop music, the "break" in the rhythm causes anticipation of the next beat and Hip-Hop DJs use the "break" to heighten the enthusiasm of the audience. The break or suspended patterning rhythm is found in African diaspora music, textiles, and art.

Jazz music is heavily influenced by polyrhythms and often uses a three against two (3:2) polyrhythm (Jones, 2006). The jazz standard *Afro Blue* is noted for its use of polyrhythms. Polyrhythms can be heard in musical pieces from the African diaspora, but they also can be seen in performing arts of dance and visual art of sculpture. The performance of *Griot New York* in the 1990's displayed the use of polyrhythms in dance, music, and sculpture (Dudar & Atkin, 1992). Three noted Black artists collaborated to create the *Griot New York* performance. Garth Fagan choreographed the piece while Wynton Marsalis wrote the music and Martin Puryear sculpted the backdrop. Fagan described the polyrhythmic movements of the dancers as using their whole bodies (i.e., legs, arms, torsos, hips, heads) while simultaneously moving to different rhythms. Marsalis' musical compositions used the polyrhythmic structure of jazz while Puryear's sculptures had multiple visual angles and curves to engage the eyes and imaginations of the audience. The diaspora African art aesthetic has a great appreciation for polyrhythms, and this extends to natural Black hairstyles.

Polyrhythm in Natural Black Hairstyles

Natural Black hairstyles are defined as those that are not chemically treated or straightened (Jones, 2020; Gathers & Mahan, 2014; Callender, McMichael & Cohen, 2004). Natural hairstyles such as Afros, locs, twists, and braids all have a sense of polyrhythm. Without a doubt, the natural hairstyles display multiple beats within one coiffure. Locs can be of different thicknesses and length in the same hairdo. Similarly, Afros and twists may appear to be puffier or more expansive in one portion of the hairdo than another. For example, an Afro may be fuller on the top and sides, but flatter in the rear. Braids may be sculpted in different directions in a single hairstyle or have multiple patterns presented in the same braided style. Bantu knots can be different sizes within the same hairstyle. The variations within the Afro, locs, twists and braids express the polyrhythmic principle. Just as the polyrhythm of Jazz brings a beautiful sound to the ear, the polyrhythm of locs presents a beautiful sight to an eye that appreciates the African aesthetic.

Natural Black hairstyles such as locs, twists, braids, and Bantu knots are a surface structure representation of the deep structure beauty found in having polyrhythms. One does not see a flat surface when one gazes at a natural Black hairstyle. Instead, one sees multiple heights, breaks, and curves which repeat in inexact or suspended patterns.

CURVILINEARITY IN THE AFRICAN AESTHETIC

Curvilinearity and repetition are complimentary elements in the African aesthetic. As the name implies, curvilinearity regards the form and shape of curves, circles, and the round (Asante & Welsh-Asante, 1990). Curvilinearity is not just a visual representation of shape, instead curvilinearity also occurs in music and literature where the beat or narrative does not follow a straight line.

Curvilinearity is present in African arts such as paintings, dance, and architecture. Indeed, curvilinearity is a prominent feature of African dance. "The motions are circular, and patterns may pass through 45 degree, 90 degree, or 180 degrees. The movements of the dance are rounded even when directed or accented" (Welsh-Asante, 2002, p. 213). Body parts, such as the knees, elbows, and waist are often bent in African dance. Thompson (1984) notes the bent knee position of classical Kongo sculptures. The bent body positions in dance and sculpture express curvilinearity. In dance, for example, bent body positions contrast with the straight lines of the classical European dance form, ballet. Thompson suggests the bent knee symbolizes vitality. In the African aesthetic, bends and curves illustrate the beauty aesthetic whereas straight lines are valued in the European aesthetic.

Curvilinearity is also expressed in African diaspora music and literature. Lawrence (2011) analyzes the fictional writing of Octavia Butler and Tananarive Due in their *Parable series* and *African Immortals series*, respectively, and finds curvilinear plots. The author also considers curvilinearity regarding the relationships between characters. Lawrence reviews the history and remembrances of characters as expressions of curvilinear interpersonal relationships. Curvilinearity can be represented visually or symbolically in long curving relationships over time.

Curvilinearity in Natural Black Hairstyles

Natural Black hairstyles can symbolically capture curvilinear human relationships. Black people can be symbolically connected to the past or communities via hairstyles. Byrd and Tharps (2014) suggest in the 1400's, natural hairstyles were not only celebrated in Africa, but they also gave clues about identity. Hairstyles could visually communicate a person's marital status, health, wealth, age, religion, ethnic group and more. Family lineage and geographic origins could be determined by hairstyle. "The Kuramo people of Nigeria, for example, were recognized by their unique coiffure – a shaved head with a single tuft of hair left on top" (Byrd & Tharps, 2014, Black Hair in Bondage, para. 2).

Curvilinearity represents the woven nature of the Africans' connection to the past and ancestors (Lawrence, 2011). Welsh-Asante (2002) refers to Epic Memory as the connective thread between the distant collective memories inherited from ancestors and current expressions of those memories in behaviors. For example, the previously mentioned African tradition of being able to determine a person's geographic origins based on the person's hairstyle continues today. Currently, Detroit, Michigan is sometimes referred to as the "Hair Capitol of the Black World" and the "over the top" hair styling is distinctively recognizable as a Detroit style. On a surface structure level, Detroit hairstyles may be represented by braids, shaved head, or cornrows; however, the deep structure significance is the curvilinear link to past heritage. The presence of curvilinearity is appreciated by persons with African aesthetic sensibilities.

REPETITION IN THE AFRICAN AESTHETIC

Repetition, in the African aesthetic, is not the exact repeating of a word or a phrase for effect or emphasis. Instead, repetition is the cycling of patterns where slight variations can occur within the pattern (Welsh-Asante, 2002). The repeating of a pattern with varied emphasis builds intensity. Call and response in music or spiritual prayer is an example of repetition. In music, the horn calls out a phrase and the drum beat responds. The pattern of call and response is repeated, and the intensity builds in the music.

Repetition is a dominant feature of African diaspora music. Repetition, where phrases are inexactly repeated to build intensity, occurs in Jazz, Gospel, Soca, Reggae, Juju, Afropop and throughout African diaspora music. Ferreira (2007) describes Candombe drumming as displaying repetition that matches the African aesthetic.

Because it is with the intensification of the movements generated by the repetition of patterns that a polarized quality emerges in the spacial axis, according to the pattern and the drum type: vertical in the small drum, horizontal in the big drum, diagonal in the medium drum in repicado pattern or alternating among the vertical, the diagonal and the horizontal axis when "talking" (Ferreira, 2007, p. 6).

Repetition begets excitement in the African aesthetic and occurs in dance. "Repetition is a distinct characteristic of the African aesthetic. It is not the refrain or chorus but the intensifying of one movement or one sequence or the entire dance until spiritual satisfaction has been reached, ecstasy, euphoria, and exhaustion" (Welsh Asante, 2002, p. 214). In the African aesthetic, repetition is evocative of call and response, communication, or dialogue. Therefore, repetition invites a communal response. Collectivism, interdependence, and group orientation are aspects of an African worldview (Jackson & Sears, 1992).

Repetition in Natural Black Hairstyles

The use of repetition is an organic way to engage a community oriented toward collectivism, groupism and interdependence. The creation of Natural Black hairstyles is often a collaboration between community members. Who twisted your locs? Who braided your hair? Are questions frequently posed by Black women to Black women who wear natural Black hairstyles. The creation of the hairstyle has a sense of collectivism. Moreover, the individual braid and twist of the hair are in a repeated pattern yet, the repetition is not precise. Instead, the loc, twist, or braid pattern repeats in a way that makes the eyes move and dance as one's gaze follows the pattern. The presence of repetition is exciting to persons who appreciate the African aesthetic.

BIAS AGAINST NATURAL BLACK HAIRSTYLES AND THE CONNECTION TO AFRICAN AESTHETICS

Afros, locs, twists, and braids are the surface structure expression of deep structure African polyrhythm aesthetic. Although natural Black hairstyles express the deep structure African aesthetic, the Black community is not a monolith in accepting natural hairstyles as beautiful or sexy. Johnson, Godsil, MacFarlane, Tropp, and Goff (2020) found differences among Black women in their rating of natural hairstyles as beautiful. The "Good Hair" Study conducted in 2016 examined implicit bias regarding Black hairstyles. Study participants viewed both natural Black hairstyles and chemically treated coiffures. Over 4,100 women and men participated in the national online study conducted in the United States and there was nearly equal representation for

Black male, Black female, White male, and White female participants. Johnson, et al. (2020) report that study participants identified as millennial naturalistas had more positive attitudes toward natural Black hairstyles (Afro, dreads, twist-out braids) than all other groups. Naturalistas are members of online communities who support natural hairstyles and provide each other advice on products and transitioning from chemically treated hair to natural hair.

Differences were found between Black women who were members of the natural hair community and those who were not (Johnson, et al., 2020). The former group had significantly more positive attitudes toward natural hair than the latter. White women were found to be more likely to rate natural hairstyles as less beautiful, less sexy, and less professional than smooth (chemically treated) hairstyles including straight, long curls, short curls, and pixie haircuts.

While polyrhythm is a facet of the deep structure African aesthetic, the expression of the aesthetic in hairstyling faces consternation from adherents of European aesthetic principles. Lopez (2009) argues that even though aesthetic principles are culturally bound, cultures are dynamic and changing. Black women's hairstyles have changed over time in response to societal pressures. Byrd and Tharps (2014) examine the many transitions in African American women's hairstyles based on encounters with bias and discrimination. According to Dawson, Karl, Peluchette, Combs, Milosevic, and Bilimoria (2019) most Black women alter their hair texture from natural to smooth and straight to avoid bias, harassment, and discrimination. The decision to alter natural curls, curves and bends in Black hair is strategically chosen by Black women to avoid experiencing bias and discrimination. Johnson, et al. (2020) conclude that one in five Black women reported social pressure to wear straight hairstyles in the workplace.

A legal case that typifies the bias and discrimination women who wear natural Black hair styles encounter is *Rogers versus American Airlines, Inc. (1981).* Renee Rogers, an 11-year employee with American Airlines began braiding or cornrowing her hair. After working for a period in a position with direct customer service, Ms. Rogers was fired from her position for noncompliance with American Airlines grooming and appearance policies which prohibited wearing braided hairstyles. Ms. Rogers sought damages against American Airlines for having a discriminatory policy. The U.S. District Court for the Southern District of New York found in favor of American Airlines and concluded that the grooming and appearance policy was not discriminatory because it applied to all employees. The court did not acknowledge braided hairstyles are a unique part of the African aesthetic. Instead, the court supported the notion that a bun or ponytail hairstyle is an appropriate parameter for the workplace grooming and appearance policy, while braids and locs are not. A signal was sent that natural Black hairstyles are not professional, conservative, or acceptable and an African aesthetic was rejected.

Black women face a series of binary choices and descriptors regarding hairstyles, (e.g., natural/altered, nappy/straight, wooly/smooth, revolutionary/conformist, manageable/unmanageable, and good/bad). The binary signifiers are counter to the principle of polyrhythm, yet they are part of the bias Black women contend with regarding hairstyles in everyday life and the workplace. Binary thinking has been both heralded and criticized as part of European thinking (Elbow, 2000). For African aesthetic expression in the United States, binaries have been oppressive.

Bias Against Natural Black Hairstyles and Binary Thinking

From Socrates to Plato, Boethius to Jung, binary thinking is an aspect of a long philosophical tradition in Western societies (Elbow, 2000). Binary thinking allows for categorizing terms into opposites (e.g., day/night, sun/moon, reason/passion, male/female). Since the enslavement period, binary thinking has been applied to Black hair (Lester, 2000). Black hair has been categorized as "good" or "bad" based on how closely the hair resembles European hair.

In the United States, "good hair" is considered to be hair that is wavy or straight in texture, soft to the touch, has the ability to grow long, and requires minimal intervention by way of treatments or products to be considered beautiful (Johnson, et al., 2020).

The favorable or "good" descriptors for hair are associated with Caucasian and Asian hair types. Conversely, African hair is categorized as "bad". Historically, African hair has been described as short, matted, kinky, nappy, coarse, brittle, and wooly (Lester, 2000, p 204). The terms used for African hair are meant to connote "bad" versus their opposite of "good" European hair.

Bias Against Natural Black Hairstyles and the Historical Context

Lester (2000) argues that good hair/bad hair is an outgrowth of the enslavement period during which forced miscegenation produced biracial offspring who were lighter in skin tone and had straighter hair than other enslaved Africans. Although the biracial children were still enslaved, under the chattel slavery system the White enslavers' offspring received privileges. Over time, a caste system was created where lighter skin tone and straighter hair is valued, and darker skin tone and coiled hair is devalued.

Therefore, the notion of upper mobility based on European phenotype is steeped in a long history. For example, an enslaved woman, Jackey Wright, used her long, straight, black hair as evidence she was an American Indian and therefore should not be held in bondage as an African woman (Donahoo & Smith, 2019). The Virginia Supreme Court of 1806 ruled in her favor and freed Ms. Wright and her children. The caste system continues to contemporary times where Black women wearing straight hairstyles is viewed as a path toward upward mobility (Donahoo & Smith, 2019).

Thompson (2009) historically places the first notions of a connection between African American women gaining greater economic opportunities if they wore straight hairstyles in the early 1900's as an idea promoted by Madam C.J. Walker. Byrd and Tharps (2014) identify C.J. Walker as the first self-made female American millionaire who amassed her fortune based on the introduction of the "shampoo-press-and-curl" method of straightening hair for African American women. African American women wearing their hair straight was considered "good" and wearing hair naturally was considered "bad".

Bias Against Natural Black Hairstyles and Compromises to Health

African American women feel so persecuted about wearing natural hairstyles that many of them are willing to compromise hair health to achieve a straight or smooth hairdo (Gathers & Mahan, 2014). For example, many Black women choose hair straightening techniques that lead to hair loss. Black women commonly experience alopecia based on use of chemical hair straightening products, thermal hair straightening methods, hair braiding for the wearing of wigs and weaves (Callender, McMichael, & Cohen, 2004).

The negative impacts of straightening natural Black hair are not limited to alopecia. Black women with thermally straightened hair report avoiding exercise out of fear that perspiration will lead to loss of the straight hairstyle (Gathers & Mahan, 2014). This is especially problematic in that weight management is a primary health concern for Black women who avoid exercise.

The good hair/bad hair binary has harmed, and continues to harm, Black youth. Woolford, Woolford-Hunt, Sami, Blake, and Williams (2016) found that Black adolescent girls avoided exercise because the perspiration made their hairstyle become nappy or puffy. The study participants view nappy or puffy hair negatively and prefer straight hair. The continued acceptance of the good hair/bad hair binary has negative impact on health outcomes. Exercise hesitancy likely contributes to prevalence of obesity for African American adolescents (Woolford, et al., 2016). There is no medical reason to avoid the natural coiling of hair. However, there are medical reasons to engage in exercise that produces perspiration.

Further, there is no medical connection between the morphology of hair (straight or coiled) and the health of hair. Callender, McMichael, Cohen (2004) describe no biochemical differences between Caucasian, Black and Asian hair types. However, there is a difference in the shape of the hair when examined under cross-section. Black hair, Caucasian hair and Asian hair is found to be elliptical, oval, and round respectively.

Bias Against Natural Black Hairstyles and Psychological Stress

The nappy/straight binary does psychological harm to the Black community. Rudman and McLean (2015) conducted a study using the aesthetic Implicit Association Test (IAT) and discovered that Blacks prefer chemically straightened hair on Black women over natural hair. The same group rates skin whitening and hair relaxing products as useful and important for Black women's beauty. Similar to how the Black community is challenged by weight management/exercise resistance based on maintaining a straight hairstyle, chemically straightened hair and chemically whitened skin have unhealthy impacts (Hunter, 2011). In all of these instances, psychological and physical health is compromised in support of a European aesthetic.

Binary thinking not only stands in contrast to the deep structure polyrhythm concept, but it can also lead to unhealthy choices. Binary thinking relates to the European aesthetic principle of balance. As suggested earlier, European aesthetic principles are internally consistent. Ascribing beauty to that which is linear, precise, and balanced is consistent with European standards. However, the aesthetic is not a characteristic of the deep structure African cannon of aesthetics. Consequentially, ascribing European aesthetic principles to Black women's natural hairstyles imparts undo psychological stress. "There is no denying that Black hair can feel like a burden rather than a blessing. Many women harbor repressed frustrations at the time, energy, and effort Black hair requires to get it into a style society deems acceptable" (Byrd &Tharps, 2014, All Grown Up, para. 4).

Bias Against Natural Black Hairstyles and the Workplace

Women who wear natural Black hairstyles have encountered bias and hostility in the workplace (Jones, 2020). Afros, locs, and braids have been described as unprofessional by some employers and banned by other employers. In 1976, the case of *Jenkins v. Blue Cross Mut. Hospital Ins., Inc.* appeared before the court. Ms. Jenkins, a three-year employee of Blue Cross Insurance, was denied a promotion by her supervisor. According to Ms. Jenkins, the supervisor asserted that her Afro hairstyle could not represent Blue Cross. The court found that Ms. Jenkins had experienced racial and sexual discrimination (Donahoo & Smith, 2019). Although the court ruled in Ms. Jenkins favor, that by no means ended the discriminatory behavior toward Black women in the workplace who have natural hairstyles. Jones suggests the standards for workplace professionalism are set by White men and the standards do not include natural Black hairstyles. Twice as many Black women compared to White women feel pressured in the workplace to straighten their hair (Johnson, et al., 2020). Based on findings from an online study, "… employment candidates with Afrocentric hairstyles were rated as less professional and less likely to succeed in Corporate America than employment candidates with Eurocentric hairstyles" (Opie & Phillips, 2015, p.5).

Multiple studies have indicated employer or societal preference for Black women wearing straightened hairstyles (Rudman & McLean, 2015; Dawson, Karl, & Peluchette, 2019; Opie & Phillips, 2015). Finding straight hairstyles visually appealing is consistent with the European aesthetic for linearity, precision, and balance. Curvilinearity and repeated patterns in hairstyles runs contrary to the European aesthetic. Dawson, Karl and Peluchette (2019) report "Afrocentric hairstyles are often labeled unprofessional, unkempt, messy, or unacceptable. These labels create an appearance stigma and determine how Afrocentric hairstyles are viewed by society in general" (p. 390).

Natural Black hairstyles that reflect a reverence for polyrhythm, curvilinearity, and repetition are so poorly regarded by the White working establishment that a legislative strategy to challenge workplace discrimination based on natural Black hairstyles was established. The Creating a Respectful and Open Workplace for Natural hair (CROWN) Act was introduced to state law makers (Jones, 2020). As of the time of this writing, 20 states have passed the CROWN Act. Although there is a degree of progress in the acceptance of Natural Black hairstyles as beautiful, professional, and appropriate, there is still work to be done in this area.

CONCLUSION TO BLACK WOMEN'S NATURAL HAIRSTYLES AND AESTHETICS

Polyrhythm, curvilinearity and repetition are three African aesthetic principles which apply to natural Black hairstyles. The concept of beauty or what is considered beautiful is relevant in cultures across time and across regions. Afros, locs, twists, braids, and Bantu knots are natural hairstyles considered beautiful in the African aesthetic across time and across regions. However, natural Black hairstyles have been disparaged in the American workplace. Discrimination and bias against natural Black hairstyles reflect bias against African aesthetic principles and preference for European aesthetics as the standard bearer of beauty.

Polyrhythm, curvilinearity, and repetition represent a reverence for multiplicity of patterns, curves, bends, and the kind of communalism found in call and response. Natural Black hairstyles such as Afros, locs, twists, braids, and Bantu knots that curve, twist, bend, and have multiple inexact repeated patterns in the same coiffure provide a visual representation of deep structure African aesthetics. Linearity, precision, balance, and symmetry exemplify the European beauty aesthetic. Women's hairstyles have demonstrated the European aesthetic via short bobs, updos, ponytails, buns, and long tresses.

The African and European aesthetic principles are meaningful articulations of cultural worldviews. Both are worthy. Problems arise when the European aesthetic principles supersede African aesthetic principles. Women of color have felt pressure to conform to European aesthetic principles and style their hair into straight, balanced, measured, and proportional hairdos.

Historically, African descended women have used chemical and thermal treatments to replicate straight, smooth, and measured hairstyles. The alteration of Black hair not only does harm to health (e.g., alopecia and exercise resistance) but the coerced alteration of hair also does psychological harm. Women of color have felt burdened with the economic cost of maintaining straight hair, chided by the workplace expectation of maintaining smooth hair, and saddled with a love/hate relationship to hair. When Black women embrace natural Black hairstyles, deep structure African aesthetics are affirmed, some psychological burdens are lifted and options for healthy routine exercise are increased. In the 21st century, the acceptance of natural Black hairstyles will lead to more favorable outcomes for women of color.

REFERENCES

Asante, M. K. (2006). *The Afrocentric idea*. Temple University Press.

Asante, M. K., & Welsh-Asante, K. (1990). Commonalities in African dance: An aesthetic foundation. In *African culture: The rhythms of unity* (pp. 71–82). Africa World Press.

Blackshire-Belay, C. A. (1996). The location of ebonics within the framework of the Africological Paradigm. *Journal of Black Studies*, *27*(1), 5–23. doi:10.1177/002193479602700101

Byrd, A. D., & Tharps, L. L. (2014). *Hair story untangling the roots of black hair in America*. St. Martin's Griffin.

Callender, V. D., McMichael, A. J., & Cohen, G. F. (2004). Medical and surgical therapies for alopecias in black women. *Dermatologic Therapy*, *17*(2), 164–176. doi:10.1111/j.1396-0296.2004.04017.x PMID:15113284

Chomsky, N., & McGilvray, J. A. (2009). Deep and surface structure. In *Cartesian linguistics: A chapter in the history of Rationalist thought* (pp. 78–92). Cambridge University Press. doi:10.1017/CBO9780511803116.006

Dawson, G. A., Karl, K. A., & Peluchette, J. V. (2019). Hair matters: Toward understanding natural black hair bias in the workplace. *Journal of Leadership & Organizational Studies*, *26*(3), 389–401. doi:10.1177/1548051819848998

Donahoo, S., & Smith, A. D. (2019). Controlling the crown: Legal efforts to professionalize black hair. *Race and Justice*, *12*(1), 182–203. doi:10.1177/2153368719888264

Dudar, H., & Atkin, J. (1992). 'Griot New York' sets the city's rhythm to dance. *Smithsonian*, *23*(6), 102.

Elbow, P. (2000). *Everyone can write: Essays toward a hopeful theory of writing and teaching writing*. Oxford University Press.

Ferreira, L. (2007). An Afrocentric approach to musical performance in the Black south atlantic: The Candombe drumming in Uruguay. *Revista Transcultural de Música/Transcultural Music Review,*11, 1-15.

Furniss, G. J. (2015). Viewing sub-saharan African art with western eyes: A question of aesthetics in the context of another culture and time. *Art Education*, *68*(6), 28–35. doi:10.1080/00043125.2015.11519345

Garber, E. (1995). Teaching art in the context of culture: A study in the Borderlands. *Studies in Art Education*, *36*(4), 218–232. doi:10.2307/1320936

Gathers, R. C., & Mahan, M. G. (2014). African American women, hair care, and health barriers. *The Journal of Clinical and Aesthetic Dermatology*, *7*(9), 26–29. PMID:25276273

Hunter, M. L. (2011). Buying racial capital: Skin-bleaching and cosmetic surgery in a globalized world. *The Journal of Pan African Studies*, *4*(4), 142–164.

Jackson, A. P., & Sears, S. J. (1992). Implications of an africentric worldview in reducing stress for African American women. *Journal of Counseling and Development*, *71*(2), 184–190. doi:10.1002/j.1556-6676.1992.tb02196.x

Johnson, A. M., Godsil, R. D., MacFarlane, J., Tropp, L. R., & Goff, P. A. (2020, June 17). *The "good hair" study*. Perception Institute. http://www.goodhairstudy.com/

Jones, R. (2006). Jazz Polyrhythms. *Jazz Education Journal*, *38*(6), 49–51.

Jones, R. (2020). What the hair: Employment discrimination against black people based on hairstyles. *Harvard Blackletter Law Journal*, *36*, 27–45.

Kaplan, R. B. (1969). On a note of protest (in a minor key): Bidialectism vs. Bidialectism. *College English*, *30*(5), 386–389. doi:10.2307/374343

Lawrence, T. (2011). *An Africentric reading protocol: The speculative fiction of Octavia Butler and Tananarive Due* [Dissertation, Wayne State University].

Lester, N. A. (2000). Nappy edges and goldy locks: African-American daughters and the politics of hair. *The Lion and the Unicorn*, *24*(2), 201–224. doi:10.1353/uni.2000.0018

López, V. (2009). The hyphen goes where? Four stories of the dual-culture experience in the art classroom. *Art Education*, *62*(5), 19–24. doi:10.1080/00043125.2009.11519033

Møller, C., Stupacher, J., Celma-Miralles, A., & Vuust, P. (2021). Beat perception in polyrhythms: Time is structured in binary units. *PLoS One*, *16*(8), 1–24. doi:10.1371/journal.pone.0252174 PMID:34415911

Opie, T. R., & Phillips, K. W. (2015). Hair penalties: The negative influence of Afrocentric hair on ratings of black women's dominance and professionalism. *Frontiers in Psychology*, *6*, 1–16. doi:10.3389/fpsyg.2015.01311 PMID:26379612

Rogers v. American Airlines, Inc., 527 F. Supp. 229 (S.D.N.Y. 1981).

Rudman, L. A., & McLean, M. C. (2015). The role of appearance stigma in implicit racial ingroup bias. *Group Processes & Intergroup Relations*, *19*(3), 374–393. doi:10.1177/1368430215583152

Sibley, F. N., Benson, J. H., Redfern, B., & Cox, J. R. (2007). *Approach to aesthetics: Collected papers on philosophical aesthetics*. Oxford University Press.

Thompson, C. (2009). Black women, beauty, and hair as a matter of *being*. *Women's Studies*, *38*(8), 831–856. doi:10.1080/00497870903238463

Thompson, R. F. (1984). *Flash of the spirit: African and Afro-American art and philosophy*. Random House.

Welsh-Asante, K. (2002). The Zimbabwean dance aesthetic: Senses, canons and characteristics. In *African dance: An artistic, historical, and philosophical inquiry* (pp. 203–220). Africa World Press.

Woolford, S. J., Woolford-Hunt, C. J., Sami, A., Blake, N., & Williams, D. R. (2016). No sweat: African American adolescent girls' opinions of hairstyle choices and physical activity. *BMC Obesity*, *3*(1), 1–8. doi:10.118640608-016-0111-7 PMID:27386139

Chapter 11
"Professionalism" and the Contentious Relationship With Black Hair:
Do You Have the Right Look?

Schnequa Nicole Diggs
North Carolina Central University, USA

Christine Heath Diggs
Independent Researcher, USA

ABSTRACT

This chapter deconstructs assumptions and standards of Black hairstyles in professional settings. Using an intersectional perspective, the authors review Black hair, culture, and identity by examining how hair takes on multiple meanings and can be used to grant or deny access to employment opportunities. The authors explore influences on socially acceptable "professional" hair through a content analysis of articles and media by decoding language, narratives, and depictions of hair with the hope of supporting claims on the ways Black women experience and internalize external pressures to conform with whitewashed standards of professional and self-identity. Authors also highlight hair discrimination lawsuits to show the complexity of grooming decisions for Black women in professional settings. The chapter proceeds with discussion on the increased visibility of Black natural hair as a means of changing perceptions of professionalism narrative and concludes with equity-focused strategies.

DOI: 10.4018/978-1-6684-8790-7.ch011

INTRODUCTION

This chapter deconstructs assumptions and standards of Black hairstyles in professional settings. The first section of the chapter introduces readers to an intersectional perspective or intersectionality to show how Black hair, as an expression of Black culture and Black identity, can take on multiple meanings and be used to deny access to employment opportunities. The authors rely on intersectionality to show how Black women experience internalized external pressures to conform to whitewashed standards of professionalism and a fractured self-identity. Throughout the chapter, the authors utilize content analysis to determine the presence of themes and decode language, narratives, and depictions of hair that influence the social definition of acceptable "professional" hair. A section on the various hair discrimination lawsuits is also included in this chapter to demonstrate the legal ramifications and complexity of grooming decisions for Black people, but more specifically Black women in professional settings. The chapter then discusses Black hair movements that challenge standards of beauty as a means to counter perceptions of traditional professional narratives. The chapter concludes with equity-focused recommendations for organizations, both public and private, to assess the ongoing barriers employees face once hired and ways to create inclusive workplaces.

Each author self-identifies as a Black woman representing two generations (the first author is a millennial – born approximately between 1977 and 1995 while the second author is a baby boomer – born approximately between 1946 and 1964). As Black women, we've experienced personal hair traumas that influence how we show up in professional settings. We made a conscious decision to narrow the focus of this chapter to the unique experiences of Black women because we understand that Black women often navigate compound barriers – race and gender biases- Black men and White women can avoid. We argue that understanding the marginalization of Black women, within the context of assumptions and standards of professionalism, will help to better understand the marginalization of other multiple intersecting identities. We start this discussion with an overview of intersectionality and its utility in understanding workplace hair discrimination.

INTERSECTIONALITY

Women and minorities are ubiquitously wedded in discourse, policy, and inquiry (Bowleg, 2012) implying a mutual exclusivity that innately produces inequities. Intersectionality is a theoretical framework, research paradigm, or analytical approach that pave the way for theoretical and empirical inquiry to redirect attention away from solidarities of sameness (Browne & Misra, 2003; Cho et al., 2013, Crenshaw,

1989; Shields, 2008). The origin of intersectionality is intellectually rooted in Black Feminist Thought and is an expression of Critical Race Theory. Black Feminist Thought uses intersectional analysis to show the path of struggle and empowerment to highlight the challenges and difficulties in combating intersecting oppression (Alinia, 2015). Intersectionality perspectives make room for the myriad ways race, gender, social class, sexual orientation, and other social descriptors combine to show a more complete story of identity and inequities (Diggs and Heckler, forthcoming).

While intersectionality has been discussed using many names, the term itself was coined by Kimberle Crenshaw. Crenshaw (1989), a legal scholar, advanced intersectionality to show how singular perspectives of identity limit an in-depth understanding of antidiscrimination doctrines in the US legal system. Her research found trends that demonstrated the significant problems Black women had filing claims of discrimination on the basis of race and gender. Myopic conceptions of discrimination undermined the narratives told by Black women which forced Black women to deny parts of their identity to find protections under the law.

Intersectionality explores ways in which identities intersect in shaping the structural, political, economic, and representational aspects across diverse societies (Crenshaw, 1995). An intersectional perspective views multiple social identities as interlocking systems of privilege and oppression (Bowleg, 2012; Collins & Bilge, 2020) and enriches our understanding of the multidimensional experience of subgroups of emergent social identities. Although the intersectional perspective remains closely associated with the study of women of color, the perspective is more inclusive of all intersecting identities at the margins of society (Bearfield, 2009; Blessett, 2020; Browne & Misra, 2003; Collins, 2000; McCall, 2005). Intersectionality, as defined, now specifies social identity beyond race, class, and gender and articulates new patterns of knowledge and different struggles for social justice (Cho et al., 2013).

Intersectionality provides a framework for understanding how categorizations of people drive social constructs of oppression and privilege (Diggs, 2022). Within the context of this chapter, intersectionality is used to show how race, as a social construct, has been contextualized as a mechanism of domination and oppression that deems segments of the population as (un)deserving and (un)worthy. We use an intersectional perspective to explore how hair is a tool of discrimination against Black women and our hair choices in professional settings. Reluctance to thoroughly interrogate deeply rooted disparity and inequity for Black people, in general, in the United States perpetuates and sustains interwoven systems of domination and oppression. Reluctance to interrogate the double disadvantages of Black women is a missed opportunity for racial justice and adopting social equity in professional settings. The following section discusses the historical context of Black identity and how it is demonstrated in Black hair and hairstyles.

HISTORICAL CONTEXT OF HAIR POSITIONING

To *position* means to alter collections of beliefs of an individual about their rights, duties, and obligations. The act of *positioning* is the mechanism through which roles are assigned or denied, either to oneself or others. Positioning describes malleable roles and storylines that determine the boundaries of future acts and the meanings of what people say or do (Elejabarrieta, 1994). Therefore, the art of *positioning* is a means of defining or redefining attitudes against Black/African American hair, people, culture, and identity and can be traced back to the start of slavery and the dehumanizing experiences of enslaved people.

Willie Morrow is one of the early Black haircare pioneers who brought African teachings of hair care to the Western world. He is known for creating a more suitable comb for teasing out surly tightly coiled afro-textured hair. In his documentary *400 Years Without a Comb: The Inferior Seed,* Morrow (1973) recounts the time of capture during the trans-Atlantic slave trade discussing how African women immediately lost autonomy and pride in their hair. Images of combs floating and settling in the water as Africans were snatched from their land and dragged across the river illustrate the start of derailing the state of the Black image in America. Morrow (1973) graphically illustrates what transpired and continues to transpire to annihilate Black features, hair, and genetics leading to self-negation and the absolute inhumanity that was inflicted upon African people.

The conditions of living in slavery without a comb did not allow for hair maintenance in the way in which African women were accustomed. Working conditions in the fields were hot, sunny, and dirty which led to handkerchiefs worn out of sheer necessity. Women who worked in the owner's homes wore wigs to present an appearance slave masters found more presentable- emulating white women. Because of the sexual exploitation of black women, by white males, many interracial children were born with a less kinky hair texture which became the preferred look. Therefore, inflicting a culturally infused competition on the basis of positioning skin complexion and hair texture against one another within the context of favorable or unfavorable perceptions of Black identity. Black women with features more closely resembling African culture (i.e. darker skin, kinky and tightly coiled hair) are viewed as less attractive which has a drastic impact on self-esteem (Byrd & Tharps, 2014; Greensword, 2021).

Hair brings one's self-image into focus; it is vanity's proving ground.

Hair is terribly personal, a tangle of mysterious prejudice.

~Shannon Alexander, American Journalist with Live Magazine (Chavannes, 2019, 0:38)

The lament of Shannon Alexanders' statement serves as a reminder of how hair is not only an expression of who people are but can tell a story of the cultural meaning of sacred traditions. The experiences of enslavement are passed down through generations and have had long-lasting effects on Black self-identity and how characteristics of Black identity, such as Black hair, are perceived and experienced. Working in chronological order, our goal is to examine the complex relationship between women of African heritage and hair retrospectively. We capture the historical positions of African hair during and post-slavery to help set the stage for hair politics as we see it today in the United States.

POLITICS OF HAIR

Greensword (2021) *defines hair politics as the ways hair is "systemically used to determine, illustrate, and exemplify who is in charge, who may impose their will upon others, who is oppressed, and who is acknowledged* (p.1). Hair has been weaponized to control, hypersexualize, and de-feminize Black women for centuries. The traumatic experiences of slavery are often passed down through a mentality that everything about Black identity is not acceptable, degrades the beauty of our hair, and dictates our perceptions of our unique identity (Greensword, 2021). However, pre-slavery and in many countries today, hair is a social and cultural signifier of a woman's fertility, marital status, age, religion, wealth, rank, or clan. Christian faith centers hair as a divine spiritual closeness to God as the highest point of the body. A passage from 1 Corinthians 11: 14-15 reads "*Does not the very nature of things teach you that if a man has long hair, it is a disgrace to him, but that if a woman has long hair, it is her glory. For long hair is given to her as a covering*". As the passage suggests, hair has a sacred value given by God, and women with long hair represent a sacred covering or blessing. Therefore, cutting hair was a common assertion of authority and power by slave captors over African people. It was an attempt to erase African cultural identity and a highly effective corrective measure for bad behavior, especially for enslaved women.

By means of positionality, hair is very political and often used to oppress Black identities. Beauty is a political prize claimed by the victors of struggles over human worth. The sting of ugliness is a weapon used by those at the top of social hierarchies to assert superiority over groups they deem inferior and therefore ugly (Collier, 2021). Afrocentric hair is therefore unacceptable, and ugly, and comes with many disadvantages that pressure Black women to conform to the perceptions of acceptable, good, and/or pretty hair. Black women quickly learn the do's and don'ts of what is expected of them regarding appearance; a generationally learned behavior.

We'd be remiss if we didn't state how hair politics parallel the politics of skin color. In *The Color Complex: The Politics of Skin Color among African Americans,* Russell et al. (1993) call attention to the harsh treatment of white racism to African Americans beyond slavery to narratives of cruel incidences of discrimination. The chapter entitled *Hair: The Straight and Nappy of it all* speaks to how discrimination continues to impact color and its relationship to status and self-worth. The authors share the story of Alvin Poussaint who points out the issue of color prejudices that persists among Black women and how deep white racism intrudes on black psyche and behavior. Among Black women, straight hair and European hairstyles have not only been considered more feminine but have sent a message about one's standing in the social hierarchy. "Good hair" has long been associated with the light-skinned middle class; whereas "Bad hair" was associated with Blacks who were less fortunate. These narratives permeate the interlocking systems of European standards of beauty, strongly influence perceptions of "professional hair", and sustain oppression for people with intersecting marginalized identities while revering privileged perspectives within the U.S. society.

Systems of privilege and oppression artificially reward certain populations over others. Although the experiences of marginalized and oppressed groups are central to intersectionality's foundation (Collins, 2000; Crenshaw, 1989, 1991, 1995), intersectionality also encompasses social identities and locations that affirm power and privilege to their members, such as whites, males, and heterosexuals (Carbado, 2013; Goodman, 2014). Privilege is the unequal opportunity between groups to access power and other resources (power, status, wealth, and opportunity) generally influenced by one's identity and social location. In this case, privilege is an expression of power or the ability to dictate the story of another person or people that rob them of their dignity (Adichie, 2009). Moreover, positions of privilege undergird hair politics and thus define the widely accepted boundaries of professionalism centering the hegemony of whiteness. We now turn the focus on understanding the term professional or professionalism within the context of privileged intersectional identity.

WORKPLACE PROFESSIONALISM AND PRIVILEGED INTERSECTIONALITY

Professionalism is a term used to demark idealized people (Adams, 2012) where workers attempt to borrow the privilege of professionals by emulating assumed behaviors, attitudes, and appearances (Ferguson & Dougherty, 2022). Professionalism allows working people to claim a desired status (Marshall, 1939), affirms a preferred social class (Cheney & Ashcraft, 2007), and is culturally embedded (Hall, 2011). Professionalism can produce unachievable expectations for success within professional spaces and is often used as an oppressive force on employees. Often ambiguous, professionalism is carefully policed and provides an unwritten and sometimes written, form of organizational control (Ashcraft, 2000).

Professionalism discourse whitewashes blackness as it maintains hegemonic ideals, values, and norms of whiteness as a privilege (Brown, 2003; Gray, 2019; Ferguson & Dougherty, 2022). Normalizing whiteness as the standard of professionalism oppresses minorities and how we- as Black women- perceive ourselves and are perceived by others. Research shows that although many Black workers believe they should conform to standards of whiteness, doing so makes them feel as if they are rejecting their blackness (Boulton, 2016; Davis, 2018), creating an unacceptable choice as they attempt to navigate through their performance. Ferguson and Dougherty (2022) refer to this as the paradox of the black professional who struggles to be seen as professional in the eyes of White standards while being true to their entire Black identity.

The identity of Black women has largely been cast invisible with very limited representational currency (Carbado, 2013). Crenshaw (1989, 1991, 1995) recognizes that when multiple marginalized identities intersect, it creates situations in which one's complete identity does not "fit" the prototypical dominant group(s) and can deny an access point to leadership positions. For example, women of all races and ethnicities are disproportionately underrepresented in leadership positions in the public and private sectors. To help explain this misrepresentation of women in leadership, the concept of "glass ceilings is offered to describe the invisible barrier for women advancing into senior leadership positions. Metaphors of "sticky floors" and "trap doors" have also been useful in explaining barriers to career advancement (Chaffin et al., 1995; Guy, 1994). Catalyst (2004) expands on this thought describing the glass ceiling as a concrete ceiling for Black women because as double outsiders' Black women are subjected to both racism and sexism simultaneously. Diggs (2022) extends this thought by offering yet another alternative to describe how barriers affect the advancement of Black women. Diggs (2022) introduces the concept of a "double-paned glass ceiling" suggesting the extra panel of glass gives the same strength of exclusion as concrete but preserves the transparency of the invisible barrier. Hair politics and other visible markers of African descent further complicate the discrimination against Black women in professional workspaces.

Workplace expectations and their underlying biases are not only pressed upon us. We've colluded on our oppression because we take it out on each other because we can't take it out on our oppressors. We judge ourselves and others harder for fear that incongruent prescriptive of professionals will reflect the negative stereotypes of Black women. For example, Opie and Phillips's (2015) study on hair penalties found that Black, as compared to White, evaluators give higher agency penalties for Black women who choose to wear Afrocentric hairstyles versus Eurocentric hairstyles in the workplace. Afrocentric hair was rated as more dominant and less professional than straight hair. The harsh reality that this study indicates is that it's not the words from our enemies but the silence of our friends that hinder workplace equity and advancement.

Privileges for Sale

To help organizations identify power relations there are various activities organizational leaders could incorporate. The first author of this chapter recently had the opportunity to participate in an interactive icebreaker designed to help participants think about diversity, equity, and inclusion (DEI) in professional settings. The activity- "Privileges for sale" invited participants to openly and honestly speak about experiences of having, or not having privileges. The goals were to acknowledge, reflect, and identify what privileges are taken for granted in our everyday lives. We were also able to determine how underrepresented groups have limited access to certain privileges and the effect that had on the lived experiences of individuals in the workplace.

The activity facilitator gave each group of participants a budget and a list of privileges we could buy. Our group was given $800 dollars. Each privilege was priced at $100 dollars so our group was only able to purchase 8 out of the 15 privileges listed. My group had approximately 12 people from diverse backgrounds all of which had a shared goal to advance DEI principles in our respective workplaces. We were asked to individually select the top three privileges we found personally important and reconvene as a group to share our experiences and convince the team to purchase the privilege. We selected our 8 privileges reflected on the activity and discussed access pathways for those lacking our selected privileges.

One of the privileges read, "*I can achieve a professional hairstyle with minimal cost, manipulation, use of chemicals, or visits to a professional cosmetologist*". A self-identified White woman in our group was the first to suggest we purchase this privilege; looking around at the Black women in the group. She prefaced her justification that although she could not directly identify with the struggles of Black hair, she could identify with hair struggles by trying to equate helmet hair-disheveled hair from riding a bike to work- to the grooming routines of Black hair. Trying to rationalize her statement given the purpose of the activity, it was hard to not question the audacity to speak to the struggles of hair from a position of privilege. In her attempt to empathize with Black women, she was unaware of how inappropriate, offensive, and minimizing her comments were to the hair traumas many Black women face on a daily basis.

This activity revealed two things: first, more often than not, Black women have to be understanding of the lack of awareness from those who ascribe to dominant narratives of privileged identities and ideologies. Second, in efforts to empathize, people from privileged identities may inadvertently invalidate and minimize the hurt and trauma hair biases cause Black women, Black men, and other people of color in society. Concerns about constructing a professional image and communicating belongingness in the professional context may cause those with marginalized identities to be particularly sensitive about how much if any, of their marginal identity traits they reveal at work (Roberts, 2005). Hair is one of the only phenotypical racial traits that can transform or mute identity (Clair et al., 2005; Opie & Phillips, 2015; Sheane, 2012) in favor of prescribed perceptions of socially acceptable hair.

PERCEPTIONS OF SOCIALLY ACCEPTABLE HAIR AND EXTERNAL INFLUENCERS

Black hair is often vilified and made a spectacle equating to animals, specifically sheep's wool (Greensword, 2021). The spectacle is subtle in tone and often disguised by inquiries such as Can I touch your hair? This can signal hidden messages to Black women which can evoke negative feelings or responses such as no, you may not, my hair is not for your entertainment. Some individuals may go as far as to reach out and touch the hair without permission followed with a condescending response; oh.... It's softer than it looks. Or maybe even, you are so lucky my hair can't do that. These comments are very hurtful, may bring feelings of shame, and speak to how Black identity as a whole has never quite measured up to the American standards of beauty. Because it doesn't flow in the wind nor fall straight, it's condemned ugly, less than.

Roseline Chavannes (2019) highlights in *Detangling the Stigma/A Natural Hair Documentary* that the wonderful thing about hair is the variety it possesses: blonde, brunette, redhead, short, mid-length, long, bone straight, wavy, curly, kinky (:55). Every strand has a unique story to tell. Chavannes (2019) is relaying a message that hair should be nothing more than what's on your head, right? The documentary presents how society categorizes hair ranking according to types. Type 1- straight hair is the preferred hair type that women of all races should strive for as the epitome of acceptable hair. Type 2 is wavy hair that is easily manageable and a step below the preferred straight hair. Type 3 and Type 4 are where you start to see curlier textured hair ranging from full-body flowy curls to tightly coiled kinky hair. Black women's hair textures generally fall in the Types 3 and 4 range.

Each hair type is subcategorized on a scale from a, b, and c; mimicking the grading scale in the American education system. Letter grades symbolize a general assessment or standard for hair acceptability in society and are used to influence standards of professionalism in the workplace. Hair typing systems are highly problematic as they strongly suggest to Black women that their natural hair is unprofessional, unattractive, or unclean. Hair typing systems perpetuate texturism-the discrimination of Afro-textured hair in favor of looser curl patterns and smooth textures (Simeon, 2021). Hair typing systems also place women in culturally infused competition with one another as they strive for more presentable, acceptable looks. The hair typing systems teach Black women how to manage their hair and the types of products that will transform hair to favorable smoother textures in a manipulative marketing scheme of beauty standards.

All across the United States, stigmatizing our unique coarse texture has become the new norm. Chavannes cites Goffman's (2009) definition of stigma and its impact on a person's health defining stigmatizing as "an attribute that is deeply discrediting, debilitating to your physical health and even cause those who are being stigmatized to grow sick and perish quicker than those who aren't stigmatized" (2:01). For many Black women, their childhood memories of short, nappy locks bring forth feelings of shame and not sweet nostalgia. Russell et al. (1993) share a story of a dark-skinned woman who remembers other children's taunts of 'your hair's so short, you can smell yo' brains'. This same woman recounts how she had it doubly hard when she was in grade school because she had short beady hair and dark skin. She remembers asking her mother to straighten her hair and how she felt forever changed and happy afterward (p. 83-84). Chavannes (2019) captures the reactions of White women as they listen to the experiences of Black women sharing the impact hair has on their careers. As the white women listed they appeared dumbfounded and perplexed by what they were hearing. The lack of awareness of White women, speaks to their positions of privilege in the workplace where they don't have to compromise or deny parts of themselves to be seen as worthy of occupying professional positions.

REGULATING HAIR AGENCY THROUGH POLICY

We assume everyone is familiar with the saying "You never get a second chance to make a first impression". This statement becomes ever so true during a job interview when the first impression counts more than in any other situation. Over the years we have learned various strategies to maneuver through the job market because we understand that appearance affects what opportunities are given and, at times, pay (Jackson, 2013). In this respect, we are taught what to wear, what colors to avoid, to ensure that our appearance looks "kept", we use proper diction, arrive to the interview early, and know how important it is to be nice to everyone because you never know who's watching. Additionally, as Black women we also learn to alter our natural appearance by straightening our hair, wearing make-up to soften our look, and acting pleasant because we don't want to come off as too aggressive.

Weller (2019) with The Center for American Progress reported that African Americans face systematic obstacles to getting good jobs. Reporting that, regardless of labor market outcomes, African Americans always fare worse than whites, with Black women often experiencing the harshest impacts. According to Byrd and Tharps (2014), Black hair in its natural state is against the rules. Natural hair refers to the natural pattern of hair that grows straight from the scalp, a state that has not been altered to change curl patterns, free from dangerous chemical processes or hot combs used to achieve straight hair. Alexander (2016) googled unprofessional hairstyles for work. The search yielded images of Black women with natural hair and hairstyles as unprofessional. Alarmed by the search results she then Googled professional hair. Images of White women with straight hair appeared. Interestingly enough we did the exact Google search to see whether natural hairstyles have gained greater acceptance, seven years later, and the specific Black hairstyles deemed unprofessional were of images we as Black women would consider as "kept" hair (e.g. braided or locs tied back into a bun). This goes to show that even as we advance in many ways the working world still associates professional and acceptable to straight flowy hair. These findings attest to natural hair limiting job opportunities for Black women (Bagalini, 2021; Byrd & Tharps, 2014; Gray, 2019; Rosette, 2020).

Although standards of behavior and appearance are imposed on all workers (Rosette and Dumas, 2007), the premise guiding these standards is problematic. The concept of professionalism within "euro" standards maintains that certain employer hairstyle prohibitions constrain African-American cultural identity and are racially discriminatory in nature (Collier, 2023). For example, grooming policies naturalize whiteness, regulate access, and are designed to preserve the integrity of whiteness and maleness in the workplace (Carbado, 2013) as superior to other ethnic, racial, and regional identities and customs (Gray, 2019). Grooming policies assert bias and regulate hair agencies where Black women rarely have full autonomy over their hair and are overly policed. Black women are constantly being told that their hair is unprofessional and/or distracting.

Collier (2023) explores whether hair prohibitions are racially discriminatory, violating Title VII protections. The study found employer hairstyle prohibitions refuse to give legitimacy to African-American hairstyle choices but do not trigger a Title VII violation. Professionalism is socially constructed and protected within coded language found in organizational policies such as grooming prohibitions. Public sector organizations, although legally bound by anti-discrimination laws, are not immune to subtle discriminatory practices. To this end, hair regulations, unwelcoming to Black hair, hinder a sense of belonging and walk a fine line on being illegal.

In many ways, employer grooming policies shape the work experiences of Black women by prohibiting natural hairstyles from being welcomed in private workplaces (Hill, 2006). We see it play out when both white and employers of color show a preference for White applicants and employees, as we all are conditioned, to some extent, to center whiteness in our perceptions of others. The earlier example found by Opie and Phillips (2015) supports claims that hair is interpretive in the nature of negative and positive organizational behaviors and performance expectations. Grooming policies also demonstrate whether organizations support diversity and inclusion. Dawson and Karl (2018) later found that women with lighter skin color and straight hair, statistically, increased their likelihood of getting promoted or put in places of high visibility in the workplace. The implications of this finding also alert us to the paradoxical meanings of Black hair. Professionalism and employer grooming policies have become coded language for White favoritism in workplace practices that privilege the values of White and Western employees (Gray, 2019) above others.

THE LAW: CODED LANGUAGE AND ITS EFFECT ON SOCIAL IDENTITY AND BELONGINGNESS

Regulating one's hair agency extends beyond working environments and can be seen in many school policies that dictate what is "appropriate" hair. For example, many followed the story of a New Jersey high school wrestler and his experience with hair discrimination as the event caught the attention of mainstream media in 2019. Viewers watched as the video of the teenager getting his locs cut on the sidelines replayed all because the referee told him he would have to forfeit the match if he refused. The incident resulted in a two-year suspension for the referee but what about the impact it will have on the student and other students of color? This is not an isolated event, cases like these happen often in our judicial system. Although this specific event followed the hair biases of a young Black male, Black girls are taught to adopt grooming practices that mimic White girls at an early age that carries into adulthood.

Judicial holdings and administrative decisions on hair discrimination claims have had mixed outcomes. This speaks to the complexity of grooming decisions for Black people and the political power of employer grooming memorandums. Collier (2023) and Carbado (2013) both examine this complexity in the legal system and the protections given to private-sector employers who prohibit certain African-American hairstyles. For example, in the case *Pitts v. Wild Adventures,* the employer grooming memorandum prohibited dreadlocks, cornrows, beads, and shells. The plaintiff, Pitts, objected to the policy claiming her hairstyle was an expression of her heritage. She later received numerous reprimands which resulted in her termination. Similarly, employers use ambiguous language in policies to specify the appearance of hair. In the case of *Booth v. Maryland,* the grooming policy stated that "hair should be neatly groomed," and the "length, bulk, or appearance of hair shall not be excessive, ragged, or unkempt". In so many words, this policy prohibited employees from wearing locked styles.

A more notable case, which is often cited, is *Rogers v. American Airlines.* In this case, American Airlines prohibited employees from wearing all-braided hairstyles- meaning a person's entire head of hair is braided. Rogers claimed that her hairstyle choice was a reflection of her culture. The courts ruled in favor of American Airlines because shortly before this incident, Bo Derek, a white actress, wore her hair in an all-braided style which popularized the hairstyle. The courts claimed that the hairstyle choice was a fashionable trend rather than a reflection of the cultural, and historical essence of Black women in American Society (Carbado, 2013; Collier 2021). The result of this case indicated that more often than not, once hairstyles are misappropriated by White people they become more socially acceptable (i.e. afros in the 1960s and early 70s and braids in the 1980s).

Legislation proposed today advocates for the protections against hair discrimination. The Creating a Respectful and Open World for Natural Hair Act, also known as the CROWN Act, is a law that prohibits race-based hair discrimination, which is the denial of employment and educational opportunities because of hair texture or protective hairstyles including braids, locs, twists or bantu knots. CROWN Act (California) is the first legislation passed at the state level that prohibited hair discrimination. In 2020 the CROWN Act passed the U.S. House of Representatives but failed to pass the Senate. It was reintroduced in 2021 to both the House and the Senate and passed House in 2022. To date, only 23 states have accepted and approached the Crown Act. The CROWN Act while a "game changer" in addressing the lack of legal protection against hair discrimination and proposing to end such discrimination, the journey of being accepted on our authentic self is still victimized and demoralized. More work is needed but this law is a step in the right direction. For many, the hair traumas experienced have affected social identity and belongingness which has a much lasting effect.

PRESSURES OF CONFORMING TO MAINSTREAM EXPECTATIONS AND THE BLACK HAIR MARKET

Black women's choices about how to wear their hair have been informed by social pressures to adopt Eurocentric standards of straight hair (Lester, 2000). Traumatic hair experiences and repeatedly hearing your hair is distracting, nappy, beady, unprofessional, and unattractive would push anyone to conform to mainstream expectations of beauty. Donahoo and Smith (2022) emphasize the fear of negative professional outcomes and constant microaggressions led black women to consider and even adopt hairstyles that emulate white beauty norms and professional expectations. However, for Black women to conform to mainstream expectations is time-consuming, requires patience, and is very costly.

We assume that many Black women can attest to hair prep rituals as little girls in our momma's kitchens. A comb, brush, hair pins, hair grease, and towels line the kitchen counters in preparation for the hairstyling process for the upcoming weeks' activities. The second author of this chapter recounts her experiences as a thick-haired little girl who was also "tender-headed". She recalls her mother taunting her questioning "How can you be nappy-headed and tender-headed at the same time". Her mom would sing *"Pull those knots 'til ya holla stop, Pulaski is read hot. They put their waters on"*. She didn't know what the quote meant, all she knew was she dreaded the tugging and pulling on Saturdays to make her hair presentable for the week and the lasting anxiety the experiences brought into adulthood.

There is a cost Black women pay when conforming to mainstream Eurocentric standards. Although Black hair is versatile, the negative side of hair straightening techniques can cause chemical burns, hair fallouts, messed up edges, and bald spots. Black women also pay the cost, financially as the largest consumers of hair products. Smith's (2009) study found that Black women spend more than 7.5 billion dollars on cosmetics annually, more than three times the amount that White women spend. Carbado (2013) suggests this is the result of Black women historically being masculinized and feeling pressure to expend more energy and resources to make themselves appear more feminine. According to a Mintel study, expenditures for black hair products in 2012 were $684 million and estimated to jump to 761 million by 2017. These figures did not include total black hair care expenditures such as money spent on hair extensions, wigs, independent distributors, and e-commerce. Black hair care is a .5 trillion-dollar industry. There are associated costs to "fit" in and these costs are disproportionately skewed to Black women. Despite newly minted legal protections, Black women are taking matters into their own hands countering the narrative of "professionalism" and influencing others to do the same through social media.

EARLY CHALLENGES TO PROFESSIONAL HAIR STANDARDS

The civil rights movements of the '60s marked a revolution in Black attitudes about their hair. Younger Black people turned away from the white aesthetic of straight hair for a more natural look. For the first time, young Black women in significant numbers stopped perming and pressing, and members of both sexes let their hair grow and go wild and free. The afro became the rage in part because it was also a political statement. During this time, the slogan "Black is beautiful" was created to offset negative stereotypes about Black beauty (hooks, 1995).

Post-sixties, the Afro turned into Jheri curls or California curls, and the old standard of defining beauty re-emerged. Honestly, the standard of defining beauty never really ever left but this was the first time it was challenged. Straight and wavy hair was still considered "good hair" while tightly curled and nappy hair remained "bad hair". Black hair continued to be a politically charged subject. There were added characteristic values dependent on how women wore hair. The style chosen reflected a woman's social consciousness, socioeconomic class, and/or lifestyle. As we've discussed Black hair has a meaning that may translate to others as a way to center power or dominance of Blackness in professional settings. This was threatening especially since Eurocentric efforts indoctrinate blacks into believing they are less valuable, respectable, and beautiful than others. Corporate America also dictates a lot of the professional standards in the workplace which pressure Black women to conform to mainstream hair expectations thus losing their hair agency.

MEDIA INFLUENCES AND COUNTER-NARRATIVES TO PROFESSIONALISM

Russell et al. (1993) believed as the twentieth century closed Black women would come to better appreciate the array of beauty they portray, despite subtle, and not-so-subtle, pressure from media, the workplace, and the larger society to conform to their standards of attractiveness. Yet they were troubled that too many still make snide and cruel comments about the politically, professional, or socially acceptable ways to wear hair. The authors suggest we would be a lot stronger as a people if we used that energy to support each other economically, emotionally, and spiritually.

As a sense of regret permeated eras since the seventies and eighties, women started to see the negative result of continuous permanent relaxers, straighteners, and chemical adjustments to their hair. By the twenty-first century, Black women have/are experiencing the physical, mental, and emotional health and financial costs of realigning their natural hair. Essentially the chemicals in relaxers break down proteins in hair and over time hair stands become thinner and weaker (Stilson,

2009). Some women experience baldness but that's just the tip of the iceberg. Black women have more occurrences of fibroids than any other group of women. Research has found that the chemicals in relaxers alter a woman's hormones and have been linked to causing reproduction and menstrual health issues. The residue of chemical relaxing goes to the brain and there are indications of chemicals linking to high rates of cancers and diseases such as high blood pressure. Hair dye is also a very common allergic reaction causing patches of hair to fall out (Titus, 2019). Chemical hair straighteners accounted for a major expenditure in the Black haircare market and have steadily declining sales as more Black women are opting to wear their hair naturally. According to a Mintel study, 70 percent of Black women acknowledged that they currently wear or have worn their hair naturally. Of that number, 53 percent have worn braids and 41 percent have worn locks within the past twelve months (Gill, 2015).

The natural hair movement has moved beyond salons which are expensive and time-consuming. Social media has made the natural hair journey more accessible, and convenient and has created dozens of social media influencers. Digital media has played a significant role in educating black women about their natural hair and has proven to be a very effective marketing tool for natural hair products (Gill, 2015). The Pandemic has also contributed to the social and digital media frenzy over natural hair.

A Forbes (2021) article *How the Pandemic Refocused Black Women's Commitment to their Wellness* revealed Black Millennials, Gen Xers, and Baby Boomers finding new ways to embrace their natural beauty. The Pandemic was particularly harsh for Black women and their typical hair maintenance routines, among other stressors. It forced Black women to find digital hair communities, heightened consciousness of racial and colorist microaggression, and mediated stronger allyship to be comfortable with their natural beauty. Digital media communities- created independently by black women entrepreneurs- support, raise awareness, and build self-esteem by documenting and sharing experiences (Greensword, 2021).

Millennials and the "woke" culture understand the need to decolonize hair. Their perception of professionalism and beauty is opposed to white-washed beauty standards and demonstrates the power to reclaim their hair agency (Orey and Zhang, 2019). Other generations have followed their lead and now we see the most visible performance of black beauty and femininity in all its glory from straight to curly, wrapped, braided, locs to wigs. Orey and Zhang (2019) say that aesthetic ideals have primarily been manufactured through the media and because of the "woke" culture, we see more natural hairstyles. Black natural hairstyles are social, cultural, and political statements that are gaining more visibility on beauty icons, supreme court rulers, presidential nominees, academics, elected and appointed government officials, CEOs, grocery stores, and in our own homes. All of which are changing the narrative that Black hair is ugly and unprofessional.

DIVERSITY, EQUITY, AND INCLUSION STANDARDS

Discrimination against Black employees, in general, is an ongoing problem in the United States (Ferguson & Dougherty, 2022), which influences the hiring, promotion, firing, and day-to-day workplace management (Gray, 2019). Black women are confronted with discriminatory race-based hairstyle biases limiting their ability or privilege to express their full cultural identity. As Black women, we have to decide how to strategically show up as fractured versions of ourselves thus denying portions of our identity in efforts to "fit in". Understandably, to some extent, everyone in the workforce may experience some form of professional maneuvering yet cultural suppression seems more common for those with marginalized identities.

Organizations advancing diversity, equity, inclusion, and accessibility (DEIA) highly focus on creating inclusive work environments. They support principles of belongingness, uniqueness, and authenticity often captured in the "bring your authentic self to work" mantra. However, DEIA fails to fully acknowledge or understand how, for some, "bringing your authentic self" to work often leads to subtle, and at times overt, stereotypes, biases, differential treatment, and microaggressions which result in limited access to job opportunities, poor performance, and low job satisfaction. The decision to construct professional identities that conform to Eurocentric norms in fear of workplace implications is an example of the inequitable ability to express one's full authentic self, identity, and culture. Discriminatory hair practices, hidden within the term "professional", hinder full access to the core principles of DEIA and illustrate how principles are not equally experienced for all members in a given workplace. This claim is supported by the creation of the Crown Act of 2019 which is an added level of protection against discrimination based on race-based hairstyles, hair texture, and the various protective hairstyles in the workplace and public schools.

However, as the number of Black women opting to wear Afrocentric hair continues to rise, organizations may find it increasingly difficult to maintain standards of professionalism that prohibit or discourage Afrocentric hairstyles. It is important for organizations to examine what purpose is served by the current culturally determined standards of appearance and how such standards relate to professionalism (Opie & Phillips, 2016). Organizations will have to start reevaluating exclusionary politics because organizations benefit from having authentic employees who feel a sense of belonging.

EQUITY-FOCUSED STRATEGIES TO CHALLENGE THE UNJUST STATUS QUO

Black women have grown tired of hiding parts of their identity and demanding policies that reflect a basic understanding of black hair. To ensure standards are fair and respectful, organizations mustn't assume that all hair grows and can be styled the same but rather consider the diversity of hair and people (Byrd & Tharps, 2014). For Gray (2019), changing professionalism is creating a culture that is fair and equitable which begins with accepting and appreciating the diversity of employees' cultures, experiences, and knowledge. It will also require a conscious effort to decentering whiteness as the standard of professionalism.

Gray (2019) provides a few examples of cooperatives and nonprofits that have begun to transform the standards of professionalism (i.e. Anti-Oppression Resource Training Alliance, Cooperative Food Empowerment Directive, Sustainable Economies Law Center, and Mondragon). The Center for Ethnic Race and Religious Understanding at Queens College, The Southwest Center for Human Relations Studies at the University of Oklahoma, and the National Conference on Race and Ethnicity in Higher Education provide additional resources to guide organizations to elevate historically marginalized people regarding hiring, gatekeeping & glass ceilings, policing, accountability, and policy for change when implementing systemic changes. Training is also provided to help organizational leaders respond, rethink, and revise discriminatory policies and practices.

The Association of College and University Educators (ACUE) equips professionals with effective and equity-promoting practices. This training is not only effective in academic settings but also applicable to public and private agencies. The courses teach strategies for managing implicit biases, ways to acknowledge and reduce microaggressions, ways to address imposter phenomenon and stereotype threats, creating an inclusive work environment, and designing equity-centered policies. Having leaders who take the time to recognize, understand, engage, prioritize, and evaluate the development and implementation of policies is necessary for organizations that wish to move beyond the status quo to achieve substantive change (Diggs et al., 2023).

CONCLUSION

It is important to understand how Black women experience and navigate discourses of professionalism. In this chapter, the study of hair in the workplace, from an intersectionality perspective, reveals how power systems have transformed the Black cultural landscape to the point where hair has become the embodiment of and metonymy for Black social identity (Greensword, 2021). Black women feel pressure to be as close to "White" as possible to gain acceptance and success within organizations even at the detriment of rejecting their blackness. All of this is rooted in systems of oppression that manifest through hair treatment and rhetoric that Afrocentric hair is the antithesis of social and professional preference. Restrictive workplace policies perpetuate whitewashed standards of professionalism and insist on standardizing whiteness as the norm for political hair structures targeting Black professional women.

The natural hair movement has evolved as an emerging yet powerful force that challenges conventional beauty standards and empowers women of African descent to embrace their unique hair textures. This movement has not only transformed perspectives on natural hair it is also challenging organizations' ability to maintain standards of professionalism that prohibit or discourage Afrocentric hairstyles. DEIA initiatives, in addition to the natural hair movement and the CROWN Act, foster a strong community that encourages self-acceptance and pride in one's heritage, uniqueness, and authentic cultural expression. Although progress is still being made, efforts to create more inclusive workplace environments that are truly receptive to marginalized social identity traits (i.e. hairstyles) continue to inspire change in how people express diversity at work and redefine the notion of professionalism for generations to come.

REFERENCES

Adams, K. F. (2012). The discursive construction of professional ism: An episteme of the 21st century. *Ephemera: Theories & Politics in Organizations*, *12*(3), 327–343.

Alexander, L. (2016). Do Google's unprofessional hair results show it is racist? *The Guardian*. https://www.theguardian.com/technology/2016/apr/08/does-google-unprofessional-hair-results-prove-algorithms-racist-

Alinia, M. (2015). On Black feminist thought: Thinking oppression and resistance through intersectional paradigm. *Ethnic and Racial Studies*, *38*(13), 2334–2340. doi:10.1080/01419870.2015.1058492

Ashcraft, K. L. (2000). Empowering "professional" relationships: Organizational communication meets feminist practice. *Management Communication Quarterly*, *13*(3), 347–392. doi:10.1177/0893318900133001

Bagalini, A. (2021). How wearing natural hairstyles harms the job prospects of Black women. *World Economic Forum*. https://www.weforum.org/agenda/2021/02/natural-hair-black-women-job-discrimination/

Bearfield, D. A. (2009). Equity at the intersection: Public administration and the study of gender. *Public Administration Review*, *69*(3), 383–386. doi:10.1111/j.1540-6210.2009.01985.x

Blessett, B. (2020). Rethinking the administrative state through an intersectional framework. *Administrative Theory & Praxis*, *42*(1), 1–5. doi:10.1080/10841806.2018.1517526

Boulton, C. (2016). Black identities inside advertising: Race inequality, code-switching, and stereotype threat. *The Howard Journal of Communications*, *27*(2), 130–144. doi:10.1080/10646175.2016.1148646

Bowleg, L. (2012). The problem with the phrase women and minorities: Intersectionality an important theoretical framework for public health. *American Journal of Public Health*, *102*(7), 1267–1273. doi:10.2105/AJPH.2012.300750 PMID:22594719

Brown, M. K. (2003). *Whitewashing race: The myth of a color-blind society*. University of California Press.

Browne, I., & Misra, J. (2003). The intersection of gender and race in the labor market. *Annual Review of Sociology*, *29*(1), 487–513. doi:10.1146/annurev.soc.29.010202.100016

Byrd, A., & Tharps, L. (2001). *Hair story: Untangling the roots of black hair in America*. St. Martin's Press.

Carbado, D. (2013). Colorblind intersectionality. *Signs (Chicago, Ill.)*, *38*(4), 811–845. doi:10.1086/669666

Catalyst. (2004). *Advancing African American Women in the Workplace: What Managers Need to Know*. Catalyst survey. https://www.catalyst.org/research/advancing-african-american-women-in-the-workplace-what-managers-need-to-know/

Chaffins, S., Forbes, M., Fuque, H. E., & Cangemi, J. P. (1995). The glass ceiling: Are women where they should be? *Education*, *115*(93), 380–387.

Chavannes, R. (2019). *Detangling the Stigma/A Natural Hair Documentary*. [Video]. YouTube. https://youtu.be/dij2lQ0-wS4

Cheney, G., & Ashcraft, K. L. (2007). Considering "the professional" in communication studies: Implications for theory and research within and beyond the boundaries of organizational communication. *Communication Theory*, *17*(2), 146–175. doi:10.1111/j.1468-2885.2007.00290.x

Cho, S., Crenshaw, K. W., & McCall, L. (2013). Toward a field of intersectionality studies: Theory, application, and praxis. *Signs (Chicago, Ill.)*, *38*(4), 785–810. doi:10.1086/669608

Clair, J., Beatty, J., & MacLean, T. (2005). Out of sight but not out of mind: Managing invisible social identities in the workplace. *Academy of Management Review*, *30*(1), 78–95. doi:10.5465/amr.2005.15281431

Collier, D. (2021). "Don't touch my hair": An examination of the exercise of privilege and power through interracial hair-centered communication interactions. *Proceedings of the New York State Communication Association, 2017*. NYCA.

Collier, D. (2023). Don't get it twisted: Why employer hairstyle prohibitions are racially discriminatory. *Hastings Race and Poverty Law Journal*, *9*(1), 33–54.

Collins, P. H. (2000). *Black feminist thought: Knowledge, consciousness, and the politics of empowerment* (2nd ed.). Routledge.

Collins, P. H., & Bilge, S. (2020). *Intersectionality*. Policy Press.

Crenshaw, K. W. (1989). Demarginalizing the intersection of race and sex: A black feminist critique of antidiscrimination doctrine, feminist theory and antiracist politics. *University of Chicago Legal Forum*, 136–167.

Crenshaw, K. W. (1991). Mapping the margins: Intersectionality, identity politics, and violence against women of color. *Stanford Law Review*, *43*(6), 1241–1299. doi:10.2307/1229039

Crenshaw, K. W. (1995). Mapping the margins: Intersectionality, identity politics, and violence against women of color. In K. Crenshaw, N. Gotanda, G. Peller, & K. Thomas (Eds.), *Critical race theory: The keys writing that formed the movement* (pp. 357–383). The New Press.

Davis, S. M. (2018). Taking back the power: An analysis of Black women's communicative resistance. *The Review of Communication*, *18*(4), 301–318. doi:10.1080/15358593.2018.1461234

Dawson, G., & Karl, K. (2018). I am not my hair, or am I? Examining hair choices of black female executives. *Journal of Business Diversity*, *18*(2).

Diggs, S. N. (2022). Intersectionality of gender and race in governmental affairs. In Shields, P. and Elias, N. (Eds.), Handbook on Gender and Public Administration. Cheltenham, UK and Northhampton, MA, USA, Edward Elgar Publishing.

Diggs, S.N. and Heckler, N. (forthcoming). *Taxonomy of Intersectionality: A Macro Intervention of Multiple Micro Identities.*

Diggs, S. N., Krewson, R. C., & McCandless, S. A. (2023). Intersectional disparities during crisis: Improving social equity through public and nonprofit management. In Intersectionality and Crisis Management, 81-100. Routledge.

Donahoo, S., & Smith, A. D. (2022). Controlling the crown: Legal efforts to professionalize Black hair. *Race and Justice*, *12*(1), 182–203. doi:10.1177/2153368719888264

Elejabarrieta, F. (1994). Social positioning: A way to link social identity and social representation. *Social Sciences Information. Information Sur les Sciences Sociales*, *33*(2), 241–253. doi:10.1177/053901894033002006

Ferguson, M. W. Jr, & Dougherty, D. S. (2022). The paradox of the black professional: Whitewashing blackness through professionalism. *Management Communication Quarterly*, *36*(1), 3–29. doi:10.1177/08933189211019751

Forbes, J. (2021). How the pandemic refocused Black women's commitment to their wellness. *Allure.* https://www.allure.com/sponsored/story/aarp-2021-survey-black-women-pandemic-beauty-wellness-habits

Gill, T.M. (2015). #Teamnatural: black hair and the politics of community in digital media. *Journal of Contemporary African Art, 37.*

Goffman, E. (2009). *Stigma: Notes on the management of spoiled identity*. Simon and Schuster.

Goodman, D. J. (2014). The tapestry model: Exploring social identities, privilege, and oppression from an intersectional perspective. In D. Mitchell, C. Y. Simmons, & L. A. Greyerbiehl (Eds.), *Intersectionality and higher education: Theory, research, and praxis* (pp. 99–108). Peter Lang.

Gray, A. (2019). *The bias of professionalism standards*. Standard Social Innovation Review.

Greensword, S. (2021). Historicizing black hair politics: A framework for contextualizing race politics. *Sociology Compass.*

Guy, M. E. (1994). Organizational architecture, gender, and women's careers. *Review of Public Personnel Administration*, *14*(2), 77–90. doi:10.1177/0734371X9401400208

Hall, S. (2011). The neo-liberal revolution. *Cultural Studies*, *25*(6), 705–728. doi: 10.1080/09502386.2011.619886

Hill, M. L. (2006). Baltimore police department has a racially insensitive appearance policy. *Jackson Free Press* retrieved from https://www.jacksonfreepress.com/news/2006/dec/20/baltimore-police-department-has-racially/

Hooks, B. ((1995). *Killing Rage: Ending racism.* New York, NY: Henry Holt and Company.

Jackson, L. (2013). *Can your hair color affect your job opportunities?* Career Addict.

Marshall, T. H. (1939). The recent history of professionalism in relation to social structure and social policy. *The Canadian Journal of Economics and Political Science*, *5*(3), 325–340. doi:10.2307/137036

McCall, L. (2005). The complexity of intersectionality. *Signs (Chicago, Ill.)*, *30*(3), 1771–1800. doi:10.1086/426800

Morrow, W., & Jefferson, A. (1973). *400 years without a comb: The inferior seed.* California Curl.

Opie, T. R., & Phillips, K. W. (2015). Hair penalties: The negative influence of Afrocentric hair on ratings on Black women's dominance and professionalism. *Frontiers in Psychology*, *6*(1311), 1–14. doi:10.3389/fpsyg.2015.01311 PMID:26379612

Orey, B. D., & Zhang, Y. (2019). Melanated millennials and the politics of black hair. *Social Science Quarterly*, *100*(6), 2459–2476. doi:10.1111squ.12694

Roberts, L. (2005). Changing faces: Professional image construction in diverse organizational settings. *Academy of Management Review*, *30*(4), 685–711. doi:10.5465/amr.2005.18378873

Rosette, A., & Dumas, T. L. (2007). The hair dilemma: Conform to mainstream expectations or emphasize racial identity. *Duke Journal of Gender Law & Policy*, *14*(1), 407–422.

Rosette, A. S. (2020). *Research suggests bias against natural hair limits job opportunities for Black women.* Duke University. https://www.fuqua.duke.edu/duke-fuqua-insights/ashleigh-rosette-research-suggests-bias-against-natural-hair-limits-job

Russell, K., Wilson, K., & Hall, R. (1993). *The Color Complex: The politics of skin color among African Americans.* Anchor Books Doubleday.

Sheane, S. (2012). Putting on a good face: An examination of the emotional and aesthetic roots of presentational Labour. *Economic and Industrial Democracy, 33*(1), 145–158. doi:10.1177/0143831X11427588

Shields, S. A. (2008). Gender: An intersectionality perspective. *Sex Roles, 59*(5-6), 301–311. doi:10.100711199-008-9501-8

Simeon, A. (2021). *The controversial history of the hair typing system.* Byrdie. https://www.byrdie.com/hair-typing-system-history-5205750

Smith, S. D. (2009). *Beauty Beat: Essence Panel Explores Beauty Purchasing.* Women's Wear Daily. http://www.ggny.com/press/51909 WWDHaspel.pdf

Stilson, J. (2009). (Director). *Good Hair.* Produced by: Nelson George, Jenny Hunter, Kevin O'Donnell, and Chris Rock.

Titus, R. (2019). *(Director). Natural Hair the Movie.* Grind Over Matter Productions.

Weller, C. E. (2019). *African Americans face systematic obstacles to getting good jobs.* The Center for American Progress. https://www.americanprogress.org/article/african-americans-face-systematic-obstacles-getting-good-jobs/

Chapter 12
Hair Bias in the Educational Organization:
An Exploration Through Qualitative Data

Thea Dirton
https://orcid.org/0000-0001-9856-1428
Independent Researcher, USA

ABSTRACT

Natural hair is both complex and simple. It so complex that legislation is required in order to protect its wearers from discrimination and bias, and it is so simple that the most controversial issues stem from the hair in its natural state. This chapter will explore the complexities and simplicities of wearers of natural hair and provide recommendations on how to move forward. Through an exploration of the legislation regarding Black hair and qualitative data, this chapter explores discrimination and hair bias and the negative effects that they have on the natural hair wearers.

INTRODUCTION

"Where do you see your career going? Do you want to be in Administration? Are you going to keep your hair like that forever?" These were questions I heard come out of the mouth of a boss I had worked under for two years. He had trusted me with leadership roles within our school building, recommended me for positions at various levels within our district, and told me that I had a bright future ahead of me. But now, it seemed like he was staking my future on the hair that grew naturally from my head. The hair that I had struggled with for the majority of my childhood and teenage years and that now grew long and strong from my head. The hair that was

DOI: 10.4018/978-1-6684-8790-7.ch012

no longer damaged and unhealthy, nor was it being treated with harmful chemicals to make it do what it did not naturally do. The hair that I had made peace with and grown to love in its present state of locs.

I am not the only one that has been faced with the issue of being blatantly or subtly questioned about their choice of hairstyle. Women in general, and more specifically, Black women, have dealt with this issue for years and based on current litigation and legislation, this will be an issue for a long time to come. Natural Hair Wearers, no matter which professional field they work in face comments, complaints, microaggressions, and other issues because they choose to wear their hair in an arguably healthier way. Although this is the case and there are common threads in this area amongst all professions, this chapter will focus on hair bias in the educational organization, with a specific emphasis on Black women who wear their hair naturally and how it negatively affects them on different levels. It is also important to note that students in educational organizations experience hair bias on a daily basis from teachers, administrators, their peers, and others such as referees as well. This book chapter seeks to highlight the issues that educators face from wearing their hair naturally in hopes that all people, students included, will benefit from the issues and recommendations presented.

HISTORICAL PERSPECTIVE

Black women wearing their natural hair in the United States have faced issues, problems, and ultimatums surrounding their hair for centuries. In an article written by Ileana Najarro, Esi Eggleston Bracey the president of Unilever USA and chief executive of North America Personal Care, states that natural hair styles worn by African-American women are discriminated against because of their connection to history (Najarro, 2022). Payne-Patterson (2023) goes further stating that hair discrimination is “yet another form of racial discrimination and yet another way to control and police Black and brown people”.

A part of this history is slavery and the way that the Ancestors of African-Americans were brought to America. Bracey states that when Africans were brought to America, the distain for certain hair styles was an effort to “a way to keep slaves docile and disconnected from that history” (Najarro, 2022). Kennedy (2020) evidences this, stating that in the early history of America, “historic publications by White travelers, newspaper articles, runaway slave advertisements, and notes of early American artists include comments about the odd growth and styling of what they refer to as Black people’s “wool” (p. 7). Slaves who worked in the slave master’s house covered their hair, wore wigs, and shaped their hair with different tools (Griffin, 2019), transitioning to the straightening of natural hair at the end of the 19th century, to current practices which are a mixture of Black women wearing their hair in different ways which include pressing, perming, braiding, and styling naturally.

The styling of Black Hair has paralleled the Black Movements in American society. During the 1960s a time of activism and fighting for Civil Rights, Black Hair provided a visual soundtrack. Griffin (2019) states "wearing an afro became a weapon in the fight for racial equality, as well as a public declaration of self-love and solidarity within the black community." Visual depictions of the 60s and early 70s portrayed both Black women and Black men boldly marching, with their afros neatly shaped, and their fists held up high. Fifty years later, The Black Lives Matter Movement featured similar images.

Jenkins v. Blue Cross Mutual Hospital Insurance in 1976 was the first discrimination case against natural hair (Griffin, 2019). In this case the U.S. Court of Appeals found that under the Title VII of the Civil Rights Act, Blue Cross Mutual Hospital Insurance Company was not allowed mandate that women could not wear afros (Griffin, 2019). Title VII of the Civil Rights Act, "covers employment discrimination based on race, color, religion, sex, national origin, or protected activity. [It's] prohibitions against race and color discrimination were aimed at ending a system in which Blacks were 'largely relegated to unskilled and semi-skilled jobs'" (EEOC, 2006). This act is extremely important to the fight to end hair bias because it is the precedence for additional anti-discriminatory legislation.

However, as time progressed, "the 1980s and 1990s ushered in more black women sporting pressed and permed hair, thanks to prevalent hair-care ads on TV and in magazines that encouraged black women to alter the texture of their hair. (Griffin, 2019)." Images on the small screen and the big screen also encouraged the braiding of hair during this time, which caused more litigation regarding black hair. One example was "In 1981, a black woman took American Airlines to court because the company demanded she not wear her hair in braids. The court sided with the airline, stating that braids were not an immutable racial characteristic—unlike the afro (Griffin, 2019)". This ruling was used to set precedence in a subsequent case resulting in the Hyatt Regency forcing Cheryl Tatum to resign because she refused to change her hairstyle, which was cornrows (Griffin, 2019).

In the 2000s artists, writers, and social media influencers "caused a shift in the cultural understanding of natural hair" (Griffin, 2019). Movies, documentaries, blogs, and videos provided space for women to "discuss their hair-care journeys, share hair tutorials, and connect with other women" (Griffin, 2019). This shift caused many black women to embrace their natural hair and move away from perming and pressing their hair. This is evidenced by data from the global research firm Mintel, which showed that "spending on perm relaxers fell 30.8 percent between 2011 and 2016" (Griffin, 2019).

Currently, as natural hair continues to be embraced by members of society and is more widely worn by women, society is changing its outlook and policies on it. Influencers and artists are continuing to document natural hair journeys and more women than ever are embracing their natural hair. Corporations and employers such as the U.S. Navy and the Army have "changed [their] grooming polici[es] to include braided styles and locs" (Griffin, 2019). The landscape of hair is changing, more women are embracing their natural hair and expressing themselves through items such as hair dye and headwraps, society is becoming more accepting of natural hair. As the new generation continues to rebel against the traditional status quo, the issues, problems, and ultimatums that Black women wearing their natural hair are facing continue to decrease.

LEGISLATION

In 2006, the U.S. Equal Employment Opportunity Commission (EEOC), a federal "organization responsible for enforcing federal laws that make it illegal to discriminate against a job applicant or an employee because of the person's race, color, religion, sex (including pregnancy and related conditions, gender identity, and sexual orientation), national origin, age (40 or older), disability or genetic information" (U.S. Equal), issued a manual that discusses and provides guidelines for natural hair and other physical characteristics in the workplace. In Section 15 of the manual, Race and Color Discrimination are addressed. In this section, the EEOC defines the terms race discrimination and color discrimination and discusses their implications in the workplace. The manual covers giving employees equal access to jobs, including hiring, promotion, and Affirmative Action and job success through equal opportunity, including racial harassment and racial bias.

The EEOC Manual is based on the broadly written Title VII Act. The Title VII Act "covers employment discrimination based on race, color, religion, sex, national origin, or protected activity" (EEOC, 2006). This act was broadly written so that it would cover all races and ethnicities, so the EEOC Manual was created in order to provide guidance on the act (EEOC, 2006). For example, the Title VII Act specifically prohibits racial discrimination; the EEOC Manual expounds upon this prohibition by explaining what racial discrimination is and what it encompasses. The manual describes eight areas in which a company cannot discriminate against their employees (EEOC, 2006). Hair is specifically, included in the physical characteristics area (EEOC, 2006), the manual defines the discrimination of employees based on their physical characteristics as "[e]mployment discrimination based on a person's physical characteristics associated with race, such as a person's color, hair, facial features, height and weight" (EEOC, 2006).

The manual goes on to provide guidance to companies so that all employees have an equal opportunity at success in their organizations. It states that "Employers cannot permit race bias to affect work assignments, performance measurements, pay, training, mentoring or networking, discipline, or any other term, condition, or privilege of employment" (EEOC, 2006). Among the examples and explanations that the manual gives in these areas is a section on "Appearance and Grooming Standards; in this section, the EEOC states, "Appearance standards generally must be neutral, adopted for nondiscriminatory reasons, consistently applied to persons of all racial and ethnic groups" (EEOC, 2006).

In the Appearance and Grooming Section, there is a specific section dedicated to hair. The manual states that, "[e]mployers can impose neutral hairstyle rules – e.g., that hair be neat, clean, and well-groomed – as long as the rules respect racial differences in hair textures and are applied evenhandedly" (EEOC, 2006). This language is problematic because the definition of those descriptions differs based on a person's perspective. Because of this, Title VII does state that employers are prohibited from preventing African-American women from wearing their hair in an Afro style (EEOC, 2006). It also "prohibits employers from applying neutral hairstyle rules more restrictively to hairstyles worn by African Americans" (EEOC, 2006). There are many court cases based on the Title VII legislation; these cases will be discussed later in the chapter.

The CROWN Act is another piece of legislation designed to provide guidance on natural hair. The act, first passed by California in 2019, supports the natural hair movement and provides a foundation for professionals to wear their hair as they see fit (Stracqualursi, 2022). The CROWN Act, which stands for "Creating a Respectful and Open World for Natural Hair" Act, has passed in 24 states and inspired similar legislation in other states (Payne-Patterson, 2023). The CROWN Act is supported by research from the national hair brand Dove, which is a section of the Unilever company (Najarro, 2022). It was introduced by members of the CROWN Act coalition, which includes members from various civil rights organizations, non-profits, and corporations, in 2019 (Najarro, 2022). The purpose of the CROWN Act is to "normalize[e] our natural hairstyles and texture, so that our hairstyles can be viewed as professional" (Najarro, 2022). The authors of the CROWN Act, including representatives from the National Urban League and the organization Color of Change, wrote the legislation so that "it makes hair texture and styles a protected trait under pre-existing civil rights legislation, namely the Fair Employment and Housing Act" (Najarro, 2022).

Efforts are also underway to get legislation like the CROWN Act passed as a federal law (Najarro, 2022). The CROWN Act Bill, sponsored by Democratic Rep. Bonnie Watson Coleman of New Jersey, passed in the House of Representatives in March of 2022 and has been sponsored in the Senate by Democratic Sen. Cory

Booker of New Jersey (Stracqualursi, 2022). In an article written about the process of getting the CROWN Act passed as a federal law, Stracqualursi (2022) states, "The Biden administration this week said it 'strongly supports' the CROWN Act and 'looks forward to working with the Congress to enact this legislation and ensure that it is effectively implemented'." The article also notes that there is opposition to the bill from Republicans, with one representative stating, "'Fourteen months of chaos and we're doing a bill on hair,' Republican Rep. Jim Jordan of Ohio said Friday, adding, 'I hope we can actually focus on the things that matter to the American people.'" Although the issue of protecting the rights of Natural Hair Wearers may seem negligible to some, it is a pervasive issue affecting millions worldwide.

While federal legislation efforts are being made, state legislation similar to the CROWN Act is continuing to be passed throughout the country. The state of Massachusetts signed a CROWN Act into law in May of 2022 and Michigan has become one of the latest states to sign CROWN Act legislation into a law this year (Marr, 2022; Payne-Patterson, 2023). The new Louisiana CROWN Act legislation, signed into law in 2022, states that "employers could require an employee tie back their locks or cover their hair at work, but not require them to cut it off or use chemicals to straighten it." (Marr, 2022). More importantly, "the law prevents employers from punishing Black hairstyles purely because they don't like the appearance" (Marr, 2022). Figure 1 is a map published in 2022 that shows the states that have outlawed hair discrimination and states that do not have a state law, but do have local bans (Marr, 2022). It should be noted that since the publication of this graphic other states such as Alaska, Minnesota, and Illinois have passed the CROWN Act (Payne-Patterson, 2023).

Figure 1. Bans on race-related hair bias
(Marr, 2022)

HISTORICAL CONTEXT ABROAD

Natural hair not only has a storied in the United States of America, but wearing naturally curly hair in other countries could also be met with disdain. In her research abroad, Marla Goins (2020) writes about her experiences and observations in countries such as the Dominican Republic and Brazil. She writes extensively about her time in the Dominican Republic and how averse the country was to hair in an afro. She relays stories from others and from her personal experience about negative reactions to afros including people calling the tightly curled hair 'bad' or making comments such as, "Look at that nest! Someone light a match!" (Goins, 2020, p. 3).

After recounting her experiences, Goins (2020) does go on to explain that after she left the Dominican Republic, it seemed to experience a hair revolution. This included many Dominicans beginning to wear their hair naturally and making statements such as "'Amo mi pajón!' ('I love my fro!')" (Goins, 2020, p. 5). However, despite the growth of natural hair in the Dominican Republic, avante guard women wearing their natural hair still faced repercussions. After being denied entry into a bar, one salon owner that specialized in natural hair "declared that 'this hair has done nothing to no one. This hair is a part of who I am. Why should I put this hair away?'" (Goins, 2020, p. 5).

This has not been the experience for all Natural Hair Wearers who have lived abroad. When interviewed, one educator stated that while living abroad in Indonesia she always received compliments on her natural hair. The educator went on to say that she never heard of any negative comments about her hair, nor did she feel hindered by her hair during her time in that country. During this interview the educator attributed the wide acceptance of her hair to the diversity of the people that she lived and worked with during her time in Indonesia and the culture of inclusion that they fostered.

Comparing the experiences of this educator with the experiences of the previous educator and the opinions of the educators in the United States reveals a glaring difference in the way that Natural Hair Wearers are treated. As one of the most diverse countries in the World, the fact that Natural Hair Wearers in the United States face such contention and opposition based on their hair choice is unacceptable.

TEACHERS HELD TO A HIGHER STANDARD

Since teaching became a profession, teachers have been held to a higher standard than most professions. Because of their work with the youngest members of society and the time and position that they have in their lives, society, legislators, and district personnel expect teachers to live morally responsible lives. In one school district, teachers and staff are required to watch a video on the district's Code of Ethics. The introduction to the video states that the district expects all students to be role models to their students and that the Code of Ethics should serve as a guide that teachers should use. This Code of Ethics includes rules on teachers obeying the law, prioritizing student health, and a rule stating that teachers should be professional in their demeanor. Every year the hundreds of teachers in the school district agree to the Code of Ethics by watching the video and agreeing to stipulations in employee handbooks. On a larger scale millions of teachers also agree to stipulations similar to these each year.

These stipulations and expectations are seen in various ways. Stipulations have been added to teachers' contracts at the district and school levels and teachers are being held accountable for the items held within them. Teachers have faced losing their job and litigation based on things unrelated to their classroom teaching and things that happened outside of school based on contract stipulations and Code of Ethics videos. Teachers have been placed on administrative leave and/or fired for social media posts that violate district policies. News outlets and social media platforms report on teachers' actions, words, and ideas any time that there is a violation by society's standards.

Discipling teachers based on society's standards is problematic because society has conflicting and changing standards. Society's standards of morality, professionalism, and beauty stem from outdated views, mainstream cultures, media, and various other areas. Esi Eggleston Bracey states that "[Natural] hair is a manifestation of a way to perpetuate the institution of racism and bias, unfortunately. And so, that shows up in the schools because we're part of a broader system, where culturally certain hairstyles are viewed as a standard and our hair texture is viewed culturally as untidy, unkept, unprofessional, unscholarly (Najarro, 2022)." There is quantitative data that supports this. In a study carried out by Dove and the professional networking website LinkedIn, "Black women's hair is 2.5 times as likely as white women's hair to be perceived as 'unprofessional.'" (Payne-Patterson, 2023).

HAIR BIAS

Hair Bias is the practice of limiting a person's opportunities, pay, or perception based on the way that they wear their hair. Hair bias can be traced back to the beginning of our time in America and can also be found in Africa. In America, "it stems from systemic bias, unconscious bias, and institutional racism. It starts back from slavery" (Najaro, 2022). Although this is against Title VII of the Civil Rights Act of 1964, it does occur. Title VII of the Civil Rights Act of 1964 "makes it unlawful for an employer to discriminate against someone because of race, color, religion, sex (including pregnancy and related conditions, sexual orientation, and gender identity), or national origin" (Laws, 2023). Based on The Civil Rights Act, employers cannot discriminate against their employees because of anything relating to their race. According to ancestry, physical characteristics, race-linked illness, culture, perception, association, subgroups of the race, or reverse discrimination (Issuing, 2023). Although hair bias is not always overtly seen in the workplace and other arenas, there is quantitative and qualitative research indicating it's existence.

Research carried out by the researcher and other scholars from prestigious organizations such as Duke University's Fuqua School of Business and companies such as Dove and Pantene provide evidence that hair bias exists and limits the success of women who wear their hair naturally. In an article published by Duke's Fuqua School of Business one researcher writes, "The impact of a woman's hairstyle may seem minute, Rosette said, 'but for Black women, it's a serious consideration and may contribute to the lack of representation for Blacks in some organizational settings' (Duke, 2020).

It should also be noted that although Black women face hair bias at very high rates and this chapter focuses predominately on their experiences, Black men also face discrimination based on how they wear their hair. In a recent conversation with a school principal who has moved into leadership in another career, he noted a marked difference between how he is treated while wear braids versus when he wore his hair cut short. In another conversation with a Black man who is not in the education field, he relayed a story similar to mine. His employer asked him "how long he was going to keep his hair like that?" indicating his newly created locs. The man responded "indefinitely", to which the employer responded that he should wear his hair like another employee that wore his head shaved bald. A few weeks later the man was fired.

Hair bias occurs in various areas because people view others through the lens of society's standards. "In many Western societies, whites have historically been the dominant social group and, as a result, the standard for professional appearance is often based on the physical appearance of whites. For women's hair, that benchmark is having straightened hair (Duke, 2020). For many members of society, women who wear their hair naturally, and do not straighten the curls out of it so that it resembles a white woman's hair are perceived to perform at lower levels than those that do.

According to the U.S. Equal Employment Opportunity Commission, "employers can impose neutral hairstyle rules – e.g., that hair be neat, clean, and well-groomed – as long as the rules respect racial differences in hair textures and are applied evenhandedly" (Issuing, 2023). Although employers have grooming policies that appear to respect the differences of all people, in practice these rules lead to consequences for employees of African-American races. Although they are supposed to be neutral, these grooming policies often "say that hair cannot be worn in protective hairstyles, braids, locs, bantu knots, or certain lengths of the hairstyles. And its discrimination because these are hairstyles that are inherent to our identity, and the natural state in which our hair grows from our head" (Najarro, 2022).

This can be seen in a case such as Hollins v. Atlantic Co., Inc., 188 F.3d 652, 661 (6th Cir. 1999) in which a company admitted to preventing a black female from wearing her hair in Fingerwaves because they thought that the hairstyle was "too eye-catching", but did not imposing the same standards to white women (EEOC, 2006). In another court case, Rogers v. American Airlines, 527 F. Supp. 229, 232-34 (S.D.N.Y. 1981), a court upheld that "an employer policy banning 'afro' hairstyles likely would be a race-based distinction in violation of Title VII because, unlike braids or cornrows, an 'afro' is the product of natural hair growth rather than artifice)" (EEOC, 2006), but this same case held that "a neutral employer policy against women wearing braids or cornrows was not a race-based distinction, and thus…would violate Title VII only if it had a disparate impact on Black women and was not job-related and consistent with business necessity, or if the policy were applied in a discriminatory manner" (EEOC, 2006).

In a professional organization, women with natural hair are discriminated against, face hiring bias, and experience inequitable treatment and microaggressions (Asare,

2022). The women are forced to deal with these harmful experiences every day and the consequences lead to feelings that create a harmful and limiting work environment.

HAIR BIAS IN THE EDUCATIONAL ORGANIZATION

An educator experiencing hair bias in his/her educational organization can be negatively affected in many areas. One area is that they may lose money, personal days, or social capital because their hairstyle could be deemed unprofessional and they are asked to change it. The Dove and LinkedIn study found that, "Over 20% of Black women ages 25–34 have been sent home from their jobs due to their hair" (Payne-Patterson, 2023). When an educator is asked to leave work due to the way that they styled their hair this causes either a loss of personal days or is an administrative issue that could impact the rest of the educator's career. If an educator is asked to change their hairstyle or chooses to change their hairstyle because they received some type of negative backlash from their peers or supervisors this will cause a loss of the time and money that the current hairstyle cost them and they may be forced to take a personal day if they are asked to go home due to the perceived administrative issue. These items could add up to hundreds of dollars wasted and hours of time lost. Both of which are a high price to pay for the average educator who only receives a small number of personal days and an inadequate salary.

An even higher cost are the ramifications that being sent home from work or having someone speak negatively about a chosen hairstyle has on the Natural Hair Wears mental health. Because "[h]air can be a declaration of personal identity and serve as a symbol of heritage and ancestry" (Payne-Patterson, 2023), having someone one think negatively about a hairstyle that the wearer has chosen could negatively impact the wearer's self-confidence and their self-esteem. It could change how they view their hair and their workplace; changes that could have devastating effects.

Along with the potential cost of having to change a hairstyle, there is an additional cost for women who wear their hair naturally. This includes "spending hours preparing their hair for work, spending entire days in the beauty salon, spending large amounts of money on hair supplies, avoiding physical activity, or avoiding going outdoors when it is raining" (Kennedy, 2020, p. 8). The time that it takes to create styles that are generally accepted as professional, such as braids, silk presses, or various other forms of heat treatment, is exorbitant; many of these styles take between two and ten hours to complete. Louisiana State Representative Brandy Fluker Oakley, a sponsor of the recently passed anti-hair bias bill, stated "As a Black woman, she has felt pressure to spend substantial time and money changing her hair to be accepted as a public school teacher, law student, and then lawyer" (Marr, 2022). Because of the hours that educators work, this means that they will have to devote entire weekends to getting their hair styled. Although these issues are widely accepted by educators who wear their hair naturally, it is important that it is highlighted as a significant sacrifice in this chapter.

During one interview with an educator, Mrs. James, who recently took on a new job at the district level, the subject stated that although she has not heard of any negative comments about her natural hair, she was conscious of the fact that wearing her hair in its naturally curly state could have a negative impact on how she was perceived. This was evidenced by her choice to wear her hair straightened when district-level personnel came to observe her teaching in her classroom or when she had district-level meetings. I can also attest to this feeling. Although no one has ever blatantly asked me to style my hair a certain way, when I knew that I was going to be observed or meeting with district-level leaders, I would re-twist my locs and/or style my hair the night before. This was because, as Mrs. James stated in her interview, "I didn't want my hair to be an issue."

In her recent research Kalen Kennedy (2020), lists African-American studies and sociology research that indicates that there are certain natural hairstyles that "can influence how Black people are perceived" (p. 7), she mentions afros and the hair style most commonly referred to as "dreadlocks" as two of these styles. These specific styles, due to their social and political context in the past are viewed negatively by many. Because of the traditional context of these hair styles, Women who wear these natural styles "are often viewed as unprofessional, aggressive, militant, incompetent, criminal, or unattractive" (Kennedy, 2020, p. 7).

This is why my principal at the time asked me if I was sure that I wanted to keep my hairstyle in locs. The educational organization is very traditional and biased in many areas. Social Influences, including the area of hair is one of those areas. My principal knew that I aspired to be an administrator one day and he knew that my locs could negatively affect my chances of promotion. I told my principal that I would be keeping my locs indefinitely, but reflecting on his question and its implications, I knew that at some point I might be faced with the decision again. A decision that Natural Hair Wearers have faced countless times. A decision that could potentially have a negative impact on my professional future, like it did for "Chastity Jones, a Black woman in Alabama, [who] was offered a customer service position, only to have it rescinded after she refused to cut her locks" (Payne-Patterson, 2023). The biased views found in professional settings, specifically the educational organization negatively impact the style wearer's social capital by limiting his/her professional and social opportunities.

If a hairstyle is deemed unprofessional, then the teacher's peers, supervisors, parents, and students develop negative opinions of the teacher's professional judgement and abilities. Mrs. General relates this concept to the researcher during an interview. In a discussion about this in the interview, Mrs. General says, "I think that when people see me in the field, they don't think that I am as qualified until they see me work. Because I have had parents say, 'I don't think that you were qualified to teach my child or judge their ability to do math'. Then they would move their child out of my class. But, the parents had to come back and apologize after they heard the same thing from another math teacher." She goes on to indicate that the type of school that she taught in made a difference when it came to her hair and her race when it came to her perceived professionalism. She says that the previously mentioned issue was more prevalent in the affluent school that she taught in.

Another area that a teacher wearing his/her hair naturally may experience is hiring bias. If a school would like to hire a teacher with a specific aesthetic and certain beliefs or morals, then their decision to hire a teacher may be based on the style of their hair. Although it is required by law that employers have an anti-discrimination law in place for hiring and all parts of employment, biases do occur. In an article published in Forbes magazine, Asare (2022) writes, "Black hair can trigger an individual's unconscious bias and make a job candidate less desirable to employers." This bias in hiring practices causes many teachers to straighten their natural hair with heat or chemicals before an interview or wear a wig on the day of the interview. The previously referenced study carried out by Dove and LinkedIn found that "approximately two-thirds (66%) of Black women change their hair for a job interview. Among them, 41% changed their hair from curly to straight" (Payne-Patterson, 2023).

When women straighten their hair with chemicals or heat, it takes hours and could cost over a hundred dollars. This cost does not include the damage that is done to the hair or to the wearers body. Heat can cause hair to become damaged and break off and chemicals have been "linked straightening products to breast and uterine cancer (Payne-Patterson, 2023). Wigs also create additional costs to women who wear them to cover their natural hair due to hair bias. Wigs can range from $40 to hundreds of dollars depending on their quality and style and take a significant amount of time to install.

Mrs. General stated that wearing a wig to her interview made her feel more professional and confident during the interview. She also stated that she didn't want her natural hair to keep her from getting a job. She "knew that she was qualified for the job and she didn't want her hair to make a possible employer think that she was not." Ms. Smith relayed this same sentiment during an interview, "you strived to have your hair tame [during interviews], because it felt like that was more professional". In an empirical study carried out by Duke University, researchers "examined participant responses to hair texture by asking a racially diverse set of participants to review professional profiles and rate the candidates on competence and professionalism. The study found that candidates with curlier hair were less likely to be recommended for hire and scored lower in assessments of professionalism and competence" (Payne-Patterson, 2023).

Not only does hiring bias affect teachers being hired for teaching positions, but it also affects teachers and other educational professionals that desire to move out of the classroom into various levels of school and district leadership. This is related to Mrs. James's comments about straightening her hair before being observed by district-level personnel and attending district-level meetings. If teachers want to move into school or district-level leadership, then they may feel pressure to change their natural hair.

When my principal asked me if I was going to leave my hair in locs and subtly implied that it might negatively impact my career, I knew that his questions didn't come from a place of spite or vengeance, but that didn't make them any less painful to hear. As I sat in his office, contemplating my future and how my hair would impact it, I knew that I could be faced with a tough decision in the future. Educators around the World have dealt with issues in their personal lives affecting their professional lives since the beginning of the profession. They have had to wear certain clothes, only associate with certain people, and behave in certain ways due to the responsibilities of their job. I felt the weight of that burden on me that day as I sat in my boss's office. Except this time, the burden was my hair.

For educators who would like to move up in their educational organization, the decision to wear their hair naturally is a complex one. They must weigh factors such as the continued use of chemical products to straighten their hair versus the physical and cultural benefits of wearing it naturally. Since the conversation that I had with my supervisor almost twenty years ago about my loc'ed hair, I have heard similar stories from other women in the educational field. These women and men, all of the African-American race, have recounted stories and told me quotes about times when their choice of hairstyle was questioned or discussed.

Women who wear their hair naturally also experience microaggressions on a daily basis. The daily derogatory comments, unnecessary questions, and physical accosting that women who wear their hair naturally face on a daily basis are exhausting and offensive. Asare, a Forbes Magazine contributor, states, "Before the pandemic, Black employees experienced being asked by non-Black employees if their hair could be touched. Even in a remote workplace setting, these racial microaggressions continue. Black employees may be asked questions about a new hairstyle they are rocking or interrogated about whether their hair is real. It is not often considered how these questions can make a person feel othered and dehumanized—these inquiries are rarely asked to non-Black colleagues" (Asare, 2022).

Incessant microaggressions create a harmful working environment for women who wear their hair naturally. Ms. Smith recounts a story of when one of her co-workers came to her and stated, "[t]he boss [a school principal] doesn't think that women should wear headwraps", deeply offended both by the statement and that it came from a co-worker and not from her boss. Ms. Smith, who wore headwraps frequently, told the co-worker that "if he wants me to stop wearing them, he needs to come and tell me himself and he needs to show me the policy that opinion is based on". Another comment relayed to me during an interview was "I like your hair when it's like that." This comment which came from a co-worker was referring to an interviewee's straightened hair. The consequences of these microaggressions are an unhealthy or hostile working environment and a possible negative effect on the employee's mental health, self-esteem, job performance, and job satisfaction.

Educators not only face these microaggressions from their peer teachers, but also have to face them from students and their parents. Educators with natural hair endure comments from the students in their classes and negative looks from the parents of the students that they teach. Parents may want their child moved to another class before the school year starts or they may question the teacher's judgement on various issues during the school year. Fighting battles like these can be very taxing on the already stressed educator. This could lead to feelings of teacher burnout and feelings of being overwhelmed. Mrs. General ended up disengaging from the student placement issues that she faced, which was to the detriment of the student. This was my method for dealing with these issues, as well. In order to avoid feelings of unfairness and helplessness, I simply let the student go.

Educators who wear their hair naturally face many situations because of their hair choice that lead to their mistreatment. Whether it is being placed on administrative leave causing a loss of pay, being overlooked for a job or promotion, or dealing with harmful comments or actions, none of these consequences are deserved and they are a palpable mistreatment of women with natural hair. In addition to these consequences, women who wear natural hair can experience mistreatment by experiencing segregation while working, receiving unwarranted negative performance reviews, and being fired (Asare, 2022).

RECOMMENDATIONS

Society has undergone many changes since its inception. Each decade, each movement, each piece of legislation, each woman that wears her hair naturally, and each administrator, co-worker, parent, and student that embraces it helps to erase the stigma associated with wearing one's hair naturally. This stigma must be completely erased for women to acquire and maintain equality in the workplace. Currently, women who wear their hair naturally are working harder than their peers in order to overcome this stigma and be seen as equals. The stigma is deleterious to their careers and mental health because it causes mistreatment in the form or hiring bias and lack of promotion, microaggressions from superiors, co-workers, and other educational stakeholders, as well as various other negative effects that can be directly or indirectly linked to how they are perceived.

One recommendation is that legislation continues to be expanded and created to protect women who are choosing to wear their hair naturally. "To be clear, hair discrimination is racial discrimination and should be protected under pre-existing civil rights legislation from the 1964 Civil Rights Act" (Najarro, 2022). Legislation such as Title VII of the Civil Rights Act and the CROWN Act offer many legal protections; however, as workplace issues continue to arise and become more prevalent, new legislation should be introduced. It should be noted here that the 24 states that have passed CROWN Acts have done so in three years; this is a testament to the urgency that is felt by legislators across the country (Marr, 2022). It should also be noted, that although 24 states have passed CROWN Act legislation, 25 states have tried to introduce CROWN Act legislation and the legislation was not passed (Marr, 2022). At the writing of this chapter CROWN Act legislation is still being introduced and passed, with Michigan passing the CROWN Act this year (Payne-Patterson, 2023). It is through the creation and enforcement of past and new legislation that businesses will continue to change their policies and perceptions of the abilities of women with natural hair.

Another recommendation is that hair in its natural state is removed from the discussion of professionalism. It is specifically prohibited by various laws to discriminate against people for naturally occurring physical characteristics; natural hair should be added to this list. Physical characteristics such as age, weight, and gender are afforded many legal protections, with costly repercussions if discovered. These same protections should be afforded to natural hair. Hairstyles should also be excluded from any conversation about dress code. Dress code should only apply to clothing items, not items that naturally grow. People who choose to do so should not be penalized for choosing to embrace their hair's natural state. This change in thinking about professionalism in organizations, means that companies will "need to train their front-line managers who make hiring, firing, and discipline decisions" (Marr, 2022).

Another recommendation is that society continues to embrace and support women who wear their hair naturally. This could include more women choosing to wear their hair naturally, expanding the market for natural hair care products, and supervisors and co-workers basing their hiring practices strictly on the candidates' abilities to carry out the job as evidenced by their previous work experiences, accomplishments, and suitability with the company. This could also include Natural Hair Wearers being given access to opportunities that have previously been denied to them. A part of society continuing to embrace this movement, is women who wear their hair naturally being willing to have open dialog about their hair. Although it may be difficult, natural women must be open to discussions and be willing to educate others about natural hair.

Early in my career, I was asked a question about my hair that changed my life. This question caused me to take a closer look at my dream job and the limitations and stipulations that I would have to face in that specific role. The question and the lines of thinking that came after them caused a shift in my focus and life. I didn't want to go into a position that was so stringent and limiting. Ultimately, I decided to go another route. I decided that I would move into a position that was less stringent and less contingent upon how I wear my hair. This is currently my fifth year in my role as an Instructional Coach and that decision was one of the best that I ever made. I get to carryout the best aspects of school-level leadership, without most of the limitations and stress that school-level administrators experience. And I get to enjoy my free-flowing, loc each and every day.

A final recommendation is that media outlets, influencers, and users continue to increase the inclusion of diverse people, including women with natural hair on their platforms. Recently, there has been an increase in the amount of diversity displayed positively on outlets such as television, social media, and video streaming services. These positive images help to change the perception of members of society each time they are viewed. Bracey states, "hairstyles can be viewed as scholarly, because you see all of us as scholars and professionals wearing the textured hairstyles" (Najarro, 2022). Intentionally sharing the images of diverse people doing positive things normalizes the existence of these occurrences and works to change the idea that these occurrences are uncommon. The more these images are seen, the more accepted they are and then they are accepted as the norm. When they become ingrained in society, societal perceptions and actions based on the perceptions change.

CONCLUSION

Women who wear their hair naturally have made the decision to not only embrace their heritage, but they have also chosen to choose a healthy path to hair care. Unfortunately, this healthy change is not well perceived by society as a whole and more specifically, by educational organizations. It is the researcher's experience and the experiences of others in the educational field and other professions that women who wear their hair naturally have been questioned, overlooked, or hurt because of the way that they wear their hair. These experiences have slowed down and impeded their professional journey. In order for women to continue to move forward in the workplace, members in the education field, those of us who wear our hair naturally and those who do not must create space for women around the world who choose to wear their hair naturally and proudly.

As an African-American woman who has been faced with the choice of wearing her hair naturally or wearing it in a more socially acceptable way if she wants to move ahead in her career, this book chapter serves as a beacon of hope. Hopefully, it provides evidence to others who are faced with the same choice that although women who have natural hair have historically faced adversity, due to legislation and biases, society's viewpoints are changing. This change is essential to the advancement of black people as a whole and black women who wear their hair naturally because it lets us know that although there is no right or wrong answer to the choice of wearing our hair naturally or not, choosing to go against the social grain means that she will not be penalized in terms of career advancement.

REFERENCES

Asare, J. G. (2022, August 16). Four ways hair bias shows up in the workplace. *Forbes*. https://www.forbes.com/sites/janicegassam/2022/08/15/four-ways-hair-bias-shows-up-in-the-workplace/?sh=4d8c943069a3

Duke's Fuqua School of Business. (2020, August 12). *Research suggests bias against natural hair limits job opportunities for black women*. Duke University. https://www.fuqua.duke.edu/duke-fuqua-insights/ashleigh-rosette-research-suggests-bias-against-natural-hair-limits-job

U.S. Equal Employment Opportunity Commission. (2006, April 19). *EEOC Compliance Manual: Section 15 race and color discrimination*. US EEOC. Office of Legal Counsel, Title VII/ADEA/EPA Division. https://www.eeoc.gov/laws/guidance/section-15-race-and-color-discrimination

Griffin, C. (2019, July 3). *How Natural Black Hair at Work Became a Civil Rights Issue*. JSTOR. https://daily.jstor.org/how-natural-black-hair-at-work-became-a-civil-rights-issue/#:~:text=The%20activist%20Angela%20Davis%20sported,black%20teens%20living%20in%20St

Kennedy, K. (2020). My Natural Hair Is Unprofessional: The Impact of Black Hairstyles on Perceived Employment-Related Characteristics. [Master's Thesis, Marquette University]. https://epublications.marquette.edu/theses_open/578

Laws we enforce. (2023, April 13). The United States Department of Justice. https://www.justice.gov/crt/laws-we-enforce#:~:text=Title%20VII%20also%20makes%20it%20unlawful%20to%20use%20policies%20or,identity)%2C%20or%20national%20origin.

Legal Defense Fund. (2023, March 22). *Natural hair discrimination faq*. NAACP. https://www.naacpldf.org/natural-hair-discrimination/

Legal Defense Fund. (2023). *Natural Hair Discrimination*. NAACP. https://www.naacpldf.org/natural-hair-discrimination/

Marr, C. (2022, August 1). Black Hair Bias Laws Spread, Including in Handful of Red States. *Bloomberg Law.* https://news.bloomberglaw.com/daily-labor-report/black-hair-bias-laws-spread-including-in-handful-of-red-states

Najarro, I. (2022, July 6). 'Our hair is our identity': What educators need to know about hair discrimination laws. *Education Week*. https://www.edweek.org/leadership/our-hair-is-our-identity-what-educators-need-to-know-about-hair-discrimination-laws/2022/07

Payne-Patterson. (2023). *The CROWN Act: A jewel for combating racial discrimination in the workplace and classroom.* Economic Policy Institute. https://www.epi.org/publication/crown-act/

Stracqualursi, V. (2022). *US House Passes Crown Act That Would Ban Race-Based Hair Discrimination.* CNN. https://www.cnn.com/2022/03/18/politics/house-vote-crown-act/index.html

Chapter 13
Why Hair Isn't Just Hair:
A Systemic Approach to Contradict DEI Initiatives and Undermine Title VII

Khadija Boyd
https://orcid.org/0000-0003-0290-9317
Northcentral University, USA

ABSTRACT

Diversity, equity, and inclusion are used with Title VII of the Civil Rights Act of 1964, which prohibits workplace discrimination, to promote the representation and participation of its employees. However, some white men feel that DEI policies are unnecessary and play an influential role in implementing DEI policies while simultaneously being a threat to them. For this chapter, the author will focus on the discriminatory definition of professionalism, its imposition on DEI, and the undermining of Title VII through hair discrimination. The author argues that white supremacy culture and its definition of professionalism engages in four mechanisms–devaluing and dehumanizing Blackness, removing Black identity and culture, forcing hegemonic ideologies rooted in anti-blackness, and controlling the bodily autonomy of Black women to answer the following research question: "Why is banning afro-textured natural hair and cultural Black hairstyles in the work environment a civil rights issue that contradicts DEI initiatives?"

DOI: 10.4018/978-1-6684-8790-7.ch013

INTRODUCTION

Diversity, equity, and inclusion (DEI) describes policies that promote the representation and participation of individuals from different ages, abilities and disabilities, cultures, ethnicities, genders, races, religions, and sexual orientations (Arsel et al., 2022) in the work environment. DEI is used in conjunction with Title VII of the Civil Rights Act of 1964, which prohibits workplace discrimination based on race, color, religion, sex, and national origin– better known as immutable characteristics (US Equal Opportunity Employment Commission, 2023). According to doctrine, a trait is immutable if it is beyond the power of an individual to change or is crucial to personal identity (Serafin, 2020). Organizations are implementing DEI efforts to bring their institutions to the forefront of their industries because enhancing workplace DEI improves creativity, engagement, and innovation (Maqsoon et al., 2023). However, the disdain for DEI efforts has been increasingly high as Black people, who have been historically marginalized and excluded, begin to take up spaces traditionally reserved for white people, specifically white men. Because of this, some white men feel that DEI policies are unnecessary (Iyer, 2022). Moreover, because of their customarily privileged position, they play an influential role in implementing DEI policies while simultaneously being a threat to them (Dover et al., 2016; Iyer, 2022).

Threats can come in many forms, but for this chapter, the author will focus on the discriminatory definition of professionalism and its imposition on DEI initiatives and the undermining Title VII. Professionalism is not an emerging concept and is enforced by the dominant group in society. In America, the dominant group has historically been white, heteronormative, English-speaking men (Boyd, 2021; 2022) who have defined professionalism through white supremacist ideologies and disguised structural racism in professionalism in the work environment. Structural racism encompasses the history that provides the foundation for white supremacy, incorporates a culture that normalizes and replicates racism, and implements systemic institutions and policies that provide reinforcements and legitimacy to sustain and preserve racism (Scott-Jones & Kamara, 2020; Lawrence & Kelecher, 2004). Therefore, to oppose DEI initiatives and undermine Title VII, employers can enforce specific guidelines about employees' appearance to enact their discrimination covertly and legally– for example, hair discrimination. Hair discrimination uses structural racism to create racist policies that exclude or force Black people, specifically Black women with afro-textured natural hair and hairstyles, into small descriptive boxes that suppress their Black identity to conform to white supremacy culture in an attempt to create a homogenous work environment. Because hair, although crucial to the culture and identity of Black women (Alexander, 2016; Barrick et al., 2019; Byrd & Tharps,

2001), is not considered an immutable characteristic or protected under Title VII (Tchenga, 2021).

Stories about Black women with afro-textured natural hair and hairstyles whose employers have asked them to change their appearance because social and political implications have increased. It has also been amplified in the last few years as more Black women continue to reject the oppression enacted through the definition of professionalism, which promotes anti-blackness and white supremacy culture. Although, to some, the impact a Black woman's afro-textured natural hair or hairstyle has on her ability to navigate their work environment may seem diminutive. Contrarywise, scholarly literature has empirically documented the damage that these elements of white supremacy culture and anti-black stereotypes associated with afro-textured natural hair and Black hairstyles have created to oppress and exclude Black women in the work environment. (Alexander, 2016; Ashe, 1995; Banks, 2000; Barrick et al., 2019; Byrd & Tharps, 2001; Craig, 2002; Dove, 2021; Ellis-Harvey, 2016; Goodman, 2021; Jones & Shorter-Gooden, 2003; Johnson & Bankhead, 2013; Johnson et al., 2017; Kipping, 2011; Koval & Rosette, 2020; Opie & Phillips, 2015; Patton, 2006; Peacock, 2019; Rooks, 1998; Tate, 2007; Webb et al., 2004).

Moreover, studies on racial phenotypical traits indicate that people with Afrocentric features, i.e., afro-textured hair, have habitually been excluded to maintain whiteness in economic, social, and educational institutions (Maddox, 2014; Opie & Williams, 2015). The evidence shows that the perception remains that afro-textured hair and hairstyles, especially those of Black women, are viewed as unprofessional (Alexander, 2016; Barrick et al., 2019; Byrd & Tharps, 2001; Dove, 2021; Goodman, 2021). Furthermore, evidence suggests that Black women with hairstyles inherent to their racial and cultural identity are viewed as childish, too outspoken, and repeatedly have their competence, professionalism, and organizational fit questioned (Dawson et al., 2019; Opie et al., 2014). Lastly, the literature indicates that Black women with afro-textured natural hair and hairstyles are burdened with a severe and deliberate variable that is attributed to maintaining the social structure of white dominance and centering whiteness, and is a significant contributing factor to the lack of representation of Black women in some work environments, their marginalization, and over-policing (Alexander, 2016; Barrick et al., 2019; Byrd & Tharps, 2001; Dove, 2021; Goodman, 2021).

Through structural racism, the definition of professionalism, as it relates to hair, has been epitomized as white (Boyd, 2020, 2021; Opie & Phillips, 2015; Peacock, 2019; Steele, 1992). The Eurocentric look is described and retained as superior, preferred, and regarded as gracious, sophisticated, refined, polished, and respectable (Johnson & Bankhead, 2013; Kennedy, 2020) to externally validate racial ideologies that value white characteristics. Moreover, this is done to preserve white spaces by prohibiting and mislabeling afro-textured natural hair and hairstyles as unprofessional to justify rejecting and removing Black women from any possibility of obtaining relevant positions and status in their work environment. Professional Black women have regularly been fired or threatened with dismissal for "looking unprofessional" because of their natural afro-textured hair and hairstyles. Black women are 30 percent more likely to receive a formal grooming policy in the workplace, 80 percent more likely to alter their natural afro-textured hair, and their hairstyles put them at 1.5 times higher risk of being sent home from work (Dove, 2021; Pitts, 2021) in contrast to other women of different races, ethnicities, and cultures.

Since the creation of negative attributes of Black hair were created during chattel slavery, the continued obsession in a post-colonial world with the texture and styles of Black women's hair remains perverted, sadistic, and warped. Moreover, to some, Black women attempting to meet white standards perpetuates a colonized or enslaved mentality, which appeases white supremacy culture and intensifies Black women's position as oppressed and owned (Giovanni, 1970) by seemingly and unconsciously admitting inferiority. Therefore, the author argues that professionalism, as it relates to hair discrimination against Black women with afro-textured natural hair and hairstyles, engages in four mechanisms– devaluing and dehumanizing Blackness, removing Black identity and culture, forcing hegemonic ideologies rooted in anti-blackness, and controlling the bodily autonomy of Black women. This chapter will expound upon these four mechanisms through an intersectional lens and the guiding theoretical framework of collective social identity to answer the following research question: "Why is banning afro-textured natural hair and cultural Black hairstyles in the work environment a civil rights issue that contradicts DEI initiatives"?

THEORETICAL FRAMEWORK

The American experience has produced a distinctive fight for Black women across the African diaspora through structural racism and discrimination against afro-textured natural hair and hairstyles. Therefore, an intersectional lens is critical in examining how racism and sexism are intertwined (Collins, 1990) and the sociological analysis and implications of how hair discrimination has habitually affected Black women. Moreover, race and gender are critical components in understanding how hair discrimination has marginalized and oppressed Black women by using the Eurocentric look as the archetype for professionalism. Through this lens, the guiding theoretical framework of collective social identity theory will link the cultural convergence to afro-textured natural hair identity as both a social category and an active social movement. This methodology will delineate the compound structure of collective social identity by incorporating a micro and macro-level analysis. The micro-level analysis of hair discrimination pertains to recognizing and categorizing Black women with afro-textured natural hair and hairstyles as a collective identity with the accompanying consequences in the work environment. The macro-level analysis of hair discrimination analyzes the contradiction of DEI efforts and undermining Title VII of the Civil Rights Act of 1964. This analysis signifies a shared awareness by the dominant group in society that implies Black women with afro-textured natural hair and hairstyles are active members of a collective who share nonconformist values intending to disrupt white supremacy culture in their work environments.

COLLECTIVE IDENTITY THEORY

Identity theories, described by Henri Tajfel in 1979, explained that people seek to categorize other individuals into groups with similar and different beliefs, including negative feelings towards those with differing beliefs (Davis et al., 2019). Alberto Melucci further developed identity theory into collective identity theory in the 1980s. He described collective identity as a homogeneous group concerned with achieving specific goals across shared beliefs through political movements. The intent was to show how political-social movements develop, generate, and sustain commitment and solidity between actors (Fominaya, 2010; Melucci, 1995). Melucci (1995) also explains how group identity is more structured and evolves into a more systematized identity embedded within social structures (Davis et al., 2019). Through a structuralist lens, the critical characteristic within collective identity implies that commonalities, i.e., ethnicity, race, or nationality, suggest structural connectedness. Therefore, structurally connected people are assumed to have a shared collective identity (Fominaya, 2010; Melucci, 1995; Snow, 2015). However, through a constructionist lens, the focus is shifted to constructing and maintaining the collective identity (Snow, 2015), which translates to creating variables that are culturally specific to the identity, for example, hairstyles.

Social movements are socially constructed groups, networks, and organizations that express cultural and social conflict through an instinctively negotiated and contested, permanently evolving collective identity (Jackson & Hogg, 2010). Social movement mobilizations also tend to be both generative of and dependent on collective identities (Bernstein, 2005; Gamson, 1991; Hunt et al., 1994; Jasper & Polletta, 2001; Melucci, 1989; Snow & McAdam, 2000; Van Stekelenberg, 2013). Moreover, these socially constructed groups can shift their focus from gender, race, and other political issues that have been involved in ongoing conflicts, which have stripped people who have been marginalized of their bodily autonomy and the ability to make sense of their lives (Melucci, 1995), culture, and traditions. Therefore, defining a collective identity is a process that leads to forming and maintaining a unified empirical actor in a social movement (Fominaya, 2010; Melucci, 1995). Correspondingly, as the oppressed identity passes through various stages, the collective actor develops a capacity to resolve the problems set by the environment and the oppressor, with the ability to produce new definitions and views of the oppressed identity (Melucci, 1995).

From the theoretical point of view, on the macro level, the liberation of the people within a collective identity who have been marginalized can be expressed through highly visible engagements and mobilization against the oppressor. In this instance and for this chapter, on the macro-level, the social movements within a collective identity are the natural hair movement of the 1960s and 2000s, the Black Power Movement, and the Black is Beautiful Movement. Within these social movements, on the micro-level, liberation is conveyed through cultural expression by rejecting white supremacy culture's behaviors and attitudes about Blackness and rejecting the hegemonic ideologies of white supremacy culture that highlight assimilation, anti-blackness, and the distorted idea of beauty, femininity, and professionalism.

HAIR DISCRIMINATION AND THE HISTORICAL IMPLICATIONS OF BLACK WOMEN'S HAIR

Apart from skin color, afro-textured natural hair and hairstyles are two of the most powerful features of Blackness that stand out in complete opposition to white supremacy culture. America is a violently racist country where the imperialist occupants created negative attributes about Black people's afro-textured natural hair and hairstyles during the transatlantic slave trade, creating an essentialist view of inferiority (Johnson & Bankhead, 2013; Kennedy, 2020). This criterion allowed white attitudes about afro-textured natural hair and hairstyles to be adverse and penalizing. Therefore, any effort to understand the abhorrence and anti-black sentiment for afro-textured natural hair and hairstyles that support the idea of being unprofessional in America begins with the enslavement and dehumanization of Africans.

Exposure to Western cultures through the transatlantic slave trade, colonialism, neo-colonialism, and globalization has transformed the meaning of Black hair and hairstyles as unconventional and uncivilized (Tchenga, 2021). During the transatlantic slave trade, racism was a social issue that segregated Africans from society, using their phenotypical features of skin color, hair type, and hair texture to justify their enslavement. Therefore, hair discrimination is a mechanism employed by white supremacy culture to enact white violence toward Black people and treat them as subhuman. Moreover, it simultaneously highlights how nuanced white supremacy culture is and solidifies that hair is not hair when the person is Black. Thus, hair discrimination is a longstanding issue of oppression toward Black people, specifically Black women.

Nonetheless, Black women's identity is indistinguishably related to their relationship to and presentation of their hair (Ashe, 1995; Byrd & Tharps, 2001; Ellis-Hervey et al., 2016; Johnson & Bankhead, 2013; Rooks, 1998; Tate, 2007; Webb et al., 2004). For Black women across the African diaspora, hair is symbolic, which extends into numerous scopes of Black culture and has played an essential socio-cultural role that has served as a method of self-expression (Byrd & Tharps, 2001; Chapman, 2007; Dash, 2006; Johnson & Bankhead, 2013; Thompson, 2009) and historically, before colonialism, played a significant role in language and communication (Chirali, 2018; Johnson & Bankhead, 2013). For example, in some West African countries, braided hair signified age, marital status, rank, religion, wealth, and geographic origin (Byrd & Tharps, 2001; Horne, 2019; Sharma, 2018). However, as stated above, although crucial to the culture and identity of Black women (Alexander, 2016; Barrick et al., 2019; Byrd & Tharps, 2001), hair is not considered an immutable characteristic or protected under Title VII of the Civil Rights Act of 1964 (Tchenga, 2021).

Black women have long suffered through expectations of conforming to Eurocentrism. Further developing the negative stigma surrounding African people's physical features, several methods were created and implemented as divisive tools during slavery (Garrin & Marcketti, 2017; Mercer, 1991; Sanders, 2011) and post-slavery. When enslaved Africans arrived in America, enslavers shaved their heads (Goodman, 2021). The idea of removing their hair set the tone to devalue the enslaved as human beings and was the first act to break them from their African culture, identity, and spirit (Goodman, 2021). From that point, enslaved African women covered their heads and growing hair with rags to combat the harsh demands of their forced labor while outside. However, those enslaved women who worked in the "big house" in proximate view of their white captures were allowed to imitate their hairstyles by wearing wigs (Randal, 2015) to be more appealing to the white gaze. As time progressed and free Black women donned elaborate hairstyles that displayed the beauty of their hair texture, Tignon Laws required Black women to wear a headscarf to hide their hair, which signified them being a member of the negro or slave class (Tchenga, 2021) regardless of their freedom status (Garrin & Marcketti, 2017; Kuumba & Ajanaku, 1998).

In an attempt to suppress African phenotypical traits post-slavery, the beauty industry purposefully targeted Black women as a high-value demographic, who developed and centered on techniques and products that emulated European-white beauty standards (Garrin & Marcketti, 2017; Kuumba & Ajanaku, 1998). After the 19th century, the hair-straightening comb or "hot comb" was invented to temporarily tame afro-textured natural hair to mimic European hair. The intent was to achieve the look of a well-adjusted Black person in a white society (Byrd & Tharps, 2001). The invention of chemical lye relaxers permanently straightened afro-textured hair, which allowed Black women an avenue for increased societal acceptance while advancing the narrative of white supremacy and the white narrative of beauty and femininity. Still, 21st-century Black women with afro-textured natural hair are subjected to the hair straightening process to peacefully exist in their social and work environments (Byrd & Tharps, 2001). Consequently, leaving them in restrictive and conceded positions. Also, it makes it challenging to adhere to the narrow beauty standards without ultimately compromising themselves and without the leverage to celebrate their culture and identity freely. These restrictions create adverse consequences and block Black women across the African diaspora from subsequently and often, making how they wear their hair less of a personal choice and more of a burden from white supremacy culture (Dove, 2021). Lastly, Black women have been gaslit to believe that these structurally racist options to use tools of assimilation are the best options to be accepted by white society, look professional, and fit in.

Subsequently, these options can force some Black women to relive the collective memory of trauma experienced by their ancestors during catalytic events (Hirschberger, 2018), making it impossible for them to be comfortable and thrive in society and work environments and serve as a reminder that the Black identity is perceived as adverse and undesirable. Nonetheless, regardless of which option they may choose, Black women are still mocked, ridiculed, tormented, and made hyper-visible for their choice. For example, when asked his thoughts on Congresswoman Maxine Waters, a Black woman, speech on patriotism, Fox News commentator Bill O'Reilly, a white man, stated, "I didn't hear a word she said; I was looking at the James Brown wig" (Cooney, 2017). Not only was his comment unwarranted and irrelevant, but it is beyond offensive and racist considering the history of mockery and marginalization white people have had over Black people's hair.

THE EMERGENCE OF A BLACK COLLECTIVE IDENTITY THROUGH THE BLACK PANTHER PARTY AND THE POLITICIZATION OF BLACK HAIR AND BLACK HAIRSTYLES

Collective identity is designed to evolve into a more systematized identity embedded within social structures (Davis et al., 2019). For social movements centered on cultural issues, collective identity is the product of consciousness and self-reflection (Melucci, 1995). In the last quarter century, the emergence of new forms of collective identity in American society has stimulated social and political movements for Black people to delegitimize white supremacy culture and white dominance. In doing so, this historically marginalized group with oppositional identities and appearances began to mirror their indigenous culture. (Garrin & Marcketti, 2017; Mercer, 1991; Sanders, 2011). The collective identities surrounding the social movements between the 1960s and 1970s involved actors fighting for civil rights for specific people and cultures (Taylor & Whittier, 1992). Established in Oakland, California, in 1966, collective actors and founders of the Black Panther Party, Dr. Huey P. Newton and Bobby Seale, created the era's most influential Black Power organization, centering ideologies of Black liberation.

Because they were disappointed in the failure of the civil rights movement to improve the social conditions of Black people outside the Southern states (Duncan, 2023; National Archives, 2023b; National Museum of African American History & Culture, 2023), the Black Panther Party created other social movements that emphasized Black pride (Duncan, 2023). The Black Panther Party used the Black Power and Black is Beautiful social movements to embrace Black culture and identity (Goodman, 2021) to create a collective identity. Specifically for Black Americans, having a collective identity allowed the visual aesthetic that embodied an affirmation that Black is beautiful by embracing African culture and their afro-textured natural hair and hairstyles, which were stripped from their identity during chattel slavery and forced assimilation post-slavery.

These social movements rejected Eurocentrism, white supremacy culture, white dominance, and its hegemonic ideologies that oppress and marginalize the Black identity while simultaneously reclaiming African pride. Furthermore, this strategy changed the physical aesthetic that allowed Black people to reclaim Afrocentrism contrary to being forcefully embedded into the same matrices of thought, culture, society, and politics as white Americans (Robinson, 2001). During the Black Power and Black is Beautiful Movements, having the Afrocentric aesthetic and sense of Black pride held on to the idea that embracing everything about being Black and Black culture was necessary to the Black identity to gain liberation instead of trying to adopt mainstream values, ideas, and traditions (Mercer, 1991).

Within these Black liberation movements, the term Black power debuted. Black power has various origins. However, its roots can be traced to the 1954 work of Richard Wright (National Archives, 2023a) and exist through iconic images that feature members of the Black Panther Party and other Black men and women with their fists in the air and natural Black hairstyles such as the afro. The afro, a natural hairstyle worn by predominately Black people, emerged during the 1960s and 1970s (Garrin & Marcketti, 2017). Wearing the afro was a form of resistance. It represented Black liberation that shifted Black people's physical aesthetic, contrary to civil rights leaders like Dr. Martin Luther King Jr., who was known for his "well-groomed" appearance. The Black Power fist and afro became a political phenomenon with distinctive cultural, political, and economic interests (Walters & Smith, 1999) that directly and ultimately disavowed a white beauty archetype that devalued phenotypical Black features. Therefore, how Black people wore their hair during this time said something about their politics (Byrd & Tharps, 2001). Natural hair, in direct opposition to white supremacy, increasingly became synonymous with Black Power, liberation, and revolution! So, Black people's hair, especially Black women's, became filled with political implications and foundational in the complex social and cultural politics because Black people's hair was never just hair, it was a characteristic to be devalued and dehumanized.

As Black Americans fought for equality and civil rights, there was enhanced recognition of looking towards traditional African culture as a source of pride and strength. Therefore, collective identity ensured the continuity and permanence of the movement over time and established the actor's limits concerning its social environment. By doing so, it regulated the membership of individuals and defined the requisites for joining the movement with criteria that allowed other members to recognize themselves (Melucci, 1995). During the Black Panther Party's involvement in the Civil Rights Movement, the afro became a monolithic symbol of unity. It established an equilibrium that the oppressor could not replicate and was a signifying identifier to the rest of society. As a symbol, the afro clearly rejected the dominant culture and its hegemonic ideologies and laid the foundation for resistance to white supremacy culture.

Furthermore, this culturally contextualized resistance allowed the Black Power Movement to become parallel to the Civil Rights Movement. However, Black civil rights activists continuously dressed in suits and ties and had "well-groomed" hair because they wanted white people to take them seriously and treat them with dignity and respect (National Archives, 2016). Contrarywise, the Black Panther Party shifted from this philosophy because the intent was not to conform by enacting their own oppression through imitating whiteness. Instead, the Black Panther Party wanted to challenge and disrupt respectability politics and white standards through acts of resistance. Other Black Americans used these efforts to distance themselves from white hegemonic ideologies in their appearance by expanding the methods of adopting other forms of Afrocentrism, i.e., clothing and jewelry, to assist in combating white supremacy culture (Garrin & Marcketti, 2017; Mercer, 1991).

The politicization of Black people's hair's encompasses many social and moral implications. Accordingly, white society viewed the Black Panther Party negatively and labeled them as anti-white, anti-law enforcement, dangerously militant, and violent, and that with their afros were meant to outwardly show transvaluation to European aesthetics and white society by defining themselves for themselves. Moreover, they viewed The Black Panther Party as defiant, rebellious, and depicted as domestic terrorists and threats to national security (National Archives, 2023b). Because of the embodied meaning behind the afro-textured natural hair, the afro hairstyle, its alignment with The Black Panther Party, Black Power, and liberation, the afro, as a political symbol, reinforced fear in other collective identities who believed that Black hair and this Black hairstyle was negative and communicated a separate Black national identity (Peacock, 2019). It also perpetuated a threat to other collectives to be disruptive and reject conformism to white supremacy culture.

DISCUSSION

This chapter expounded upon these four mechanisms through an intersectional lens using collective social identity as a guiding theoretical framework to answer the following research question: "Why is banning afro-textured natural hair and cultural Black hairstyles in the work environment a civil rights issue that contradicts DEI initiatives"? History shows how Black people have been discriminated against since the inception of America in every aspect of its creation. However, some, if not most, people do not consider the employment practices perpetuating Black people's subordination through hair discrimination and forced assimilation as a civil rights issue because, on a federal level, courts have determined that racial discrimination in the workplace must be based on immutable characteristics (US Equal Opportunity Employment Commission, 2023), which allows hair discrimination based on hair texture and hairstyles because it is not a protected class detailed in Title VII. However, the author disagrees as no other hair textures, based on race and gender, carry the historical weight and negative connotations of afro-textured natural hair and hairstyles as Black women (Crown Coalition, 2023).

Black hair and hairstyles, especially that of Black women, have been aspersed, scandalized, and villainized. Moreover, it was labeled pro-Black and anti-white. Therefore, in the shared delusions of the collective identity of white people, pro-Black translates to anti-American. So, it is no coincidence that in the summer of 2008, when the New Yorker mocked former First Lady Michelle Obama as a drawn character, she was sketched as an anti-American, militant, Black radical with afro-textured natural hair styled in an afro (Desmond-Harris, 2009; Johnson & Bankhead, 2014). This identity strategy implemented by the illustrator attempted to construct, define, and devalue Mrs. Obama's identity to shape others' beliefs and feelings about her and her hair to achieve the maximum impact of being viewed negatively. Also, to question Mrs. Obama's credibility as a leader, undermine and degrade the collective identity associated with afro-textured natural hair and hairstyles.

In reality, the Black revolutionary figures that the New Yorker was attempting to mock remain fearful of the symbolic power of Black hair as it remains a catalyst for dismantling the collective myth of white supremacy. Black social movements assault the most deeply rooted notions of white dominance and instill fear in its antagonists and adversaries. So, it is no coincidence that the response to the first Black First Lady of the United States was negative because white people responded with the same tactics that they always do– devalue and dehumanize. However, that drawn character representing Black people's hair and hairstyles does not dictate the dichotomy of meanings of Black hair and represents a long and storied cultural significance across the African diaspora that symbolizes collective identities rooted in counter-hegemonic efforts.

Politically linking afro-textured natural hair and hairstyles associated with Blackness to the Black Power movement, the correlation specifically caused Black women with natural hair and hairstyles to be pigeonholed in certain negative terms (Peacock, 2019). Besides the afro, traditional Black hairstyles, i.e., cornrows, Bantu knots, braids, and twists, are subject to discrimination and deemed unprofessional in work environments. When Black women wear the afro and other natural hairstyles, it implies a dominant, overbearing woman who would participate in a racial revolution with employers (Kelly, 1997; Opie & Williams, 2015). Therefore, by penalizing certain hair textures and hairstyles linked culturally to the African diaspora that fall outside of Eurocentric norms, discriminatory grooming policies in the work environment are among the many pillars of structural racism that affect Black women by contradicting DEI initiatives to support other race, genders, and cultures, while simultaneously undermining Title VII by attacking characteristics not deemed immutable.

Expanding on cultural violence through hair discrimination in work environments and why hair isn't just hair, the author concludes that amid the Black Power and Black is Beautiful Movements, Black women were advocating transvaluation using their hair to promote that cause. Therefore, when implementing DEI initiatives, white people created an image of professionalism to control Black women as human capital, degrade them as commodities, and exclude them from work environments. Since the Black body can no longer be physically exploited and controlled through peonage, chattel slavery, and Tigon Laws, Black hair is the most apparent controllable phenotypical feature to justify rejecting and removing Black women from any possibility of obtaining relevant positions and status in society and their work environment.

While all employers do not have grooming policies that explicitly address Black hair and hairstyles in the workplace, the evidence shows that the perception remains that Black hair and hairstyles, especially those of Black women, are viewed as unprofessional, which allows employers to refuse to hire and terminate Black women who do not fit into their definition of professionalism. Moreover, because of the prevalent stigma of Black women's natural hair signifying the forfeiture of conformism and choosing liberation by directly challenging white supremacy culture, white America's recollection of the collective identity during the time of the Black Panther Party only induces fear of Black women. Specifically, it labels them angry, aggressive, argumentative, defiant, and confrontational. Hair discrimination continues to fuel the racist economic, social, and political treatment of Black women with afro-textured natural hair and hairstyles, specifically in the work environment to preserve white spaces.

The critical element of this research is that outside of the physical and mental trauma Black people endured during the chattel slavery, they have historically lacked bodily autonomy since their forcible arrival in America because white people hold a morbid fascination with the differences in Black people's hair and hairstyles, especially those of Black women. Although human anatomy and Black bodies have been heavily researched, most of the time without consent, Black women's hair cannot escape this perversion and the perception of vulgarity as being seen as dirty, matted, unkempt, ugly, untamed, and lacking social capital relating to beauty, femininity, and professionalism. Also, forcing Black women to change their hair constitutes an act of submission, removing them from the perceived dominant position. Thus, making them assimilate to gain their humanity and footing in economic, social, and political positions. Lastly, still having control over the bodily autonomy of Black women continues to advance the white narrative of superiority and a never-ending attempt to remove the cultural identity associated with Blackness and the notions of racial inferiority.

Black social movements united actors in support of Black causes, which created a strong association of afro-textured natural hair and hairstyles with Black Power, liberation, and reclaiming as a systemic threat to white supremacy culture. Therefore, white supremacy culture continues to argue that Black women are not presenting their best selves to the world in their Afrocentric state and are better served by society imitating whiteness and enacting their own oppression instead of resisting it. Black women's hair remains a trait that needs to be conquered. Truthfully, the problem exceeds Black hair–the problem with American society has always been with Blackness itself, and afro-textured natural hair and hairstyles represent Blackness. Thus, the erasure of Blackness remains necessary and fundamental to the psychological and cultural conversion of Black people's socialization as a subordinate group rather than a self-determining one. So, the policies prohibiting the expression of Black culture through afro-textured hair and hairstyles are foundationally rooted in structural racism, which overextend into Black women's civil freedoms while simultaneously denying them bodily autonomy. Accordingly, making hair discrimination a civil rights issue that directly contradicts DEI initiatives in the work environment.

Although Title VII protects against workplace discrimination, the definition of immutability is fundamentally flawed and leaves space for racist policies about hair to be implemented against Black women in work environments, especially with the abundance of empirical evidence that signifies hair discrimination exists. Oppression through hair discrimination is not imaginary and has been a systemic threat to Black people across the African diaspora since the transatlantic slave trade. Considering the historical implications that afro-textured hair and hairstyles are fundamental to

Black culture and identity, the triviality of something as simple as hair still having the potential to encompass discrimination, stereotypical behaviors, and negative attitudes, while remaining unprotected under federal law is astounding.

FUTURE RESEARCH

As political movements fade and activism transitions, individuals move into different roles and life stages, which allows the focus on afro-textured natural hair and hairstyles to change. Because when a Black woman is working, it is assumed that they will adhere to the approved dress code created through structural racism. As a result, hair discrimination has led many Black women to assimilate to survive in mainstream society by linking Eurocentric ideologies of hair to advance in their professional environments. Bell (1990) and Bell et al. (2001) speak to the tension Black women experience when their values differ from the prevailing values of their work organizations. Moreover, how racist views on Black hair have negative psychological implications and historically shaped the lives of Black women and the way they appear in society and their work environment. As Black women provide an inauthentic version of themselves, they are emotionally laboring their mental and physical being under the misconception that they must do so to meet white expectations (Boyd, 2020; 2021). Rather than adjust their racist policies, the arrogance of white supremacy culture leads these organizations to ignore the fundamentals of DEI, undermine Title VII, and justify their discriminatory actions in the beliefs of unsubstantiated ideals based on European dogma.

In order to explore this phenomenon further, the author recommends theoretical research into the political damage of immutable characteristics through Facades of Conformity as a response to racial conflict when Black women create false physical representations of themselves to appear as if they embrace organizational values (Hewlin, 2003;2009; Perrigino & Jenkins, 2022) and Optimal Distinctiveness Theory to ensure job security by constructing a Eurocentric professional image to communicate belongingness in the professional context (Leonardelli et al., 2010; Ma & Rast, 2017).

Also, how Black women use emotional intelligence as a filter of racial awareness to cater to white comfort by self-regulating to be seen as acceptable and suitable for the work environment to avoid disruption in white supremacy culture (Boyd, 2020; 2021).

Lastly, Black Feminist Thought considering the matrix of domination and how the intersections of oppression (structural, disciplinary, hegemonic, interpersonal) are structurally organized against Black women (Collins, 2000). Black Feminist Thought is critical in applying a complex analysis of structural racism and how it has specifically implemented a negative association with everything culturally and socially linked to Black womanhood. Future research of immutable characteristics through these theoretical frameworks can highlight the effect, if any, it has on Black women who decide to opt-out, soften, or disguise their marginalized identity, such as an Afrocentric hairstyle, to protect their professional image by carefully choosing which characteristics from their marginalized identity they will show to fit in the professional environment. Also, it expounds upon how Black women's civil rights, as it relates to bodily autonomy, have been continuously infringed upon to maintain structures of white dominance.

CONCLUSION

For the Black Collective, hair provides self-definition and is crucial to their identity. Also, it is a sacred means of Black liberation and revolution that would change the power dynamic for Black people to control their own destiny. Moreover, asserting and reclaiming the identity their oppressor has denied them allows them to regain control of their bodily autonomy so that it is no longer subjected to oppression. Furthermore, enacting social change to shift culture and institutions made explicitly for white people and creating an equally strong association with dismantling the power structure of white dominance. Lastly, Black cultural identity is important in fostering organizational environments that encourage authenticity through diversity, equity, and inclusion and how Black women with afro-textured natural hair and hairstyles should not have to change or suppress their culture and identity or navigate their careers by centering whiteness. Therefore, on a federal level, laws must be written to protect Black women considering their history of oppression that defines their social and economic position, their current position relative to that of other women in society, and whether employment practices perpetuate the subordination through forced assimilation to uphold systems of white supremacy culture to gatekeep white spaces. Until then, culturally contextualized acts of resistance to disregard the patterns of oppression and forced assimilation will be used to disrupt the status quo and dismantle the effects of white dominance.

REFERENCES

Alexander, L. (2016, April 8). Do Google's "unprofessional hair" results show it is racist? *The Guardian*. https://www.theguardian.com/technology/2016/apr/08/does-google-unprofessional-hair-results-prove-algorithms-racist-

Arsel, Z., Crockett, D., & Scott, M. L. (2022). Diverstity, Equity, and Inclusion (DEI): A Curation of Research Agenda. *The Journal of Consumer Research*, *48*(5), 920–933. doi:10.1093/jcr/ucab057

Ashe, B. D. (1995). "Why don't he like my hair" Constructing African American Standards of Beauty in Toni Morrison's Song of Solomon and Zora Neale Hurston's Their Eyes Were Watching God. *African American Review*, *29*(4), 579–592. doi:10.2307/3042151

Barrick, M. R., Shaffer, J. A., & DeGrassi, S. W. (2009). What you see may not be what you get: Relationships among self-presentation tactics and ratings of interview and job performance. *The Journal of Applied Psychology*, *94*(6), 1394–1411. https://psycnet.apa.org/doi/10.1037/a0016532. doi:10.1037/a0016532 PMID:19916651

Bell, E. L. (1990). The bicultural life experience of career-oriented black women. *Journal of Organizational Behavior*, *11*(6), 459–477. doi:10.1002/job.4030110607

Bell, E. L., & Nkomo, S. M. (2001). *Our separate ways: Black and white women and the struggle for professional identity*. Harvard Business School Press.

Bernstein, M. (1997). Celebration and Suppression: The Strategic Uses of Identity in the Lesbian and Gay Movement. *American Journal of Sociology*, *103*(3), 537–565. doi:10.1086/231250

Boyd, K. (2021). The Surface Act: Exercising Emotional Intelligence as a Filter of Racial Awareness as a Means of Survival at PWIs. *The Vermont Connection*, *42*(1). https://scholarworks.uvm.edu/tvc/vol42/ iss1/6

Boyd, K. (2022). An Open Letter to the Marginalized Academic: Divesting from Colonial Indoctrination. *The Vermont Connection, 43*(1). 13–18. https://scholarworks.uvm.edu/cgi/siteview.cgi/tvc/vol43/iss1/5

Byrd, A. D., & Tharps, L. L. (2001). *Hair Story: Untangling the Roots of Black Hair in America, Print.* Macmillan. https://us.macmillan.com/books/9781250046574/hairstory

Chapman, Y. (2007). *"I am not my hair! Or am I?": Black women's transformative experience in their self-perceptions of abroad and at home*. [Master's thesis, GSU]. http://digitalarchive.gsu.edu/anthro_theses/23

Chirali, S. (2018). *Africans Used Their Hairstyles to Hide Escape Maps from Slavery in Their Hairstyles*. ED TIMES. https://edtimes.in/africans-used-to- hide-escape-maps-from-slavery-in-their-hairstyles.

Collins, P. H. (1990). Defining Black Feminist Thought. In *Feminist Theory Reader*. Local and Global.

Collins, P. H. (2000). *Black Feminist Thought: Knowledge, Consciousness, and the Politics of Empowerment.* Routledge. https://books.google.com/books?id=cdtYsU3zR14C&printsec=frontcover&source=gbs_ge_summary_r&cad=0#v=onepage&q&f=false

Cooney, S. (2017). Bill O'Reilly Apologizes for Saying Maxine Waters' Hair Looked Like a 'James Brown Wig.' *Time.* https://time.com/4715552/bill-oreilly-maxine-waters-hair-james-brown-wig/

Craig, M. L. (2002). *Ain't I a Beauty Queen: Black Women, Beauty, and the Politics of Race.* Oxford University Press. doi:10.1093/acprof:oso/9780195152623.001.0001

Crown Coalition. (2023). *About Us.* The CROWN Act. https://www.thecrownact.com/about

Dash, P. (2006). Black hair culture, politics, and change. *International Journal of Inclusive Education*, *10*(1), 27–37. doi:10.1080/13603110500173183

Davis, J.L., Love, T.P., & Fares, P. (2019). Collective Social Identity: Synthesizing Identity Theory and Social Identity Theory Using Digital Data. *Social Psychology Quarterly, 82*(3) 254–273. doi:10.1177/0190272519851025

Dawson, G. A., Karl, K. A., & Peluchette, J. V. (2019). Hair Matters: Toward Understanding Natural Black Hair Bias in the Workplace. *Journal of Leadership & Organizational Studies*, *26*(3), 389–401. doi:10.1177/1548051819848998

Desmond-Harris, J. (2009). Why Michelle's hair matters. *Time*, *174*, 55–57.

Dove, M. L. (2021). *The Influence of Colorism on the Hair Experiences of African American Female Adolescents. Genealogy, 5(1), 5.* MDPI AG. doi:10.3390/genealogy5010005

Dover, T. L., Major, B., & Kaiser, C. R. (2016). Members of high-status groups are threatened by pro-diversity organizational messages. *Journal of Experimental Social Psychology*, *62*, 58–67. doi:10.1016/j.jesp.2015.10.006

Duncan, G. A. (2023, March 27). Black Panther Party. *Encyclopedia Britannica.* https://www.britannica.com/topic/Black-Panther-Party

Ellis-Hervey. Doss, A., Deshae, D., Nicks, R. & Arazia, P. (2016). African American Personal Presentation: Psychology of Hair and Self-Perception, *Journal of Black Studies, 47*(8), 869–882. https://www.jstor.org/stable/26174232

Fominaya, C. F. (2010). Collective Identity in Social Movements: Central Concepts and Debates. *Sociology Compass*, *4*(6), 393–404. doi:10.1111/j.1751-9020.2010.00287.x

Garrin, A. R., & Marcketti, S. B. (2017). The Impact of Hair on African American Women's Collective Identity Formation. *Clothing & Textiles Research Journal*, *36*(2), 104–118. doi:10.1177/0887302X17745656

Giovanni, N. (1970). Of Liberation. Black Feeling Black Talk/Black Judgement. New York: William Morrow & Co., 1979.

Goodman, M. (2021). Wearing My Crown to Work: The Crown Act as a Solution to Shortcomings of Title VII for Hair Discrimination in the Workplace. *Touro Law Review*, *37*(2). https://digitalcommons.tourolaw.edu/lawreview/vol37/iss2/17

Hewlin, P. F. (2003). And the Academy Award for Best Actor Goes to: Facades of Conformity in Organizational Settings. *Academy of Management Review*, *4*, 633–642. https://www.mcgill.ca/humanrights/files/humanrights/irndi-patricia_hewlin-facade_conformity.pdf

Hewlin, P. F. (2009). Wearing the cloak: Antecedents and consequences of creating facades of conformity. *The Journal of Applied Psychology*, *94*(3), 727–741. doi:10.1037/a0015228 PMID:19450009

Hirschberger, G. (2018). Collective Trauma and the Social Construction of Meaning. *Frontiers in Psychology*, *9*, 1441. doi:10.3389/fpsyg.2018.01441 PMID:30147669

Horne, M. (2019). *A Visual History of Iconic Black Hairstyles*. HISTORY. https://www.history.com/news/black-hairstyles-visual-history-in-photos

Iyer, A. (2022). Understanding advantaged groups' opposition to diversity, equity, and inclusion (DEI) policies: The role of perceived threat. *Social and Personality Psychology Compass*, *16*(5), e12666. doi:10.1111pc3.12666

Jackson, R. L., & Hogg, M. A. (2010). Social Movements. SAGE Publications. *Inc.*, *1*(1). doi:10.4135/9781412979306

Johnson, A. M., Godsil, R. D., MacFarlane, J., Tropp, L. R., & Goff, P. A. (2017). The "good hair" study: Explicit and implicit attitudes toward Black women's hair. *Perception Institute*. https://perception.org/wp-content/uploads/2017/01/TheGood-HairStudyFindingsReport.pdf

Johnson, T. A., & Bankhead, T. (2014). Hair It Is: Examining Experiences of Black Women with Natural Hair. *Open Journal of Social Sciences*, *2*(1), 86–100. doi:10.4236/jss.2014.21010

Jones, C., & Shorter-Gooden, K. (2003). *Shifting: The double lives of Black women in America*. HarperCollins.

Kelley, R. (1997). Nap time: Historicizing the afro. *Fashion Theory*, *1*(4), 339–352. doi:10.2752/136270497779613666

Kennedy, K. (2020). *My Natural Hair Is Unprofessional: The Impact of Black Hairstyles on Perceived Employment-Related Characteristics*. [Master's Thesis, Marquette University]. https://epublications.marquette.edu/theses_open/578

Kipping, M. (2011). Hollow from the start? Image professionalism in management consulting. *Current Sociology*, *59*(4), 530–550. doi:10.1177/0011392111402727

Kuumba, M. B., & Ajanaku, F. (1998). Dreadlocks: The hair aesthetics of cultural resistance and collective identity formation. *Mobilization: An International Quarterly (San Diego, Calif.)*, *3*(2), 227–243. doi:10.17813/maiq.3.2.nn180v12hu74j318

Lawrence, K., & Kelecher, T. (2004). Chronic disparity: strong and pervasive evidence of racial inequalities poverty outcomes: Structural racism. *Race and Public Conference.*

Leonardelli, G., Pickect, C. L., & Brewer, M. B. (2010). Optimal Distinctiveness Theory. *Advances in Experimental Social Psychology*, *43*, 63–113. doi:10.1016/S0065-2601(10)43002-6

Ma, A. C., & Rast, D. E. (2017). Optimal Distinctiveness Theory. In V. Zeigler-Hill & T. Shackelford (Eds.), *Encyclopedia of Personality and Individual Differences*. Springer. doi:10.1007/978-3-319-28099-8_1144-1

Maddox, K. (2014). Perspectives on racial phenotypicality bias. *Personality and Social Psychology Review*, 8383–8401. doi:10.120715327957pspr0804_4 PMID:15582860

Maqsoom, A., Musarat, M. A., Mubbasit, H., Alaloul, W. S., Ashraf, H., Rabbani, M. B. A., & Shaheen, I. (2023). Extrinsic workforce diversity factors: An impact of employee characteristics on productivity. *Ain Shams Engineering Journal*, *14*(10), 102170. doi:10.1016/j.asej.2023.102170

Melucci, A. (1985). The Symbolic Challenge of Contemporary Movements. *Social Research*, *52*, 789–816.

Melucci, A. (1995). *The Process of Collective Identity*. The University of Minnesota Press. https://www.jstor.org/stable/10.5749/j.ctttt0p8.6

National Archives. (2016). *Revolutionary Movements Then and Now: Black Power and Black Lives Matter*. National Archives. https://rediscovering-black-history.blogs.archives.gov/2016/10/11/revolutionary-movements-then-and-now-black-power-and-black-lives-matter/

National Archives. (2023a). *Black Power*. National Archives. https://www.archives.gov/research/african-americans/black-power

National Archives. (2023b). *The Black Panther Party*. National Archives. https://www.archives.gov/research/african-americans/black-power/black-panthers#bpintro

National Museum of African American History & Culture. (2023). *The Black Panther Party: Challenging Police and Promoting Social Change*. NMAAHC. https://nmaahc.si.edu/explore/stories/black-panther-party-challenging-police-and-promoting-social-change

Opie, T. R., & Phillips, K. W. (2015). Hair penalties: The negative influence of Afrocentric hair on ratings of Black women's dominance and professionalism. *Frontiers in Psychology*, *31*(6), 1311. doi:10.3389/fpsyg.2015.01311 PMID:26379612

Patton, T. O. (2006). Hey Girl, Am I More than My Hair? African American Women and Their Struggles with Beauty, Body Image, and Hair. *NWSA Journal*, *18*(2), 24–51. doi:10.2979/NWS.2006.18.2.24

Peacock, T. N. (2019). *African American Hair and Beauty: Examining Afrocentricity and Identity Through the Reemergence and Expression of Natural Hair in the 21st Century*. Scholar Commons. https://scholarcommons.sc.edu/etd/5252

Perrigino, M.B. & Jenkins, M. (2022). Antecedents of facades of conformity: when can employees "be themselves?" *Journal of Humanities and Applied Social Sciences*. doi:10.1108/JHASS-04-2022-0045

Pitts, B. (2021). Uneasy Lies the Head that Wears the Crown: A Critical Race Analysis of the CROWN Act. *Journal of Black Studies*, *52*(7), 716–735. doi:10.1177/00219347211021096

Polletta, F., Goodwin, J., & Jasper, J. (2000a). *Political Passions: Emotions and Social Movements*. University of Chicago Press.

Polletta, F., & Jasper, J. M. (2000). Collective Identity and Social Movements. *Annual Review of Sociology*, *27*(1), 283–305. doi:10.1146/annurev.soc.27.1.283

Robinson, D. (2001). *Black Nationalism in American Politics and Thought*. Cambridge Univ. Press. https://books.google.com/books?hl=en&lr=&id=d_5xjlv7VekC&oi=fnd&pg=PP11&ots=7JmJfowI-u&sig=WKd-_L1xpoE0rGgiIvFryO6WOps#v=onepage&q&f=false doi:10.1017/CBO9780511606038

Scott-Jones, G., & Kamara, M. R. (2020, November 7). CAADC; Kamara MR; PE. The Traumatic Impact of Structural Racism on African Americans. *Delaware Journal of Public Health*, *6*(5), 80–82. doi:10.32481/djph.2020.11.019 PMID:34467171

Serafin, N. (2020) In Defense of Immutability, *Brigham Young University Law Review 275, 2*(8). https://digitalcommons.law.byu.edu/lawreview/vol2020/iss2/8

Steele, C. (1992, April). Race and Schooling of Black Americans. *Atlantic (Boston, Mass.)*, 1–12. https://www.theatlantic.com/magazine/archive/1992/04/race-and-the-schooling-of-black-americans/306073/

Stryker, S., Owens, T., & White, R. (2000). *Self, Identity, and Social Movements*. University of Minnesota Press.

Tate, S. (2007). Black beauty: Shade, hair and anti-racist aesthetics. *Ethnic and Racial Studies*, *30*(2), 300–319. doi:10.1080/01419870601143992

Taylor, V., & Whittier, N. (1992). Collective Identity and Lesbian Feminist Mobilization. In A. Morris & C. Mueller (Eds.), *Frontiers of Social Movement Theory*. Yale University Press.

Tchenga, D. S. N. (2021). Black Women's Hair and Natural Hairstyles in the Workplace: Expanding the Definition of Race Under Title VII. *Virginia Law Review Online, 107,* 272–299, https://virginialawreview.org/wp-content/uploads/2021/11/Nguenang_Book_107.pdf

Thompson, C. (2009). Black women, beauty, and hair as a matter of being. *Women's Studies*, *38*(8), 831–856. doi:10.1080/00497870903238463

U.S. Equal Opportunity Employment Commission. (2023). *Title VII of the Civil Rights Act of 1964*. EEOC. https://www.eeoc.gov/statutes/title-vii-civil-rights-act-1964

Walters, R. W., & Smith, R. C. (1999). *African American Leadership*. State University of New York Press. https://books.google.com/books?hl=en&lr=&id=xArrb8_3iNQC&oi=fnd&pg=PR11&ots=SLB36Nvy5F&sig=fkLR8wEOuruvl_nsXYqwihaN5vI#v=onepage&q&f=false

Webb, T., Looby, J., & Fults-McMurtery, R. (2004). African American men's perceptions of body figure attractiveness: An acculturation study. *Journal of Black Studies*, *34*(3), 370–385. doi:10.1177/0021934703254100

ADDITIONAL READING

Boyd, K. (2021). The Surface Act: Exercising Emotional Intelligence as a Filter of Racial Awareness as a Means of Survival at PWIs, *The Vermont Connection, 42*(1), 52–60. https://scholarworks.uvm.edu/tvc/vol42/iss1/6

Boyd, K. (2023). *The Matrix of Domination: The Structuralized Oppression of Black Women in the United States Army and its Effect on Leadership Development. Black Women's Formal and Informal Ways of Leadership*. IGI Global. doi:10.4018/978-1-6684-3827-5.ch006

KEY TERMS

Cultural Convergence: Cultural convergence is when cultures become more alike with increased interaction. With high degrees of exposure to each other, two or more cultures' beliefs, behaviors, ideologies, and languages "converge", and take on one another's characteristics.

Diversity, Equity, and Inclusion (DEI): This describes policies that promote the representation and participation of individuals from different ages, abilities and disabilities, cultures, ethnicities, genders, races, religions, and sexual orientations.

Immutability: The state of not changing; or being unable to be changed.

Intersectionality: The interconnected nature of social categorizations such as race, class, and gender as they apply to a given individual or group, regarded as creating overlapping and interdependent systems of discrimination or disadvantage.

Title VII of the Civil Rights Act of 1964: Prohibits discrimination in hiring, promotion, discharge, pay, fringe benefits, job training, classification, referral, and other aspects of employment, on the basis of race, color, religion, sex or national origin.

White Supremacy Culture: A form of racism centered upon the belief that white people are superior to people of other racial backgrounds and that whites should politically, economically, and socially dominate non-whites.

Compilation of References

'Fashion rules' suffocate medical students. (2010, February 4). *Education Times*. https://www.educationtimes.com/article/campus-beat-college-life/69558655/fashion-rules-suffocate-medical-students

Adams, K. F. (2012). The discursive construction of professional ism: An episteme of the 21st century. *Ephemera: Theories & Politics in Organizations*, *12*(3), 327–343.

Aguirre, A. (2000). *Women and minority faculty in the academic workplace: Recruitment, retention, and academic culture*. Jossey-Bass.

Alexander, L. (2016). Do Google's unprofessional hair results show it is racist? *The Guardian*. https://www.theguardian.com/technology/2016/apr/08/does-google-unprofessional-hair-results-prove-algorithms-racist-

Alexander, L. (2016, April 8). Do Google's "unprofessional hair" results show it is racist? *The Guardian*. https://www.theguardian.com/technology/2016/apr/08/does-google-unprofessional-hair-results-prove-algorithms-racist-

Alinia, M. (2015). On Black feminist thought: Thinking oppression and resistance through intersectional paradigm. *Ethnic and Racial Studies*, *38*(13), 2334–2340. doi:10.1080/01419870.2015.1058492

Alleyne, A. (2005). Invisible injuries and silent witnesses: The shadow of racial oppression in workplace contexts. *Psychodynamic Practice*, *11*(3), 283–299. doi:10.1080/14753630500232222

Anderson, E. (2022). Black. In *White Space*. The University of Chicago Press.

Arsel, Z., Crockett, D., & Scott, M. L. (2022). Diverstity, Equity, and Inclusion (DEI): A Curation of Research Agenda. *The Journal of Consumer Research*, *48*(5), 920–933. doi:10.1093/jcr/ucab057

Asante, M. K. (2006). *The Afrocentric idea*. Temple University Press.

Asante, M. K., & Welsh-Asante, K. (1990). Commonalities in African dance: An aesthetic foundation. In *African culture: The rhythms of unity* (pp. 71–82). Africa World Press.

Asare, J. G. (2022, August 15). Four Ways Hair Bias Shows Up In The Workplace. *Forbes.* https://www.forbes.com/sites/janicegassam/2022/08/15/four-ways-hair-bias-shows-up-in-the-workplace/?sh=4be6402469a3

Asare, J. G. (2022, August 16). Four ways hair bias shows up in the workplace. *Forbes.* https://www.forbes.com/sites/janicegassam/2022/08/15/four-ways-hair-bias-shows-up-in-the-workplace/?sh=4d8c943069a3

Ashcraft, K. L. (2000). Empowering "professional" relationships: Organizational communication meets feminist practice. *Management Communication Quarterly*, *13*(3), 347–392. doi:10.1177/0893318900133001

Ashe, B. D. (1995). "Why don't he like my hair" Constructing African American Standards of Beauty in Toni Morrison's Song of Solomon and Zora Neale Hurston's Their Eyes Were Watching God. *African American Review*, *29*(4), 579–592. doi:10.2307/3042151

Awad, G. H., Norwood, C., Taylor, D. S., Martinez, M., McClain, S., Jones, B., Holman, A., & Hillard, C. C. (2015). Beauty and Body Image Concerns Among African American College Women. *The Journal of Black Psychology*, *41*(6), 540–564. doi:10.1177/0095798414550864 PMID:26778866

Badu, E. (1997). *On & On*. Baduizm. Kedar Records and Universal Records.

Bagalini, A. (2021). How wearing natural hairstyles harms the job prospects of Black women. *World Economic Forum.* https://www.weforum.org/agenda/2021/02/natural-hair-black-women-job-discrimination/

Banks, B. M., & Landau, S. E. (2021). Cognitive effects of racial microaggressions directed at Black college women. *The Journal of Negro Education*, *90*(1), 84–95.

Barrick, M. R., Shaffer, J. A., & DeGrassi, S. W. (2009). What you see may not be what you get: Relationships among self-presentation tactics and ratings of interview and job performance. *The Journal of Applied Psychology*, *94*(6), 1394–1411. https://psycnet.apa.org/doi/10.1037/a0016532. doi:10.1037/a0016532 PMID:19916651

Bearfield, D. A. (2009). Equity at the intersection: Public administration and the study of gender. *Public Administration Review*, *69*(3), 383–386. doi:10.1111/j.1540-6210.2009.01985.x

Bell, E. L. (1990). The bicultural life experience of career-oriented black women. *Journal of Organizational Behavior*, *11*(6), 459–477. doi:10.1002/job.4030110607

Bell, E. L., & Nkomo, S. M. (2001). *Our separate ways: Black and white women and the struggle for professional identity*. Harvard Business School Press.

Bellinger, W. (2007). Why African American Women try to Obtain "Good Hair.". *Sociological Viewpoints*, 63.

Berdahl, J. L., & Moore, C. (2006). Workplace Harassment: Double Jeopardy for Minority Women. *The Journal of Applied Psychology*, *91*(2), 426–436. doi:10.1037/0021-9010.91.2.426 PMID:16551193

Berkemeyer, C. (2020). New Growth: Afro-Textured Hair, Mental Health, and the Professional Workplace. *The Journal of the Legal Profession*, *44*(2), 279–292.

Bernstein, M. (1997). Celebration and Suppression: The Strategic Uses of Identity in the Lesbian and Gay Movement. *American Journal of Sociology*, *103*(3), 537–565. doi:10.1086/231250

Bettencourt, B. A., & Sheldon, K. (2001). Social roles as mechanism for psychological need satisfaction within social groups. *Journal of Personality and Social Psychology*, *81*(6), 1131–1143. doi:10.1037/0022-3514.81.6.1131 PMID:11761313

Blackshire-Belay, C. A. (1996). The location of ebonics within the framework of the Africological Paradigm. *Journal of Black Studies*, *27*(1), 5–23. doi:10.1177/002193479602700101

Blessett, B. (2020). Rethinking the administrative state through an intersectional framework. *Administrative Theory & Praxis*, *42*(1), 1–5. doi:10.1080/10841806.2018.1517526

Blessett, B., Dodge, J., Edmond, B., Goerdel, H. T., Gooden, S. T., Headley, A. M., Riccucci, N. M., & Williams, B. N. (2019). Social equity in public administration: A call to action. *Perspectives on Public Management and Governance*, *2*(4), 283–299. doi:10.1093/ppmgov/gvz016

Boulton, C. (2016). Black identities inside advertising: Race inequality, code-switching, and stereotype threat. *The Howard Journal of Communications*, *27*(2), 130–144. doi:10.1080/10646175.2016.1148646

Bourdieu, P., & Passeron, J. C. (1998). Foundations of a Theory of Symbolic Violence. Reproduction in Education, Society, and Culture. *Sage (Atlanta, Ga.)*.

Bowleg, L. (2012). The problem with the phrase women and minorities: Intersectionality an important theoretical framework for public health. *American Journal of Public Health*, *102*(7), 1267–1273. doi:10.2105/AJPH.2012.300750 PMID:22594719

Boyd, K. (2021). The Surface Act: Exercising Emotional Intelligence as a Filter of Racial Awareness as a Means of Survival at PWIs. *The Vermont Connection*, *42*(1). https://scholarworks.uvm.edu/tvc/vol42/ iss1/6

Boyd, K. (2022). An Open Letter to the Marginalized Academic: Divesting from Colonial Indoctrination. *The Vermont Connection*, *43*(1). 13–18. https://scholarworks.uvm.edu/cgi/siteview.cgi/tvc/vol43/iss1/5

Boyd, A. (2023). Hair me out: Why discrimination against black hair is race discrimination under title vii. *The American University Journal of Gender, Social Policy & the Law*, *31*(1), 75–106.

Breslin, R. A., Pandey, S., & Riccucci, N. M. (2017). Intersectionality in public leadership research: A review and future research agenda. *Review of Public Personnel Administration*, *37*(2), 160–182. doi:10.1177/0734371X17697118

Brice, A. L., Mansueto, C. S., & McCombs Thomas, A. (2007). *Hair pulling and its affective correlates in an African-American university sample*. Science Direct. https://www.sciencedirect.com/science/article/pii/S0887618506001204. doi:10.1016/j.janxdis.2006.08.004

Browne, I., & Misra, J. (2003). The intersection of gender and race in the labor market. *Annual Review of Sociology, 29*(1), 487–513. doi:10.1146/annurev.soc.29.010202.100016

Brown, M. K. (2003). *Whitewashing race: The myth of a color-blind society*. University of California Press.

Byrd, A. D., & Tharps, L. L. (2001). *Hair Story: Untangling the Roots of Black Hair in America, Print*. Macmillan. https://us.macmillan.com/books/9781250046574/hairstory

Byrd, A. D., & Tharps, L. L. (2014). *Hair story untangling the roots of black hair in America*. St. Martin's Griffin.

Byrd, A., & Tharps, L. (2001). *Hair story: Untangling the roots of black hair in America*. St. Martin's Press.

Byrd, A., & Tharps, L. (2014). *Hair story: Untangling the roots of Black hair in america* (Second Edition, Revised). St. Martin's Griffin.

Byrd, A., & Tharps, L. (2014). *Hair story: Untangling the Roots of Black Hair in America* (Second Edition, Revised). St. Martin's Griffin.

California S. O. (2019, July 3). *Governor Newsom Signs Legislation to Protect Employees from Racial Discrimination Based on Hairstyle*. California Governor. https://www.gov.ca.gov/2019/07/03/governor-newsom-signs-legislation-to-protect-employees-from-racial-discrimination-based-on-hairstyle/

Callender, V. D., McMichael, A. J., & Cohen, G. F. (2004). Medical and surgical therapies for alopecias in black women. *Dermatologic Therapy, 17*(2), 164–176. doi:10.1111/j.1396-0296.2004.04017.x PMID:15113284

Carastathis, A. (2016). *Intersectionality: Origins, Contestations, Horizons*. University of Nebraska Press. doi:10.2307/j.ctt1fzhfz8

Carbado, D. (2013). Colorblind intersectionality. *Signs (Chicago, Ill.), 38*(4), 811–845. doi:10.1086/669666

Carter, R. T., Forsyth, J. M., Mazzula, S. L., & Williams, B. (2005). *Racial Discrimination and Race-Based Traumatic Stress: An Exploratory Investigation: Handbook of Racial-Cultural Psychology and Counseling: Training and Practice* (R. T. Carter, Ed.). Vol. II). John Wiley & Sons, Inc.

Carton, A. M., & Rosette, A. S. (2011). Explaining bias against Black leaders: Integrating theory on information processing and goal-based stereotyping. *Academy of Management Journal, 54*(6), 1141–1158. doi:10.5465/amj.2009.0745

Catalyst. (2004). *Advancing African American Women in the Workplace: What Managers Need to Know*. Catalyst survey. https://www.catalyst.org/research/advancing-african-american-women-in-the-workplace-what-managers-need-to-know/

Chaffins, S., Forbes, M., Fuque, H. E., & Cangemi, J. P. (1995). The glass ceiling: Are women where they should be? *Education*, *115*(93), 380–387.

Chapman, Y. (2007). *"I am not my hair! Or am I?": Black women's transformative experience in their self-perceptions of abroad and at home*. [Master's thesis, GSU]. http://digitalarchive.gsu.edu/anthro_theses/23

Cha, S. E., Hewlin, P. F., Roberts, L. M., Buckman, B. R., Leroy, H., Steckler, E. L., Ostermeier, K., & Cooper, D. (2019). Being your true self at work: Integrating the fragmented research on authenticity in organizations. *The Academy of Management Annals*, *13*(2), 633–671. doi:10.5465/annals.2016.0108

Chavannes, R. (2019). *Detangling the Stigma/A Natural Hair Documentary*. [Video]. YouTube. https://youtu.be/dij21Q0-wS4

Cheney, G., & Ashcraft, K. L. (2007). Considering "the professional" in communication studies: Implications for theory and research within and beyond the boundaries of organizational communication. *Communication Theory*, *17*(2), 146–175. doi:10.1111/j.1468-2885.2007.00290.x

Chirali, S. (2018). *Africans Used Their Hairstyles to Hide Escape Maps from Slavery in Their Hairstyles*. ED TIMES. https://edtimes.in/africans-used-to- hide-escape-maps-from-slavery-in-their-hairstyles.

Choi, I., & Choi, M. (2009). A Study of Hindu God's and Goddess' Hairstyle. *The International Journal of Costume Culture*, *12*(1), 26–37.

Chomsky, N., & McGilvray, J. A. (2009). Deep and surface structure. In *Cartesian linguistics: A chapter in the history of Rationalist thought* (pp. 78–92). Cambridge University Press. doi:10.1017/CBO9780511803116.006

Cho, S., Crenshaw, K. W., & McCall, L. (2013). Toward a field of intersectionality studies: Theory, application, and praxis. *Signs (Chicago, Ill.)*, *38*(4), 785–810. doi:10.1086/669608

Clair, J., Beatty, J., & MacLean, T. (2005). Out of sight but not out of mind: Managing invisible social identities in the workplace. *Academy of Management Review*, *30*(1), 78–95. doi:10.5465/amr.2005.15281431

Cohen, P. (2021, March 18). Black women were half as likely to be hired for state or local jobs than White men, a report says. *The New York Times*. https://www.nytimes.com/2021/03/18/business/black-women-hiring-discrimination.html

Collier, D. (2021). "Don't touch my hair": An examination of the exercise of privilege and power through interracial hair-centered communication interactions. *Proceedings of the New York State Communication Association, 2017*. NYCA.

Collier, D. (2023). Don't get it twisted: Why employer hairstyle prohibitions are racially discriminatory. *Hastings Race and Poverty Law Journal*, *9*(1), 33–54.

Collins, P. H. (2000). *Black Feminist Thought: Knowledge, Consciousness, and the Politics of Empowerment.* Routledge. https://books.google.com/books?id=cdtYsU3zR14C&printsec=frontcover&source=gbs_ge_summary_r&cad=0#v=onepage&q&f=false

Collins, P. H. (1990). Defining Black Feminist Thought. In *Feminist Theory Reader*. Local and Global.

Collins, P. H. (2000). *Black feminist thought: Knowledge, consciousness, and the politics of empowerment* (2nd ed.). Routledge.

Collins, P. H., & Bilge, S. (2020). *Intersectionality*. Policy Press.

Cooney, S. (2017). Bill O'Reilly Apologizes for Saying Maxine Waters' Hair Looked Like a 'James Brown Wig.' *Time*. https://time.com/4715552/bill-oreilly-maxine-waters-hair-james-brown-wig/

Cooper, D., & Wolfe, J. (2020, July 9). Cuts to the state and local public sector will disproportionately harm women and Black workers. *Economic Policy Institute*. https://www.epi.org/blog/cuts-to-the-state-and-local-public-sector-will-disproportionately-harm-women-and-black-workers/

Corbin, J., & Strauss, A. (2008). Basics of qualitative research: Techniques and procedures for developing grounded theory, 3rd ed (pp. xv, 379). Sage Publications, Inc. doi:10.4135/9781452230153

Cortina, L. M., Kabat-Farr, D., Leskinen, E. A., Huerta, M., & Magley, V. J. (2013). Selective incivility as modern discrimination in organizations: Evidence and impact. *Journal of Management*, *39*(6), 1579–1605. doi:10.1177/0149206311418835

Cortina, L. M., Magley, V. J., Williams, J. H., & Langhout, R. D. (2001). Incivility in the workplace: Incidence and impact. *Journal of Occupational Health Psychology*, *6*(1), 64–80. doi:10.1037/1076-8998.6.1.64 PMID:11199258

Couch, K. A., & Fairlie, R. (2010). Last hired, first fired? Black-White unemployment and the business cycle. *Springer, 47*(1), 21.

Cox, E. (2018). Black Girl Magic sparkles again: Netflix's "Nappily Ever After" is the hair representation we've been looking for. *UWIRE Text*, 1.

Craig, M. L. (2002). *Ain't I a Beauty Queen: Black Women, Beauty, and the Politics of Race*. Oxford University Press. doi:10.1093/acprof:oso/9780195152623.001.0001

Crenshaw, K. (1991). Mapping the Margins: Intersectionality, Identity Politics, and Violence Against Women of Color. *Stanford Law Review*, *43*(6), 1241–1299. doi:10.2307/1229039

Crenshaw, K. W. (1989). Demarginalizing the intersection of race and sex: A black feminist critique of antidiscrimination doctrine, feminist theory and antiracist politics. *University of Chicago Legal Forum*, 136–167.

Crenshaw, K. W. (1995). Mapping the margins: Intersectionality, identity politics, and violence against women of color. In K. Crenshaw, N. Gotanda, G. Peller, & K. Thomas (Eds.), *Critical race theory: The keys writing that formed the movement* (pp. 357–383). The New Press.

Creswell, J. W. (2003). *Research design qualitative, quantitative, and mixed method approaches* (2nd ed.). Sage.

CROWN Act Resources — The Official CROWN Act. (n.d.). The Official CROWN Act. https://www.thecrownact.com/research-studies

Crown Coalition. (2023). *About Us.* The CROWN Act. https://www.thecrownact.com/about

Daley, D. M. (1996). Paths of glory and the glass ceiling: Differing patterns of career advancement among women and minority federal employees. *Public Administration Quarterly*, 143–162.

Dash, P. (2006). Black hair culture, politics, and change. *International Journal of Inclusive Education*, *10*(1), 27–37. doi:10.1080/13603110500173183

Davis Tribble, B. L., Allen, S. H., Hart, J. R., Francois, T. S., & Smith-Bynum, M. A. (2019). "No [right] way to be a Black woman": Exploring gendered racial socialization among Black women. *Psychology of Women Quarterly*, *43*(3), 381–397. doi:10.1177/0361684318825439 PMID:35237026

Davis, J.L., Love, T.P., & Fares, P. (2019). Collective Social Identity: Synthesizing Identity Theory and Social Identity Theory Using Digital Data. *Social Psychology Quarterly, 82*(3) 254–273. doi:10.1177/0190272519851025

Davis, S. M. (2018). Taking back the power: An analysis of Black women's communicative resistance. *The Review of Communication*, *18*(4), 301–318. doi:10.1080/15358593.2018.1461234

Dawson, G. A., Karl, K. A., & Peluchette, J. V. (2019). Hair matters: Toward understanding natural Black hair bias in the workplace. *Journal of Leadership & Organizational Studies*, *26*(3), 389–401. doi:10.1177/1548051819848998

Dawson, G., & Karl, K. (2018). I am not my hair, or am I? Examining hair choices of Black female executives. *Journal of Business Diversity*, *18*(2), 46–56.

Dawson, G., & Karl, K. (2018). I am not my hair, or am I? Examining hair choices of black female executives. *Journal of Business Diversity*, *18*(2).

DeLongoria, M. (2018). Misogynoir: Black Hair, Identity Politics, and Multiple Black Realities. *Africology*, *12*(8), 39–49.

Desmond-Harris, J. (2009). Why Michelle's hair matters. *Time*, *174*, 55–57.

DiAnglelo, R. (2011). White Fragility. *The International Journal of Critical Pedagogy*, *3*(3), 54–70.

Diggs, S. N. (2022). Intersectionality of gender and race in governmental affairs. In Shields, P. and Elias, N. (Eds.), Handbook on Gender and Public Administration. Cheltenham, UK and Northhampton, MA, USA, Edward Elgar Publishing.

Diggs, S. N., Krewson, R. C., & McCandless, S. A. (2023). Intersectional disparities during crisis: Improving social equity through public and nonprofit management. In Intersectionality and Crisis Management, 81-100. Routledge.

Diggs, S.N. and Heckler, N. (forthcoming). *Taxonomy of Intersectionality: A Macro Intervention of Multiple Micro Identities.*

Djan, N. (2020, September 19). Taking Up "Hair" Space: 8 Black Women Talk About What Natural Hair Means to Them. *PopSugar*. https://www.popsugar.com/beauty/black-women-talk-about-their-natural-hair-47350427

Don't compel girl students to plait hair: child rights body to Kerala schools. (2016). *Asianet Newsable*. https://newsable.asianetnews.com/south/dont-compel-girls-to-plait-their-hair-tells-commission-to-schools

Donahoo, S. (2022). Working with Style: Black women, black hair, and professionalism. *Gender, Work and Organization*, *2*(30), 596–611. doi:10.1111/gwao.12838

Donahoo, S., & Smith, A. D. (2022). Controlling the crown: Legal efforts to professionalize Black hair. *Race and Justice*, *12*(1), 182–203. doi:10.1177/2153368719888264

Dove LinkedIn 2023 Workplace Research Study. (2023, January). The Crown Act. https://www.thecrownact.com/research-studies

Dove. (2023). *2023 CROWN Workplace Research Study*. The official CROWN Act. https://www.thecrownact.com/research-studies

Dove, M. L. (2021). *The Influence of Colorism on the Hair Experiences of African American Female Adolescents. Genealogy, 5(1), 5*. MDPI AG. doi:10.3390/genealogy5010005

Dover, T. L., Major, B., & Kaiser, C. R. (2016). Members of high-status groups are threatened by pro-diversity organizational messages. *Journal of Experimental Social Psychology*, *62*, 58–67. doi:10.1016/j.jesp.2015.10.006

Dudar, H., & Atkin, J. (1992). 'Griot New York' sets the city's rhythm to dance. *Smithsonian*, *23*(6), 102.

Duke's Fuqua School of Business. (2020, August 12). *Research suggests bias against natural hair limits job opportunities for black women*. Duke University. https://www.fuqua.duke.edu/duke-fuqua-insights/ashleigh-rosette-research-suggests-bias-against-natural-hair-limits-job

Duncan, G. A. (2023, March 27). Black Panther Party. *Encyclopedia Britannica*. https://www.britannica.com/topic/Black-Panther-Party

Elbow, P. (2000). *Everyone can write: Essays toward a hopeful theory of writing and teaching writing*. Oxford University Press.

Elejabarrieta, F. (1994). Social positioning: A way to link social identity and social representation. *Social Sciences Information. Information Sur les Sciences Sociales*, *33*(2), 241–253. doi:10.1177/053901894033002006

Ellington, T. N. (2015). Social networking sites: A support system for African-American women wearing natural hair. *International Journal of Fashion Design. Technology and Education*, *8*(1), 21–29. doi:10.1080/17543266.2014.974689

Ellington, T. N. (2023). *I'm Free Now! The Self-Esteen and Self-Schema of African American Women Wearing Natural Hair* (T. N. Ellington, Ed.). The Kent State University Press.

Elliott, J. R., & Smith, R. A. (2004). Race, gender, and workplace power. *American Sociological Review*, *69*(3), 365–386. doi:10.1177/000312240406900303

Ellis, G. (2001). The Psychology of American Race Prejudice. In E. Cashmore & J. Jennings (Eds.), *Racism: Essential Readings* (pp. 10–17). Sage Publications. doi:10.4135/9781446220986.n2

Ellis-Hervey. Doss, A., Deshae, D., Nicks, R. & Arazia, P. (2016). African American Personal Presentation: Psychology of Hair and Self-Perception, *Journal of Black Studies, 47*(8), 869–882. https://www.jstor.org/stable/26174232

Equal Employment Opportunity Commission v. Catastrophe Management Solutions, No. 14-13482 (11th Cir. 2017). (2017, December 5). Justia Law. https://law.justia.com/cases/federal/appellate-courts/ca11/14-13482/14-13482-2017-12-05.html

Everett, J. E., Camille Hall, J., & Hamilton-Mason, J. (2010). Everyday conflict and daily stressors: Coping responses of Black women. *Affilia*, *25*(1), 30–42. doi:10.1177/0886109909354983

Express News Service. (2016, August). Schools girls not to be compelled to plait hair: Protection of child rights. *The New Indian Express*. https://www.newindianexpress.com/cities/kochi/2016/aug/24/Schools-girls-not-to-be-compelled-to-plait-hair-Protection-of-Child-Rights-1512355.html

Farley, Y. O. (2016). *An exploration of the identity and career development of African American women in higher education leadership: Does hair style make a difference?* (Publication No. 10248737). [Doctoral dissertation, Old Dominion University.] ProQuest Dissertation Publishing.

Ferguson, M. W. Jr, & Dougherty, D. S. (2022). The paradox of the black professional: Whitewashing blackness through professionalism. *Management Communication Quarterly*, *36*(1), 3–29. doi:10.1177/08933189211019751

Ferreira, L. (2007). An Afrocentric approach to musical performance in the Black south atlantic: The Candombe drumming in Uruguay. *Revista Transcultural de Música/Transcultural Music Review,* 11, 1-15.

Fleeson, W., & Wilt, J. (2010). The Relevance of Big five trait content in behavior to subjective authenticity: Do high levels of within-person behavioral variability undermine or enable authenticity achievement? *Journal of Personality*, *78*(4), 1353–1382. doi:10.1111/j.1467-6494.2010.00653.x PMID:20545814

Fominaya, C. F. (2010). Collective Identity in Social Movements: Central Concepts and Debates. *Sociology Compass*, *4*(6), 393–404. doi:10.1111/j.1751-9020.2010.00287.x

Forbes, J. (2021). How the pandemic refocused Black women's commitment to their wellness. *Allure*. https://www.allure.com/sponsored/story/aarp-2021-survey-black-women-pandemic-beauty-wellness-habits

Ford, K. A. (2011). Race, gender, and bodily (mis)recognitions: Women of color faculty experiences with White students in the college classroom. *Journal of Higher Education (Columbus, Ohio)*, *82*(4), 444–478. doi:10.1353/jhe.2011.0026

Furniss, G. J. (2015). Viewing sub-saharan African art with western eyes: A question of aesthetics in the context of another culture and time. *Art Education*, *68*(6), 28–35. doi:10.1080/00043125.2015.11519345

Garber, E. (1995). Teaching art in the context of culture: A study in the Borderlands. *Studies in Art Education*, *36*(4), 218–232. doi:10.2307/1320936

Garrin, A. R., & Marcketti, S. B. (2017). The Impact of Hair on African American Women's Collective Identity Formation. *Clothing & Textiles Research Journal*, *36*(2), 104–118. doi:10.1177/0887302X17745656

Garrod, A., Kilkenny, R., & Gomez, C. (2013). *Mixed: Multiracial college students tell their life stories* (1st ed.). Cornell University Press. doi:10.7591/9780801469169

Gathers, R. C., & Mahan, M. G. (2014). African American women, hair care, and health barriers. *The Journal of Clinical and Aesthetic Dermatology*, *7*(9), 26–29. PMID:25276273

Gill, T.M. (2015). #Teamnatural: black hair and the politics of community in digital media. *Journal of Contemporary African Art, 37.*

Gillespie, C. H. (2013). *Down to the roots: A qualitative analysis of the psychological impacts of messages black women receive regarding their hair.* (Publication No. 3587989). [Doctoral Dissertation.] ProQuest Dissertations Publishing.

Giovanni, N. (1970). Of Liberation. Black Feeling Black Talk/Black Judgement. New York: William Morrow & Co., 1979.

Glace, N., & Waldstein, A. (2022). Spiritual hair: Dreadlocks and the bodies multiple in Rastafari. *Journal of the Royal Anthropological Institute*, *28*(1), 279–296. doi:10.1111/1467-9655.13660

Glesne, C. (2011). *Becoming qualitative researchers: An introduction* (4th ed.). Pearson.

Goffman, E. (2009). *Stigma: Notes on the management of spoiled identity*. Simon and Schuster.

Goodman, D. J. (2014). The tapestry model: Exploring social identities, privilege, and oppression from an intersectional perspective. In D. Mitchell, C. Y. Simmons, & L. A. Greyerbiehl (Eds.), *Intersectionality and higher education: Theory, research, and praxis* (pp. 99–108). Peter Lang.

Goodman, M. (2021). Wearing My Crown to Work: The Crown Act as a Solution to Shortcomings of Title VII for Hair Discrimination in the Workplace. *Touro Law Review*, *37*(2). https://digitalcommons.tourolaw.edu/lawreview/vol37/iss2/17

Goodman, M. (2021). Wearing my Crown to Work: The Crown Act as a Solution to the Shortcomings to the Title VII for Hair Discrimination in the Workplace. *Touro Law Review*, *37*(2), 1001–1025.

Goodman, M. (2021). Wearing My Crown to Work: The Crown Act as Solution to Shortcomings of Title VII for Hair Discrimination in the Workplace. *Touro Law Review*, *37*(2), 1001–2021.

Gray, S. (2017). *"To curl up or relax? That is the question: Tenured Black female faculty navigation of black hair expression in academia.* (Publication No. 10266906). [Doctoral dissertation, Southern Illinois University Carbondale]. ProQuest Dissertation Publishing.

Gray, A. (2019). *The bias of professionalism standards*. Standard Social Innovation Review.

Greensword, S. (2021). Historicizing black hair politics: A framework for contextualizing race politics. *Sociology Compass*.

Griffin, C. (2019, July 3). *How Natural Black Hair at Work Became a Civil Rights Issue.* JSTOR. https://daily.jstor.org/how-natural-black-hair-at-work-became-a-civil-rights-issue/#:~:text=The%20activist%20Angela%20Davis%20sported,black%20teens%20living%20in%20St

Guy, M. E. (1994). Organizational architecture, gender, and women's careers. *Review of Public Personnel Administration*, *14*(2), 77–90. doi:10.1177/0734371X9401400208

Hair straightening chemicals associated with higher uterine cancer. (2022, October 17). National Institutes of Health (NIH). https://www.nih.gov/news-events/news-releases/hair-straightening-chemicals-associated-higher-uterine-cancer-risk

Hall, S. (2011). The neo-liberal revolution. *Cultural Studies*, *25*(6), 705–728. doi:10.1080/09502386.2011.619886

Harter, S. (2002). Authenticity. In *Handbook of positive psychology* (pp. 382–394). Oxford University Press.

Heidegger, M. (1962). *Being and time*. Harper & Row.

Hervey, N. E., Doss, A., Davis, D., Nicks, R., & Araiza, P. (2016). African American Personal Presentation: Psychology of Hair and Self-Perception. *Journal of Black Studies*, *47*(8), 869–882. https://www.jstor.org/stable/26174232. doi:10.1177/0021934716653350

Hewlin, P. F. (2003). And the Academy Award for Best Actor Goes to: Facades of Conformity in Organizational Settings. *Academy of Management Review*, *4*, 633–642. https://www.mcgill.ca/humanrights/files/humanrights/irndi-patricia_hewlin-facade_conformity.pdf

Hewlin, P. F. (2009). Wearing the cloak: Antecedents and consequences of creating facades of conformity. *The Journal of Applied Psychology*, *94*(3), 727–741. doi:10.1037/a0015228 PMID:19450009

He, Y., Cao, Y., Nie, B., & Wang, J. (2023). Mechanisms of impairment in hair and scalp induced by hair dyeing and perming and potential interventions. *Frontiers in Medicine*, *10*, 1139607. doi:10.3389/fmed.2023.1139607 PMID:37275367

Hill Collins, P. (2000). *Black Feminist Thought | Knowledge, Consciousness, and the Politics of*. Routledge. https://www-taylorfrancis-com.libproxy.lib.unc.edu/books/mono/10.4324/9780203900055/black-feminist-thought-patricia-hill-collins

Hill, M. L. (2006). Baltimore police department has a racially insensitive appearance policy. *Jackson Free Press* retrieved from https://www.jacksonfreepress.com/news/2006/dec/20/baltimore-police-department-has-racially/

Hilliard, A. G. (1979). Respect the Child's Culture. *Young Children*, *34*(5), 2–3. https://www.jstor.org/stable/42642722

Hiltebeitel, A., & Miller, B. (1998). *Hair: Its Power and Meaning in Asian Cultures*. State University of New York Press.

Hirschberger, G. (2018). Collective Trauma and the Social Construction of Meaning. *Frontiers in Psychology*, *9*, 1441. doi:10.3389/fpsyg.2018.01441 PMID:30147669

Holler, S. E. (2023). Braids, Locs, and Bostock: Title VII's Elusive Protections for LGBTQ+ and Black Women Employees. *The Journal of Gender, Race & Justice*, *26*(1), 223–270.

Honeycutt, J. M., & Wright, C. N. (2017). Predicting Affectionate and Aggressive Teasing Motivation on the Basis of Self-Esteem and Imagined Interactions With the Teasing Victim. *The Southern Communication Journal*, *82*(1), 15–26. doi:10.1080/1041794X.2016.1265577

Hooks, B. ((1995). *Killing Rage: Ending racism.* New York, NY: Henry Holt and Company.

Horne, M. (2019). *A Visual History of Iconic Black Hairstyles*. HISTORY. https://www.history.com/news/black-hairstyles-visual-history-in-photos

HughesB. T.SrivastavaS.LeszkoM.CondonD. M. (2022, September 28). Occupational Prestige: The Status Component of Socioeconomic Status. doi:10.31234/osf.io/6qgxv

Hunter, M. L. (2011). Buying racial capital: Skin-bleaching and cosmetic surgery in a globalized world. *The Journal of Pan African Studies*, *4*(4), 142–164.

IANS. (2019, August). Indians still stuck in sexist prejudices; prefer long, straight hair on women, says survey. *National Herald.* https://www.nationalheraldindia.com/lifestyle/indians-still-stuck-in-sexist-prejudices-prefer-long-straight-hair-on-women-says-survey

Iyer, A. (2022). Understanding advantaged groups' opposition to diversity, equity, and inclusion (DEI) policies: The role of perceived threat. *Social and Personality Psychology Compass*, *16*(5), e12666. doi:10.1111pc3.12666

Jackson, A. P., & Sears, S. J. (1992). Implications of an africentric worldview in reducing stress for African American women. *Journal of Counseling and Development*, *71*(2), 184–190. doi:10.1002/j.1556-6676.1992.tb02196.x

Jackson, L. (2013). *Can your hair color affect your job opportunities?* Career Addict.

Jackson, R. L., & Hogg, M. A. (2010). Social Movements. SAGE Publications. *Inc.*, *1*(1). doi:10.4135/9781412979306

Jeffries, R. B., & Jeffries, D. (2014). Reclaiming our roots: The influences of media curriculum on the Natural Hair Movement. *Multicultural Perspectives*, *16*(3), 160–165. doi:10.1080/1521 0960.2014.926747

Johnson, A. M., Godsil, R. D., MacFarlane, J., Tropp, L. R., & Goff, P. A. (2017). The "good hair" study: Explicit and implicit attitudes toward Black women's hair. *Perception Institute*. https:// perception.org/wp-content/uploads/2017/01/TheGood-HairStudyFindingsReport.pdf

Johnson, A. M., Godsil, R. D., MacFarlane, J., Tropp, L. R., & Goff, P. A. (2020, June 17). *The "good hair" study*. Perception Institute. http://www.goodhairstudy.com/

Johnson, A. M., Goff, P., Tropp, L., MacFarlane, J., & Godsil, R. (2020, June 17). *The "good hair" study*. Perception Institute. http://www.goodhairstudy.com/

Johnson, C. M. E. (2019). *"Each New Curl Howling a War Cry": Black Women, Embodiment, and Gendered Racial Formation*. (Publication No. 27802372, [Doctoral dissertation, University of Southern California].ProQuest Dissertations Publishing.

Johnson, T., & Bankhead, T. (2014). Hair It Is: Examining the Experiences of Black Women with Natural Hair. *Open Journal of Social Sciences*, *02*(01), 86–100. doi:10.4236/jss.2014.21010

Jones, C., & Shorter-Gooden, K. (2003). *Shifting: The double lives of Black women in America*. HarperCollins.

Jones, R. (2006). Jazz Polyrhythms. *Jazz Education Journal*, *38*(6), 49–51.

Jones, R. (2020). What the Hair: Employment discrimination against black people based on hairstyles. *Harvard Blackletter Law Journal*, *36*(12).

Jones, R. (2020). What the hair: Employment discrimination against black people based on hairstyles. *Harvard Blackletter Law Journal*, *36*, 27–45.

Jones, S. R., Arminio, J. L., & Torres, V. (2014). *Negotiating the complexities of qualitative research in higher education: fundamental elements and issues* (2nd ed.). Routledge. doi:10.4324/9780203123836

Kalra, V. (2015, November 20). Tightly-wound to knotted, a history of Indian hairstyles. *IndianExpress*. https://indian express.com/article/india/india-news-india/tightly-wound-to-knotted-a-history-of-indian-hairstyles/

Kaplan, R. B. (1969). On a note of protest (in a minor key): Bidialectism vs. Bidialectism. *College English*, *30*(5), 386–389. doi:10.2307/374343

Karl, K., Peluchette, J. V., & Dawson, G. (2022). Why so much ado about a hairdo? Examining how the hair choices of Black women vary by occupation. *Journal of Business Diversity*, *22*(1), 10–22.

Karl, K., Peluchette, J. V., & Dawson, G. (2022). Why So Much Ado About a Hairdo? Examining How the Hair Choices of Black Women Vary by Occupation. *Journal of Business Diversity*, *22*(1), 10–22. https://www.proquest.com/scholarly-journals/why-so-much-ado-about-hairdo-examining-how-hair/docview/2643280738/se-2

Kedia, S. (2022, December 12). South Asians are reclaiming their curly hair. *The Juggernaut*. https://www.jgnt.co/south-asians-reclaiming-curly-hairCurly hair movement

Kelley, R. (1997). Nap time: Historicizing the afro. *Fashion Theory*, *1*(4), 339–352. doi:10.2752/136270497779613666

Kennedy, K. (2020). *My Natural Hair Is Unprofessional: The Impact of Black Hairstyles on Perceived Employment-Related Characteristics*. [Master's Thesis, Marquette University]. https://epublications.marquette.edu/theses_open/578

Kennedy, K. (2020). My Natural Hair Is Unprofessional: The Impact of Black Hairstyles on Perceived Employment-Related Characteristics. [Master's Thesis, Marquette University]. https://epublications.marquette.edu/theses_open/578

Kerala School girl shows us how it's done: Hair plaiting can't be made compulsory, says govt. (2016, October 24). *The News Minute*. https://www.thenewsminute.com/article/kerala-school-girl-shows-us-how-its-done-hair-plaiting-cant-be-made-compulsory-say-govt

Khedkar, S. (2022, October 4). Despite the science, hairy stereotypes still plague curly hair. *Science. The Wire*. https://science.thewire.in/health/curly-hair-science-stereotypes/

King, D. K. (1988). Multiple jeopardy, multiple consciousness: The context of a Black feminist ideology. *Signs (Chicago, Ill.)*, *14*(1), 42–72. doi:10.1086/494491

King, V., & Niabaly, D. (2013). The politics of Black womens' hair. *Journal of Undergraduate Research at Minnesota State University, Mankato*, *13*(4), 1–19.

Kipping, M. (2011). Hollow from the start? Image professionalism in management consulting. *Current Sociology*, *59*(4), 530–550. doi:10.1177/0011392111402727

Koval, C. Z., & Rosette, A. S. (2021). The natural hair bias in job recruitment. *Social Psychological & Personality Science*, *12*(5), 741–750. doi:10.1177/1948550620937937

Kuumba, M. B., & Ajanaku, F. (1998). Dreadlocks: The hair aesthetics of cultural resistance and collective identity formation. *Mobilization: An International Quarterly (San Diego, Calif.)*, *3*(2), 227–243. doi:10.17813/maiq.3.2.nn180v12hu74j318

Laird, J. (2017). Public sector employment inequality in the United States and the Great Recession. *Demography*, *54*(1), 391–411. doi:10.100713524-016-0532-4 PMID:28092072

Lakritz, T. (2022, August 19). 'The Princess Diaries' portrayed my curly hair as a problem. I've since learnt to embrace it. *Business Insider*. https://www.businessinsider.in/entertainment/news/the-princess-diaries-portrayed-my-curly-hair-as-a-problem-ive-since-learned-to-embrace-it-/articleshow/93647697.cms

Lawrence, T. (2011). *An Africentric reading protocol: The speculative fiction of Octavia Butler and Tananarive Due* [Dissertation, Wayne State University].

Lawrence, K., & Kelecher, T. (2004). Chronic disparity: strong and pervasive evidence of racial inequalities poverty outcomes: Structural racism. *Race and Public Conference.*

Laws we enforce. (2023, April 13). The United States Department of Justice. https://www.justice.gov/crt/laws-we-enforce#:~:text=Title%20VII%20also%20makes%20it%20unlawful%20to%20use%20policies%20or,identity)%2C%20or%20national%20origin.

Leath, S., Jerald, M. C., Perkins, T., & Jones, M. K. (2021). A qualitative exploration of jezebel stereotype endorsement and sexual behaviors among Black college women. *The Journal of Black Psychology*, *47*(4-5), 244–283. doi:10.1177/0095798421997215

Lee, J. (2017). Self-esteem and reflected appraisals of Women's Hair in College Women. *Journal of Interdisciplinary Undergraduate Research, 9.* https://doi.org/https://knowledge.e.southern.edu/jiur/vol9/iss1/2

Legal Defense Fund. (2023). *Natural Hair Discrimination.* NAACP. https://www.naacpldf.org/natural-hair-discrimination/

Legal Defense Fund. (2023, March 22). *Natural hair discrimination faq*. NAACP. https://www.naacpldf.org/natural-hair-discrimination/

Leonardelli, G., Pickect, C. L., & Brewer, M. B. (2010). Optimal Distinctiveness Theory. *Advances in Experimental Social Psychology*, *43*, 63–113. doi:10.1016/S0065-2601(10)43002-6

Lester, N. A. (2000). Nappy edges and goldy locks: African-American daughters and the politics of hair. *The Lion and the Unicorn*, *24*(2), 201–224. doi:10.1353/uni.2000.0018

Letter from a Birmingham Jail [King, Jr .]. (n.d.). UPenn. https://www.africa.upenn.edu/Articles_Gen/Letter_Birmingham.html

Lewis, J. A., Mendenhall, R., Harwood, S. A., & Browne Huntt, M. (2016). "Ain't I a woman?": Perceived Gendered racial microaggressions experienced by Black women. *The Counseling Psychologist*, *44*(5), 758–780. doi:10.1177/0011000016641193

Llorens, J. J., Wenger, J. B., & Kellough, J. E. (2008). Choosing public sector employment: The impact of wages on the representation of women and minorities in state bureaucracies. *Journal of Public Administration: Research and Theory*, *18*(3), 397–413. doi:10.1093/jopart/mum020

Lloyd, C. (2021, March 5). *Black Women in the Workplace*. Gallup.Com. https://www.gallup.com/workplace/333194/black-women-workplace.aspx

López, V. (2009). The hyphen goes where? Four stories of the dual-culture experience in the art classroom. *Art Education*, *62*(5), 19–24. doi:10.1080/00043125.2009.11519033

Lumpkin, T. (2022). *What I Like: Chronicles of Black Males' Perspectives of Black Women's Hair* (Publication No. 29164066) [Doctoral dissertation, University of Maryland, Baltimore County]. ProQuest Dissertations Publishing. https://www.proquest.com/docview/2677022697/B66F6D9656254E41PQ/1

Luney, L. T. (2021). *Coping to survive in the "wild west": Black college womxn and femmes enduring anti-black gendered racism in a university of the American West*. (Publication No. 28549089). [Doctoral dissertation, University of Colorado]. ProQuest Dissertations Publishing.

Ma, A. C., & Rast, D. E. (2017). Optimal Distinctiveness Theory. In V. Zeigler-Hill & T. Shackelford (Eds.), *Encyclopedia of Personality and Individual Differences*. Springer. doi:10.1007/978-3-319-28099-8_1144-1

Maddox, K. (2014). Perspectives on racial phenotypicality bias. *Personality and Social Psychology Review*, 8383–8401. doi:10.120715327957pspr0804_4 PMID:15582860

Madu, P., & Kundu, R. (2014). Follicular and Scarring Disorders in Skin of Color: Presentation and Management. *American Journal of Clinical Dermatology*, *15*(4), 307–321. doi:10.100740257-014-0072-x PMID:24820821

Makkar, J. K., & Strube, M. J. (1995). Black Women's Self-Perceptions of Attractiveness Following Exposure to White versus Black Beauty Standards: The Moderating Role of Racial Identity and Self-Esteem. *Journal of Applied Social Psychology*, *25*(17), 1547–1566. doi:10.1111/j.1559-1816.1995.tb02632.x

Mantri, G. (2018, June 28). 'Curly is beautiful': This movement is helping Indian women accept their natural hair. *The News Minute*. https://www.thenewsminute.com/article/curly-beautiful-movement-helping-indian-women-accept-their-natural-hair-83844

Maqsoom, A., Musarat, M. A., Mubbasit, H., Alaloul, W. S., Ashraf, H., Rabbani, M. B. A., & Shaheen, I. (2023). Extrinsic workforce diversity factors: An impact of employee characteristics on productivity. *Ain Shams Engineering Journal*, *14*(10), 102170. doi:10.1016/j.asej.2023.102170

Marr, C. (2022, August 1). Black Hair Bias Laws Spread, Including in Handful of Red States. *Bloomberg Law*. https://news.bloomberglaw.com/daily-labor-report/black-hair-bias-laws-spread-including-in-handful-of-red-states

Marshall, T. H. (1939). The recent history of professionalism in relation to social structure and social policy. *The Canadian Journal of Economics and Political Science*, *5*(3), 325–340. doi:10.2307/137036

Mbilishaka, A. (2018). Black Lives (and Stories) Matter: Race Narrative Therapy in Black Hair Care Spaces. *Community Psychology in Global Perspective*, *4*(2), 22–33.

Mbilishaka, A. M., & Apugo, D. (2020). Brushed aside: African American women's narratives of hair bias in school. *Race, Ethnicity and Education*, *23*(5), 634–653. doi:10.1080/13613324.2020.1718075

Mbilishaka, A. M., Hudlin, M., Clemons, K., Warner, C., & Jones, D. (2020). Don't Get It Twisted: Untangling the Psychology of Hair Discrimination Within Black Communities. *The American Journal of Orthopsychiatry*, *90*(5), 590–599. doi:10.1037/ort0000468 PMID:32463256

Mbilishaka, A. M., Mitchell, D. S. B., & Conyers, C. (2020). Grandma's Hands: Memories of Hair Styling Interaction with African American Grandmothers: Research. *Journal of Intergenerational Relationships*, *18*(2), 139–155. doi:10.1080/15350770.2019.1658008

McCall, L. (2005). The complexity of intersectionality. *Signs (Chicago, Ill.)*, *30*(3), 1771–1800. doi:10.1086/426800

McCann, C. R., & Kim, S. K. (2013). *Feminist Local and Global Theory Perspectives Reader*. Routledge. doi:10.4324/9780203598313

McCluney, C. L., Durkee, M. I., Smith, R. E. II, Robotham, K. J., & Lee, S. S.-L. (2021). To be, or not to be...Black: The effects of racial codeswitching on perceived professionalism in the workplace. *Journal of Experimental Social Psychology*, *97*, 104199. doi:10.1016/j.jesp.2021.104199

McCluney, C. L., & Rabelo, V. C. (2019). Conditions of visibility: An intersectional examination of Black women's belongingness and distinctiveness at work. *Journal of Vocational Behavior*, *113*, 143–152. doi:10.1016/j.jvb.2018.09.008

Melucci, A. (1995). *The Process of Collective Identity*. The University of Minnesota Press. https://www.jstor.org/stable/10.5749/j.ctttt0p8.6

Melucci, A. (1985). The Symbolic Challenge of Contemporary Movements. *Social Research*, *52*, 789–816.

Merriam, S. B. (2009). *Qualitative research: A guide to design and implementation*. Jossey-Bass.

Miller, W., Kerr, B., & Reid, M. (2010). Descriptive representation by gender and race/ethnicity in municipal bureaucracies: Change in US multiethnic cities, 1987–2001. *Journal of Women, Politics & Policy*, *31*(3), 217–242. doi:10.1080/1554477X.2010.496641

Mitchell Dove, L., & Powers, L. E. (2018). Exploring the complexity of hair and identity among African American female adolescents in foster care. *Children and Youth Services Review*, *95*, 368–376. doi:10.1016/j.childyouth.2018.10.043

Møller, C., Stupacher, J., Celma-Miralles, A., & Vuust, P. (2021). Beat perception in polyrhythms: Time is structured in binary units. *PLoS One, 16*(8), 1–24. doi:10.1371/journal.pone.0252174 PMID:34415911

Moronta, G. (2022). Why do you care about my hair? A Proposal for remedying Hair Discrimination in the Workplace on a Federal Level. *Cardozo Law Review, 43*(4).

Moronta, G. (2023). Why Do You Care About My Hair? A Proposal For Remedying Hair Discrimination In The Workplace On A Federal Level. *Cardozo Law Review, 43*(4), 1715–1746.

Morrow, W., & Jefferson, A. (1973). *400 years without a comb: The inferior seed.* California Curl.

Moustakas, C. (1994). *Phenomenological research methods.* Sage. doi:10.4135/9781412995658

Naaz, H. (2016, December 23). "I will not tie my hair": Sexism in Educational Institutions. *Feminism in India.* https://feminisminindia.com/2016/12/23/hair-educational-institutions-campus-sexism/

Najarro, I. (2022, July 6). 'Our hair is our identity': What educators need to know about hair discrimination laws. *Education Week.* https://www.edweek.org/leadership/our-hair-is-our-identity-what-educators-need-to-know-about-hair-discrimination-laws/2022/07

National Archives. (2016). *Revolutionary Movements Then and Now: Black Power and Black Lives Matter.* National Archives. https://rediscovering-black-history.blogs.archives.gov/2016/10/11/revolutionary-movements-then-and-now-black-power-and-black-lives-matter/

National Archives. (2023a). *Black Power.* National Archives. https://www.archives.gov/research/african-americans/black-power

National Archives. (2023b). *The Black Panther Party.* National Archives. https://www.archives.gov/research/african-americans/black-power/black-panthers#bpintro

National Museum of African American History & Culture. (2023). *The Black Panther Party: Challenging Police and Promoting Social Change.* NMAAHC. https://nmaahc.si.edu/explore/stories/black-panther-party-challenging-police-and-promoting-social-change

Nichols, E. G., & Kenny, E. (2017). *Beauty around the world: A cultural encyclopedia* (1st ed.). ABC-CLIO.

NilepC. (2006). "Code Switching" in sociocultural linguistics. *Colorado Research in Linguistics.* doi:10.25810/hnq4-jv62

Norwood, C. R. (2018). Decolonizing my hair, unshackling my curls: An autoethnography on what makes my natural hair journey a Black feminist statement. *International Feminist Journal of Politics, 20*(1), 69–84. doi:10.1080/14616742.2017.1369890

Oathes, D., & Ray, W. (2008). Dissociative Tendencies and Facilitated Emotional Processing. *Emotion (Washington, D.C.), 8*(5), 653–661. doi:10.1037/a0013442 PMID:18837615

Oberfield, Z. W. (2016). Why are some agencies perceived as more committed to diversity than others? An analysis of public-sector diversity climates. *Public Management Review*, *18*(5), 763–790. doi:10.1080/14719037.2015.1045017

Okazawa-Rey, M., Robinson, T., & Ward, J. V. (1986). Black women and the politics of skin color and hair. *Women's Studies Quarterly*, *14*(1/2), 13–14.

Opie, T. R., & Phillips, K. W. (2015). Hair penalties: The negative influence of Afrocentric hair on ratings of Black women's dominance and professionalism. *Frontiers in Psychology*, *6*, 1311. doi:10.3389/fpsyg.2015.01311 PMID:26379612

Orey, B. D., & Zhang, Y. (2019). Melanated millennials and the politics of Black hair. *Social Science Quarterly*, *100*(6), 2458–2476. doi:10.1111squ.12694

Oriowo, D. O. (2016). *Is it easier for her? Afro-textured hair and its effects on Black female sexuality: A mixed methods approach.* (Publication No. 10120152). [Doctoral dissertation, Widener University]. ProQuest Dissertations Publishing.

Oxford University Press. (2023, March). *Bias.* OED Online. www.oed.com/view/Entry/18564

Oxford University Press. (2023, March). *Implicit Bias.* OED Online. https://www-oed-com.fgul.idm.oclc.org/view/Entry/88686775

Painter, D. H. (1976). Women in America. *Current History (New York, N.Y.)*, *70*(416), 224–227.

Patkar, K. (2008). Herbal cosmetics in ancient India. *Indian Journal of Plastic Surgery, 41*(S 01), 134-137. doi:10.1055/s-0039-1700484

Patton, M. Q. (2002). *Qualitative research and evaluation methods* (3rd ed.). Sage.

Patton, T. O. (2006). Hey girl, am I more than my hair? African American women and their struggles with beauty, body image, and hair. *NWSA Journal*, *18*(2), 24–51. doi:10.2979/NWS.2006.18.2.24

Payne-Patterson. (2023). *The CROWN Act: A jewel for combating racial discrimination in the workplace and classroom.* Economic Policy Institute. https://www.epi.org/publication/crown-act/

Peacock, T. N. (2019). *African American Hair and Beauty: Examining Afrocentricity and Identity Through the Reemergence and Expression of Natural Hair in the 21st Century.* Scholar Commons. https://scholarcommons.sc.edu/etd/5252

Perrigino, M.B. & Jenkins, M. (2022). Antecedents of facades of conformity: when can employees "be themselves?" *Journal of Humanities and Applied Social Sciences.* doi:10.1108/JHASS-04-2022-0045

Phelps-Ward, R. J., & Laura, C. T. (2016). Talking back in cyberspace: Self-love, hair care, and counter narratives in Black adolescent girls' YouTube vlogs. *Gender and Education*, *28*(6), 807–820. doi:10.1080/09540253.2016.1221888

Pitts, B. (2021). Uneasy Lies the Head that Wears the Crown: A Critical Race Analysis of the CROWN Act. *Journal of Black Studies*, *52*(7), 716–735. doi:10.1177/00219347211021096

Polletta, F., Goodwin, J., & Jasper, J. (2000a). *Political Passions: Emotions and Social Movements*. University of Chicago Press.

Polletta, F., & Jasper, J. M. (2000). Collective Identity and Social Movements. *Annual Review of Sociology*, *27*(1), 283–305. doi:10.1146/annurev.soc.27.1.283

Randle, B. (2015). I am not my hair: African American women and their struggles with embracing natural hair. *Race, Gender & Class (Towson, Md.)*, *22*(1-2), 114–121.

Randle, B. A. (2015). I am not my hair; African American Women and their Struggles with Embracing Natural Hair! *Race, Gender & Class (Towson, Md.)*, *22*(1), 114–121.

Reynolds-Dobbs, W., Thomas, K. M., & Harrison, M. S. (2008). From mammy to superwoman: Images that hinder Black women's career development. *Journal of Career Development*, *35*(2), 129–150. doi:10.1177/0894845308325645

Riccucci, N. M. (2009). The pursuit of social equity in the federal government: A road less traveled? *Public Administration Review*, *69*(3), 373–382. doi:10.1111/j.1540-6210.2009.01984.x

Rice, M. (2004). Organizational culture, social equity, and diversity: Teaching public administration education. *Journal of Public Affairs Education*, *2*(2), 143–154. doi:10.1080/15236803.2004.12001354

Roberts, L. M. (2005). Changing faces: Professional image construction in diverse organizational settings. *Academy of Management Review*, *30*(4), 685–711. doi:10.5465/amr.2005.18378873

Robinson, D. (2001). *Black Nationalism in American Politics and Thought*. Cambridge Univ. Press. https://books.google.com/books?hl=en&lr=&id=d_5xjlv7VekC&oi=fnd&pg=PP11&ots=7JmJfowI-u&sig=WKd-_L1xpoE0rGgiIvFryO6WOps#v=onepage&q&f=false doi:10.1017/CBO9780511606038

Rogers v. American Airlines, Inc., 527 F. Supp. 229 (S.D.N.Y. 1981).

Rosette, A. S. (2020). *Research suggests bias against natural hair limits job opportunities for Black women.* Duke University. https://www.fuqua.duke.edu/duke-fuqua-insights/ashleigh-rosette-research-suggests-bias-against-natural-hair-limits-job

Rosette, A. S., & Dumas, T. L. (2007). The hair dilemma: Conform to mainstream expectations or emphasize racial identity makeup, identity performance & discrimination. *Duke Journal of Gender Law & Policy*, *14*(1), 407–422.

Rosette, A. S., Koval, C. Z., Ma, A., & Livingston, R. (2016). Race matters for women leaders: Intersectional effects on agentic deficiencies and penalties. *The Leadership Quarterly*, *27*(3), 429–445. doi:10.1016/j.leaqua.2016.01.008

Rosette, A., & Dumas, T. L. (2007). The hair dilemma: Conform to mainstream expectations or emphasize racial identity. *Duke Journal of Gender Law & Policy*, *14*(1), 407–422.

Rowe, K. L. (2022). Tangled: Black Hair and Texturism in ethnodrama. *Cultural Studies ↔. Cultural Studies, Critical Methodologies*, *22*(1), 32–43. doi:10.1177/15327086211049708

Rudman, L. A., & McLean, M. C. (2015). The role of appearance stigma in implicit racial ingroup bias. *Group Processes & Intergroup Relations*, *19*(3), 374–393. doi:10.1177/1368430215583152

Russell, K., Wilson, K., & Hall, R. (1993). *The Color Complex: The politics of skin color among African Americans*. Anchor Books Doubleday.

Saldaña, J. (2013). *The coding manual for qualitative researchers* (2nd ed.). SAGE.

Santiago, R., Nwokoma, N., & Crentsil, J. (2021). Investigating the implications of code-switching and assimilating at work for African American professionals. *Journal of Business Diversity*, *21*(4), 72–81.

Schwandt, T. A. (2001). *Dictionary of qualitative inquiry* (2nd ed.). Sage.

Scott-Jones, G., & Kamara, M. R. (2020, November 7). CAADC; Kamara MR; PE. The Traumatic Impact of Structural Racism on African Americans. *Delaware Journal of Public Health*, *6*(5), 80–82. doi:10.32481/djph.2020.11.019 PMID:34467171

Scott-Ward, G., Gupta, N., & Greene, E. (2021). *back to natural* and the intergenerational healing of the natural black hair movement. *Journal of Humanistic Psychology*, *62*(6), 925–941. doi:10.1177/00221678211009078

Section VII- Proving Discrimination- Disparate Impact. (2021, February 3). CRT Department of Justice. https://www.justice.gov/crt/fcs/T6Manual7#D

Sehra, R. (2020, March 3). Indian women open up about the pressure to keep their hair long and straight. *HuffPost*. https://www.huffpost.com/entry/indian-women-hair-pressure-long-straight_l_5e54236ec5b66729cf6064e3

Seité, S., Dantec, G. L., Demessant-Flavigny, A., & Kerob, D. (2023). Survey of Hand Issues Encountered by Hairdressers and Hairdresser Related Professionals: From Epidemiological Data to Clinical Observational Survey Results. *Clinical, Cosmetic and Investigational Dermatology*, *16*, 111–117. doi:10.2147/CCID.S385681 PMID:36698444

Sekayi, D. (2003). Aesthetic resistance to commercial influences: The impact of the eurocentric beauty standard on Black college women. *The Journal of Negro Education*, *72*(4), 467–477. doi:10.2307/3211197

Serafin, N. (2020) In Defense of Immutability, *Brigham Young University Law Review 275, 2*(8). https://digitalcommons.law.byu.edu/lawreview/vol2020/iss2/8

Sheane, S. (2012). Putting on a good face: An examination of the emotional and aesthetic roots of presentational Labour. *Economic and Industrial Democracy*, *33*(1), 145–158. doi:10.1177/0143831X11427588

Shields, S. A. (2008). Gender: An intersectionality perspective. *Sex Roles*, *59*(5-6), 301–311. doi:10.100711199-008-9501-8

Sibley, F. N., Benson, J. H., Redfern, B., & Cox, J. R. (2007). *Approach to aesthetics: Collected papers on philosophical aesthetics*. Oxford University Press.

Simeon, A. (2021). *The controversial history of the hair typing system.* Byrdie. https://www.byrdie.com/hair-typing-system-history-5205750

Sini, R. (2016, May 15). Wear a weave at work—Your afro hair is unprofessional. *BBC News*. https://www.bbc.com/news/uk-36279845

Smith, S. D. (2009). *Beauty Beat: Essence Panel Explores Beauty Purchasing*. Women's Wear Daily. http://www.ggny.com/press/51909 WWDHaspel.pdf

Smith, A. E., Hassan, S., Hatmaker, D. M., DeHart-Davis, L., & Humphrey, N. (2021). Gender, race, and experiences of workplace incivility in public organizations. *Review of Public Personnel Administration*, *41*(4), 674–699. doi:10.1177/0734371X20927760

Snider, S. R., & Rosenberg, J. (2006). The relationships of skin tone and hair to perceived beauty among African American students. *The University of Alabama McNair Journal*, 201-211.

Soni, V. (2000). A Twenty-first-century reception for diversity in the public sector: A case study. *Public Administration Review*, *60*(5), 395–408. doi:10.1111/0033-3352.00103

Staszak, J. F. (2008). Other/otherness. International Encyclopedia of Human Geography, 1-7.

Steele, C. (1992, April). Race and Schooling of Black Americans. *Atlantic (Boston, Mass.)*, 1–12. https://www.theatlantic.com/magazine/archive/1992/04/race-and-the-schooling-of-black-americans/306073/

Steele, C. M., & Aronson, J. (1995). Stereotype Threat and the Intellectual Test Performance of African Americans. *Journal of Personality and Social Psychology*, *69*(5), 797–811. doi:10.1037/0022-3514.69.5.797 PMID:7473032

Stemberger, R. M. T., Thomas, A. M., Mansueto, C. S., & Carter, J. G. (2000). Personal toll of trichotillomania: Behavioral and interpersonal sequelae. *Journal of Anxiety Disorders*, *14*(1), 97–104. doi:10.1016/S0887-6185(99)00028-6 PMID:10770238

Stilson, J. (2009). (Director). *Good Hair.* Produced by: Nelson George, Jenny Hunter, Kevin O'Donnell, and Chris Rock.

Stokes, M. N., Hope, E. C., Cryer-Coupet, Q. R., & Elliot, E. (2020). Black Girl Blues: The Roles of Racial Socialization, Gendered Racial Socialization, and Racial Identity on Depressive Symptoms among Black Girls. *Journal of Youth and Adolescence*, *49*(11), 2175–2189. doi:10.100710964-020-01317-8 PMID:32955702

Stracqualursi, V. (2022). *US House Passes Crown Act That Would Ban Race-Based Hair Discrimination.* CNN. https://www.cnn.com/2022/03/18/politics/house-vote-crown-act/index.html

Stryker, S., Owens, T., & White, R. (2000). *Self, Identity, and Social Movements*. University of Minnesota Press.

Sue, D. W., & Spanierman, L. (2020). *Microaggressions in everyday life*. John Wiley & Sons.

Summers, D., Davis, T., & Kosovac, B. (2022). Hair we grow again: Upward mobility, career compromise, and natural hair bias in the workplace. *The Career Development Quarterly*, *70*(3), 202–214. doi:10.1002/cdq.12302

Swanagan, M. (2014). *Developing a critical consciousness: Black women and the intersection of hair and power* (Publication No. 1571649). [Master's thesis, Southern Illinois University at Edwardsville.] ProQuest.

Tate, S. (2007). Black beauty: Shade, hair and anti-racist aesthetics. *Ethnic and Racial Studies*, *30*(2), 300–319. doi:10.1080/01419870601143992

Taylor, T. (2023). *Going Natural: Black Women's Didactic Hair Culture* (T. N. Ellington, Ed.).

Taylor, V., & Whittier, N. (1992). Collective Identity and Lesbian Feminist Mobilization. In A. Morris & C. Mueller (Eds.), *Frontiers of Social Movement Theory*. Yale University Press.

Tchenga, D. S. N. (2021). Black Women's Hair and Natural Hairstyles in the Workplace: Expanding the Definition of Race Under Title VII. *Virginia Law Review Online, 107,* 272–299, https://virginialawreview.org/wp-content/uploads/2021/11/Nguenang_Book_107.pdf

Tchenga, D. S. N. (2021). Black women's hair and natural hairstyles in the workplace: Expanding the definition of race under title vii. *Virginia Law Review*, *107*, 272–299.

The Deloitte Global 2022 Gen Z and Millennial Survey. (2023, May 17). Deloitte. https://www.deloitte.com/global/en/issues/work/genzmillennialsurvey-2022.html

The Kent State University Press. (n.d). *The CROWN Act.* Kent State University Press. https://www.thecrownact.com/

The Perception Institute. (2016, August). *The "Good Hair" Study Results*. The Perception Institute. https://perception.org/goodhair/results/

The Sister Study: Home. (n.d.). Sister Study. https://sisterstudy.niehs.nih.gov/English/index1.htm

Thompson, C. (2009). Black women, beauty, and hair as a matter of *being*. *Women's Studies*, *38*(8), 831–856. doi:10.1080/00497870903238463

Thompson, R. F. (1984). *Flash of the spirit: African and Afro-American art and philosophy*. Random House.

Titus, R. (2019). *(Director). Natural Hair the Movie*. Grind Over Matter Productions.

Treiman, D. J. (1976). A Standard Occupational Prestige Scale for Use with Historical Data. *The Journal of Interdisciplinary History*, *7*(2), 283–304. doi:10.2307/202737

Trüeb, R. (2017). From hair in India to hair India. *International Journal of Trichology*, *9*(1), 1. doi:10.4103/ijt.ijt_10_17 PMID:28761257

U.S. Equal Employment Opportunity Commission. (2006, April 19). *EEOC Compliance Manual: Section 15 race and color discrimination*. US EEOC. Office of Legal Counsel, Title VII/ADEA/ EPA Division. https://www.eeoc.gov/laws/guidance/section-15-race-and-color-discrimination

U.S. Equal Opportunity Employment Commission. (2023). *Title VII of the Civil Rights Act of 1964*. EEOC. https://www.eeoc.gov/statutes/title-vii-civil-rights-act-1964

van den Bosch, R., & Taris, T. W. (2014). Authenticity at work: Development and validation of an individual authenticity measure at work. *Journal of Happiness Studies*, *15*(1), 1–18. doi:10.100710902-013-9413-3

van Manen, M. (1990). *Researching lived experience: Human science for an action sensitive pedagogy*. SUNY Press.

Walters, R. W., & Smith, R. C. (1999). *African American Leadership*. State University of New York Press. https://books.google.com/books?hl=en&lr=&id=xArrb8_3iNQC&oi=fnd&pg=PR11&ots=SLB36Nvy5F&sig=fkLR8wEOuruvl_nsXYqwihaN5vI#v=onepage&q&f=false

Webb, T., Looby, J., & Fults-McMurtery, R. (2004). African American men's perceptions of body figure attractiveness: An acculturation study. *Journal of Black Studies*, *34*(3), 370–385. doi:10.1177/0021934703254100

Welbourne, J., Gangadharan, A., & Sariol, A. (2014). Ethnicity and cultural values as predictors of the occurrence and impact of experienced workplace incivility. *Journal of Occupational Health Psychology*, *20*(2), 205–217. Advance online publication. doi:10.1037/a0038277 PMID:25365631

Weller, C. E. (2019). *African Americans face systematic obstacles to getting good jobs*. The Center for American Progress. https://www.americanprogress.org/article/african-americans-face-systematic-obstacles-getting-good-jobs/

Welsh-Asante, K. (2002). The Zimbabwean dance aesthetic: Senses, canons and characteristics. In *African dance: An artistic, historical, and philosophical inquiry* (pp. 203–220). Africa World Press.

Who is protected from employment discrimination ? (n.d.). US EEOC. https://www.eeoc.gov/employers/small-business/3-who-protected-employment-discrimination

Wilkins, A. C. (2012). Becoming Black women: Intimate stories and intersectional identities. *Social Psychology Quarterly*, *75*(2), 173–196. doi:10.1177/0190272512440106

Wilson, I.-P., & Mbilishaka, A. M., & Lewis, M. L. (2018). "White folks ain't got hair like us": African American mother–daughter hair stories and racial socialization. *Women, Gender, and Families of Color, 6*(2), 226–248.

Wingfield, A. H. (2015, October 14). Being Black—but not too Black—in the workplace. *The Atlantic*. https://www.theatlantic.com/business/archive/2015/10/being-black-work/409990/

Wong, N., Williams, K., Tolliver, S., & Potts, G. A. (2023). Hair length in association with hair care regimen and healthy habits in Black women. *Journal of Cosmetic Dermatology*, *22*(8), 2361–2363. doi:10.1111/jocd.15696 PMID:36994547

Woolford, S. J., Woolford-Hunt, C. J., Sami, A., Blake, N., & Williams, D. R. (2016). No sweat: African American adolescent girls' opinions of hairstyle choices and physical activity. *BMC Obesity*, *3*(1), 1–8. doi:10.118640608-016-0111-7 PMID:27386139

Yancy, G., & Ryser, T. A. (2008). Whiting Up and Blacking Out: White Privilege, Race, and White Chicks. *African American Review*, *42*(3-4), 731–746. https://www.jstor.org/stable/40301264

Yoshino, K. (2001). Covering. *The Yale Law Journal*, *111*(4), 769–940. doi:10.2307/797566

About the Contributors

Kula A. Francis is a tenured Associate Professor of Political Science, and the Interim Director of the Virgin Islands Caribbean Cultural Center (VICCC) in the College of Liberal Arts and Social Sciences at the University of the Virgin Islands. A native of St. Thomas, Dr. Francis earned a Bachelor of Arts Degree in Social Sciences from the University of the Virgin Islands. She also holds a Master of Public Administration, and a PhD in Urban Studies and Public Affairs, from the University of Akron, in Ohio. She teaches a variety of courses at UVI, including, political science, history, public administration, and the social sciences. Her research interests include Virgin Islands history and culture, social equity, disaster management, Burnout in public agencies, and STEM mentorship. She has published in a number of refereed academic journals, has written many book chapters, and has served as Principal Investigator on Federally and locally funded grants.

Anna M. Clarke, DSW, CSW earned a Doctor of Social Work and Master of Social Work degrees from Walden University, Master of Education Administration from the University of the Virgin Islands, and Bachelor of Social Work from Clark Atlanta University. She worked as a Social Worker, Educator, Therapist, and Administrator at various agencies throughout her over thirty-year career. Dr. Clarke serves as the Director of Practicum Education for the Bachelor and Master programs within the Social Work department at UVI. She holds membership in Zeta Phi Beta Sorority Inc., National Association of Social Workers, National Association of Black Social Workers, Phi Alpha Social Work and Golden Key Honor Societies, and National Society of Leadership and Success.

Carolyn Allen received her PHD in African American Studies from Temple University in 1997. She also received a Master of Arts in African American Studies from Temple University in 1994 and a Master of Social Service degree from Bryn Mawr College in 1986. Dr. Allen has 28 years of teaching experience at the university level in both brick-and-mortar and online programs. She is currently Associate Professor of Social Work at the University of the Virgin Islands.

Destiny Bell is a mother, early childhood educator, and senior undergraduate researcher majoring in Psychology at Georgia State University. Upon conferring her degree, she plans to become an Educational Psychologist centering Black and Brown children from birth to 3rd grade. By using her experience as an early childhood educator and researcher, Destiny plans to study emerging learning styles and implement creative strategies for teaching and learning through play.

Khadija Boyd is a Retired United States Army Combat Veteran. She received her Ph.D. in Organizational Leadership from Northcentral University in 2020. Her research and previous publications focus on race and gender discrimination in the military as identified as military colorblindness and military gestational loathing. Also, the use of Emotional Intelligence (EQ) as a filter of racial awareness. She is currently an Editor for the Journal of Veterans Studies and Section Editor for the Journal of Veterans Studies.

Kimalee Dickerson is an assistant professor of public leadership at the University of North Carolina at Chapel Hill School of Government. She earned a PhD from the University of Virginia School of Education and Human Development and a JD from the University of North Carolina at Chapel Hill School of Law. Dr. Dickerson writes and presents widely on issues of equity and inclusion in the public sector.

Christine Diggs is a retired faculty member of social work where her research and practice interests included intergenerational trauma, multicultural competence, wellness and resilience, and Black privilege.

Schnequa Nicole Diggs is a faculty member in the Department of Public Administration where she teaches courses in the MPA core curriculum and select electives in the Urban & Regional Planning specialization. Dr. Diggs completed her Ph.D. in Public Administration from Florida Atlantic University where she examined factors that influence emergency medical services level of cultural competence. Her research interest focuses on social justice advocacy and crafting effective policies to reduce generational inequalities in interrelated policy areas: housing, planning, health, and environmental. Dr. Diggs has a strong commitment to educate and encourage future public administrators furthering their education in graduate studies. She currently service as the Vice President of the Conference of Minority Public Administrators (COMPA) and an executive board member with the Section on Democracy and Social Justice (DSJ), she also co-chairs the NASPAA DEI Committee. In Durham, NC she serves on the Durham Affordable Housing Implementation Committee and with the Coalitions for Affordable Housing and Transit.

Thea Henderson Dirton is an Educational Leader in her community. She studies and documents the effect of research-based strategies on her educational organization and the educational system as a whole. She attended Winthrop University and Capella University obtaining Bachelor's, Master's, and Doctorate degrees. She has taught in a variety of different school settings after attaining her life-long goal of becoming a teacher. Dr. Dirton is a leader in her community, serving on the Board of Directors for two non-profit organizations that serve underserved populations and she is an active member of Zeta Phi Beta, Sorority Inc, which includes serving as one of the youth coordinators for her chapter. She is a peer-reviewed author of many book chapters and articles and presented at national, state, and local conferences.

Amanda E. Fehlbaum is an Associate Professor of Sociology and Director of Women's and Gender Studies at Youngstown State University in Youngstown, Ohio.

Whitney Harris Christopher (she/her) is an award-winning multimedia journalist, researcher, and voiceover artist. She currently serves as a Professorial Lecturer in the School of Communication at American University. Whitney's expertise is shooting, writing, editing, reporting, and producing broadcast news stories for local television network affiliates. She also uses this expertise in TV news as the basis for her research and publications exploring hair-based discrimination in the broadcast news industry, particularly for Black women and women of color. Before entering the education field, Whitney was an anchor, reporter, and multimedia journalist for several local news affiliates including ABC, NBC, and CBS. She received an Associated Press award for her multi-platform coverage of a news story and her work has been nominated for several other awards such as regional Emmys and Murrow awards. Whitney has covered numerous crime scenes, car accidents, fires, and high-profile court cases, but what she really enjoys are human interest stories. As a morning anchor and reporter at the ABC-News affiliate in Richmond, Virginia she created several community-oriented video series including one about outstanding teachers called Above and Beyond the Classroom and a series about different ways to get active in her community called Get Fit RVA. She also profiled a convicted felon's journey to having his voting rights restored, and one man's discovery of his family's ties to slavery on a nearby plantation. Whitney is passionate about telling impactful stories and is thrilled to share those insights with students to help the next generation of journalists. Whitney previously taught for nearly five years in the Digital Media department at the University of the District of Columbia and served as an adjunct professor at American University. In addition to her work in video broadcasting, Whitney also serves as a professional voiceover artist for a local government contracting company.

Cryshanna A. Jackson Leftwich is a Professor of Public Affairs and Politics at Youngstown State University where she also serves as the Urban Internship Coordinator of the Political Science Program.

Nicole Dezrea Jenkins is an Assistant Professor in the Department of Sociology and Criminology at Howard University. She received her Doctoral degree from the University of Nevada Las Vegas in the Department of Sociology in 2020. She obtained an M.A. in Sociology in 2017 and B.A. in Sociology in 2015 from the University of Nevada Las Vegas. In 2013, she received an A.A. in Criminal Justice after serving six years of active duty in the United States Air Force as Military Police. She is a proud advocate for social justice and is committed to teaching with such emphasis on topics such as Sociology of Poverty and Problems of the Black Community. As a qualitative researcher and urban ethnographer, she incorporates intersectional and critical feminist frameworks into her own research, centering the experiences of women in the African Diaspora. Her recent research project incorporates two years of ethnographic data collection in a Las Vegas African hair braiding salon. She finds that Black women's identity-making process is complex and perceptions of Black womeness often impede the process. She is the recipient of the Princeton University Press -Supportive Diverse Voices, Book Proposal Development Grant 2021.

Tunisia Lacy-Lumpkin is an energetic, multi-talented professional, with a plethora of work experience in diverse fields. Currently a Human Resources Specialist with the federal government, has held positions in the financial industry and higher education. She holds a PhD in Language, Literacy and Culture from the University of Maryland, Baltimore County.

Camaron Loritts is a proud native of North Carolina. Her career in higher education was extensive and impactful, with significant roles in programs like the McNair Scholars Program and her contributions to Wake Forest's Center for Research, Engagement, and Collaboration for African American Life. Camaron's work focused on the sociocultural impact of Black women's aesthetics and hair on their experiences in higher education. In a remarkable transition, Camaron Loritts shifted her skills and knowledge to the tech industry, with the intent of merging her background in higher education with her passion for advancing Black hair culture. This visionary move allowed her to incorporate her academic insights into a new journey, where she's committed to making a difference. Camaron is the proud owner of Froxy Beauty, a social impact beauty business that empowers Black women and Black-owned beauty businesses. Her venture provides not only high-quality beauty products but also serves as an educational and uplifting platform. Camaron's commitment to diversity and inclusion is evident in her work, where she redefines beauty standards and encourages self-confidence. With two degrees from UNC Greensboro, including a Master's in Women, Gender, and Sexuality Studies, Camaron Loritts' lifelong dedication to education, empowerment, and beauty innovation continues to inspire others on their own unique journeys.

Afiya Mbilishaka is a therapist, educator, research-scientist, hair historian, and hairstylist. She is the owner of Ma'at Psychological Services, a private practice in Washington, DC focused on promoting balance and restoring order to the lives of her clients. She focuses on understanding and using traditional African cultural rituals for contemporary wholistic mental health practices. She is a graduate of the University of Pennsylvania. She studied the psychological significance of race within lives and earned a Ph.D. in Clinical Psychology from Howard University at the age of 26. She is the former Association of Black Psychologist DC chapter president. Dr. Mbilishaka innovated the practice and research of, "PsychoHairapy," where she uses hair as an entry point for mental health services in beauty salons and barbershops, as well as through social media. She is the principal investigator of the PsychoHairapy Research Lab. Dr. Mbilishaka has published over 20 peer-reviewed journal articles, 10 book chapters, and 2 books. She has presented at over 40 universities and conferences. Dr. Mbilishaka has been identified as a subject matter expert by the Senate and House of Representatives, testifying nationally on the behalf of the CROWN Act, an anti-discrimination law to protect Black hair. She has now gone international, leading cultural and mental health focused trips to Cuba and to various African countries. Dr. Mbilishaka is a natural hairstylist at N Natural Hair Studio in Silver Spring, Maryland where she loves creating art with locs, twists, and afros.

Nicolette Powe is an Associate Professor in Graduate Studies in Health & Rehabilitation Sciences at Youngstown State University.

Kernysha L. Rowe, PhD is the Assistant Dean of Students and Adjunct Professor at American University in Washington, D.C. She teaches undergraduate courses about social identity formation, race and ethnicity, and intersectionality in the School of Education and is responsible for adjudicating student discipline and using restorative justice principles to heal and repair the campus community. She received her PhD from Morgan State University in Higher Education Administration and was awarded outstanding dissertation of the year. Her dissertation centers Black women medical and law students, with natural Black hair and hair texture, and their professional identity construction within their respective fields. Her research agenda examines race and identity within higher education, with research interests spanning interdisciplinary topics including JEDI (justice, equity, diversity, and inclusion), organizational leadership, feminism, Black esthetics, and texturism. She earned a Bachelor of Science in Public Relations from Florida International University, an MBA from the University of Phoenix, and an MAEd in Higher Education Administration from The George Washington University.

Indumathi Somashekar is an Assistant Professor at the Department of Media Studies, (CHRIST) Deemed to be University - BGR Campus, Bangalore, India. She has over a decade of experience in teaching media studies and communication at premier universities in India. She teaches subjects like Film Studies, Gender Studies, and Media and Culture Studies.

Joanne Simon Walters is the Chief Operating Officer at a technology company that partners with defense customers to protect critical infrastructure from cyber-attacks and unlock previously siloed information to monitor, diagnose, and respond faster to events in real time. In addition, Joanne develops and delivers online training courses for LinkedIn Learning a plethora of leadership and human resources courses. Joanne is the co-author of five HR certification preparation manuals published by McGraw-Hill. In July 2017, Joanne delivered a TEDx Talk on workplace civility. Joanne earned a Ph.D. in Creative Leadership for Innovation and Change. The focus of her research was the Role of Transformational Leadership in Facilitating the Ascent of Black Women into Executive Leadership. Additionally, Joanne earned a Master of Business Administration (MBA) with a concentration in Technology Management and a Bachelor of Business Administration with a concentration in Finance. Joanne is a certified Senior Professional in Human Resources (SPHR), SHRM-Senior Certified Professional (SHRM-SCP), certified Crucial Conversations trainer, Prosci Change Management Practitioner, and a trained paralegal specializing in employment law. When Joanne is not working, she is spending time with her family on her favorite Caribbean beaches in her birthplace of St. Thomas, US Virgin Islands, and her parents' native country, Antigua, West Indies.

Index

C

D

E

G

H

www.ingramcontent.com/pod-product-compliance
Lightning Source LLC
LaVergne TN
LVHW080643011026
849160LV00014B/1302